CRIME, PUNISHMENT, AND RESTORATIVE JUSTICE

To Brian

Frest wishes/
and good luck!

Ross

CRIME, PUNISHMENT, AND

RESTORATIVE JUSTICE

A Framework for
Restoring Trust

Ross London

WIPF & STOCK · Eugene, Oregon

Wipf and Stock Publishers
199 W 8th Ave, Suite 3
Eugene, OR 97401

Crime, Punishment, and Restorative Justice
A Framework for Restoring Trust
By London, Ross
Copyright©2011 Lynne Reiner Publishers
ISBN 13: 978-1-4982-0057-8
Publication date 12/3/2014
Previously published by First Forum Press, 2011

Restorative Justice Classics Series Foreword

THE PHRASE "RESTORATIVE JUSTICE" was unknown before the 1970s. Forty years later restorative justice is a vast international movement: nearly a million pages on the Internet refer to it; Google Scholar lists 16,600 books and essays on restorative justice; many states around the world have written it into law; and more important, hundreds of thousands of people and communities have had their fear and shame transformed by encounters with and efforts of those practicing restorative justice.

Along the way, while having intentions to repair harm, restorative justice initiatives have also added to harm. The growth of this mass movement is not without missteps and failures, some very painful. If this movement is to be advanced wisely into the future, its advocates need to remember both fruitful attempts and painful ones.

The Restorative Justice Classics Series is an attempt to help create foundations and share memories for those interested in restorative justice. In a movement that grows and changes so incredibly fast and in so many diverse places, this book series creates space for cultivating restorative justice memory. Amidst the frenzy of work, growth, and missteps, this book series represents a commitment to bring back into print those restorative justice books and articles that could be considered classic. The label "classic" is used here loosely to refer to books that have shaped the restorative justice movement and whose writing continues to be worth remembering, worth sharing, and worth reconsidering amidst the changing scene. In most cases there is still a need for the content and thus a continuing demand for the books.

Books are chosen in this series because they will be of special on-going value to practitioners and scholars of restorative justice. Wipf and Stock Publishers, at the instigation of Series Editor Ted Lewis, has set up the series in such a way that the books will stay in print and remain available. Anyone wanting to understand the origins, history, diverse practices, and spirit of restorative justice will find the series particularly helpful.

Jarem Sawatsky, Series Consultant
Canadian Mennonite University
Winnipeg, Manitoba
April 2009

To see a complete listing of books in this series, go to www.wipfandstock.com and click on "Advanced Search" to locate the Restorative Justice Classics Series in the series box. Recommendations for further reprints in this series can be directed to Ted Lewis, Series Editor, at tedlewis@wipfandstock.com or can be made by calling 541-344-1528.

Preface to the 2014 Edition

WHY IS RESTORATIVE JUSTICE still ignored by the criminal justice mainstream? What can possibly be objectionable about wanting our justice system to be *restorative*?

We can begin answering these questions by acknowledging that while the goal of restoration is shared by almost everyone interested in criminal justice reform, the meaning of "restoration" has remained unclear. What, exactly, do we want to restore? In the absence of a clearly defined meaning of restoration, the restorative justice movement has become known through its most controversial procedural innovations: face-to-face dialogue between victim and offender instead of state-controlled prosecutions, and apology and restitution instead of punishment. These are features that remain controversial to this day and which unfortunately limit restorative justice to petty crimes and juvenile offenders. The controversies surrounding the issues of privatized justice and non-punitive sanctions will remain unresolved, I believe, as long as the restorative justice movement fails to articulate a clear meaning of restoration. After all, procedures are simply means to an end. *But to what end?*

In this book I attempt to put forward an answer that is understandable, workable, and is shared by us all regardless of political orientation: the goal of restorative justice is *the restoration of trust.*

Trust? To many readers, this might seem to be rather obvious or perhaps even a bit trite. To others, it may seem too fuzzy and idealistic to be taken seriously by busy criminal justice practitioners. If so, please bear with me. I do have a very specific meaning for "trust" that needs to be developed over the course of several chapters: trust is "the presumption of reciprocity by others."

If you follow the argument, I believe you will come to appreciate its power to transform the way we view the nature of crime, the harm of crime, and the path to repairing that harm. Forgive me if this sounds grandiose. The last thing I want is for this book to be regarded as merely an exercise in clever argumentation; a feather in my academic cap. In writing it, there were many times that I wished the idea of trust as the presumption of reciprocity had occurred to another writer, a better writer, to John Braithwaite, for example. But, alas, this conception did occur to me one summer afternoon as I was delving into the arcane worlds of socio-biology, economics and game theory, and I knew at once that I was somehow in possession of an idea that needed to be shared with my colleagues in criminal justice. It wasn't just an idea suitable for publication in an academic journal. It was about something true about us; it was about what makes us thrive as social beings.

Crime, I will argue, is the intentional violation of the presumption of reciprocity in others (i.e., the violation of trust). The fundamental harm of crime, therefore, is the destruction of trust, both personal and social. Accordingly, the fundamental object of restorative justice is the restoration of trust.

But can the trust that was damaged or destroyed by crime ever be repaired? The answer, I will argue, is "Yes." Trust can be and has been repaired innumerable times in our own lives and in those of our neighbors. People are imperfect and crime exists everywhere, yet the endurance of social life throughout the world and across hundreds of generations stands as vivid testimony to the ability of society to heal those injuries and restore the trust that crime has damaged. Trust, in short, can be repaired; perhaps not completely, but sufficiently to ensure the health of society and of individual crime victims. What we need to do as social scientists and criminal justice reformers is to learn how trust is actually restored in communities and in the lives of crime victims and to apply those lessons in fashioning effective criminal justice policies and procedures that best promote the restoration of trust.

One final note. Although this books discusses at some length the issue of punishment within restorative justice, this theme, while controversial, is very secondary to the primary issue of restoring trust. An offender's voluntary submission to a deserved punishment in cases of serious crime, I will argue, is certainly one of the means by which trust in that offender and for society can be repaired. On the other hand, many other offenses require no more than a non-punitive "diversionary" approach as presently used today in the vast majority of restorative justice cases. But even in those cases in which some measure of punishment is thought to be required for the sake of restoring trust in the victim, in society and in the offender, the restoration-of-trust model operates as a mean of responsibly *minimizing* resort to punishment by *maximizing* all other means of restoring trust.

With those words in mind, I invite you to explore this new approach to criminal justice reform.

Ross London
Berkeley College, NY
May 2014

Contents

Figures

Preface

Restorative justice began as a vision of a better way to do criminal justice and, in hundreds of programs throughout the world, it has proven to be just that. It has helped victims to feel more satisfied with the process and more secure in their personal safety. It has increased offenders' compliance with restitution orders without adversely affecting recidivism rates. Yet it has not nearly reached its potential for transforming the conventional criminal justice system because it has failed to articulate a theory or set of policies applicable to the kinds of cases that most concern us: serious crime and adult offenders. Restorative justice has been readily adapted to juvenile and petty offenses, but what it has to offer in those cases is not a significant departure from the conventional policies that already favor conflict resolution and remediation over formal prosecution and punishment. Whether or not restorative justice can effectively deal with serious cases and adult offenders represents its primary challenge today because, unless it can do so, it shall remain on the sidelines of criminal justice practice, "doomed to irrelevance and marginality."[1]

The intent of this book is to help bridge the gap between "the margin and the mainstream" of criminal justice practice—not by abandoning or compromising restorative core values, but by building on them and extending their reach. Given the extraordinary diversity of opinions within the restorative justice "movement," I begin by focusing on the unique perspective it offers, a perspective that sets it apart from conventional approaches to criminal justice: *viewing crime as a source of harm that must be repaired.*

But what exactly is that harm? And what must be done to repair it? This book is an attempt to help answer these questions in a way that draws upon traditional criminal justice values and morality. Yet it also endeavors to expand upon those values by encompassing them under an all-embracing goal of restoration that is sought by the victim, by the community, by the offender, and by the larger society: *the restoration of trust.*

Of course, there are many other important human values that a criminal justice system ought to advance. Thus, it may be questioned at the outset whether *trust* should be regarded as any more important than values such as security, respect, or, indeed, justice itself. Is the restoration of trust just another lofty, unattainable ideal to add to the already voluminous restorative justice "wish list"?

The answer, I have come to believe, is that there is, indeed, something uniquely important about the notion of restoring trust that qualifies it to function as an overarching goal of criminal justice policies and practices. The conception of *trust*—its preservation, its loss, and its repair—is central to our understanding of interpersonal relations, our development of "moral emotions," and our innate concerns for fairness and reciprocity in dealings with others. It enriches our knowledge about the nature of crime and the function of criminal sanctions. It helps us to better comprehend the needs of the victim, the community, and the larger society in the aftermath of crime. The goal of restoring trust is an intuitive, specific, and, above all, useful guide for criminal justice professionals in their search for a sensible path through a maze of competing goals. Throughout this book, I return to a simple basic question, one to help guide our judgment in a multitude of all-too-familiar, but frustratingly complex, problems. For any offense and its offender, I ask: What must be done to restore trust in this person and in society?

This approach is not presented as a radically different conception of criminal justice that would cast aside conventional values. Neither is it merely an additional consideration to add to the complex interplay of values and goals that already exist in our system of criminal justice. Rather, it is a comprehensive means of prioritizing and evaluating those values and goals.

Unlike most books on restorative justice, this one considers not only juvenile and petty crimes, but also the "hard cases"—serious offenses and adult offenders—that are at the forefront of public concern about crime. Today's restorative justice programs, with few exceptions, are limited to juvenile, non-violent offenses, but what they offer for these cases may not differ substantially from already well-established remedial programs. For many years, the criminal justice system has sought to involve family, neighbors, and community resources in devising remedial solutions to youthful offending, and it has installed thousands of programs throughout the country to divert petty cases away from formal criminal prosecution. An increasing number of those cases are diverted to restorative justice programs, many of which have achieved high praise from their participants.

Yet our success in implementing restorative justice programs for juvenile and petty crime matters cannot be easily extrapolated to serious adult crimes. Important issues of personal accountability, security, expectations of justice, and adherence to the law, which may be of secondary interest in juvenile and petty crimes, are of primary interest in the realm of adult offending. My intent in this book is to look at all of these issues with candor.

Unless we do, the opportunity will be lost for restorative justice to escape from its niche as an exotic diversionary strategy and emerge as an important agent for change throughout the mainstream of criminal justice practice.

Note

[1] Dignan, "Restorative Justice and the Law," p. 179.

Acknowledgments

Not long after the dazzling debut of restorative justice several decades ago, inspiring us with a new vision of criminal justice, British scholar Andrew Ashworth cautioned that unless major changes were to be proposed, restorative justice was "unlikely to provide the basis for a theoretically respectable or socially respectable system of dealing with serious crime."

In the intervening years, criminal justice professionals, policy analysts, and legislators have still not been persuaded that restorative justice is capable of handling cases of serious crime. And so, despite its early promise, restorative justice has largely been relegated to administering cases involving petty offenses and juvenile offenders, far from the mainstream of criminal justice.

It is the vastly immodest goal of this book to meet Ashworth's challenge "head-on" and put forward not only a conception of restorative justice that attempts to be sensible and coherent, but one that *just might work* in the real world of serious crime: the "restoration of trust." To accomplish this task, I have drawn upon the work of some very great thinkers whose ideas inspired this project: John Braithwaite for permitting us to fundamentally re-think the basic objectives of criminal justice by his advocacy of "reintegration"; Howard Zehr for raising Braithwaite's proposal to a new level, thereby bringing to the world what we know as "restorative justice"; Robert Trivers for showing how trust—*the presumption of reciprocity*—is fundamental to our success as social beings; Susan Dimock, who explained that trust has not only a personal but a social dimension that must be maintained; and Norval Morris for providing the sentencing framework that provides the key for reconciling these two levels of trust—a key, I will argue in these pages, that makes restorative justice applicable to serious as well as minor crimes and that permits victims and offenders to participate in the process without jeopardizing fundamental social values.

A tall order indeed! But, I believe the best way to honor their remarkable contributions is to put their ideas to use in the "real world," adding what I can to make it accessible to students, practitioners, law-makers—and, indeed to anyone in search of a better way for criminal justice in our country.

I am indebted to many scholars, teachers, and practitioners whom I have consulted in the development of this project, both in its initial phase of social psychology and criminology research and in subsequent research in criminal justice policy, including: Prof. David Wilder and Prof. Harold Siegel of Rutgers University, Dr. Neil Vidmar of Duke University, Prof. Judith Lewis Herman of Harvard University, Prof. Gordon Bazemore of Florida Atlantic University, Prof. Stephen Garvey of Cornell University, Prof. Antony Duff of the University of Stirling, and Prof. Norval Morris of the University of Chicago. I'd like to thank my wonderful teachers at the Rutgers University School of Criminal Justice for providing me with a rich background in criminology theory and social science methodology, including: Prof. Freda Adler, Prof. Gerhardt Mueller, Prof. Jeffrey Fagan, Prof. Marcus Felson, Prof. Andrew von Hirsch, Prof. James Finckenauer, and the indispensable Phyllis Schultz, our most knowledgeable and helpful librarian. I am particularly grateful to Prof. Ronald Clarke, Prof. George Kelling, and Prof. Todd Clear, who brought to the task of reviewing my research a wealth of knowledge, creativity, and scholarly integrity that is known throughout our profession. My special thanks go to my friend and colleague Prof. Candace McCoy for reviewing an early draft of this book and making many valuable suggestions, and most of all to my dear friend Catharine, without whose inspiration and encouragement this work could not have been completed.

Finally, I would like to thank my wonderful family, Diana, Danny, and Annie Rose; my brother and sister, Peter and Rabbi Tsurah, and my brother-in-law, Yosaif; my innumerable and beloved relatives and in-laws—the Londons, the Shifrins, the Shumans; my friends and colleagues, from the old days practicing law in Hoboken to the new days teaching criminal justice; and, lastly, the loving memory of my dear mom and dad, for providing emotional support, spiritual uplifting, patience, and love all along the way. Thank you and bless you, everyone.

1
Introduction:
Restoring Trust

The genesis of this book began on a train trip from New York to Boston. Traveling alone on my way to a criminal justice conference, I had a chance to do some thinking. I took out my legal pad and started jotting down notes.

* * *

After 25 years of practicing law—as a private attorney, public defender, prosecutor and culminating as a municipal court judge—I had recently enrolled as a graduate student in criminology because I was seeking answers to a number of perplexing questions about the system of which I had been a part. These questions essentially boiled down to one: Is this *really* the best we can do?

Despite the efforts of many brilliant minds and the expenditure of vast sums, we have managed to create a criminal justice system that transforms innumerable personal misfortunes into yet other calamities. Victims, who have suffered the trauma of a crime, enter the portals of this system with high expectations of justice, only to find themselves wandering its halls feeling bewildered, unfulfilled, and used. For those accused of a crime, entry into the system portends the beginning of a personal nightmare of dehumanization, ruinous financial losses, and unending suspicion. As a criminal justice professional, I came in contact with hundreds of human beings caught up in this labyrinth. Time and again, I saw the same look of despair on those who emerged from the process embittered, exhausted, and defeated.

Paradoxically, although I shared many of the frustrations of both the victims and offenders, I grew to admire the values of the system and the means we have adopted to uphold those values. The U.S. criminal justice system was never fully planned; it *evolved* over time in response to the competing demands for protection against crime and from oppressive prosecution. Every innovation we have proposed to apprehend, detain, adjudicate, and sentence offenders has been counterbalanced with rules and procedures designed to protect the innocent. In a sense, the system has emerged from the clash of two nightmares: the nightmare of brutal, uncontrolled crime in the streets and the nightmare of false accusation. By many measures, we have done a good job at this balancing act. For most Americans, we have managed to keep crime to a tolerable level while continually expanding on a list of basic rights that are well beyond those in place when the Constitution was adopted.

Yet as respectful as I had become of the criminal justice system, I increasingly came to believe that it was fundamentally flawed, and not simply because of the personal inadequacies of those who administer it: the police who mishandle evidence, overzealous prosecutors, unprepared defense attorneys, inattentive jurors and overworked, underpaid court staff and probation officers. Much more troubling to me was the realization that, even when the system functions as it should (i.e., when cases are adjudicated swiftly, fairly, and conscientiously), we still don't seem to achieve very much. I worked hard to improve the fairness and efficiency in my own courtroom. Yet even on the best days—the days when all the parties arrived on time, when all the notices were properly served, when cases that could be settled were settled, and when other cases were tried to completion—even then, I had the hollow feeling that we didn't go far enough.

For criminal justice professionals (the judge, the staff, the attorneys), the conclusion of a case means the closing of one file and the opening of the next file. But what about the other lives that are involved? For the convicted offender, the conclusion of a case means a descent into a world of disdain and rejection that can be endured only by hardening the shell of denial and defiance that already sets him apart as a "criminal." *(Throughout this book, I refer to the defendant as male to reflect the statistical predominance of male criminality.)* For the victim, the conclusion of a case brings new questions: What happens now? When is the offender coming back? How will I be paid for my losses? How can I be protected from retaliation? As for the community at large—those who have to live in fear every day that a similar crime might happen to them—their questions, concerns, and voices are hardly ever heard.

It seemed to me that, in devoting all of its efforts to the tasks of determining culpability and imposing sanctions, the criminal justice system had succeeded in becoming an efficient instrument for condemnation and exclusion, but had utterly failed as an instrument of healing and reconciliation. The system that had evolved as a powerful instrument for apprehending criminals, assessing blame and imposing punishment was oddly indifferent to the need of the victim, the offender, and the community to break the cycle of crime, blame, and punishment.

Unlike the experience of many judges in large cities, I returned home at the end of the day only a few blocks from the courtroom, into the same community lived in by the victims and, in many cases, by the offenders. I often wondered if all we were doing in court was "spinning our wheels." I kept running into the same faces, the same families and the same problems. Having come of age in the uproarious '60's and therefore being constitutionally indisposed to accept limitations on what the system can and cannot do, I started to become more interested in finding solutions than in merely "disposing cases." In a city the size of Hoboken, New Jersey—one square mile and a population of about 35,000—the chances were good that the victim and the offender either knew each other already or would bump into each other again sometime soon. For many cases, perhaps the majority, trials did not provide anything remotely like a sense of closure. In our "winner-take-all" adversary system, success for one side means defeat for the other—hardly a formula for peaceful coexistence.

Whenever possible, therefore, I tried to see if the parties themselves could come to agreement about what should be done in their case. The parties were almost always resistant to settling their differences at first. The victims wanted vindication, the defendants wanted exoneration, and neither side wanted compromise. And so, I did not propose compromise. Instead, I asked the victim a fairly simple, straightforward question, "What do you want to accomplish in this case?" Amazingly enough, with that one question, doors that seemed permanently shut started to open, feelings that seemed forever hardened started to thaw and possibilities emerged that had seemed impossible.

Of course, I had a decided advantage over other mediators. As the presiding judge, after listening to all of their stories and evaluating the quality of evidence, I was able to give the parties my "professional opinion" concerning their prospects if they insisted on a trial before my alternate judge. (I was obliged to recuse myself from cases that I mediated). Attorneys were particularly grateful for this advice because it punctured their clients' misconceptions about what they could achieve at trial. Both prosecutors who had to handle "prima donna" cops and defense attorneys who had to handle their "kings and queens of denial" thereby became facilitators of mediation, not obstacles to it. Moreover, this professional opinion helped ensure that the resulting agreements were in line with the outcomes that could be expected at trial (guilty pleas, fines, community service, restitution, probation). But now, because the terms of the agreements were entered into voluntarily by the parties, unusually satisfying results could be achieved. Instead of feeling neglected or abused, the victim was fully involved. The defendant was able to stop lying to himself, his family, and his lawyers and accept responsibility "like a man." The prosecutor got his conviction. The defense attorney avoided yet another embarrassing defeat. And, as for me, I felt that I had accomplished something more than just sending another misfit off to jail. Beyond these results, the mediation sessions provided the opportunity for face-to-face dialogue, expressions of remorse, and creative solutions that could never be accomplished at trial. I developed a set of techniques for encouraging productive dialogue and continued to refine these techniques as a referee in the juvenile court once my term as municipal court judge was over. There, the motivation to resolve neighborhood problems—vandalism, bullying, assault, and gang rivalries—was even greater and obviously preferable to formal adjudication.

So maybe there was a better way after all! But I needed something more than my gut instinct to guide me. Once enrolled in graduate school, I embarked on a journey of intellectual discovery to find out if my grab bag of techniques and my instinctual desire for a more humane and responsive criminal justice system was supported by the findings and opinions of leading criminologists. Along the way, I found that criminologists have quite a lot of interesting things to say, but little agreement, as to the causes of crime and the best means for reducing it. What particularly interested me were ideas about the overall goals of the process; especially, the goals of criminal justice sentencing. I was searching for a comprehensive theory of criminal justice that not only accounted for and justified the system, but one that pointed the way to a more expansive vision of what we could achieve.

I was surprised to discover that the academics, far removed from the battlefield of the courtroom, are hardly less confrontational than my trial attorney brethren. Worse yet, their intellectual battles are far more insidious and enduring than legal confrontations, where courtroom theatrics are often followed by a round of drinks among "worthy adversaries." Perhaps because attorneys realize that their cause, in the end, is not their own and that their effectiveness is constrained by the often inconvenient *facts* of the case, most develop a fairly detached view that can be described as fatalistic or, perhaps, cynical. In short, attorneys tend to be good sports about the whole thing. But the academics who, having labored mightily to create an edifice of ideas, often come to view rival theories and theorists as threats to their standing among their peers.

This may account for the divisiveness that I noticed among sentencing theories and sentencing theorists. The advocates of "deterrence" and "incapacitation" regarded "rehabilitation" as hopelessly naïve and ineffectual, a feeling shared by "retributionists" who, further, claimed that all so-called "utilitarian" theories such as deterrence, incapacitation, *and* rehabilitation are morally deficient and potentially dangerous. To these charges, the utilitarians responded that retributionism, lacking a socially useful goal, is essentially irrational.

The uncompromising position of many of these sentencing theorists concerning the validity of their claims and the invalidity of rival claims was disconcerting to me, not only because it showed that criminologists had come no closer to agreement on these basic issues than the views of the average layman, but also because their insistence on the supremacy of one sentencing ideal over all others failed to reflect the reality of sentencing practice I had seen in every courtroom I had ever entered. Judges (with precious few exceptions) are no fools. They understand the strengths and weaknesses of competing sentencing goals. And so, in devising a reasonable sentence for any particular case, they do not pick only one sentencing goal to the exclusion of others. Instead, they try to find a sensible combination of goals that simultaneously reflects the need to deter future crime, to incapacitate dangerous offenders, to provide rehabilitation, and to impose retribution as a reflection of society's values. What I was looking for in my graduate studies was a principle that could help prioritize and guide this balancing of goals. Moreover, I was looking for a principle that could *go beyond* the limitations of each of these conventional theories; one that would promote the possibility of healing and reconciliation that the system, for all its virtues, seemed incapable of achieving.

In the course of my search for a more expansive conception of criminal justice, I came across the work of John Braithwaite. Braithwaite is a rarity among criminologists. Having achieved the reputation of a tough-minded analyst of corporate crime, he gained further renown as a communalistic visionary. In his influential work *Crime, Shame and Reintegration,* Braithwaite proposed a new way to deal with offenders; a way that, ironically, is far older than the existing system. The most potent means of controlling behavior, he argued, is the social network of the family and community. In ignoring the power of social approval, the modern criminal justice system relies on ever-harsher sanctions that not only are less effective than social approval, but they also result in the kind of stigmatization that produces further crime. A system dedicated to the goal of reintegration, he maintained, offers the possibility of crime control and reabsorption of offenders often found in traditional societies.

Braithwaite's conception of community-based justice and his understanding of the need for reintegration were encompassed in Zehr's more expansive vision, one that was graced by a most sublime and beguiling name: *restorative justice.* I'm sure I was not alone in practically swooning over the possibilities for a new, better, more transformative kind of justice that is suggested by this name. And indeed, for many people, restorative justice became the long-sought alternative to a system they had come to loathe for a variety of reasons—political, personal, and religious. To the radicals of the Left, restorative justice meant an alternative to the oppressive power of the state. To prisoners' rights advocates, restorative justice meant an alternative to incarceration. To victims' groups, restorative justice meant the possibility of genuine involvement and concern for their welfare. For Native American and aboriginal groups, restorative justice meant the possibility of a return to traditional practices and values. For Mennonites and other Christian groups, restorative justice meant the replacement of Old Testament retributionism with New Testament forgiveness. And for all those in search of a better way, restorative justice provided hope. I recognized that no theory can be all things to all people, and that restorative justice—the theory with the seductive name—looked more like a "Noah's Ark" of criminal justice critics, idealists, and reformers rather than a well-formulated theory capable of practical application. There was a distinct danger that, by becoming a vehicle for everyone's fantasy, restorative justice might end up on the scrap heap of other panaceas that periodically arise in criminal justice to raise our hopes to dizzying heights before dashing them.

And so, as I started to read through the outpouring of literature on this newly emerging development in criminal justice, I tried to separate the "wheat from the chaff." My objective was to identify the primary values of restorative justice that resonated most with my own conception of justice and respect for the rule of law but were also capable of application in the real world of my personal experience both in and out of court.

Reading through the works of many authors on restorative justice, all with their own well-defended pet theories, the theme that consistently struck me as wholly original and crucial to the restorative justice perspective was *the goal of repairing the harm of crime.* By identifying this goal, restorative justice had not only envisioned an important alternative to traditional sentencing theory, but a fundamentally new orientation for the criminal justice system as a whole. Specifying the ways in which this goal was to be achieved was, as I saw it, a secondary consideration. Once the goal of repairing harm was viewed as a guiding principle, it was possible to imagine any number of procedural innovations that could help to accomplish this task.

Now my focus turned to more specific questions. If the key goal of restorative justice is repairing the harm of crime, what exactly *is* the harm of crime that needs repairing? Is it injury, property loss, psychological damage, or all of these? What can the system do to repair that damage? And what, if anything, can the defendant do to repair the damage he has caused?

* * *

Such were my thoughts as the train chugged along the coast of Connecticut and on up to Boston. By now, my legal pad was filled with notes—most of which were quite illegible to the average mortal—all cumulating in one boldly marked question: **What is the victim's basic loss?**

I paused for a moment of reflection, and then wrote down a single-word answer: *trust.*

What distinguishes crime from other types of injuries, it seemed to me, is that it represents a fundamental breach of trust. For the victim, the experience of crime results in a loss of trust in the offender and in the society that failed to provide basic security. The offender, now having been labeled as being "untrustworthy," is an outsider to the law-abiding community. He has become, literally, an "outlaw." Further questions raced into my mind: Is it really possible to restore trust? Is there anything an offender can do to regain trust, or must he remain a permanent outsider? Is there anything the criminal justice system can do to promote the restoration of trust?

In contemplating answers to these questions as well as related ones, I found that focusing attention on the goal of regaining trust not only helped to clarify the basic principles, strategies, and procedural innovations of restorative justice both but also helped to address some of its major dilemmas. I am grateful for the opportunity afforded me by graduate school to contemplate these issues at my leisure rather than in the midst of a hectic court calendar. In the course of my studies, I had the chance to question some of my core beliefs about the use punishment, the value of forgiveness, and the role of the victim in criminal sentencing. I also came to appreciate and eventually utilize the tools of social science research to find answers based on empirical data and not simply on opinions, no matter how compelling they might appear to be.

Overview of the Book

The result of that process of study, soul-searching, and number crunching is this volume. In the first half, I invite the reader to explore a *comprehensive* approach to restoration; attempting to resolve the major issues that have prevented restorative justice from bridging the gap between the margin and the mainstream of criminal justice practice. In the second half, we will consider the practical implications this approach can have upon the way we handle criminal justice in this country—from policing to corrections.

Our exploration begins in the following chapter, Chapter 2, in which I describe the basic concepts of restorative justice and trace its development from an idealistic vision of a new criminal justice "paradigm" to a worldwide movement. The chapter ends by focusing on the two major issues faced by restorative justice as it moves from the margins to the mainstream of criminal justice: (1) the problem of private justice and (2) the problem of punishment. To resolve these issues, I attempt to distinguish between the core mission of restorative justice and the host of collateral values with which it has been associated.

In Chapter 3 I advance the claim that the greatest innovation of restorative justice is not in creating new *criminal justice practices*, but in creating a new *criminal justice goal*: repairing the harm of crime. By focusing on this as an overarching goal, I argue, we employ a powerful tool to examine and to reform every aspect of the criminal system. If the central goal of restorative justice is repairing the harm of crime, the next task is to identify *what* is the essential harm of crime. I argue that the kind of harm essentially associated with the commission of a crime is the *loss* of trust. The core mission of restorative justice, then, is the *restoration* of trust. But what is needed to restore personal trust? The guiding insight here is that, given our human fallibilities, breaches of trust are commonplace in human relations; yet we somehow manage to repair those breaches and restore relationships of trust. If we can figure out how this is done on an interpersonal level, we might be able to apply those lessons to the problem of repairing the harm of crime. In this chapter, I invite readers to brainstorm about various ways that trust might be restored in the aftermath of several crime scenarios: beginning with a simple property offense and ending with a violent crime.

In Chapter 4, this analysis of restoring personal trust undergoes a significant transformation. Here, I argue that we cannot design a comprehensive criminal justice system based on lessons learned from the model of restoring personal trust unless we also consider another dimension of trust: trust in society. This expanded analysis of trust presents the key to solving one of the most crucial problems facing the development of restorative justice: reconciling the goal of informal justice (based on personal encounters between the victim and offender) with the requirements of law and principles of equality. After discussing a number of proposed solutions to this problem, I introduce my own solution based on the analysis of Canadian philosopher Susan Dimock who distinguishes between two dimensions of trust. Because trust has both a personal and a social dimension, the restoration of trust also must operate on *both* an individual and a societal level. For a criminal sanction to address both levels of trust, I propose a procedural solution whereby the conditions for regaining social trust operate as "outer boundaries" of sentencing severity reflecting society's interest in maintaining norms of conduct, but within those boundaries we are free to explore conditions to regain personal trust in the individual offender. Distinguishing between these two levels of trust enable us not only to solve the problem of private, informal justice, but also to integrate a host of competing sentencing theories under a single all-encompassing goal of restoration.

My purpose in Chapter 5 is to deepen our understanding of the importance of repairing trust. To do so, I explore the remarkably convergent findings of sociobiologists and economists concerning the evolution of cooperative behavior and its associated emotional responses, all of which have a bearing on the relation between trust and justice. My argument here is that the establishment of trust is not simply an incidental benefit of life in society. It is, instead, an essential precondition of social cooperation. Yet all these theoretical discussions could amount to nothing more than an intellectual exercise unless they resonate with and are confirmed by our powerful, instinctual responses to the experience of justice and injustice. My belief is that the prospect of restoring trust taps into these instinctual responses in a way that genuinely respects the needs of crime victims. Furthermore, I attempt to explain why understanding the role of trust in social relations helps us to comprehend the nature of crime and the process of identifying, punishing, and excluding offenders as well as what is necessary to bring them back into the "fold."

The next two chapters are devoted to a major theme of this book: *the pathway back for victims and offenders.* In Chapter 6, I argue that the "maximalist" model of restoration that utilizes apology, restitution, and the voluntary submission to a deserved punishment affords crime victims a foundation for the healing and closure that they seek. Here, I examine the competing views between restorative justice theorists concerning the role of punishment in a system dedicated to restoration, and contrast the claims of those who regard punishment as the antithesis of restoration with those who look upon punishment as a necessary instrument of restoration. In this review, I present the results of my own empirical research: The imposition of what the victim regards as a deserved punishment and, more importantly, *the perceived failure to impose a deserved punishment* are significant factors in the emotional recovery of crime victims. These findings indicate further that, while punishment is certainly a necessary component of criminal justice, its use can be minimized in a responsible manner if punishment is coupled with other effective means of engendering trust. It is the nexus of apology, restitution, and deserved punishment, I argue, that offers crime victims a realistic and encouraging pathway to genuine healing and forgiveness. In Chapter 7, I examine how the criminal justice system acts as a kind of rite of passage by which offenders are excluded from the "moral community." But is it truly possible to move on from that exclusion to inclusion? In this chapter, I maintain that the pathway back to inclusion is indeed possible within a criminal justice system designed to facilitate the restoration of trust in the offender by employing the critical nexus of apology, restitution and voluntary submission to a deserved o punishment.

Guided by the principle of restoring trust, in Chapter 8 I examine a number of important issues in criminal sentencing theory and practice while always keeping in mind the question: What must be done to regain trust in the offender and in society? Using this approach, the possibilities for significant change become manifest to anyone with an open mind—and an open heart.

Chapter 9 explores the interaction of trust and community; that is, how the community serves the development of trust and how relations of trust enhance the life of the community. In this chapter, I also examine some of the key issues surrounding the participation of community members at restorative justice conferences. In Chapter 10, I pause to apply the theory of restorative justice to a number of crime scenarios in a restorative justice "workshop." By comparing the restoration of trust approach with both conventional criminal justice administration and other forms of restorative justice practices, readers of this chapter will gain a deeper appreciation of the impact of these differing models on the achievement of justice and restoration for the victim, the community, and the offender. Chapter 11 extends our analysis to one of the most troubling problems in the U.S. criminal justice system today: the disproportionate incarceration of minority offenders. I have attempted to approach this issue with a degree of candor that is often avoided in such discussions. But if nothing else were to be achieved by writing this volume, the communication of its pragmatic and hopeful message to those who live in and those who serve the minority community would make these efforts worthwhile.

Chapter 12 is all about the issue of openness to new ideas. Here, I acknowledge that for many of those who have been attracted to restorative justice as a purely nonpunitive alternative to the conventional system, the restoration of trust model that I am putting forward—one that includes punishment as a sentencing alternative—will represent a corruption of the purity of the original restorative justice paradigm. I confront that issue directly, and in some depth, because I consider the problem of conceiving restorative justice as a new "paradigm" to be the single greatest conceptual impediment to open discussions of restorative justice theory and practice. To readers unfamiliar with the issue, it might seem as if the controversy over paradigms is a matter of concern only to academicians. But this is an intellectual barrier that must be confronted if any of the issues that I discuss are to be considered with an open mind.

In Chapter 13, I apply the restoration of trust approach to a wide range of criminal justice reforms ranging from policing to corrections. The final chapter, Chapter 14, not only sums up what has come before, but also serves as an invitation to readers to expand and extend these restorative justice concepts to the real world that they experience.

At its core, this book seeks answers to the question: What must be done to restore trust in the offender and in society in the aftermath of crime? My hope is that this query will stimulate innovative thinking by the criminal justice theorists, the practitioners, and, most of all, the students whose own search for a "better way" is just beginning.

2

A New Paradigm Arises

Restorative justice as both a philosophy and an implementation strategy developed from the convergence of several trends in criminal justice: the loss of confidence in rehabilitation and deterrence theory, the rediscovery of the victim as a necessary party, and the rise of interest in community-based justice.

In the 1970s and 1980s, the America's faith in the criminal justice system was severely shaken. The optimistic beliefs of earlier decades that crime could eventually be eradicated by addressing the "underlying causes" of poverty, urban congestion, and discrimination had by now eroded. President Lyndon Johnson's Great Society had failed to materialize and the hopefulness of the civil rights movement had been undone by a succession of inner-city race riots that shattered the stability of cities throughout the country. After nearly a century of attempts to reform and rehabilitate offenders, the inconsistent results of these efforts generated a pervasive sense that "nothing works."[1] The traditional concept of penance had long since been discarded, and even the efficacy of crime prevention by deterrence was questioned by criminologists who argued that a free society is unlikely to provide the inevitability of detection, apprehension, and swift punishment that is required for effective deterrence.[2] Crime theorists, no longer convinced that offenders could be induced to change by either threats or therapy, resurrected biological theories of criminality and stressed the need to identify and incarcerate the hard-core "incorrigibles" who were thought to be responsible for a disproportionate amount of crime. Even if the threat of incarceration does not deter people from committing crimes, they argued, the walls and iron bars of prison effectively (if expensively) incapacitate offenders from further menacing the public as long as they are kept inside.[3] Other theorists argued for the merits of retributive justice, claiming that the state should impose punishment as a morally based response to blameworthiness of offenses rather than an attempt to change the character of offenders through rehabilitation.[4] During the

1980s, political leaders perceived a shift in public opinion away from rehabilitation and toward greater punitivity. Understanding full well that being labeled "soft on crime" was the kiss of death for their careers, politicians throughout the country withdrew their support for rehabilitation programs and began enacting ever-tougher sentencing laws with longer jail terms, mandatory sentences, elimination of parole, lifetime incarceration for repeat offenders, and juvenile "waivers" for treatment as adults. Then, to accommodate the flood of inmates that ensued, they appropriated millions for the construction of new prisons.

Yet despite creating the highest levels of incarceration in our nation's history and one of the highest rates of incarceration among developed nations, crime rates during the early 1980s continued to rise. Not only was the criminal justice system seen by many critics as ineffectual, unable to stem the epidemic of drug use, and, through its "get tough" tactics, the cause of further alienation and rebellion in the inner cities,[5] the system was increasingly deemed unresponsive to the needs of crime victims and their communities. The growing victims' rights movement sought to gain judicial acceptance of victims' entitlement to increased services, financial compensation and restitution, and intervention in the criminal justice process.[6] Some saw restitution not simply as a necessary component in sentencing, but as the basis of a new philosophy of justice in which accountability is achieved by offenders through actions to repair the damage they have caused rather than merely by accepting punishment.[7] Social critics from the Left renewed their attacks on the criminal justice system as a means of social control exercised by a repressive state,[8] and proposed decentralized, informal alternative means of resolving conflicts.[9] Prisoners' rights groups, with the support of a number of Christian groups, stressed the need to reintegrate, rather than permanently exclude, offenders.[10] The 1980s also saw a rise in interest in community-based problem solving and indigenous justice.[11] During this period, the "just deserts" theory, initially embraced by legislators as a principled solution to the problem of sentencing disparities that resulted from unbridled discretion, came under strenuous attack for being rigid, obsessed with punishment, retrospective, and more concerned with "uniformity rather than resolving genuine conflict and addressing underlying juvenile and interpersonal problems."[12]

Out of this amalgam of critiques of the existing criminal justice system grew an interest in a new conception of justice, one based on healing injuries rather than the assignment of blame and punishment for legal transgressions. This "restorative justice" alternative was envisioned to be essentially informal and nonpunitive. The adversarial nature of the prevailing criminal justice system, designed to protect the rights of the accused, was now seen as inherently non-restorative by discouraging candor and cooperation on the part of the accused and excluding the participation of the victim. These restorative justice theorists sought an alternative to a system that placed undue reliance on attorneys and judges, and in which many victims felt they were treated as little more than a "piece of evidence"[13] and who were "twice victimized, first by the offender and then by an uncaring criminal justice system that doesn't have time for them"[14] To some, this emphasis on victim restoration called for an end to criminal law, replacing it with the civil law protection of an individual's personal and property rights.[15]

This new vision of justice was understood to be an entirely new paradigm, not merely a means of reforming the system, but one in which retributive justice would be replaced by a justice that "grows out of love" and "seeks to make things right."[16] Under the "old paradigm," the system operated as an arena for the conflict between two adversaries having entirely different goals: (1) the state, which sought to control crime by obtaining a speedy conviction and a severe punishment; and (2) the defendant who sought protection against unfair and oppressive prosecution. In this adversarial system, the truth of accusations was to be determined by the clash of professional combatants who were well trained in complex rules and procedures designed to establish guilt or innocence without impairing the rights of the accused. Because a crime was prosecuted on behalf of the state, the victim of the crime had no separate standing in the courtroom and, consequently, was merely a witness rather than a party whose individual interests were to be protected. Under the "new paradigm" of restorative justice, however, the victim would become a central decision maker in a process of personal encounters and joint negotiation.

Ironically, restorative justice advocates contended that the new goal of repairing harm through informal encounters was not really a new innovation at all but, in fact, represented a return to ancient and tribal practices from which Western societies could learn a great deal. In ancient times, they claimed, an offense was not against the state, but against a person and a community.[17] The goal of conflict resolution therefore was not simply to assign blame for legal transgressions, but to restore wholeness to individuals and the community. Aboriginal justice, they maintained, involved more than just a resolution of a dispute or the proper assessment of legal liability; there also was an active effort to repair material, psychological, and relational damage. Beyond the harm suffered by the individual members of the group, crime represented a threat to the stability and peace of the community. Clan loyalty required collective retaliation for transgressions and, without a mechanism for negotiating conflicts, the danger of resort to a cycle of violent retaliation was very real. Thus, mediation was typically used to address transgressions within the clan and to establish peace between clans.

The basic features of this new but, in many ways, more traditional way of achieving justice began to coalesce during the 1990s. What was achieved was not so much a set of principles as a set of shared values and goals:

> • Viewing crime as a source of harm, not simply as a transgression of law, and, consequently, specifying the mission of the criminal justice system as the repair of harm instead of only the determination of guilt and imposition of punishment;
> • Involving the victim, the offender, and relevant community members to the fullest extent possible in voluntary negotiations;
> • Providing compensation for the victim and achieving social reintegration of the offender; and
> • Conducting personal encounters between the victim and offender to establish community peace, and not merely conformity to the law.

The original vision of restorative justice practice therefore consisted of informal, voluntary face-to-face encounters between the victim, the offender, and relevant community members. Through this dialogue, the parties come to greater understanding and empathy, the offenders express remorse, and all negotiate a plan for repairing the harm of crime, resulting in an agreement that emphasizes reparative solutions such as restitution, apology, and community service rather than only punishment.

Growing Pains:
Searching for Fundamentals and Confronting Challenges

As the restorative justice approach grew during the 1990s from an idealistic vision to implementation in actual practice—with more than 1,500 programs throughout the world and over 300 programs in the United States—certain strains developed between those who claimed to represent the "original, pure" vision of restorative justice and those who sought a larger role in determining the course of mainstream criminal practice. These tensions centered on two fundamental challenges to restorative justice theory and practice: (1) reconciling its advocacy of a nonpunitive response to crime with the public's insistence on deterrence and retribution; and (2) reconciling the value of private, informal justice with the needs of society and the rule of law.

Critics of the radically informal approach of restorative justice, both in academia and in the general public, questioned how such a system would be able to cope with the problems of protecting public safety, promoting offender rehabilitation, and ensuring the rights of the accused to a fair trial.[18] The resolution of cases by private negotiation, they contended, would contribute to greater lawlessness by substituting the interests of individual crime victims for the rule of law and by ignoring the interests of the general public not privy to that agreement.[19] Private grievants might be satisfied by the payment of compensation or the entry of consensual restraining order, for example, but the public at large might still be faced with the presence of a dangerous offender in their midst. Even in cases where a victim genuinely comes to forgive his or her assailant, the interests of the general public not privy to their agreement are not necessarily considered. Just as the state under the old paradigm was blind to the needs of victims, under this new system of private justice, the victim may be blind to the needs of society. Worse yet, if economically powerful offenders and criminal organizations are able to buy their way out of trouble, they can continue their criminal enterprises as before, writing off the occasional payment of restitution as the "cost of doing business."

As in the case of conventional prosecutions where the community representatives do not necessarily reflect the concerns of the victim, so too the victim does not necessarily concern himself or herself with the welfare of the community. Recognizing the greater ability of the formal criminal justice system to protect the interests of the general public—its insistence on public safety and its concern for "consistency, fairness, and efficiency"[20] in criminal procedure and sentencing—many restorative justice theorists have sought a balance between formal and informal justice. The danger of arbitrary and disparate sentences stemming from victim-offender settlements was intended to be controlled by judicial review, and the concern for community safety was meant to be protected by community participation. To some, however, the inclusion of the community as an interested party to the proceedings threatened a return to the retributive model[21] and a source of "net widening."[22] More fundamentally, the incorporation of the traditional legal system into restorative justice for the purpose of ensuring procedural safeguards and maintaining standards became viewed as a potential degradation to the core value of personal, informal encounters between the victim and offender.[23]

In addition to the problems raised by the new paradigm of informal, personal encounters, restorative justice had to address the issues raised by its rejection of punishment. Eliminating punishment would mean removing a sanction that many, if not most, citizens view as a necessary component of justice. Although there is universal agreement among restorative justice theorists that the singular fixation of traditional criminal justice with assigning blame and imposing punishment is incompatible with restoration, the legitimate use of punishment within a restorative context has been the subject of considerable debate. While the view of the "penal abolitionists" has been the abandonment of punishment altogether[24] or its replacement with a restitution model,[25] others concede a limited role in enforcing settlements or as a last resort for those incorrigibles who have proven to be unreceptive to restorative programs.[26] As against these views, some new voices have entered the debate in recent years: a small, but growing, minority of restorative justice theorists who have argued for a restorative function of punishment.[27]

Concern for public safety and a desire to include the community as an equal participant in the restorative justice process has resulted in the adoption by the Office of Juvenile Justice and Delinquency Prevention (OJJDP), U.S. Department of Justice, of a "balanced and restorative approach" to restorative justice.[28] Under the OJJDP approach, restoration is seen to consist of three major components: (1) accountability of the offender (responsibility, empathy toward the victim, and reparation), (2) community safety, and (3) competency development (what was once referred to as "rehabilitation"). This approach sees the harm of crime not only as individual harm to the victim, but also as harm to the general public. Additionally, it recognizes the need for reintegration of the offender even after his individual debt to the victim has been satisfied. The OJJDP approach clearly demonstrates a desire to accommodate the needs of both the individual victim and society. But without a coherent theoretical model, this kind of accommodation can be viewed as a compromise of essential restorative justice values.[29]

Searching for Fundamentals

Through its simultaneous emphasis on reparation to the victim, accountability to the community, and responsiveness to the rehabilitation needs of offenses, the concept of "restorative justice" has become increasingly inclusive but also increasingly amorphous. Furthermore, attempts that have been made to accommodate due process protections demonstrate the difficulty of creating a full-scale alternative to the existing system. Bazemore and Walgrave argued that the problems associated with privatization could be solved by recommending that legal institutions oversee individual encounters to ensure that minimal protections of the rights of the accused are respected.[30] Yet it is in defining the nature and extent of these minimal protection that difficulties arise. The United States Constitution grants to the accused such rights as the right to counsel, the presumption of innocence, the right to remain silent, and the right to trial. Restorative justice programs cannot compromise these rights by calling for "minimal" adherence: The Constitution has already defined what those minimal rights must be for all criminal cases.

As a result of these and other considerations, the growth of restorative justice has resulted in a constellation of values rather than a unified vision. After reviewing various formulations of restorative justice core principles, Bazemore and Walgrave concluded that "a full-fledged restorative justice alternative should offer as many legal safeguards as the traditional justice system, but it should be socially more responsible, provide more standing and support for crime victims and offer at a minimum no fewer opportunities for offender rehabilitation and reintegration than systems grounded in individual treatment assumptions."[31] In other words, at the same time as it accomplishes the goal of reintegrating the offender into the community, restorative justice ought to include all of the protections of the due process model and the offender benefits of the rehabilitation model as well as satisfying the need of the crime victim for reparation and the need of the community for safety.

The danger, of course, is that, in fashioning a program from such an all-inclusive wish list, not only will the original focus of restorative justice be lost, but individual components of the program also will suffer. On the other hand, the cost of maintaining allegiance to a vision of restorative justice as a *radical alternative* to existing criminal justice theory and practice is the continual marginalization of restorative justice to juvenile offenders and petty offenses.

If restorative justice is to play a role in reformation or transformation of the criminal justice system, it cannot proceed by a withdrawal into an arcane orthodoxy applicable only to petty juvenile offenses. Neither can it progress by simply acquiring more and more "tools," more vectors of interest, and more principles. What is thereby gained in comprehensiveness is lost in increasing incoherence. Thus, restorative justice theorists must propose a persuasive concept of restoration that can be applied to all offenders—juvenile and adult offenders, first-timers and repeat offenders. Furthermore, as restorative justice grows from a vision to an implementation strategy in the real world, it must develop a reasonable jurisprudence—one that provides a rational basis for the rule of law, procedural fairness, and just enforcement. The wholesale rejection of a positive role of the state in establishing and enforcing law in favor of private justice, which is advanced by some theorists, not only is a political barrier to greater acceptance of restorative justice, but it also neglects the vital role of government in ensuring the due process rights, equality treatment, and protection of minorities.

The ability of restorative justice to help victims and communities recover from their losses and offenders gain reintegration cannot be based on a yearning for an idealized past or a homogeneous, communitarian society. Instead, it must be relevant to the inner cities as well as suburbs, small towns, and Native American reservations. It must apply to the hard cases as well as the easy cases, to violent crime as well as property crime, and to repeat offenders as well as first-timers. It must be appropriate for the cases that now fill the prisons as well as the cases that are routinely diverted away from the criminal justice system. The future of restorative justice therefore involves a critical choice: Should it remain as an exotic alternative to the conventional system, applicable to only a limited category of offenses and offenders? Or should it enter the criminal justice "mainstream" by offering a *comprehensive* model applicable to the widest variety of cases?

Finally, restorative justice must be embraced by the victims' rights community as a better way of doing justice. Remarkably, despite the streams of rhetoric extolling restorative justice as a means of victim empowerment and healing, little support has been forthcoming from victims rights' and victims' advocacy groups. Indeed, an extensive survey of victims' advocacy groups noted widespread dissatisfaction with restorative justice policy and practices involving feelings of "injustice, disrespect, exclusion, lack of empathy and irrelevance."[32] Some of this concern centered on the ambiguity of restorative justice goals and values, which derived from a "fractious collection of interests and personalities."[33] A criminal justice alternative dedicated to the interests of crime victims cannot afford to be regarded as "tone deaf to their aspirations."[34]

And so, as restorative justice continues into its third decade, with programs throughout the world and an ever-growing literature by its advocates, practitioners, and critics, it still can be aptly described as a "work in progress."[35] Devised by criminal justice visionaries in the 1980s as a new paradigm to replace what was viewed as a structurally flawed and misdirected system, criticized as a naïve rejection of hard-won constitutional rights, and fragmented into factions with different outlooks and strategies, restorative justice remains a promising but marginal development in criminal justice, still "in search of fundamentals."[36] It is to an examination of those fundamentals that we now turn.

Notes

[1] Lipton, Martinson & Wilks, "The Effectiveness of Correctional Treatment."
[2] Sherman, et al., "Preventing Crime;" Blumstein et al., Deterrence and Incapacitation.
[3] Wilson & Herrnstein, Crime and Human Nature.
[4] von Hirsch, Doing Justice: The Choice of Punishments.
[5] Wright, Justice for Victims and Offender.
[6] Elias, The Politics of Victimization.
[7] Barnett & Hagel, "Assessing the Criminal," p. 15.
[8] Pepinsky, The Geometry of Violence and Democracy.
[9] Christie, "Conflicts as Property," pp. 1–15.
[10] Colson & Benson, "Restitution as an Alternative to Imprisonment."
[11] Wright & Galaway, Mediation and Criminal Justice.
[12] Bazemore & Walgrave, "Restorative Juvenile Justice: In Search of Fundamentals," p. 46.
[13] Cardenas, Juan, "The Crime Victim and the Prosecutorial Process," p. 371.
[14] Umbreit, Coates & Kalanj, Victim Meets Offender, p. 196.
[15] Barnett, "Assessing the Criminal: Restitution, Retribution and the Legal Process."
[16] Zehr, Changing Lenses, p. 139.
[17] Van Ness & Strong, Restoring Justice (3rd Ed.), p. 7.
[18] Feld, "Rehabilitation, Retribution and Restorative Justice, pp. 17–44.
[19] Ashworth, "Some Doubts About Restorative Justice," pp. 277–299.
[20] Van Ness, "New Wine and Old Wineskins," p. 264.
[21] McCold, "Paradigm Muddle," 2004.
[22] Van Ness, supra, p. 272.
[23] McCold, "Toward a Holistic Vision of Restorative Justice," pp. 357–358.
[24] Bianchi & Van Swaaningen, Abolitionism: Toward a Non-Repressive Approach to Crime; Christie, Limits to Pain.
[25] Barnett, "Restitution: A New Paradigm," pp. 279-301.
[26] Braithwaite, "Restorative Justice and De-Professionalization," p. 29.
[27] Daly, "Restorative Justice: The Real Story," pp. 58-60; Barton, "Empowerment and Retribution in Criminal Justice," p. 67; Miller & Blackler, "Restorative Justice: Retribution Confession and Shame," p. 88
[28] Office of Juvenile Justice and Prevention, Guide for Implementing the Balanced and Restorative Justice Model.
[29] McCold, "Paradigm Muddle."

[30] Bazemore & Walgrave, "Restorative Juvenile Justice: In Search of Fundamentals."

[31] Bazemore & Walgrave, "Reflections on the Future of Restorative Justice," pp. 363-364.

[32] Mika, *et al.*, "Listening to Victims," p. 35.

[33] *Id.*

[34] *Id.* p. 40.

[35] Bazemore & Walgrave, "Reflections on the Future of Restorative Justice," p. 359.

[36] Bazemore & Walgrave, "Restorative Juvenile Justice: In Search of Fundamentals," p. 45.

3
Restoration of Personal Trust

In order to create a comprehensive model of restorative justice that will be applicable to a wide variety of offenses and to both adult and juvenile offenders, it is essential to go back to the basics.

First, we require a clear definition of *restorative justice*. One definition that has be well received was put forth by Marshall: "Restorative justice is a process whereby all parties with a stake in a particular offence come together to resolve collectively how to deal with the aftermath of the offense and its implication for the future."[1] This widely adopted definition offers a fair summary of restorative justice practice, but little guidance with respect to its core values. As Bazemore and Walgrave have pointed out, Marshall's emphasis on a unique restorative justice process makes the definition at once too broad and too narrow.[2] It is too broad because the solutions derived from personal encounters are not necessarily restorative. Without a specific orientation toward repairing the harm of crime, the agreed-on results of these conferences are as likely to be recriminatory as they are to be reparative. Marshall's definition also appears to restrict the application of restorative justice to those cases in which both the victim and offender agree to directly participate, thus removing the operation of restorative principles from the many cases in which one or the other party declines to participate.

A comprehensive approach to restorative justice would therefore reject a restrictive definition like Marshall's, and seek the application of restorative justice to the widest possible variety of cases and procedural contexts. But can restorative justice achieve such a comprehensive range without thereby "losing its soul"? To answer this question, we must attend to more fundamental questions: What, exactly, is the soul of restorative justice? Is there a core value that unites the various strains of restorative justice theory and practice, and can offer the possibility of system-wide reform?

What sets restorative justice apart from the conventional approach is not a body of specific procedures, but a conception of criminal justice that is capable of application in different settings. As Bazemore and Walgrave have suggested: "We need openness to the possibility that reparation and restitution is achieved in different circumstances, for different victims and for different victimized communities." [3] Therefore, the fundamental innovation of restorative justice is not in any particular application, but instead in its *intent*. Whereas the traditional goals of the criminal justice system are to deter, censure, incapacitate, and rehabilitate offenders, restorative justice poses an entirely new and original goal: *repairing the harm of crime*. Bazemore and Walgrave have proposed a definition that stresses this unique goal of restorative justice: "restorative justice is every action that is primarily oriented towards doing justice by repairing the harm that is caused by crime."[4]

What, then, is the essential harm of crime? Clearly, the harm of crime involves a material loss, but mere recompense for material losses is not fully restorative to a crime victim if the offender shows no remorse or acceptance of responsibility. The commission of a crime against a person, whether it results in bodily harm or property loss, is an insult to the dignity of that victim, a fundamental expression of contempt, and, ultimately, an act of dehumanization that cannot be repaired or restored merely by the payment of money. Then too, if repayment for material losses was all that mattered, the fear and anxiety associated with threatened or repeated offenses would go uncompensated. Furthermore, even if material and psychological damages of an individual victim were somehow to be compensated monetarily (as we attempt to do in civil cases), payment alone would do little to assuage the fears of the community. As we attempt to understand why the payment of money cannot adequately restore the losses suffered by a victim and the community as a consequence of crime, we can better understand why the advocates of restitution as a new basis for criminal sanctions fundamentally misconceive the difference between criminal harms (crime) and civil harms (torts). These two types of harm may not differ markedly in terms of intent: Both crimes and torts may be intentional, reckless, or, at times, negligent (in the case of crime, "criminally negligent"). Their fundamental difference lies in the fact that a crime is more than an injurious act because the victim is not merely *harmed* but is also *wronged*.[5] Even if it were possible to restore a victim's psychological damage through therapy, medication, or the acquisition of better "coping skills," the injustice to him or her would persist and would require some form of redress.

A more insightful conception of the essential harm of crime, one that takes into account the disrespect and degradation suffered by crime victims, is the damage to relationships. This is closer to the real concern of crime victims but, in many cases, there is no preexisting relationship that is disturbed by crime. If we expand the conception of "relationship" to include an offender's relationship with the community,[6] the definition gains applicability to a much wider variety of offenses. In many cases in which there is a preexisting relationship between a victim and offender (as in the case of domestic violence), while the victim may have no desire to restore that relationship, the victim still often expresses a desire to restore her relationship with the community.[7]

Even so, identifying the essential harm of crime as the damage to relationships seems rather to identify the *result* of the harm rather than the harm itself. Personal relationships can be damaged by a host of psychological factors such as failure to communicate, jealousy, and insensitivity. And social relationships can be damaged by factors such as class and racial discrimination. The key question is: What is it about *crime* that damages relationships? Additionally, if we conceive of the essential harm of crime as damage to relationships, there is an implicit message that restoring a relationship involves a preference for a return to the status quo. But attempts to reconcile a relationship often ignore the oppressive nature of the relationship that gives rise to the offense. In these cases, the goal should be to transform the relationship rather than to restore the preexisting inequality.

The Fundamental Value of Trust

Still lacking from the concept of the harm of crime as a material loss and partially, although not fully, comprehended by the concept of harm to relationships is the notion that crime is not just a cause of injury; it is a betrayal of the most basic understandings of what we can expect of our kindred human beings. What needs to be restored is the security of the individual and group in the knowledge that we all play by the same rules and that we can rely on each other in our interpersonal dealings without fear of force or fraud to overcome our will. In short, what needs to be restored in the aftermath of crime is a *sense of trust in the individual who broke the rules.*

Certainly, the idea of regaining trust in the offender does not envision the establishment of *perfect trust*, something that does not exist even among nonoffenders, but rather reestablishing *basic trust*, the degree of trust that we accord to members of the general public with whom we might come into contact in the ordinary course of life.

Accordingly, this notion of trust does not assume a preexisting relationship between a victim and offender. Even if the parties are unknown to each other, everyone in society has a right to assume that others will not victimize them. Trust can be regarded as a reasonable presumption of "fair play" that enables us to conduct our normal affairs in society without crippling fear. Crime represents a fundamental breach of that trust. In order for us to regain trust in such a person, we need to know that the offender has a conscience, that he is capable of empathy and has comprehended the consequences of his actions, has done his best to repay the losses, and, in some fundamental way, has undergone a significant life change. Unless the offender has suitably demonstrated this, he can neither be trusted nor successfully reintegrated into society.

When a person transgresses the rules of social or commercial interaction, the state properly discharges its function by providing effective modes of redress. If the transgression is accidental, unintended, or innocently mistaken, the state provides a mechanism for compensation through the *civil law*. In civil cases, there is no moral approbation associated with the infliction of harm by another person. However, certain harms require more than material compensation in order for restoration of trust to occur. Here, the *criminal law* has a central role to play in guaranteeing the maintenance of bonds of trust that have been ruptured by intentional acts of force or fraud.[8]

The possibility of achieving real and lasting restoration of trust is not an idealistic fantasy. We have all experienced the process of regaining trust in a personal manner within the context of family, friendship, and marital relations. Insults, lies, assaults, theft, and property damage occur frequently in these intimate relationships, and yet we seem to find ways to mend those harms eventually and to maintain those bonds. That social relationships do not inevitably disintegrate from breaches of trust is vivid testimony to humanity's capacity to resolve disputes—not merely to the end of assessing blame and exacting punishment, but to the end of real restoration and reintegration. The trust-based concept of restorative justice takes this intimate model seriously because it provides the basis for understanding the elements of regaining trust in a full range of offenses.

How do we respond to a person who has lied to us, cheated us, or intentionally injured us? Those who violate our trust by their words or deeds remain forever distrusted unless they do something to earn our reacceptance. But what can they do? What must they do? These are exactly the kinds of questions we should ask in order to generate a "to do" list for offenders who seek to be re-accepted by society, and we can start exploring the answers from our own, personal experience of having our trust betrayed in some manner. Ordinarily, we would require that the transgressor at least accept responsibility for the offending action, provide compensation for the material harm inflicted, and thereafter manifest a personal transformation in order to be restored to a position of trust. Mere words are not enough. Words are easy to mouth and are especially suspect when they come from people whose trustworthiness has already been placed into question by their actions. Repayment of losses, although necessary, is not enough to restore trust if the person does not understand, acknowledge, and atone for their moral fault. Even more is required: a sense of shame with a visible manifestation of conscience. We humans respond positively to contrition because it is only then that we can view that person as having, in some way, personally experienced a measure of the pain, suffering, and loss they inflicted on us. It is this manifestation of empathy with the victim's suffering and shame for having caused it that enables us to see the offender's anguish as genuine remorse and not merely self-pity. The offender's demonstration of remorse that permits us to perceive his underlying humanity in turn makes it possible for us to eventually accept and forgive him.[9]

In this context of family and social relations, we do not require the inner suffering associated with shame and contrition as an end in itself or as a means of exacting revenge. Neither do we require suffering as some sort of behavioral conditioning or deterrence device, especially in our adult relationships. The goal at all times is to create the conditions under which the family or the relationship can be restored. A person who breaches our trust by words or conduct has manifested an inadequate moral brake to his behavior. The people we trust are those who regulate their personal interactions by genuine empathy and respect for the rights, feelings, and values of others, and therefore do not require external means of controlling their behavior. They are part of our moral community—a community defined not by geographical boundaries, but by mutual adherence to moral obligations. [10] Those who violate this trust must somehow prove that they deserve to be readmitted and reaccepted as "one of us." As impossible as it may seem at first, trust *can* be reestablished, wounds *can* be healed, and relationships *can* be repaired—never by a simplistic and vain attempt to "turn back the clock," but rather by a process of transformation that creates a new relationship. Out of an understanding of the conditions for reaccepting those who have injured us in personal relations, we can begin to derive concrete ideas on how to reaccept offenders into the larger community and to devise solutions for the task of healing the wounds of crime.

Therefore, in envisioning a criminal justice system dedicated to the restoration of trust, I pose a simple, central question: What must be done to restore our trust in the offender? Answering this question does not require any philosophical, political, or religious assumptions. It is an empirical question, amenable to the research tools of social science, which may provide important insights for the development of restorative sentencing policies.

Let's start looking for answers. To do so, it will be helpful to engage in an act of imagination. For any particular crime, and any particular offender, consider what you (as the victim) *would require of him* so that, at some point in the future, you would trust him enough to allow him back into your community with normal social relations.

It is necessary to concede at the outset that the wounds of crime never entirely heal, even in the case of minor crimes, and that the loss of trust is never perfectly recovered. Many physical wounds leave permanent scars, and the wounds of crime are no different. However, insofar as it is possible, try to identify those actions that an offender might take, however burdensome and over whatever length of time, in order to restore a basic, minimal level of trust that might be accorded to the ordinary man in the street. Consider the following incident:

On your way to your car, you notice that the passenger side window is broken and the ground is covered with shattered glass. Inside the car, your personal belongings are strewn about—and your radio is gone. Later that week, a 25-year-old man is arrested for breaking into your car and stealing the car radio. He has no prior criminal record. Your total losses (including the radio, damage to the car and lost time from work) amount to $1,000.

What will it take to restore your trust in this offender? At first blush, the idea of ever "trusting" this person again seems ridiculous. If you never trusted this stranger before, it makes little sense to start trusting him now that he has shown himself to be untrustworthy. But recall that, by the use of the term "trust," I am not referring to honesty but rather basic trust: that minimal level of trust we require for any and all people living in our community. In the case of this automobile break-in, for example, you know that we cannot imprison this person forever. He is coming back some day. So the question is not whether he will be permitted back into the community, but whether he will come back with your consent or against your wishes. What we will explore here are those conditions of regaining minimal basic trust that will make your consent more or less likely. Therefore, while we cannot ever hope to establish an exact and comprehensive formula for regaining trust, we can begin to identify those factors *without which* regaining trust is unlikely to occur.

And so, from the point of view as the victim of this crime, what specifically must be done to restore your trust in this offender? *(My personal reactions are indicted in italics. You may wish to compare your reactions to the following scenarios).*

1. Apology.

He must apologize. He must show he has a conscience, a sense of morality. He must demonstrate that he appreciates the full extent of the damage he has caused me. He must show he is ashamed of his conduct.

For both juvenile and adult offenses, a required part of the "core sequence" of repairing personal relations is the delivery of an apology in which the offender acknowledges his fault and demonstrates shame and remorse.[11] This basic requirement is as instrumental to the healing of the injury of crime as it is to noncriminal episodes we accept as a normal part of life. If the offender does not accept responsibility for the damage he has caused and does not indicate an awareness of any moral fault on his part, we can be justified in considering that person to be fundamentally untrustworthy: a personal and community danger, despite his having been convicted and serving a sentence.

Just as it is critical to the restoration of trust that the offender expresses remorse, so too is it instrumental for the victim to have the opportunity to express himself or herself so that the offender may understand the impact of his crime and, perhaps, empathize with the victim. While the limited empirical findings so far suggest that the generation of empathy has not been particularly successful, either because of a victim's skepticism of the offender's real motives or an offender's preoccupation with minimizing exposure to punishment[12] the goal of instilling empathy as part of the restoration process should not be dismissed. Certainly, there is little reason to believe that offenders (other than those already predisposed toward empathy) will suddenly become transformed as a result of an emotionally charged encounter session, as many restorative justice advocates have imagined. As Levrant *et al.* cautioned, this model of offender rehabilitation based on a sudden insight into the harmful effect of crime on the victim is fundamentally at odds with the empirical findings of "what works."[13]

Yet by encouraging the expression of remorse through personal encounters, rather than by discouraging them as we routinely do in the adversarial system, the opportunities for instilling genuine empathy and expressing genuine remorse are undoubtedly expanded. Although we may never know an offender's real intent, the very act of offering an apology by one who was previously a victimizer—even if performed in the hope of gaining lenient treatment—is inherently empowering to the victim because it grants him or her the authority to evaluate the sincerity of the offender and to accept or reject the offer of apology. Furthermore, as Daly found in her study of Australian restorative justice programs, whether or not the offenders had a genuine change of heart, the expression of remorse by offenders was significantly related to reduction in the fear of crime experienced by victims.[14] For those offenders whose remorse is regarded as insincere or inadequate, a range of options designed to elicit empathy (including counseling and victim assistance services) might also be useful in the restorative process, and may constitute a further ground for mitigating the severity of punishment. Performing volunteer work in a hospital, for example, can offer an offender the opportunity to empathize with those who suffer, and to comprehend the consequences of his crime. Therefore, even if empathy is not aroused by a victim-offender encounter, empathy may be instilled by appropriate sentencing options that are specifically intended for that purpose, thereby minimizing resort to punishment.

2. Restitution.

He must agree to pay for my losses and come up with a realistic plan for repayment.

An obvious component in the process of regaining trust in a person who has caused material damage is full and voluntary restitution. Restitution must be regarded as a necessary, although not sufficient, precondition for regaining trust. Unlike the imposition of fines, which are intended as punishment and therefore vary with the seriousness of the offense and culpability of the offender, the only valid consideration in setting the limits of restitution is the quantum of damages suffered by the victim. No upper or lower limit can be predetermined as an objective condition: If the parties fail to agree, the victim must prove his or her losses in a civil proceeding. Restitution is important both as an end itself and also as an indication of the sincerity of the offender's remorse. Without the agreement to compensate a victim fully, the offering of an apology can be seen as an expedient means to escape further consequences. Furthermore, while it may be easy to promise to pay restitution, the promise sets up a specific, measurable test of trustworthiness. Those who fail to repay the loss may be forgiven. But can they be trusted?

3. Explanation.

He must tell me why he did it. For my own peace of mind, I am entitled to know why I was singled out. I need to know why it did not bother him to victimize me.

If we are to regain some kind of trust in the offender, we must know his reasons for committing the offense. For money? For thrills? Because of rage? Whatever the motives, he has to do something serious about addressing those "needs." Also, if we do not determine that the offender has an extraordinary need for money or an identifiable psychological problem that manifests in a lack of control, it may be that he simply thought he could "get away with it." If that is the case, we will have to find out much more about him: his childhood, education, family, employment experiences, and peer groups. Anything that can be thought of as a "cause" of his misconduct—whether it be a positive motivation to commit a crime or, more likely, a failure to restrain his impulses—may then become a source of a reparative solution. What must be avoided is a perception that the offender's actions are incomprehensible because, if they were, there would be an unbridgeable chasm between him and the moral community. He would be a permanent outsider—the unknowable and untrusted "other"—whose presence in the community could mean only an occasion for fear, avoidance, and rejection.

4. Rehabilitation.

If it were clear that his criminal conduct is strongly linked to some problem that can be helped through rehabilitation, I would insist that he undergo the necessary treatment program.

Some restorative justice advocates have questioned the role of rehabilitation within the restorative justice paradigm, arguing that it constitutes an offender-oriented rather than a victim-oriented approach to restoration.[15] The premise that justifies rehabilitation in a trust-based conception of restorative justice is that an offender who is incompetent to manage his affairs and who, by his misconduct, demonstrates a disregard for the rights of others, is reasonably held in distrust. Above and beyond anything that is needed for personal forgiveness of that offender's moral failure is tangible proof that he has sufficiently overcome his physical, mental, or educational disabilities to qualify for a minimally acceptable life in society without resort to crime. Furthermore, just as empathy-building mechanisms may help to reduce the need for punishment in the process of reestablishing trust, so too can rehabilitation help to reduce the need for punishment. A drug-dependent offender, for example, cannot be reasonably expected to exercise elementary caution or self-control and, thus, is justifiably distrusted so long as the addiction remains in effect. For such an offender, a term of incarceration might be viewed as a less desirable than an appropriate treatment, when sentencing options are judged by the standard of their ability to promote trust and, thereby, social reintegration.

5. Social Network.

He must convince me that he is responsive to people who share my values and who will act as guardians and intermediaries.

In order for the offender to be trusted in the community, he must show that he is part of a responsible social network, be it family, employment, or religious affiliation. Ideally, the offender should have at least one sponsor to act as an intermediary until his supervisory period is over and to exercise a degree of interpersonal control over him. An offender who is responsive to the moral expectations of intermediaries provides hope that he will learn and grow from the experience of rehabilitation. The offender's trust in the intermediary will promote the community's trust in the offender.

6. Probationary Time.

The offender is literally and figuratively "on probation" until some time has passed and I have seen a demonstration of his commitment to change. Trust is not earned overnight, and it is not achieved by words alone.

Even if the offender fulfills all of the previous requirements, he cannot be considered socially trustworthy until a certain amount of time has passed in which he has complied with all of the agreed-on conditions and has refrained from any crime. As impressive as an emotionally charged encounter between a victim and offender can be, the real proof of a genuine transformation in the offender occurs through his actions over a period of time during which judgment as to his trustworthiness remains in a state of suspension. Sudden epiphanies make for good television dramas, but for bad criminal justice planning.

7. Punishment.

If the above conditions are followed; that is, if the offender apologizes, agrees to pay restitution, submits to rehabilitation, and stays out of trouble, I won't insist on punishment, or perhaps will require only some minimal punishment in the form of community service. On the other hand, if he does not apologize or show remorse and if he fails to honor any of his agreements, he should be punished.

This assessment accords fairly well with the claim advanced by many restorative justice theorists that, from a victim's point of view, what is genuinely restorative is an apology, a personal encounter between the victim and offender, restitution, and a commitment to change. Punishment plays no significant role in this formulation; it becomes a factor only if the voluntary restorative model fails and some external means of enforcement must be applied. This is the purist conception of restorative justice as a voluntary, personalized, and nonpunitive alternative to the traditional system. Punishment is the antithesis of this ideal, but it must remain as a tool of enforcement in the event that non-punitive measures prove to be inadequate.

Now, let us imagine several variations of this hypothetical crime. The following example involves the same crime but, here, the offender has been previously convicted of a similar crime:

On your way to your car, you notice that the passenger side window is broken and the ground is covered with shattered glass. Inside the car, your personal belongings are strewn about—and your radio is gone. Later that week, a 25-year-old man is arrested for breaking into your car and stealing the car radio. He has a record of one prior conviction for a similar offense. Your total losses (including the radio, damage to the car, and lost time from work), amount to $1,000.

As a victim of this crime, what will it take to regain your trust in this repeat offender?

1. Apology.

I would still need an apology, as in the case of a first-time offender, but I would be far more skeptical and the effect of the repeat offender's apology would be considerably diminished.

2. Restitution.

As in the case of the first-timer, I would insist on restitution, but I would have lower expectations of it being paid by the repeat offender.

3. Explanation.

I would be skeptical about any explanations offered by the repeat offender and would want to know why he didn't learn his lesson the first time.

4. Rehabilitation.

I would need to know why his rehabilitation needs were not addressed before and, if they were, why they failed. I would have much less confidence in the effectiveness of rehabilitation for a second offense, but would require it anyway for specific, treatable problems such as drug addiction and illiteracy.

5. Social Network.

This is still an important consideration, but I would want to know why the social network failed for the repeat offender. Perhaps there is a way to increase its effectiveness by involving a specific person who both the offender and I could trust as a go-between.

6. Supervision and Restriction.

Because my trust in this repeat offender is not easily restorable by his words and promises, I would insist on stricter external controls: more intensive supervision and greater restrictions on his liberty.

7. Punishment.

I just don't trust him. In the case of this repeat offender, I don't believe that imprisonment is necessary in order to guarantee my personal safety, as long as he is under intensive supervision. However, I believe he must receive punishment—possibly in the form of incarceration—to ensure that he "gets the message," a message he might not have actually absorbed the first time he was convicted and released into the community. Also, he should receive a punishment simply as a matter of justice. None of us is perfect, and so the first offense may have been a one-time-only aberration. But a second offense implies a degree of deliberateness that requires a strong message of condemnation.

The case of a repeat offender represents a challenge to the nonpunitive orientation of restorative justice. In our first encounter with offender, he demonstrated remorse, empathy, and willingness to change, coupled with the prospect of personal growth through rehabilitation and responsiveness to a social network. All of these factors came into play in our decision to reject the need for punishment for his first offense. However, at least from these preliminary observations, it appears that each of the factors that mitigated against punishment are so undermined by the occurrence of a repeat offense that punishment now becomes a necessary component of sentencing if some measure of trust is ever to be restored in the future.

Now, instead of focusing on an automobile break-in, let's consider a violent crime:

As you are walking alone in a downtown shopping area at night, you are grabbed from behind by a man and pushed up against a wall. He shows you a gun and demands your money. You hand over your wallet, and he runs around the corner. Later that week, the robber, a 25-year-old man with no prior criminal record, is arrested after he attempted to use your credit card. Your total losses (including your wallet and its contents, and lost time from work) amount to $2,000.

As a victim of this crime, what will it take to regain your trust in this offender?

1. Apology.

Because this crime is far more serious and devastating to me personally, the need for an apology is particularly important if my trust is ever to be restored. Certainly, the absence of an apology or, worse, the refusal to offer an apology would eliminate any chance of restoring trust. However, as in the case of the repeat offender in the automobile break-in scenario, the apology must be backed up by actions to show that it is credible.

2. Restitution.

I expect restitution not only to pay my bills, but also to show that the offender's words are believable. This is particularly important if the payment of restitution involves some degree of personal sacrifice by the offender (as opposed to, say, payment from an insurance policy or by an affluent relative).

3. Explanation.

I need an explanation. Without an explanation, I cannot judge whether or not I will ever be able to consider him socially trustworthy.

4. Rehabilitation.

I would require rehabilitation only if the need is obvious such as in the case of drug addiction or a neurological disorder. In any case, rehabilitation must be coupled with a full and complete admission of responsibility. Otherwise, it might appear to me to be a means of excusing the behavior or mitigating the offender's responsibility in order to receive a lighter sentence.

5. Social Network.

Of course, any indication of social control or social responsiveness would be a good sign, but it would be a small factor since it obviously was not enough to prevent my victimization. Furthermore, by the commission of this serious offense, this offender has exhibited such entrenched criminality that his social network is very likely to be involved in his criminal lifestyle. For me to be able to trust him again, he must permanently sever his ties with his network of offenders and participate in a new network of law-abiding citizens.

6. Supervision and Restriction.

Even though this is a first offense, I will not feel safe in this community if he is at large. He needs to be confined initially, and then closely supervised with enforceable restrictions on his movements (i.e., curfew, electronic monitoring devices) once released.

7. Punishment.

Even if the offender apologizes, agrees to pay restitution, offers an explanation, submits to rehabilitation, and agrees to a new network, he still should be incarcerated in order to prevent further crimes, by showing him clearly what he will face if he relapses. Also, anyone who commits a crime of this nature should be punished, if only as a matter of justice.

8. Extended Probationary Period.

After the offender's release from jail, with suitable restrictions on his movements, I will continue to consider him a risk. Sometime in the future, when it is clear that he has truly changed, I will be able to accept him back into my neighborhood as a "reformed sinner."

From my reactions to these three cases—a property offense, a repeat property offense, and a violent crime_it might appear that, as long as restorative justice insists on a purely nonpunitive approach, its use must be restricted only to juvenile cases and, for adult offenders, first-time property offenses. This is a serious limitation, one that would render restorative justice all but irrelevant to the vast majority of criminal cases.

Of course, my personal responses to these scenarios cannot be used as the foundation for a model of restorative justice, however restrictive or comprehensive. It is certainly possible that many readers, in thinking through and "feeling through" these scenarios, will have a much different analysis of what is necessary for restoration, including the restoration of trust. Regaining trust in an offender after all, is a highly subjective matter. For victims who are motivated to regain trust in the offender because there has been a prior relationship, there is little reason to believe that imposing a punishment will make future trust more likely, and considerable reason to believe that insisting on punishment (especially after an apology and payment of restitution) might be counterproductive. For victims who have had no prior relationship with the offender, the imposition of punishment might do little to restore trust because there was no particular reason to trust him to begin with. In my commentaries on the scenarios, the reasons for demanding punishment mostly had to do with societal goals such as "teaching a lesson" or obtaining justice rather than restoring trust. Yet some readers might believe there is a greater possibility of achieving genuine understanding during the process of interpersonal dialogue between a victim and offender without the sanction of punishment looming in the background, which could induce insincere apologies for the sake of expediency. Therefore, while there may be general agreement on the utility of apology, restitution, explanation, supervision, and the successful passage of a probationary period toward the goal of restoring trust in the offender, the utility of imposing a punishment toward the attainment of this goal is not at all obvious.

Later in the book, there will be much more about the relationship between punishment and trust but, at this juncture, let us simply note that the imposition of punishment on an offender is not universally acknowledged as a requirement or precondition for restoring trust in him. A nonpunitive version of restorative justice might yet be envisioned that could apply to a wide variety of criminal cases, subject only to the limitation that it be used solely for those victims who do not insist on punishment. This would, of course, limit the reach of restorative justice but, if that is the price that must be paid for maintaining its integrity—its "soul"—then, so be it.

But restricting the application of restorative justice to cases in which a victim does not seek punishment for the offender raises other issues, which, if uncorrected, would render restorative justice ineligible to administer *all but the most trivial* criminal cases. To understand why this is so, we now must consider the key problem inherent in a system of justice that focuses exclusively on the restoration of a victim's trust in the offender: the problem of private justice.

Notes

[1] Marshall, "The Evolution of Restorative Justice," p. 37
[2] Bazemore & Walgrave, "Restorative Juvenile Justice: In Search of Fundamentals," p. 48.
[3] *Id.* p. 52.
[4] *Id.* p. 48.
[5] Duff, *Punishment. Communication and Community*, p. 46; "Restorative Punishment and Punitive Restoration," pp. 84–88.
[6] Bazemore, "After Shaming," pp. 161–163.
[7] Herman, "Justice from the Victim's Perspective," p. 585.
[8] Gottfredson & Hirschi, *A General Theory of Crime.*
[9] Neiburh, *God's Justice and Mercy.*
[10] Opotow, Moral Exclusion and Injustice," pp. 2–6.
[11] Retzinger & Scheff, "Strategy for Community Conferences," pp. 316–317.
[12] Daly, "Mind the Gap," pp. 224–225.
[13] Levrant, *et al.*, "Reconsidering Restorative Justice."

[14] Daly, "Restorative Justice: the Real Story."
[15] Wright, *Justice for Victims and Offenders*; McCold, "Toward a Holistic Vision of Restorative Juvenile Justice," p. 358.

4

The Restoration of Social Trust

To understand what "private justice" is and why it is represents problem for the development of restorative justice, consider the following outcomes that might arise if criminal sanctions were determined by the mutual agreement of the victim and offender rather than by public prosecutions:

1. **The Overly Forgiving Victim.** Mr. Jones is mugged on his way home from the bank by a young man with a lengthy criminal record. At the restorative justice conference, he accepts the offender's apologies and remorse and, believing fully in the power of forgiveness, agrees to drop any demand for incarceration.
2. **The Selfish Victim.** Mrs. Taylor's house, along with many others on the block, is burglarized by a young man with a lengthy record, and her jewelry is stolen. At the conference, she agrees to drop demands for incarceration if her wedding ring is returned and the defendant agrees to stay away from her house.
3. **The Fearful Victim.** Mr. Todd's store is robbed by a gang member. He drops demands for imprisonment because he's afraid of retaliation from other gang members.
4. **The Favorably Biased Victim.** Mr. Reed's car is vandalized by a group of young men. He demands imprisonment—except for the son of his coworker.
5. **The Negatively Biased Victim.** Mrs. Fisher's car is vandalized by a group of young men. She agrees to probation for the white youths, but insists on a prison term for the two black youths in the group.
6. **The Vindictive Victim.** Mr. Smith's daughter is verbally harassed by a homeless man. Smith, a retired police officer, gets the offender to agree to a 4-month prison sentence.

7. The Partner in Crime. Mr. Rawls and Mr. Jeffers, members of the same gang, engage in a bloody brawl. Because both have extensive criminal histories, they decide to drop all charges against each other.

The point of these hypotheticals, of course, is that, as much as we can envision value in criminal sentencing based on satisfaction of the demands of the victim,[1] there are other factors besides the interests of the victim that must be taken into consideration. Specifying the conditions for regaining trust is useful in inventorying the various means of bringing about restoration both for both the victim and the offender, but is *not* an adequate basis for social policy. Given the enormous amount of individual variability among both victims regarding their requirements for regaining trust and their willingness to forgive, leaving sentencing decisions to the unlimited discretion of victims would likely result in great disparities and neglect of the community's right to safety.

The kind of justice that is achieved by the victim and the offender in the course of their negotiations, is a form of *private justice;* justice that is responsive only to the litigants' private interests. The central problems of private justice, accordingly, involve its lack of concern for impartiality and uniformity of treatment and its disregard for the welfare of other citizens.

How, then, can a restorative criminal justice system dedicated to repairing the harm suffered by the victim avoid the problem of disparities, arbitrariness, bias, and neglect of the public interest that arise in a fully privatized model of justice? One solution that has been offered to address problems arising from the victims' subjectivity is the inclusion of representatives from the police department, prosecutor's office, or probation department in victim-offender restorative justice conferences, a procedural solution that often is used in restorative justice programs in the United Kingdom and Canada. Although this undoubtedly serves to protect the public interest and to ensure a degree of uniformity, it can easily lead to domination of such hearings by the professionals, thus detracting from the kind of empowerment and degree of candor that are sought in victim-offender dialogue.

Another proposed solution to the problem of private justice is the inclusion of community representatives in restorative justice conferences. However, even if a community representative participates in a restorative justice conference session, the inherent limitations of the subjective perspective remain because the issue to be considered by the participants is whether the offender can be trusted to reenter the community and, if not, what are the reasonable conditions he must satisfy to regain trust. To answer this question, the participants must take a "holistic" view of the offender. They must try to understand his upbringing, education, employment, rehabilitation needs, and prior experience with the law in order to evaluate his apparent honesty, the sincerity of his remorse, his empathy for the suffering of the victim, and his capacity and willingness to pay restitution. They must find out about—and communicate with—his family in order to determine what kind of supervision and support he will have once the case is concluded. It is certainly proper to conduct such an analysis in order to guide the victim and the community representative in their assessment of whether the offender is worthy of some degree of trust, given certain conditions, or whether incarceration is required. But such a high degree of individualization would inevitably lead to enormous disparities in sentencing. The sentence for a case of arson, for example, might be a lengthy term of incarceration for some offenders and probation for others, depending on the characteristics of the particular offender—his ability to communicate, his network of support, and his likability. As we would have others forgive our own faults, we are apt to forgive those who most remind us of ourselves.

Yet by giving favorable treatment to offenders with whom we can identify, a problem arises with respect to offenders who do not communicate well, have no great network of support, and are not regarded by the victim or the community as likable. This is the problem of *prejudice*. Private justice unconstrained by notions of equality and proportionality is not necessarily benign. Victims and community representatives are as likely to be overly vindictive as they are to be naïvely forgiving.[2] More importantly, they are apt to regard the members of their own ethnic or class group as basically good people who can be worked with and are apt to regard those outside their circle with varying degrees of suspicion, contempt, or fear. Even people who think of themselves as being entirely free from prejudice are more likely to believe in the possibility of restoring trust in the sons and daughters of their peers than in strangers.[3]

Furthermore, even if we lived in an ideal world totally free of prejudice, sentencing decisions based entirely on the characteristics of a particular offender would still result in class-based disparities. It has been shown in the works of Braithwaite and Hirschi that the most effective kinds of control against antisocial behavior are social controls.[4] An offender who is embedded in a social matrix that provides support and encouragement for good conduct and that induces unbearable shame for misconduct does not need the imposition of a prison term to ensure that he will not reoffend. By contrast, those whose social environment is disorganized or dysfunctional are rightfully viewed as greater risks to security of the community. The end result of privatized justice is justice that places no value on the ideal of equality of treatment. It necessarily discriminates against people raised in socially disadvantageous environments, especially if incarceration is used as a last resort for only those who lack adequate social controls. Using community members in restorative justice victim-offender conferences sessions may be an appropriate solution to the problem of crime victims who fail to consider the needs of their neighbors, but is *not* a solution to the problem of inequality of treatment.

One idea that has been advanced to cope with the disparities that arise from the subjectivity of victim-offender conferences is to eliminate all those social inequalities that tend to classify some people as requiring incarceration more than others. Braithwaite, for example, rails against the hypocrisy of the traditional liberal insistence on equality of treatment, claiming it to be simply a tool for subjugating the poor and minorities in a capitalist, racist system:

> The formal equality of the liberal justice model—equal punishment for equal wrongs—unfortunately creates an oppressive system in which domination is rampant. In practice, the equal justice model delivers just deserts to the poor and impunity to the rich because of the way the dominations of punishment interact with the dominations of unequal wealth.[5]

Braithwaite argues further that a restorative system that has no such rules of "formal equality" may nonetheless support the value of equality, so long as the economic, political, and social system itself is non-exploitive. However, it would not work in a capitalist society: "Empirically, we argue that individualistic, privatized societies do not have the capacity to mobilize community disapproval against violations of rights that assure non-dominated freedoms."[6]

Indeed, he argues, restoration itself is an undesirable goal if what is being restored is an unequal, exploitive system:

> "Restoring balance" is acceptable as a restorative justice ideal only if the "balance" between offender and victim that prevailed before the crime was morally decent. There is no virtue in restoring the balance by having a woman pay for a load of bread she has stolen from a rich man to feed her children.[7]

I take this to mean that only when such a non-exploitive society is achieved, where one group has no economic advantage over another and where bigotry and intolerance are unknown, can the criminal justice system operate in a nondiscriminatory manner. This may actually be true. The criminal justice system does not operate in a vacuum, and the effects of discrimination in the larger society are bound to show up in the manner in which we differentiate between offenders. It does seem, however, that the existence of class, race, and social discrimination in society as a whole should make us *more insistent* on protections against arbitrary, subjective, and discriminatory sentencing rather than less so, as would be the case if we were to abandon rules of equality and proportionality in sentencing. There is indeed a value in ensuring that justice is blind, and that, to best of our ability, we strive to create a system of criminal justice based on the equal application of law.

The problem of private justice also represents a fundamental challenge to the theory of restoring trust. Our analysis of the core mission of restorative justice—repairing the harm of crime—has led us to identify the *loss of trust* as the essential harm of crime and, consequently, to identify the *restoration of trust* as the central goal of restorative justice theory and practice. Furthermore, I have argued that the goal of restoring trust is not unattainable in human affairs. Breaches of trust between individuals involved in every variety of interpersonal relationships are commonplace and yet every society, including ours, has evolved methods of repairing those breaches and successfully restoring those relationships. Were this not so, social life as we experience it would hardly be possible. Our "game plan" for the development of a restorative justice theory and practice therefore has been to examine how breaches of trust are repaired on an interpersonal level and to utilize these techniques and insights as the basis for envisioning criminal justice reform. To appreciate this point, consider what would happen if we were to use the tools and tactics of the criminal justice system to deal with personal breaches of trust that occur, say, within our own homes. Surely, the result would be more misery and more distrust. The model of restoring personal trust has to be a "better way" than the crude and impersonal techniques that are used for the serious breaches of trust we label as crimes.

And yet, the model of restoring personal trust, however effective it might be in interpersonal relations, cannot be an adequate basis for devising criminal justice policy because it cannot adequately address the problems associated with private justice. On the contrary, the model of restoring personal trust is itself a form of privatized justice and, as such, is vulnerable to the associated problems of inequality, subjectivity, abandonment of the rule of law, and neglect of the public good. Indeed, one may argue that, in addressing the private concerns of individuals affected by crime rather than the concerns of society as a whole, the model of restoring personal trust fails to minimally qualify as a "criminal justice system" at all because criminal justice, as opposed to civil justice, is expected to satisfy public, rather than purely private interests.[8]

Speaking personally, my growing awareness of the inadequacy of the model of restoring personal trust as a basis for sentencing policy marked the end of one phase of my thinking on the subject of trust, and the beginning of another. As a criminal court judge and as a criminal justice graduate student, I was especially interested in developing a theory of sentencing based centered on the restoration of trust as a core goal. The prospect of gleaning the world's wisdom in methods for restoring trust and applying those lessons to the reform of criminal sentencing was, I must admit, an intoxicating possibility. Given mankind's success in repairing breaches of trust among family, friends and community members, it was altogether disheartening that the criminal justice system, despite the billions spent yearly on its maintenance and expansion, remained stubbornly blind to this fundamental goal. The model of restoring personal trust, I believed, could provide the basis for fundamental reform of sentencing policies because we can see it in operation every day in our closest relationships that certainly do not rely on punishment or coercion.

But the optimistic promise of this approach—utilizing the model of repairing breaches of interpersonal trust to inform sentencing policy—was disturbed by the inadequacy of the interpersonal model to deal with the above-mentioned vulnerabilities of private justice. These considerations are of no particular importance when dealing with one's family. Who, after all, would insist on a child being punished out of a concern for "justice" when a little kindness and wise counseling could work perfectly well? Who would insist on adherence to the "law" when a simple apology would suffice? But just as the rules we would apply to strangers would be inappropriate for our loved ones, I had to concede that the rules applicable to family relations could not be an adequate basis for social policy. This realization was a devastating blow to me because it raised the possibility of abandoning restorative justice as a realistic alternative to the "conventional" system.

My initial responses to the problems inherent in the administration of private justice were very much akin to the standard postures of many other restorative justice advocates in defending their "new paradigm" from criticisms by the upholders of traditional criminal justice values:

1. **Defiance.** From this perspective, if a system of criminal justice based on the restoration of trust does not conform to certain societal-level values (such as uniformity of treatment and the supremacy of the rule of law), it is simply because it represents a fundamentally different alternative to a system that sacrifices the interests of the individual to the needs of the state. Rather than apologize for or attempt to excuse its failure to address societal concerns, the validity of those conventional concerns of criminal justice could be denied as being mere by-products of "statism." The much-vaunted ideal of equality of treatment is simply illusory, it might be argued, because the uniform application of the law can only result in the oppression of disfavored minorities in a society corrupted by racism and economic inequality.[9] The ideals of protecting public safety and the supremacy of the law are also but ideological constructs used to ensure the domination of the state.[10]

2. **Retreat.** From this viewpoint, the problem of privatized justice is avoided by regarding restorative justice as an alternative means of resolving criminal justice problems only in those cases in which matters of public safety are not of great importance. For more serious cases, the traditional methods might yet apply as a "fall-back" option.

3. **Wishful Thinking.** From this outlook, the objectionable features of privatized justice are apparent to only those who are inured to the values of the conventional system. Over time, once the restorative justice model becomes the conventional method of doing justice, the expectations of justice will change and the problems associated with privatized justice will evaporate. Only if the ultimate goal of criminal justice is punishing offenders, for example, do we care about uniformity. If, however, the goal is "healing," we can expect highly individualized and diverse treatment without resentment for lack of uniformity, the same as we would respond to individualized treatment of patients suffering from a variety of medical ailments. And just as in the case of family interactions, the present concern for rigid adherence to legal precedent along with a belief in the necessity for punishment to ensure order will eventually appear unnecessary and oppressive.

4. **Contempt.** From this point of view, those who are troubled by the failure of restorative justice to address conventional values "just don't get it." They haven't yet been able to change the lens through which they see the world of this new paradigm, and so

are in no position to understand, much less judge, its features. The task for restorative justice advocates thus is not to reconcile the new restorative justice approach with conventional values, but to persuade others—including crime victims—to appreciate the values implicit in the new paradigm, even if this involves discarding conventional notions of "justice," which are only derivatives of the old way of seeing things.[11]

5. **Avoidance.** For those who are still encumbered by conventional notions of justice such as equality, proportionality, public safety, and the rule of law, the development of restorative justice could be regarded as a "work in progress," in which the basic features are established, but certain "loose ends" await further theoretical development. Perhaps it is expecting too much that such a radical program for change can offer solutions to every problem. The details, in short, can be worked out later.

If these reactions sound familiar to readers, they should, because each one can be seen in the work of almost every leading restorative justice advocate who has attempted to cope with the problems associated with private justice. For my own part, I believed that identifying "loss of trust" as the focal concern of restorative justice enabled it to become a fully fledged alternative to the conventional way of doing justice. I was satisfied that the basic difficulty in applying restorative justice to a wide variety of cases was essentially solved, and that other problems associated with privatized justice would be resolved over time.

The trouble was, those "loose ends" associated with private justice were more than temporary annoyances. Instead, they represented a fundamental flaw in any approach to criminal justice that operated exclusively on a personal level. Even if the option of imposing punishment for serious offenses could be incorporated into restorative justice, public safety could not be guaranteed if sentencing decisions were left in the hands of victims more interested in their own well-being than the welfare of the community. What protections would exist to oppose favoritism, racism, intimidation, undue vindictiveness, and incompetence? Ultimately, I had to ask myself whether we would really be better off under a system dedicated to the restoration of personal trust in the offender or whether this was simply an idealistic fantasy that could not—and perhaps should not—replace the conventional system.

It was at this juncture that I decided to explore the notion of restoring trust even further. In so doing, I came across a remarkable article by Susan Dimock.[12] To be perfectly candid, it was initially disheartening to find that, in addition my conceptual problems concerning private justice, Dimock had introduced a dimension of trust that I had neglected to consider. Just as I was in the throes of defending my notion of the restoration of *personal* trust as a model for criminal justice reform, Dimock compelled me to also consider a *societal* dimension of trust. Instinctively, I fought to preserve the purity of my interpersonal ideal, insisting (in the spirit of restorative justice advocacy) that the concept of restoring trust in society was nothing more than an accommodation to statist values. But the more I considered Dimock's analysis, the more I had to conclude, reluctantly, that she was right. What I did not realize at first, however, was that Dimock's analysis of trust not only was something I was obliged to recognize in my own analysis, but that, far from representing a conceptual obstacle to a trust-based theory of restoration, it provided the conceptual key to unlocking the dilemma of reconciling private justice with public justice.

According to Dimock, the trust we require in order to conduct the daily business of living can be understood to have two levels of meaning: (1) subjective trust in individuals and (2) objective trust in society. Subjective conditions of trust depend on a specific, personal knowledge of the person to be trusted. For other persons, such as strangers or those with whom we have infrequent contact, we must rely on objective conditions of trust that pertain to people and to society in general. This is the kind of impersonal trust that Dimock calls "metatrust" or "trust-in-trust."[13] It represents a pervasive background of trust into which individual relations of trust are embedded. For Dimock, a serious breach of trust that, if uncorrected, would tend to undermine the great network of trust relations in society is that which we properly characterize as a criminal offense, and it requires mandatory correction on the part of the state.[14] One objective condition for mistrust, applicable to all persons, is the inability or unwillingness of society to correct these breaches. Restoring objective trust means *restoring trust in the society that failed to protect the victim's security.* In addition to restoring trust in a particular offender, members of a society need to believe it has enforceable standards of behavior that can be relied on. When society fails to carry out its promise to enforce these standards, the state "mocks its own legitimacy."[15] Furthermore, the failure of a society to enforce its own laws—to fulfill the terms of its social contract—mocks the efforts of all those who exercise self-restraint under the belief that such sacrifices were required of everyone. For this reason, all members of society have a legitimate interest in seeing to it that crimes are prosecuted and agreed-on sanctions are imposed. The objective conditions of trust complement the subjective conditions as mandatory mechanisms of enforcement, applicable to all persons and all offenses defined as "criminal." The fulfillment of objective conditions of trust makes more reasonable the possibility of personal trust in any one person. This not only guarantees the public interest in maintaining compliance with the law but, because of its applicability to all persons and all offenses, supports a value that is entirely absent from subjective considerations: *equality of treatment.* The principle of equality is fundamental to the idea of law, and it is through the application of the rule of law that the dangers inherent in a purely subjective approach can be remedied.

The subjective approach to justice implies wide discretion and highly individualized sentencing choices, based on the many unique characteristics of both the offender and the victim. As we have seen above, what is necessary to regain trust in one offender may be quite different from what is needed in another. Additionally, while the use of punishment may be an instrumentality to regain trust for some offenders, it may not be necessary for others. Indeed, it is easy to envision situations in which requiring punishment may be counterproductive, by arousing defensiveness and defiance rather than remorse and cooperation. Punishment is therefore a contingent factor for regaining subjective trust. On the other hand, the uniform application of the law is required as a necessary condition of objective trust. Because the failure to enforce the law is an objective condition for distrust of others that may prevail in a society, it is only by the rigorous application of the law that objective-level trust can be restored.

The importance of Dimock's analysis of trust can scarcely be overstated. Instead of adopting one or more of the above-mentioned positions typically taken by restorative justice advocates when confronted with the problem of privatized justice—defiance, retreat, wishful thinking, self-criticism, and avoidance—the recognition that trust operates on both an interpersonal and a societal level requires restorative justice theory to recognize the validity of values associated with *both* private justice and public justice. Rather than ignore or reject societal demands for equality of treatment, assurance of public safety, and the uniform application of the law as somehow being outside the restorative justice paradigm, the dual-level conception of trust compels us to fully integrate the values of both private and public justice. *(To make the distinction between "subjective trust" and "objective trust" a bit clearer, I will be using the equivalent terms "personal trust" and "social trust" throughout the remainder of this book.)*

But can this integration of values be achieved, or is the recognition of a societal and a personal level of trust merely the expression of an irreconcilable conflict between public and private justice? If so, the restoration of trust approach, far from being a useful "guide to the perplexed," becomes yet another sentencing consideration along with the conventional goals of retribution, rehabilitation, and deterrence, thereby making the job of sorting out sentencing options even more perplexing. What is needed is a conceptual framework for prioritizing the multiplicity of competing sentencing goals. Although there are advantages and disadvantages to each such an endeavor, it is clear that, rather than attempting to select one goal to the exclusion of others, it is preferable to draw on the advantages afforded by each within an "orderly plurality" of sentencing goals. How, then, can such an order be achieved?

The answer, I believe, can be found by adopting the "limit-setting" approach of Morris, in which competing sentencing goals are placed in a rational framework.[16] The foundation for such a framework is the recognition that moral considerations must always have precedence over practical considerations: An immoral sentencing formulation is to be rejected despite any practical advantages it may offer society. We can begin by examining the fundamental weakness of all approaches to sentencing that seek to promote the utilitarian goal of crime prevention, whether it be deterrence, incapacitation, or rehabilitation. In each of these approaches, the criminal sanction is seen as a means of preventing crime, and therefore is judged strictly on the basis of its ability to achieve that goal. Advocates of deterrence have argued that controlling crime requires the imposition of powerful disincentives, advocates of rehabilitation have claimed that crime prevention can be achieved only by addressing the offender's personal deficiencies, and advocates of incapacitation have argued that the only certain way to prevent crime is by making the commission of crime a physical impossibility. Although we may have greater or lesser confidence in the efficacy of these utilitarian approaches to sentencing, they all suffer from the same defect: In pursuing the goal of crime prevention, they have no inherent moral limits. If crime prevention were thought to be the only legitimate goal of sentencing, then it would be permissible to sentence offenders to many years of incarceration for a trivial offense if by so doing the crime rate for that offense would be significantly reduced. Even using the benign principle of rehabilitation as the best way to prevent crime, we can conceive of any number of oppressively invasive procedures that the authorities might deem useful in transforming an offender into a law-abiding citizen. In short, unless the reach of sentences devised to achieve the utilitarian goal of crime control are limited by principles of morality, they may well become the instruments of injustice. In constructing a reasonable framework for sentencing, it therefore is necessary to constrain all utilitarian considerations within boundaries of *deservedness*. If sentencing policy is to conform to moral values, no punishment may be imposed that offends the moral standards of excessive severity or undue leniency, regardless of any social or personal benefit that may be intended or achieved.

Clearly, every sentence must be a deserved sentence, but a significant problem with this approach is that it is almost impossible to specify with any precision exactly what sentence is appropriate in any given case. This very imprecision in determining a deserved sentence, which could be used as an argument against the use of just deserts as a meaningful principle in sentencing, is the foundation of the framework for sentencing I shall propose.

In recognizing that a deserved sentence cannot be exactly specified, Morris argued that agreement may nonetheless be reached as to a *range* of permissible sentences (i.e., sentences that do not overstep insight into what is undeservedly harsh or undeservedly lenient). The same considerations apply to individual decision making: As difficult as it may be to decide the exact sentence that is due in any given case, we have no hesitation in protesting against a sentence that goes too far. The best we can do, therefore, is to establish a *range* of deserved sentences—from most to least severe. Any sentence falling within that upper and lower range is necessarily a deserved sentence, one that adheres to the principle of proportionality. This procedure accords fully with the "limited scope" alternative expressed by von Hirsch et al. for implementation of restorative justice practices "within certain limits established by a larger sentencing framework emphasizing proportionality."[17]

Within these outer boundaries of deservedness is another set of boundaries representing the minimum and maximum severity of sanctions thought to be necessary for the protection of public safety. Together, the boundaries of deservedness and protection of public safety represent matters of public policy and, as such, are legislatively determined for an entire class of offenses. The boundaries of deservedness correspond to the requirements of retributory justice and reflect society's standards of moral proportionality in sentencing. These outer boundaries of deservedness limit the scope of all utilitarian considerations. Therefore, regardless of whether a particular sentence is expected to result in greater crime prevention, it cannot exceed the point at which it is regarded as undeservedly harsh. Conversely, a sentence that may be regarded as unnecessary for the protection of public safety may yet be required solely by considerations of morality. The prosecution and punishment for an old, previously unsolved crime, for example, may do little to protect society from an elderly defendant, but morality would be offended by a dismissal of the charges altogether.

The outer boundaries of sentencing severity represent societal standards for the maintenance of social trust among members of society generally. They provide a consistent, predictable background that ensures the stability of social relations. In terms of traditional sentencing theory, the outer boundary of deservedness corresponds to the notion of retributory justice, and the outer boundary of protection of public safety corresponds to the utilitarian goals of general deterrence. Adherence to these outer boundaries engenders faithfulness to the principles associated with public justice: equality of treatment, proportionality in sentencing, public safety, and the supremacy of the rule of law. Therefore, these values ensure the maintenance of social trust that must be upheld regardless of the particularities presented by any one case. Within the boundaries that represent conditions necessary for social trust, we can consider all those factors that bear upon personal trust in the individual offender. A simplified model of this conceptual and procedural framework of the restoration of trust is presented in Figure 4.1.

Figure 4.1 The Restoration of Trust:
A Conceptual and Procedural Framework

Undeservedly lenient sentences	Deserved sentences: neither undeservedly lenient nor undeservedly harsh	Undeservedly harsh sentences
	Area for free operation of personal trust (trust in the offender)	
Less than the minimum necessary for social trust (trust in society)		More than the maximum necessary for social trust (trust in society)

Within the societal-level limitations of morality and general deterrence, applicable to all cases, sentences can be fine-tuned to reflect a host of personal factors applicable to any individual case. In this zone of highly individualized justice, societal values such as uniformity of treatment, public safety, and supremacy of law need not be considered by the decision makers because any sentence that falls within the range of inner and outer boundaries of social trust has been predetermined to conform to those societal-level concerns. In other words, because we have determined by law the range of conditions that must be satisfied in order to restore trust in society, we are free to consider any conditions within that range that may operate to restore trust in an individual offender. These are all highly subjective considerations because there can be no agreed-on formula for assessing such characteristics as honesty, sincerity, empathy, willingness to change, and, ultimately, trustworthiness. It is this very subjectivity that makes the assessment of personal trust particularly suitable to victim-offender dialogue as well as judicial sentencing. Any offender who agrees to participate in this dialogue is encouraged to offer a sincere apology, an honest explanation, and a realistic plan for repayment, all of which are necessary for the repair of the material and emotional losses suffered by the victim. Of course, these personal considerations are likely to result in sentencing disparities, but that is the inevitable consequence of individualized sentencing. The range of these disparities, however, is restricted by law. As in the case of current sentencing guidelines, the legislative challenge is to create sentencing parameters that are broad enough to permit flexibility and creativity by the individual participants, but narrow enough to ensure proportionality, uniformity, and the rule of law.

Locating a purely discretionary range of sentencing options available within boundaries that conform to the rule of law would help resolve the problem of informal versus formal justice that has impeded the acceptance of restorative justice into the mainstream of criminal justice. By defining a role for personal trust within the boundaries established by law to maintain social trust, we can exercise significant sentencing discretion without jeopardizing public safety and without violating basic principles of equality, proportionality, and adherence to the rule of law.

But who should exercise this sentencing discretion? The sentencing framework that I have described is applicable to a full range of options from traditional to "alternative" decision making. Traditional sentencing, in which the criminal sanction is solely within the purview of the judge, can utilize the proposed social and personal trust framework as an equivalent to the sentencing guidelines now in effect throughout the country. But in addition to defining the permissible scope of subjective sentencing discretion, the framework also provides guidance for the exercise of that subjectivity. Having satisfied the societal demands for retributive justice and public safety, a sentencing judge may exercise considerable flexibility and creativity in specifying the conditions that he or she believes to be necessary in order to restore trust in a particular offender. A judge's complex task of sentencing may be guided by a series of simple, but penetrating, questions: Why don't I trust this person to reenter society right now? What must he do, and over what period of time must he do it, to demonstrate that he can be sufficiently trusted to reenter society? This sentencing framework may also be used in nontraditional settings by involving a victim and offender in the search for a suitable disposition, which may result in a recommendation to the sentencing judge. The advantages and disadvantages of involving a victim and offender in this kind of dialogue will be explored in depth later. But whichever alternative for decision making is selected, be it conventional or nonconventional, the trust-based sentencing framework may be utilized for the same goal: the creation of criminal justice sanctions that serve simultaneously to protect the public interest, to repair the material and emotional losses suffered by the victim, and to offer to the offender a pathway back to social acceptance.

Notes

[1] *See, e.g.* Fattah, "Gearing Justice to Victim Satisfaction."

[2] Acorn, *Compulsory Compassion, p.* 51.

[3] Robinson, "The Virtues of Restorative Processes," p. 382

[4] Braithwaite, *Reintegrative Shaming*; Hirschi, *Causes of Delinquency.*

[5] Braithwaite & Parker, "Restorative Justice is Republican Justice," p. 105.

[6] *Id.* p. 104.

[7] Braithwaite, "Restorative Justice," p. 329

[8] Ashworth, "Responsibilities, Rights and Restorative Justice."

[9] Braithwaite & Parker, "Restorative Justice Is Republican Justice," p. 105.

[10] Quinney, *Class, State, and Crime.*

[11] For a closer examination of the use of "paradigm" terminology in restorative justice, see Chapter 12, "Problems in Paradigms."

[12] Dimock, "Retributivism and Trust."

[13] *Id.* at 51. A similar and very useful distinction between "strategic trust" and "moralistic trust" is drawn by Eric Uslaner in *The Moral Foundations of Trust.* While strategic trust is based upon specific facts known to an individual, "moralistic trust is a moral commandment to treat people *as if* they were trustworthy." "Moralistic trust is based upon some sort of belief in the goodwill of the other and that others will not try to take advantage of us." Uslaner, p. 18.

[14] Dimock, *supra*, p. 51

[15] Clear, *Harm in American Penology*, p. 128.

[16] Morris, "Desert as a Limiting Principle."

[17] von Hirsch, *et al.*, "Specifying Aims and Limits for Restorative Justice," p. 40.

5

The Primacy of Trust

Within the conventional criminal justice system, there exists a polar tension between the fundamental goal of controlling crime and the goal of protecting the "due process" rights of the accused.[1] The unique contribution of restorative justice is to introduce an entirely new criminal justice goal; a goal that subsumes this traditional duality: *repairing the harm of crime.* Building on an understanding that the loss of trust is the essential harm associated with crime that must be repaired, I have proposed that the restoration of trust—in both its personal and social dimensions—should be considered the overarching goal of criminal justice policy and practice.

But while the goal of restoring trust may be desirable in human relations, what is so special about trust that we should regard it as an essential value that must be restored in the aftermath of crime? Isn't it simply another dreamy New Age ideal? And even if we acknowledge its importance, why shouldn't this new goal of restoring trust simply be added to our list of criminal justice goals, rather than being considered as an "overarching" goal as I have claimed?

My thesis is that trust is no ordinary virtue; it is a necessary precondition for life *in society.* To understand why this is so, we must first consider a problem that lies at the center of one of the most important intellectual developments in evolutionary and economic theory: the problem of altruism. It is from an analysis of this issue that the key concept of "reciprocal altruism" has emerged; a concept, I will argue, that forms the socio-biological underpinnings of trust and that establishes trust as the *sine qua non*—the fundamental prerequisite—for successful social interaction.

Reciprocal Altruism and the Origins of Justice

The stunning achievements of the human species could not have occurred without cooperative efforts. Alone, we are incapable of the most rudimentary survival on this planet. But in society, we conquer the planet, for good or for ill. In order for cooperation to thrive, we must be motivated to behave in ways that benefit others and not merely ourselves. In attempting to identify how this extraordinary capacity for cooperative behavior came about, researchers investigating this issue have arrived at a number of important insights into the origin and function of interpersonal control as well as the origin and function of law, justice, and the state.

A frequent theme in early speculation on the origin of law is the view well expressed by Hobbes that the natural state of man is a life that is "nasty, poor, brutal, and short." In this view, without the restraining influence of law, there is a perpetual state of war between isolated individuals selfishly pursuing their own ends. Because life under these conditions would be intolerable, so Hobbes argued, humans came to devise the state as the instrument for regulating harmful conduct. They willingly relinquished a portion of their freedom to a paramount authority, granting to it a monopoly on physical coercion in exchange for which the remaining freedom—the core human values they regarded as their "rights"—were secured. Thus, the "social contract" was born, an idea that has always been more a philosophical construct than a factually accurate account of the origins of law and the state.[2] Various formulations of the social contract have been expressed through the ages from Socrates in ancient Greece to Hobbes, Hume, Locke, and Rousseau in the Enlightenment to Rawls and Nozick in the current era. For each of these thinkers, the law is regarded as the product of man's reason in opposition to man's passions; a rational framework for cooperation that controls man's innate selfishness.[3] These views of man's essential nature before the formulation of law—his "original condition"—were reinforced by the social Darwinists both past and present.[4] Given the competitive climate in which social animals such as we humans exist, they argued, it is only natural that the strong will pass on their characteristics to a new generation and that the weak will not. Aggression is instinctual under this theory because it has been a successful strategy for survival. Because animals will always multiply to the limit of an area necessary to support life, as Malthus noted, the aggressive defense of territory is an economic necessity. The sharing of dwindling resources is a recipe for slow extinction of the selfless while the survival of the fittest is a recipe for a thriving life for the selfish. The notion of man as an egotistical, predatory, and aggressive creature has gained widespread attention in the popular works of Lorenz and Audrey.[5] The function of law, in this view, is just as Hobbes had envisioned it: an institutional suppression of man's instinctual aggression by means of the social contract.

However, a different view concerning the development of the social contract has emerged in recent years. First, the idea that humans actually "sat down" and agreed on rules to govern their innate egoism and aggressiveness is obviously fictitious. If we were indeed such selfish and aggressive creatures, the likelihood of us agreeing to something that contradicts our essential nature would be rather remote. Secondly, the idea that we had a prehistory as independent, selfish, and aggressive beings before the creation of a state is contrary to everything we know about our evolution as social animals.[6] As Singer pointed out: "Human beings are social animals and we were social before we were human."[7] Because both we and our predecessors, as social organisms, existed in stable social groups long before the creation of law, our capacity to regulate harmful conduct and to ensure cooperation within the group was itself an evolutionary development. The natural condition of human beings is lived in society and the human "passion for justice,"[8] which is necessary for the regulation of harmful behavior, is essential to our nature and not merely a rational construct intended to curtail our natural aggressiveness and egotism. Social cooperation requires both restraint of actions and a "justice motive" that induces retaliation against those who fail to restrain their conduct. Yet despite the benefits to group survival that result from self-restraint and the justice motive, the evolutionary origin of these traits is not easily explained by Darwinian analysis that focuses on those traits that confer a competitive advantage to individuals. This is because self-restraint and the justice motive are essentially *altruistic* in that they primarily function to benefit the group while exacting a cost to the individual.[9] Indeed, retaliation involves considerable risk to the individual actor for a reward that primarily benefits others because it functions to discourage future offenses to other possible victims. The challenge to evolutionary theory therefore has been to account for the rise of such altruistic behavior by the operation of natural selection.

One way to account for the evolution of altruistic behavior is to consider how such behavior introduces a selective advantage to the group in its competition with other groups. In a world of competitive bands of hunter-gatherers, the group with the greater degree of social cohesion made possible by the genetic predisposition of its members toward intragroup altruism will tend to pass on their genes to further generations of humans more efficiently than the noncohesive group. Yet it is not enough to claim that altruism helps the *group* to survive in accounting for the evolutionary basis for cooperation because it is only by the transmission of genes through *individuals* that certain genes will either be retained or eradicated. The trait of altruism must therefore confer some evolutionary advantage to the individual in order for the trait to gain ascendancy within the group. Unfortunately, those altruistic individuals whose actions promote the welfare of others at their own expense do not individually fare as well as those who are content to benefit from the altruism of others. The very quality of courage that helps the group to survive, for example, is likely to be extinguished because the brave are more apt to die without passing their genes to a new generation than the cowards who benefit from the courage of others. In a world dominated by egocentric aggression, the appearance of a cooperative, altruistic "mutant" has rather less chance of survival than his or her nonaltruistic neighbors. This is a problem noted by Darwin himself in *The Descent of Man* and it remained a central problem in the emerging field of sociobiology.[10]

To be sure, a purely altruistic instinct can be found throughout the animal kingdom in the powerful bond between parents and offspring, but this type of altruism is, in fact, merely an extension of genetic egotism because the child is the means by which the parents' genes survive.[11] "Kin altruism," which in reality is the operation of the "selfish gene,"[12] not only is seen in the case of parents who share 50% of the genes of their children, but also in siblings who share a similar proportion as well as other relatives such as first and second cousins to correspondingly lesser degrees. The closer the relation, the higher the proportion of shared genes and the greater the degree of seemingly altruistic behavior that is exhibited. What remains to be explained is a mechanism by which the altruism necessary for social cohesion is selectively advantageous to the individual who possesses it for relations *outside* the family. How can the trait of benefiting strangers confer a competitive advantage to the altruist?

The answer to this dilemma—finding a selfish advantage for selflessness—has been articulated by sociobiologists as the principal of reciprocal altruism. Reciprocal altruism, to be sure, is quite different from "pure altruism." Pure altruism, in which personal sacrifices are made for the good of others without any demand for payment, is a good strategy for group survival, but it is a bad strategy for individual survival. Moreover, if it is a bad strategy for individual survival, it has little likelihood of being incorporated into the gene pool over successive generations. But although altruism does not tend to thrive in isolated encounters, it may become a successful evolutionary development in the context of reciprocal relations in which a person's propensity for altruism is accompanied by an *expectation that it will be returned.* In the case of parents, no such quid pro quo is required—the altruistic act is rewarded by the survival of the offspring that transmit the parents' genes. For non-kins, however, the expectation of return is crucial to cooperative behavior.

In order to understand the biological evolution of reciprocal altruism, it is useful to consider its logical evolution in the context of game theory, employing a familiar non-zero-sum game: the prisoner's dilemma. In the classical version of the prisoner's dilemma, two men are arrested by the authorities and placed in separate cells with no possibility of communication. Each is offered the same deal: If you inform on the other prisoner, you will be set free while the other will be executed. Of course, this cannot happen if they both agree to inform on each other and so, if both prisoners inform on each other, they will face a moderately severe penalty. On the other hand, if neither informs on the other, both prisoners believe that they will receive a minimal punishment, reasoning that if there were sufficient evidence, the prosecutors wouldn't have offered them a reduction in severity in exchange for their testimony. In an ideal world, the prisoners would clearly benefit by cooperating with each other. They should choose to do as little harm to each other as possible. Moreover, by cooperating with each other, each individually achieves a favorable outcome and, collectively, they achieve an optimal outcome. That is what they *should* do. But is it what they *will* do? Whatever advantages attached to cooperation with each other must be weighed against the possibility that the other prisoner might refuse to cooperate and accept the prosecutor's offer. Despite any moral training that he has received, there remains the possibility that one prisoner might prefer the certainty of living by informing on the other over the possibility of dying by the other informing on him. Additionally, there is the sobering thought that the very reason one prisoner has for distrusting the other is the same that the other has for distrusting him. The result is that the spirit of altruism, which would have benefited both, is crushed by the logic that favors egotism.

If egotism has such an evolutionary advantage, how could altruism have a chance to thrive and become incorporated into the human gene pool? By what mechanism could the logic of egotism be annulled? Unless some missing factor were detected, game theory would therefore predict the extinction of cooperation over time and the eventual triumph of egotism. This is a key problem for evolutionary biology, but is also a problem for economics because it undermines the possibility of cooperative behavior, without which there would be a reversion to Hobbesian conditions of suspicion, isolation, conflict, and mutual impoverishment. Researchers in both evolutionary biology and economics thus embarked on a search for an evolutionarily stable strategy for group and individual survival in which it is advantageous to cooperate and disadvantageous to cheat, using both game theory and population genetics to aid in their inquiry. Through computer simulation and mathematical modeling, it was quickly discovered that neither pure altruism nor pure selfishness resulted in a stable strategy for group survival. In a population of hawks and doves, the doves were quickly decimated and the hawks were forever involved in bloody conflicts. More to the point, in a population of cooperators and cheaters, the cooperators were found to be driven to extinction by the cheaters (because it is more economical to profit from another's altruism without having to return the favor), and the remaining cheaters soon found that there was no one left who they could cheat and therefore were also eventually driven to extinction.

But what if the cooperators turn non-cooperative on those who cheat them? What if the doves turned hawkish against the hawks? This is the kernel of the idea of reciprocal altruism; altruism that is extended to, and only to, those who cooperate. Take the example of grooming among chimpanzees. A distinct disadvantage of having a body covered by fur is the annoying presence of lice and fleas lodging in inaccessible places. A chimpanzee who wishes to be rid of these vermin cannot do it alone, but must rely on the help of others. Who can be counted on to do a good job? A careful job of grooming cannot be expected from someone who is forced to do so. Yet considering what we know about biological beings, waiting for someone to be of assistance out of the sheer goodness of their heart would likely involve a good deal of waiting. There is, however, one effective strategy that is seen in primates all over the world: Groom your neighbor carefully and conscientiously with the expectation that like services will be returned, coupled with the imposition of unpleasant consequences if they are not returned. This is the strategy of reciprocal altruism (or, in the colorful language of game theory, "tit for tat"). Reciprocal altruism differs from pure altruism in its insistence on return. In the case of the simian groomers, the receiver of a good and careful grooming might well be inclined to cheat by not returning the favor. After all, why bother spending hours grooming your neighbor if he or she is willing to do it for free? If cheaters are permitted to "get away with it," the non-cheaters not only would be exploited, but they might eventually lose the incentive to help others altogether. Without some personal advantage to the benefactor, it is difficult to understand how a strategy of mutual help could evolve.

By contrast to the unconditional do-gooders, those who subscribe to reciprocal altruism are not so easily exploited. For them, the performance of an altruistic action like grooming automatically raises the expectation of return. The disappointment of these expectations is experienced viscerally as resentment against the cheater—a feeling that persists until the cheater is punished. It is through this act of retaliation that the economic advantages of cheating are erased and cooperation can become the norm rather than the exception or, in the language of game theory, can become an evolutionarily stable strategy. That, at least, is the predicted outcome of reciprocal altruism. When this strategy is applied to a single case or to a single choice, however, reciprocal altruism is still defeated by cheaters. That is because the power of reciprocal altruism is realized only by shaping subsequent behavior over time. The key breakthrough in the development of reciprocal altruism theory came about as the contrasting strategies were put through repeated computer simulations.[13] At first, the cheaters gained the upper hand because they had an easy field of cooperators to exploit, especially the doves, who had no means of self-protection. After the doves were driven to extinction, the cheaters were faced with the prospect of dealing with the reciprocal altruists—the "grudgers"—who were on to their game and were willing to impose consequences. The cheaters fared poorly in this phase of the match. The grudgers refused further dealings with the cheaters and, at the same time, forged mutually beneficial alliances with other grudgers. The reciprocal altruism strategy offered a consistent advantage to cooperation and a consistent disadvantage to noncooperation.

Here at last was an evolutionary stable model of cooperative behavior—one that could survive in the Darwinian world of survival of the fittest. The features of this strategy of reciprocal altruism were set forth in a seminal article by Robert Trivers.[14] In reciprocal altruism, the actor does not heedlessly (or even empathetically) strew beneficence on others. In a competitive world with scarce resources, such persons may be beloved, but do tend to die early without passing on their virtuous genes. Instead, reciprocal altruism requires a concomitant expectation of return which, if unfulfilled, engenders a sharp and inescapable feeling of resentment. Very likely, this is the primordial "justice response"—a feeling that is associated not so much from the experience of *justice* as it is with the experience of *injustice*. It is a prerational response of unfairness that underlies and guides our ethical intuitions. Contrary to the view that justice is a rational suppression of aggressive urges, it is this feeling of resentment that is the foundation for justice because "unless justice is personally felt, there can be no justice at all."[15] The resentment that arises from our disappointed expectations of reciprocity, in turn, is the powerful emotional motivation for punishment, without which the system of reciprocal altruism must collapse. If the failure to fulfill the terms of reciprocity were not punished, there would be no obvious disadvantage for a cheater or a deadbeat to take without giving.[16] Indeed, why would it ever be to anyone's advantage to return a favor if there were no disincentive to freeloading and, moreover, if the favors continued to be received without any reciprocity? Why would it ever be to someone's advantage to "play by the rules" rather than to exploit those who foolishly make themselves vulnerable by giving to others with the mere expectation of return? Cheating loses its competitive edge only by operation of the resentment that automatically and inescapably accompanies the disappointment of expectations of reciprocity and that motivates retaliation against the non-reciprocator.

In order for reciprocal altruism to work, each participant must have some reasonable assurances that their altruism will be returned. They must be able to distinguish between those who have subscribed to this plan for mutual cooperation and those who have exploited it, a task that requires intelligence and memory.[17] The sociobiology of altruistic behavior helps us to understand the ubiquity of the obsession with detecting and punishing cheaters. A chimpanzee whose painstaking grooming of another is reciprocated by a perfunctory or careless job is no less adept in detecting cheaters by the intuitive guide of resentment or any less insistent on imposing consequences on the offender than is a trained jurist. The subscribers to the plan for mutual cooperation—those who have demonstrated self-restraint and reciprocity—can be regarded as members of the "moral community."[18] This group of cooperators may originate in a kinship network where reciprocal obligations are well understood and expected to be enforced by social pressure, but the circle of those who are bound by the rules of social reciprocity may widen with increased interpersonal knowledge. The individual, innate "justice response" is modified and broadened in our social interactions, resulting in norms of reciprocity we expect of each other. The scope of altruism grows as we feel a greater sense of belonging to a wider social group within which adherence to these norms of reciprocity is both expected and enforced.[19] Conversely, the cost to the freeloader—the person who has exploited the system of reciprocal altruism to his selfish advantage—is punishment and exclusion. Punishment is, literally, "the wages of sin." It operates on the group level as a means of enforcing the system of reciprocal altruism and operates on the individual phenomenological level as the means of satisfying the resentment of the victim.

The moral emotions associated with reciprocal altruism are basic biological responses to injustice that predate law, predate language, and, very likely, predate our evolution as humans. Just as the moral emotion of resentment is an essential motivation for retaliation against cheaters so is the discomfort of resentment relieved by the act of retaliation. Feelings of moral outrage are assuaged by punishing violators because punishment signals restoration of fairness as well as the presumption of reciprocity in others.[20] From this perspective, punishment is not so much a source of pleasure as it is relief from the pain of resentment. This accords with several criminological theories that have attempted to account for the insistence on just deserts. These include the notions that crime causes the victim to lose faith in the assumption of a just world (just world theory)[21] and that, because the essence of crime is a destabilization of equity, the resentment associated with this destabilization is restored by a counterbalancing penalty (equity theory).[22]

Whatever theory one subscribes to, it does appear that each is a kind of *rationalization for what one already knows*—a groping for the right words to describe an intuitive, emotional response to wrongdoing. And, indeed, the emotions that not only are associated with, but are integral to, the genetic strategy of reciprocal altruism should be understood in the same way that other emotions operate. They "animate, focus and modify neural activity in ways that lead us to choose certain responses."[23] Emotional responses motivate complex behavior essential to survival in ways that seemingly bypass and even contradict rationality. They are "involuntary and innate" limbic system responses shaped by natural selection that adjusts behavior in social situations.[24] This may be the reason why a victim's search for justice is seemingly irrational and obsessive.[25] The genetic strategy of reciprocal altruism makes us amazingly sensitive to cheaters, but sensitivity alone is only "stage one" of the process. In order for the strategy of reciprocal altruism to work, it is not sufficient for cheats to be merely *detected*—we must *act* on the expectation of reciprocity to inflict negative consequences on the wrongdoer, whatever the cost. But if these feelings are irrational and persist despite their apparent irrationality or futility, does this not mean that they conflict with economic theory and, consequently, evolutionary theory? That is, if the moral instincts associated with wrongdoing subject us to urges that divert us from more productive and efficient economic activities and impel us to expend enormous time and effort in the pursuit of such an apparently useless thing as "justice," how can they form a part of an evolutionarily stable strategy or confer a selective advantage?

The answer is that these emotions impel actions that have short-term costs, but long-term advantages. Over time, they help us by removing the cheaters from our zone of interaction and free us to obtain the great benefits of cooperation from those who return the favor. These long-term advantages may not be readily apparent. The emotions connected with a genetically based life strategy function as "overrides" that motivate conduct that enhances long-term reproductive fitness in ways that might not be readily apparent to the conscious mind.[26] The seeming irrationality of retaliation against the wrongdoer is, in essence, its lack of short-term benefit. Without the powerful motivating influence of resentment and its relief through the imposition of a consequence on the cheater, the sociobiological mechanism to identify and punish cheaters would not operate, and the possibility of cooperative behavior and the maintenance of relationships of trust would be greatly diminished.

The operation of retaliation against those who would disturb our expectation of reciprocity and the social advantages of such a strategy has been ingeniously tested in human subjects.[27] Respondents in experiments designed to demonstrate economic choices showed a remarkable tendency to expend precious resources to punish those who refuse to cooperate or who act unfairly toward others. Their retaliatory response is called "altruistic punishment" in that the punishment is costly to them and yields no material results. The utility of altruistic punishment to human groups has been demonstrated in these studies which show a significant increase in over-all levels of cooperation when respondents are permitted to retaliate against those "cheat" or who they perceive as being unfair to others. "Cooperation flourishes if altruistic punishment is possible, and breaks down if it is ruled out." [28] Moreover, the studies have confirmed that the impetus for these actions which have short-term losses but long-term gains for the group, is attributable to the actor's *feelings:* "the evidence indicates that negative emotions toward defectors are the proximate mechanism behind altruistic punishment." [29] In other words, without the powerful feelings associated with the perception of cheating or unfairness by others, the extraordinary mutual benefits brought about by social cooperation might not be possible.

Therefore, our passion for justice is not to be thought of as a construct of pure reason that constrains instinctual aggression. Instead, from a socio-biological perspective, it is an innate emotional response that has thereafter been abstracted and generalized into law.[30] This is an especially important insight for restorative justice because its goal is to create a justice system that works not only to serve the needs of the state, but also to satisfy the needs and expectations of individual crime victims. In demanding justice, victims demand the restoration of respect.

The criminal act, here understood as the willful breach of the norms of reciprocity,[31] is an act of disrespect. The symbolic message of crime is: "You may have to play by the rules, but I don't. I hold myself over and above the rules that I expect everyone else to obey."[32] Resentment is the moral response to this disrespect. That is why a person who does not resent a moral injury done to him or her is almost necessarily a person lacking self-respect.[33] What a victim has to "gain" by punishment is personal vindication of his or her self-worth. The false message of contempt must be publicly cancelled. In this manner, victims "profit" from punishment on an emotional level, not by gloating over the suffering of the offender, but by the quelling of their resentment. It is not necessarily a joyous occasion; it is simply a return to some semblance of normalcy because, at last, the distress of resentment is alleviated. That is why the failure to punish is so debilitating: The victim's emotional distress arising from the experience of victimization is compounded by the failure of society to satisfy his or her expectation of justice.

The resentment that involuntarily arises from the betrayal of expectations of reciprocity is central to the operation of reciprocal altruism because, without it, there is no spur to actions that make cheating disadvantageous. The moral emotions associated with reciprocal altruism therefore motivate actions that have long-term benefits to the individual by reinforcing bonds of cooperation rather than immediate selfish rewards. The moral emotions are prosocial emotions, and are culturally favored as virtuous because we conceive of virtue, essentially, as prosocial behavior and vice as antisocial behavior. Building on these primal moral emotions, we have created principles of morality by articulating the circumstances under which we are justified in our resentment. Every society devotes enormous amounts of time and energy to the task of specifying the rules of reciprocity and codifying them into rules in order to vouchsafe the presumption of reciprocity. The greater the scope of such presumptions, the greater is the capacity to trust. The less we have to fear in our interactions with others, the greater is the scope of our freedom.

It is necessary to take note of the fact here that the failure to reciprocate does not always arouse resentment, as in the cases of young children and adult family members, and these circumstances also should be closely considered. We may feel vexed or angry at young children, but we hardly ever feel *resentful* at their misconduct because we do not consider them to be fully formed and mature enough to exercise good judgment. We know they are prone to error and rashness. In essence, although we always want them to behave themselves, we don't fully expect them to behave. We know they are *kids*. We love them, but we have no reason to trust them. Therefore, when they do misbehave, our reaction is hardly ever one of resentment. If they hurt us, abuse us, cheat us, or defy us, we do not seek justice. And if we feel the need to punish them, it is done in order to help them in the process of socialization rather than to satisfy any urge toward retaliation. This absence of resentment is an amazingly acute guide in differentiating between juvenile misbehavior and adult offending, and informs all of our subsequent responses. It is also an accurate guide in distinguishing between intentional harms and accidental harms. As Justice Holmes famously noted: Even a dog knows the difference between being stumbled on and being kicked.[34] In tort cases, the resentment is not aroused by the harmful act itself, but is intensely aroused by a subsequent refusal to acknowledge the fault and to pay for losses. In the case of crimes (cases that involve the willful violation of expectations of reciprocity), the status of the perceived offender as a member in good standing in the moral community becomes unsettled: His trustworthiness can no longer be presumed.

Even in the case of adult family members, the violation of reciprocity is experienced as something quite different from the feelings aroused by the misdeeds of strangers. For one thing, expectations of reciprocity are wholly different among family members. To them, we give freely of our labor and resources without demanding repayment. Among family members, mutual dependency is such that offenses are experienced as emotional wounds associated with the loss of love. We do not require justice or the steadfast application of the law. We forgive endlessly and punish rarely. The reason that we treat family so differently from others is that our responses to family members are based on an entirely different genetic strategy altogether. We cooperate with kin and offer every type of advantage to them, often at great cost, but not in order to receive payment. We do it because, by helping them, we are actually helping ourselves in the incessant drive to populate the planet with our genes. We sustain our family members in the same way that we sustain our own bodies: They are the means by which our genes get passed down. In short, the rules applicable to the family are inapplicable to strangers, and vice versa. This may appear to be an obvious truism, but it has important implications in moral and political theory. It has long been the dream of social reformers to treat others as we treat our family,[35] but the dream can be only an illusion so long as people are driven by instinctive demands for justice among those outside the bonds of kinship.

It is beguiling to imagine the possibility that the love and unconditional forgiveness that works so humanely and effectively for the misdeeds of family members could become the basis for criminal justice policy in this complex, industrial society. It would be heavenly to live in a world where everyone treats each other as a brother or sister. But this can happen only if human beings are capable of substituting a genetic strategy of altruism based on kinship for a genetic strategy of reciprocal altruism that evolved specifically for non-kinsmen.

This strategy of reciprocity is not a recipe for oppression and domination. It is instead a *recipe for fairness*. Indeed, the intuitive, affective response of resentment that arises when our expectations of reciprocity are disappointed brings the notion of fairness into being in a world of mere factuality. This visceral experience of resentment is our first, instinctual indication that something is not as it should be. We know something is wrong before we can articulate *why* it is wrong. Resentment, rather than being a source of stress that ought to be cast off, is actually a powerful guide to moral behavior. Indeed, our systems of morality can be thought of as rationalizations for what we already know intuitively through our feelings. When our intuitive, emotional responses conflict with abstract principles, we tend to revise those principles rather than question our responses.[36] This is also how the law evolves. I again quote Justice Holmes: "The life of the law has not been logic; it has been experience."[37] When the application of abstract principles of law would offend our intuitive sense of justice, it is the set principles we have constructed, not the intuition, that must be questioned, reconsidered, and modified.

The search for justice, from the sociobiological perspective, is thus not a rational construct that constrains primitive drives. It is a highly evolved strategy that has come down through the ages because of its ability to promote social cooperation. It is part of our human nature. It is, perhaps, the source of the Platonic concepts of innate and immutable moral ideals that guide the judgment of fairness in any concrete application. As any teacher of law or ethics knows from personal experience, students can be led to discover legal and ethical principles by examining their personal responses to a variety of hypothetical cases. Their intuitive sense of fairness is their unerring guide, regardless of their prior knowledge of legal principles. What they learn in class is not so much how to resolve a problem, but how to articulate in terms of rational principles the result that they understood intuitively. This is what we call the Socratic method (after Plato's mentor): guiding the student to the articulation of general principles by a succession of contrasting hypothetical problems. But how could they resolve these hypothetical problems in the first place unless they, in some sense, already possess knowledge of the governing ethical principles? The

Platonic view is that these fundamental ethical principles must be innate, and that our common agreement on the resolution of ethical problems points to their universality. In sociobiological terms, we might agree with Plato that ethical discernment is innate, but explain its origin as an evolutionally advantageous trait: an unrelenting insistence on reciprocity, coupled with the ability to detect and retaliate against those who willfully violate the presumption of adherence to the norms of reciprocity (i.e., those who violate our trust).

The theory of reciprocal altruism, in summary, provides a comprehensive account for the biological origins of justice that enriches the understanding of how we humans, as social beings, emotionally respond to wrongdoing. We have seen how some form of retaliatory response to those who violate the norms of reciprocity is necessary for the survival of society and how the retaliatory response of individuals provides an altruistic function by serving the interests of others rather than merely those of the individual victim, often at considerable risk and cost to the victim. Indeed, it is because of the apparent "uselessness" of punishment to the interests of the individual victim that retaliation against the offender has been criticized as irrational and needlessly cruel. What the theory of reciprocal altruism has to offer is a plausible mechanism for the societal value of compliance with group norms to become selectively advantageous to the individual. Reciprocal altruism, which insists on punishment for those who, by failing to respect our expectation of reciprocity, arouse intense feelings of resentment, gives a genetic advantage to those who comply as well as a genetic disadvantage to those who do not. It thus becomes a powerful force for group cohesion, thereby conferring a competitive advantage over other, noncohesive groups.

Lest this model of strict retaliatory justice appear too harsh, the sociobiologists assure us that there is, indeed, a place for forgiveness. This conclusion is not based on a desire to placate those moralists who might object to a purely Darwinian view of human nature, but on the tangible outcomes of experimental research. In early computer modeling of various strategies of interaction, those who did not insist on retaliation were easy prey for the cheaters and, as a result, were ultimately eradicated. Only the grudgers (who subscribe to the retaliatory tit-for-tat credo) successfully competed with the cheaters and, indeed, outlasted the cheaters by simultaneously building cooperative associations with cooperators and depriving non-cooperators of necessary resources.

But the story does not end there. Subsequent computer modeling revealed that a significant improvement was made in the strict tit-for-tat model by the introduction of occasional forgiveness to transgressors. This improvement came about, not by design but by the introduction of random "mistakes," hence replicating the Darwinian mechanism of random mutation. In these simulations, the winning formula had all the attributes of tit for tat with one exception—it tolerated occasional defections by non-reciprocators.[38] In this "generous" version of tit for tat, there was no retaliation for approximately one third of the first-time violators. If generosity were extended to all cheaters, a "green light" would be given to potential cheaters to exploit the goodwill of others without any disincentive to do so. On the other hand, occasional forgiveness was found to be effective in counteracting the tendency of tit-for-tat strategies to devolve into "cycles of mutual recrimination."[39] In human terms, the strategy of occasional (and unpredictable) forgiveness represents an acknowledgment of the possibility of an occasional honest mistake, a possibility that is certainly not tolerated in the case of a second offense. This acknowledgment of fallibility, which in the computer model is a function of randomly introduced "mistakes," operates in the human world to reinforce relationships rather than weaken them. To be sure, no such mechanism is required for close kin because the genetic basis for cooperative behavior in these cases does not necessarily require a retaliatory strategy.

What is remarkable about the work of Nowak and Sigmund is that a certain measure of forgiveness was found to be an evolutionarily successful addition to the strictly retaliatory model, even in the case of non-kinsmen. Unfortunately, the generous tit-for-tat strategy did not evolve into a fully stable strategy because of its tendency to permit other strategies to evolve, which eventually permitted the cheaters to take over. This defect led Nowak and Sigmund to consider a further refinement of the tit-for-tat strategy. Instead of simply remembering (and reacting to) the opponent's last move, the new strategy of "win-stay, lose shift" considers both parties' last moves and retaliates only when the last move is disadvantageous. Hence, "forgiveness" (the absence of retaliation to cheating) occurs only after both the parties "defect."[40] A further refinement focuses on the actions of the cheater. While tit-for-tat promotes the well-being of cooperators by their retaliation against cheaters, the cooperators are still prone to further retaliatory responses from those who they have punished. The net result is a cycle of violence within the community that eventually plays out as a slow extinction of both cooperators and non-cooperators. But in the "contrite" version of tit for tat, the cheater who is retaliated against will abstain from a further retaliatory response.[41] This effectively breaks the cycle of violence because there is no provocation to the cooperator victim who has retaliated against the cheater. By accepting punishment without protest, the cheater is effectively forgiven and normal interaction resumes.

In short, the theory of reciprocal altruism does indeed favor some leeway in the bestowal of forgiveness; especially, if that forgiveness is achieved through the acceptance of a "deserved" retaliatory response from a victim. However, it is easy to confuse this achievement of forgiveness with a general policy of forgiveness that is incapable of dealing with cheaters. In *Beyond Revenge: The Evolution of the Forgiveness Instinct*,[42] psychologist Michael McCullough, after reviewing the various formulations of reciprocal altruism, concluded that forgiveness is a feature of every evolutionarily stable strategy: "Whatever the details of the evolution of human cooperation, it seems, the organisms that survived the evolutionary winnowing process had forgiveness in their cognitive toolkits."[43] What McCullough failed to note is that the forgiveness feature of these strategies primarily results in evolutionary stability when it follows the infliction of a retaliatory response from the victim together with a demonstration of cooperation by the cheater either by a random (tit for tat) or, better yet, a programmed withholding of further retaliation by the cheater (contrite tit for tat). This is "earned" forgiveness (forgiveness that follows successful retaliation by the aggrieved party) rather than the unconditional forgiveness that McCullough advocated as an antidote to the insistence on revenge.

In *Evolutionary Psychology and the Origins of Justice*, Anthony Walsh described the history of the theory of reciprocal altruism and cited the findings that a "measure of forgiveness may work even better in some instances" than "those who strictly apply the rules of tit-for-tat"[44] as reasons for embracing a nonpunitive restorative justice model. But the "generous tit for tat" is not at all a nonpunitive model: It is a modified form of an essentially retaliatory approach, and one that has not proven to be evolutionarily stable at that. Where Walsh got it perfectly right, however, was in his understanding that the retaliatory response is more effective if the retaliation does not bar the door to eventual reconciliation. Ideally, the form of retaliation will itself encourage rehabilitation. The model of unconditional forgiveness fails as an instrument for reintegration because it is not an evolutionarily stable strategy. In Chapter 6 we explore the shortcomings of unconditional forgiveness as a means toward victims attaining genuine emotional recovery and offenders gaining genuine reintegration. We also examine the linkage between these two important goals—victim recovery and offender reintegration—and argue that neither of these goals can be attained without addressing the violation of the presumption of reciprocity inherent in the criminal act. My central thesis is that the very actions necessary to restore this presumption of adherence to reciprocity, such as the submission by the offender to a deserved punishment, the offering of a genuine apology, and the payment of fair compensation, simultaneously operate to restore trust in the offender and in society. In so doing, they are instrumental in the victim's attainment of emotional well-being and the offender's eventual reintegration into society.

Depersonalizing Retaliation: The Role of the Community and the State in Administering Sanctions

Reciprocal altruism depends on the ability of members of society to detect, to remember, and to retaliate against the actions of those who violate the rules of reciprocity. It therefore operates effectively on the limited number of people anyone knows and with whom they have repeated dealings. As the group expands, this kind of "personal justice" is not only more risky and less consistent, it also is open to attack by the cheaters who take advantage of the "free pass" given to first-time offenders, thereby subverting the presumption of trust in others and impairing social cooperation. One consequence of the distrust of strangers is the shrinking of the circle of social and economic relations, coupled with an emphasis on kin loyalty that is already favored by the instinctual bias toward genetic relations. Kin loyalty also makes retaliation more effective because the victim's resentment is shared by his or her clan. And by virtue of the same principal of shared identity, the blame for the offense is quickly transmuted to the kin of the offender. Hence, personal retaliation becomes clan retaliation with all its destructive consequences to the larger society. In short, as society has expanded from small bands of hunter-gatherers, for whom social exclusion meant a member's social and even physical death, to ever-larger groupings, the principal of reciprocal altruism through personal—or through kin-related—retaliation has become increasingly less capable of promoting social cohesion.

As societies grow, the expansion of the circle of reciprocal altruism requires that enforcement of these shared expectations be administered by persons other than the victim and his or her kinsmen. Only then can the public be assured that their willingness to trust one another in social and communal relations was not an invitation to disaster. In other words, while a small homogenous group of interdependent beings whose happiness and very existence depend on their inclusion in the moral community can be maintained by the personal administration of reciprocal altruism, this biological principal requires further refinements in order to apply to larger groups. Two effective strategies have emerged for the "depersonalization" of the retaliatory response: (1) the sharing of a victim's resentment and urge toward retaliation by others in the community, and (2) the administration of sanctions by a universally recognized, paramount authority within the group.

Informal Sanctions: The Shared Response by Community Members

Not only the victim's "passion for justice" is aroused by a crime. These powerful feelings are also experienced by non-victims who share the genetic legacy of reciprocal altruism. Those who fail to respect the norms of reciprocating—those who cheat—are threats both to the victim and to all those who subscribe to the pact of reciprocity. Accordingly, the same moral inducements to punishing cheaters exist in non-victims in order to ensure the survival of the reciprocal altruism strategy. This does not mean that we were necessarily "designed" to detect and punish cheaters. Instead, from an evolutionary perspective we can see that a genetic aptitude for identifying with crime victims is likely to survive and flourish in succeeding generations because the selective advantages of the strategy of reciprocal altruism are enhanced by the vicarious experience in non-victims of resentment and its associated relief through punishing cheaters. It therefore is not surprising that we have evolved the capacity for non-victims to powerfully empathize with the victim. They literally *feel* what the victim feels. This is one reason why crime stories continue to dominate the news, entertainment media, and ordinary conversations. Even without the actual experience of victimization, we all know what it feels like. We share the moral outrage at the prospect of an offender "getting away with it," and are relieved when justice is administered. These shared intuitions of moral outrage, shaped by culture, form the basis of a moral code. Because all of us can imagine ourselves in the position of another, those personal feelings of resentment solidify into a group code with socially acceptable standards of what should be done to an offender who violates the expectation of reciprocal dealings.[45] The resentment that is vicariously, but in a real sense, *actually* experienced by members of the community and that motivates their retaliation against the offender is also a powerful expression of group solidarity.[46] Victims of crime whose suffering is regarded as solely their private misfortune are likely to feel isolated and, indeed, disrespected by the moral community. Only when a victim's resentment and demand for justice are shared by the group can the victim feel restored to full membership in the moral community.

The ability of other persons to empathize with a victim is the foundation of a crucial component of crime control: the "collective efficacy" of a community.[47] Crime is poorly controlled by the retaliatory action of individual victims and, indeed, is also poorly controlled by government through the police. Communities that offer a pervasive network of social control over their residents provide a potent means of crime prevention. An accident may be only a private misfortune, but a crime—a willful violation of the norms of reciprocity—is a threat to the well-being of the group. And it is through the shared feeling of outrage at the suffering of a crime victim that the full power of social control is mobilized.

Formal Sanctions: The Response of the State

Another important strategy for depersonalizing a victim's retaliatory response is administration of sanctions, not by the victim directly, but by a universally recognized, paramount authority within the group. This delegation of personal retaliation to others is one of the hallmarks of law as an instrument of social control. This development is undoubtedly a great cultural achievement, but there is reason to believe that it too has strong sociobiological roots that are worth considering. Many sociobiologists do not conceive that the transition from personal retaliation to retaliation by a paramount authority is accomplished by the quelling of our "animal instincts" through the exercise of reason a là Hobbes, Rousseau, and other social contract theorists. Instead, a closer inspection of the "law of the pack" reveals an evolutionary basis for both personal vengeance and retributive justice.

The distinction between vengeance and retribution is often blurred, principally in the context of attempts to account for an origin to the human justice instinct. Some have claimed that retribution is nothing more than a polite euphemism for revenge,[48] and that retribution is "only vengeance in disguise."[49] In its simplest equation, retribution and vengeance are thought to be identical payback responses to wrongdoing: "you hurt me and I will hurt you . . . and if I cannot hurt you myself, I demand that you should be hurt by others."[50]

Important differences do exist, however, between retribution and vengeance as a moral response to crime.[51] Vengeance can be defined as a personal response to wrongdoing, outside the rule of law. It is accompanied by intense feelings of hatred and is intended to exact suffering and to vanquish the opponent rather than to achieve a just solution. Since it operates outside the rule of law, it tends to destabilize the group and, indeed, often leads to internecine cycles of violence of aggression and retaliation.

Once understood as a personal response to harm, the utility of vengeance and the characteristics of vengeance become intelligible. Vengeance is a form of self-protection, but is different from actions we would describe as "self-defense." Acts of self-defense arise in a context in which physical force is immediately necessary to protect a person from harm. The utility of self-defense is therefore obvious. Vengeance, on the other hand, is a retaliatory response that is *not* immediately necessary to protect against harm. For this very reason, vengeance is rejected as a legitimate "affirmative defense" in the law. Acts of vengeance may occur at any time after a crime has been committed, but certainly not during the commission of a crime. Since the harm already has been suffered by the victim, what possible utility can there be in expending additional resources in causing harm to another person rather than repairing the harm you have suffered?

How, indeed, does anyone benefit from the infliction of additional suffering? It all seems so irrational and economically wasteful until we examine the victim's motives, as economist Robert Frank encouraged us to do. [52] From the perspective of a person who has been victimized, the ultimate purpose of retaliation is clear—it is to send a message about the victim's character: I will not be trifled with.   I will not suffer victimization passively. I will retaliate against those who harm me, no matter how long it takes and no matter what hardships I must endure. Implicit in this message is that the actor is obsessive, compulsive and unrestrained by boundaries of reason or proportionality.   A reputation for fierce retaliation might be extremely useful in signaling that you will not tolerate mistreatment. The retaliation "after the fact" may lack short-term benefits and carry considerable risks, but it may have significant *long term* benefits in preventing future harms.

Being reasonable and moderate is not in your self-interest if your aim is to establish a reputation of intolerance for being victimized. You seek to discourage any future attempts to harm you, and this might very well involve a devastating "overreaction." Your reputation for ferocity is established if you show you are completely unconcerned about the cost of exacting vengeance and that you have no interest in precisely calibrating your responses so as not to exceed the boundaries of propriety.   In vengeance, there is no desire for intersession by others, since this also indicate weakness. There is no desire for legal procedures, because this delays operation of retaliation. Also, in order to send out the message of fearfulness, retaliation is not necessarily limited to the instigator himself but also to anything or anyone he holds dear. Since vengeance can be exacted from persons other than the actor, there is no insistence on innocence or guilt, and no necessary linkage between punishment and any notion of deservedness. Vengeance occurs outside the strictures of legal precedents or procedures, so the context of conflict in which vengeance operates is more analogous to warfare than law. In war, the innocent will die. It is preposterous in war to limit one's responses only to those who actually committed some offense against you. War is only terminated when the opponent's will to wage war is ended, either in defeat or in a stand-off.

Retribution, on the other hand, can be understood as a rational, measured and impersonal response to wrongdoing. From this perspective, retribution is rooted in the principle of proportionality and the belief that a society must set moral limits on the amount of punishment to be inflicted on wrongdoers. Unlike vengeance, which often results in endless rounds of retaliation, the intended result of retribution is the restoration of social peace. Although it is conceivable that a measured, proportional response to wrongdoing can occur on a purely personal level, retaliation against wrongdoing that *requires* proportionality, rationality and a necessary linkage with deservedness, together with the goal of establishing justice and social order must be administered by a paramount authority who is not personally involved in the criminal incident.[53] For this reason, I will use the terms "retribution" and "retributory justice" to mean punitive sanctions administered by a legitimate authority (i.e. a *legal* authority) whose goal is to uphold norms of conduct within the group (i.e. the *law* of the group). In this way, retribution can be understood as justice *within the law* as opposed to the "personal justice" of vengeance.[54]

Thus, there are obvious advantages to justice administered within the law as opposed to personal vengeance. Here too, sociobiology provides insights into a possible evolutionary basis of the transition from vengeance to retribution. Of course, the complete story of the evolution of human society will always be shrouded in mystery, and our attempts to reconstruct it can only be reasonable speculations. But we are not entirely ignorant of our origins, and the more we know of how we survived for millennia as social animals, the richer is our understanding of things regard as most basic to our nature.

Let us consider the hunting pack. The hunting pack is a good model for human society because individual survival is inconceivable outside of the group. The group functions as a kind of a "super-organism" in the same way as the human body is a super-organism for the survival of individual cells. From this perspective, the Hobbesian idea of man's natural condition as a state of war waged by all against all cannot be sustained. Cooperation is not invented for the convenience of individuals but is a *precondition* for individual survival. Furthermore, the survival of human groups over the long course of evolution not only was a struggle to obtain resources from nature, but also involved conflict with other human groups for these scarce resources as well as conflicts within the group itself. Given the fallibility of human nature and the relentless operation of individual desires, it is impossible to imagine a society without what we would call "crime." However, if the only responses to crime within the group were personal retaliation or exclusion, these mechanisms for social control would soon become the seeds of the group's eventual fragmentation and disintegration unless there were a powerful moderating and reintegrating feature of norm maintenance. Inequalities in strength between the victim and the offender leads to retaliation by surrogates—typically based on kinship—which often devolves into irresolvable intra-group conflict. Hence, the need for a form of social control that does not depend on personal retaliatory.

While the social contract theorists have maintained that the transition from personal retaliation to "official retribution" was the product of a deliberate agreement by individuals to cede power to the state, evolutionary biologists have stressed the role of dominance hierarchies in bringing about social peace. A member of the group whose resentment is aroused by a criminal act does not necessarily retaliate because to do so against a dominant member would surely be suicidal. The choice, instead, is between retaliation to an inferior or protest to those who are superior in the social order. As De Waal noted, the sense of social regularity is "a set of expectations about the way in which oneself (or others) should be treated and how resources should be divided. Whenever reality deviates from these expectations to one's (or the other's) disadvantage, a negative reaction ensures most commonly protest by subordinates individuals and punishment by dominant individuals."[55]

For an individual pack member who has been victimized or "bullied," the availability of recourse to the leader relieves the victim of the unwinnable problem of retaliation against a superior power. Allegiance to the leader guarantees the member's access to superior power. Through the exercise of the leader's power to provide redress for transgressions to any member of the group, every member is assured of protection from harm and therefore can expand the scope of social trust and, consequently, his or her freedom. The group thereby prospers as a well-integrated organism, both in its attempts to wrest resources from the environment and in its struggle with competitive neighbors.

Two features of the leader's exercise of dominance through his administration of justice are notable:

1. **Proportionality.** The leader's retaliatory response to transgressions is motivated by the conservative desire to maintain dominance by demanding demonstrations of loyalty. Unlike the case of personal retaliation, the leader has no interest in inflicting harm on an offender for the purpose of self-protection or to "get back." Therefore, while the motive for personal vengeance "ceases only when exhausted . . . after it has destroyed the source of harm,"[56] the retributive justice administered by the paramount authority seeks no more than what is necessary to induce submission. It therefore is a more measured and less emotional response to wrongdoing than personal retaliation through vengeance.

2. **Rites of submission.** The administration of retaliatory justice by the group leader can also be accomplished with a minimum of physical violence. Both the actions of the leader and of the offender are highly ritualized and symbolic. Because it is the goal of the leader to assert his dominance without losing a valuable member, his power is demonstrated symbolically by impressive public displays. In return, the object of his wrath demonstrates his allegiance to the prevailing power hierarchy by a pantomime of submission: He literally exposes his neck. Once it is clear that the offender has offered himself up as a sacrifice, it is now the leader's turn to show magnanimity by desisting from actual violence and reaccepting him as a member of the group.

These studies of animal behavior offer fascinating insights into our own evolution as social beings—but whether they represent a historically accurate account of our past is speculative at best. What does seem undeniable is that the retaliatory instinct implicit in reciprocal altruism has been successfully channeled into socially acceptable communal responses by countless generations of humans. This mode of retaliation within the "law"—whether it is viewed as evolutionary development or as a purely cultural artifact—has proven to be capable of quelling the resentment that arises from the disturbance of reciprocity. It therefore draws upon and satisfies our emotional responses to injustice in a way that promotes community peace rather than enduring conflict.

The ritual of exclusion and reintegration, repeated countless times in both animal and human populations, is such an organic part of social control that, in our efforts to devise a criminal justice system responsive to the need of victims, offenders, and society as a whole, we would be wise to heed its lessons. One clear lesson is that the system must be based on a shared understanding that those who violate basic expectations of adherence to the norms of reciprocity will forfeit their membership in the group, but nevertheless can obtain readmission upon demonstration that they are again fit to be trusted as a member of society. Furthermore, whether or not the goal of restoring trust in any particular offender is achieved, the goal of restoring trust in society in the aftermath of wrongdoing is necessary and achievable both for a victim and for all who participate in the life of society.

Reciprocity and Trust

There is an intimate and powerful relation between reciprocal altruism and trust. Understanding the linkage between reciprocity and trust enriches our understanding of the nature of crime, the etiology of crime, the psychology of victimization and the means by which the presumption of reciprocity may be restored, both on an individual and a societal level. Let us therefore explore some of the important implications of the theory of reciprocal altruism on criminal justice theory and policy.

Whereas pure altruism is selectively advantageous only in the context of family relations, social cooperation beyond the family unit requires reciprocal altruism. For reciprocal altruism to function, there must be an expectation of reciprocity. Those who participate in the system of reciprocal altruism, and therefore profit from the many benefits of social cooperation, must agree to play by the rules. Each member of the moral community is thus acutely sensitive to violations of reciprocity by their experience of resentment.

But what, exactly, is it that a reciprocal altruist offers to others for which he or she expects a like return? It is not simply services (as in the case of grooming) or material possessions (as in the case of a seller who parts with merchandise on the expectation of being paid). More importantly, the reciprocal altruist offers *desistance from self-protective force*. This means, in effect: "I will not harm you, with the expectation that you will not harm me. I will not steal from you, cheat you, or hurt you, even if it is to my advantage to do so, with the expectation that you will do likewise." There is a tangible risk involved in such desistance. It is a form of voluntary disarmament that makes the reciprocal altruist vulnerable to predators because trust involves a belief in the goodwill of others,[57] a belief that they will not try to take advantage of us.[58] Trust is the basis of cooperative behavior, but blind trust cannot exist for long. It must be based on a realistic expectation that it will be returned and that those who betray our trust will face appropriate consequences. The kind of trust that is at the core of social interactions—the loss of which constitutes the essential harm of crime—can therefore be defined as *the presumption of adherence to the norms of reciprocity in others*. Willful violations of the presumption of reciprocity that are regarded by the public as being of sufficient magnitude to jeopardize relations of trust generally and that, accordingly, require a public response, are what we call *crimes*.

This presumption of reciprocity, so essential for interpersonal relations, necessarily involves the risk that the benefits that we grant to others—by being honest in our dealings and by refraining from the use of violence—may be exploited to our disadvantage. A commitment to renounce the use of force and fraud in dealings with others based on the expectation of reciprocity makes us vulnerable to those who are not committed to playing by the rules. In other words, in social relations outside of our families, we need to know whom we can trust. Those who subscribe to the requirements of reciprocal altruism and who thereby agree to play by the rules constitute the moral community of those who can be trusted. Those who do not subscribe to these rules are the "outlaws." They have done things that deliberately violate the rules of reciprocity and, as criminologists and as members of society, we want to know how to eliminate, or at least how to minimize these violations and thereby extend the scope of mutual trust.

Undoubtedly, the uniform and consistent enforcement of rules, which operates at a societal level, makes the possibility of trust in any one person more reasonable.[59] In societies that competently administer the rule of law, adherence to reciprocity can be reasonably presumed for any citizen in any social encounter, even perfect strangers. Just as new highways and cell phone towers help foster an integrated, cohesive society, so do relations of trust enable a society to prosper by facilitating every kind of social interaction. Conversely, the loss of trust destroys relationships. It destroys the individual relationship between a victim and offender as well as the relationship between an offender and the larger social group. If actions that destroy interpersonal trust go unpunished, then a time may come when it is no longer reasonable for members of society to expect and presume reciprocity, and thus the circles of trust wither into isolated contentious fragments. Crime "atomizes" communities by inducing fear and suspicion, and is therefore both a result and a cause of social disorganization.

The Bernard Madoff scandal is a disturbing illustration of the consequences of betraying trust. Madoff built an immense financial empire on little more than trust. He personally managed billions of dollars in investments that uncannily yielded ample, although non-sensational returns, despite market fluctuations. Investors trusted his judgment and felt privileged to be part of a select group of individuals and institutions lucky enough to have Bernie Madoff manage their funds. But it all turned out to be a tissue of lies, a vast Ponzi scheme in which income was derived not from sound investments, but from the pockets of new investors. Ultimately, this scheme was bound to fail, and fail it did, leaving in its wake hundreds of angry investors who lost millions, even billions, by their misplaced trust. As horrendous as those losses were, however, the damage done to the larger investing community was even greater because once people lose confidence in financial institutions, they stop investing. Investing requires a high degree of faith in the legitimacy and integrity of the system. Of course, the system cannot entirely eliminate risk, but it can ensure that the risks undertaken by investors are fully disclosed and knowingly accepted. A fraud such as Madoff's subverts the trust necessary for investment and, as a result, the personal wealth that might have become available as capital lies dormant. Therefore, when trust is lost, the economy contracts, jobs are lost, businesses close, and the very basis of the economy—our way of life—is jeopardized. For society as well as for individuals, the stakes for losing and for restoring trust are therefore very high indeed.

Those who try to cheat the system by obtaining the vast benefits of reciprocal altruism without respecting its pledge of mutual restrictions have broken the bonds of trust. According to the rules of the game and, on a visceral level in order to quell the moral resentment of its members, the offender must be punished. But punishment alone is insufficient to restore trust in the offender. The failure of modern society to reintegrate its growing population of offenders—and perhaps its failure to reduce recidivism—is largely attributable to the neglect of this basic principle: *The punishment that is necessary to maintain trust in society does not operate as a means of restoring trust in the offender when it is merely imposed upon him.* That is why the restoration of trust theory has something important to contribute to the understanding of the uses of punishment. If criminal sanctions are to be used to repair the harm of crime, the loss of trust in society requires the imposition of an appropriately severe sanction, but the loss of trust in an individual offender requires more. It requires the voluntary submission of the offender to a deserved punishment as only one necessary component, along with restitution, apology, and rehabilitation. By voluntarily submitting to a deserved punishment, the offender indicates that he respects the rules of the game of reciprocal altruism; by his apology, he expresses his renunciation of the contempt he has shown for the rights of the victim and for all those who play by the rules; by his agreement to make restitution, he expresses his agreement not to profit from his freeloading; by his voluntary agreement to submit to rehabilitation, he expresses his desire and commitment to change; and, finally, by the totality of these actions and expressions, he indicates his desire to return to the good graces of the moral community.

The very capability that we have to detect violations of reciprocity by others also makes us acutely aware of our own choices. Despite any immediate benefits we might achieve, we are involuntarily subject to powerful emotions that favor prosocial, long-term benefits over egotistical short-term gains.[60] When a potential offender desists from crime only by his concern for the possibility of detection, prosecution, and punishment, it is only his fear of detection, prosecution and punishment that acts as a deterrent. But when he desists from crime by his awareness of the suffering he would cause in others, not only does he become immediately aware of the social cost from his network of relations, he also experiences a sensation of self-condemnation borne of empathy: the experience of guilt. Guilt can be understood as the counterpart of resentment. Among those who genetically subscribe to the reciprocal altruistic "game plan," the act of cheating arouses guilt in the offender just as the detection of cheaters by others arouses resentment in the victim. And just as the imposition of punishment tends to assuage the resentment of the victim, so does the acceptance of punishment for those who failed to exercise self-control assuage the guilt of the offender through the act of atonement.[61]

For those who do not subscribe to the reciprocal altruistic game plan, the impact of punishment has a fundamentally different character. Here, punishment acts simply as a negative reinforcer to conduct. An offender does not thereafter desist from crime because it is wrongful or shameful, but because he has not found the right opportunity to test his luck. He can be "trusted" only as long as his fear restrains him. This is why it is essential to the restoration of trust that the offender demonstrates empathy for the suffering of the victim. If no empathy is shown, there is good reason to doubt his capacity for experiencing guilt. Therefore, the offender cannot be trusted to exercise self-restraint in his dealings with others as a moral choice. He cannot be accepted as "one of us." Those who exhibit guilt, on the other hand, identify themselves as subscribers to the reciprocal altruistic pact. Because a sense of guilt arises only in those who value their inclusion in the group and who subscribe to its rules and its authority, the expression of guilt by an offender is an expression of his allegiance to the group in his desire to become reintegrated. He renounces his contempt and the false assertion of superiority implicit in the crime by humbling himself. By submitting to the punishment, he demonstrates his respect for the system and his willingness to pay the moral debt. The doors of social rejection can only now begin to open.

Trust is really at the heart of this matter. As a member of society, we must relinquish our weapons and armor that would otherwise protect us from harm, but only with the understanding and the expectation that others will also do so. We agree to play by the rules, even though that limits our freedom, with the expectation that others will do so too. The widening of this circle of trust is a basic attribute of civilization, one that makes possible the prosperity that is achieved by the efficiencies of trade. "A nation's well-being, as well as its ability to unite, is conditioned by a single, pervasive attribute—the force of trust inherent in the society."[62] This growth of trust is not a naïve faith in human goodness. Far from it. It is an outgrowth of evolved social instincts that retaliates against the abusers of trust, but that seeks their eventual reintegration rather than their elimination.

The presumption of reciprocity in others (i.e., our trust in others) is implicit in the Golden Rule that serves as a model of ethical discernment in many cultures. There are actually two versions of the Golden Rule: one positive and one negative. We are mostly familiar with the positive version: "Do unto others as you would have others do unto you." By contrast, the negative version states: "Do not do to others that which you would not want others to do to you." Which is preferable? The positive version appears more enlightened, humane, and generous while the negative version seems somewhat stingy (as well as being harder for kids to memorize), but the real test is whether they are *useful* in resolving moral questions. In this regard, the negative version may win out because it draws its discriminatory power from the emotion of resentment that involuntary arise from the disappoint of our expectations of reciprocity. Resentment is our guide to right conduct because we know it and feel it immediately, powerfully, and unrelentingly. It is the central mechanism that makes reciprocal altruism operational and, as such, is largely responsible for our success as social animals. In deciding what is right to do in any situation, we can merely ask: How would I feel if that were to happen to me? By knowing the instinctual response of resentment at conduct that disappoints our expectations of fair treatment, we can tell instantly whether any conduct passes or fails the "resentment test."

If the negative version of the Golden Rule tells us what *not* to do, the positive version of the Golden Rule is designed to tell us what we must do. Here, we are not guided by resentments at the bad things people may do to us, but by our wishes for the good things they could do for us. I would like people to be kind to me, therefore I should be kind. I would like people to love me, therefore I should love others. But herein lies a problem: Sometimes the things I want for myself would not be feasible or even desirable if granted to others. For example, I would like people to give me special attention and special privileges. I would like my faults to be overlooked. I would like to be given a second chance, or even a third or fourth. There are many things I would like to get from other people. But does that mean that it is therefore my obligation to do these things to others, even if I get nothing at all from them? If it were my ethical obligation to do so, without regard to any return, I would be offering advantages to others without any corresponding utility to myself. Accordingly, the positive version of the Golden Rule is a rule of unconditional altruism and, as such, is prone to extinction by cheaters. Furthermore, even if this positive mandate to do unto others could survive in a competitive world, it may not be such a good idea to bestow on everyone those benefits that I would like for myself. Would it really be wise to give everyone a second and third chance if, by doing so, potential offenders knew that they had one or more free passes? Although I may be able to generalize the negative claim that robbing a person is wrong (because I would not want to be robbed), it is more difficult to generalize the positive claim that I should give to the poor. While I can state categorically that robbing a person is wrong, no matter how much money is taken, I cannot easily claim how much money must be given to the poor, what qualifies as being "poor," how many people I should give it to, and how much money I should be left with. Certainly, as much as we would like to receive special treatment from others, wish them to overlook our faults, or give us a second or third chance, the prospect of converting these positive wishes into universal moral requirements is neither likely nor desirable.

The negative version of the Golden Rule is easier to administer because it alone is based on the genetic strategy of reciprocal altruism. Indeed, the Golden Rule can be regarded as the verbal expression of reciprocal altruism, and its operation would continue to govern human affairs (at least for non-kinsmen) whether or not it was consciously adopted as a guiding principle. Whatever actions impair trust, and thereby arouse our resentment, are bad because trust is the underpinning of (non-kin) relationships. They are *universally* bad because, if the act were done by everyone, organized life in society would be impossible. Lying is bad, for example, because it impairs trust in the liar. And unless justified by a more crucial societal value, such as the protection of innocent life from wrongful actions,[63] it is categorically bad because, if everyone were to lie, it would be devastatingly harmful to life in society. That is also why stealing is bad, or bullying is bad: They harm individual relations of trust and, if universalized, harm societal relations of trust. The same is true about every act that intentionally violates the expectations of reciprocity: They violate our basic trust, arouse our resentment, destroy personal relationships, and, if universalized, destroy societal-level cooperation.

Reciprocity is essential to life in society and therefore stands as a guiding principle for social interactions. This was recognized by a wise man thousands of years ago:

> *Tse-kung asked, "Is there one word that can serve as a principle of conduct for life?"*

> *Confucius replied, "It is the word 'shu'—reciprocity."* (Analects of Confucius, 15:23)

Trustworthiness, of course, is a moral virtue of the highest order. But since it is essential for human interactions, is not at all a rare quality, such as is the case of courage or wisdom. The principle of reciprocal altruism presumes *all* members of society to be sufficiently trustworthy to fully engage in the life of the society unless they demonstrate untrustworthiness by their failure to reciprocate. The deliberate failure to honor the basic presumption of trust, if sufficiently serious, is a crime, and the consequences to both a victim and offender are catastrophic. The victim has been deprived of his or her presumption of the trustworthiness of others, and the offender has forfeited his position among those who may be trusted. This defect in trust was not brought about by the failure to do unto others something beneficial that the offender would wish for himself, but rather by deliberately doing something harmful that he would resent if anyone did it to him.

We can now return to the question posed at the beginning of this chapter: What is so special about trust that we should regard it as an essential value that must be restored in the aftermath of crime? By understanding the importance of reciprocity in regulating social behavior and promoting social cooperation, we can now understand why the goal of restoring the presumption of reciprocity—restoring trust—should not be regarded as simply another vector in field of competing criminal justice goals. Beyond adding to the familiar dichotomy of crime control and protection of due process rights, restoring trust necessarily subsumes these goals, and also enriches our understanding of these traditional values. By understanding the effect of crime on our fundamental presumption of trust in others, we can also see how the control of crime is a necessary aspect of restoring trust but, by the same token, we can no longer can be satisfied with punitive measures designed merely to control unwanted behavior by fear alone. Guided by the goal of restoring trust, the sanctions imposed by the criminal justice system can not only be more humane and creative, but also more effective in accomplishing the traditional goals of sentencing. By insisting that an offender take personal responsibility for his offense; by involving the offender, his family, and the community in devising a solution; and, in short, by using the criminal justice process as a way to regain trust in the offender instead of as a means of disenfranchising him, greater crime control can be obtained from the very sanctions that are presently administered by the conventional system.

The restoration of trust also necessarily involves an insistence on justice. A criminal justice disposition that is not fair cannot be restorative. This is manifestly so for crime victims, but also is true for offenders. A sentence—even a deserved sentence—that is obtained through a process that violates the rights of the accused will be regarded as unfair an oppressive. As such, it cannot operate as an instrument of restoring trust, but rather serves an instrument of engendering greater distrust between the offender and society. The restoration of trust for a crime victim requires the precondition of justice because the expectations of reciprocity involved in relations of trust, as well as the human reactions to the disappointment of these expectations, are inextricably linked to the innate perceptions of justice. These subjective reactions to justice, and to the absence of justice, must be taken seriously by criminal justice system. It is the instinctual passion for justice that ensures the stability of reciprocal relations of trust, relations that are central to our ability to survive and flourish as social beings.

Of course, not everyone's conception of justice is particularly restorative. Indeed, this obsessional insistence on justice and the vindication of honor has been cited as the motivation behind the dangerous strategy of vengeance: "A common denominator among the severe, intentional harms that elicit the desire for revenge is that they violate the victim's sense of honor."[64] This is certainly epitomized in the hideously cruel practice of "honor killings" in which family members (typically female) who have dishonored the family name (typically by an exercise of sexual freedom) are ritually killed by another member of the family. In Western societies, a more familiar example of honor killings is the use of violence to redress a perceived insult. The more insistent that someone is on preserving their honor, it would appear, the more mindlessly brutal they are in their vindication. If justice is required as a prerequisite to the restoration of trust, are we not therefore condoning or promoting personal violence?

The concern about escalating violence based on exaggerated notions of personal or family honor is very real, but the restoration of trust perspective, rather than elevating these concerns, should help alleviate them. In both cases of honor killings—for unchastity or personal insult, for example—the allegedly harmful conduct, though likely harming personal trust in the individual, has no bearing on trust in society. The failure to sanction the offensive conduct does not constitute a threat to general relations of trust in the community because, if it did, that same conduct would be considered a *crime* for which the appropriate remedy would be public prosecution and sanctions. In these cases, however, the retaliation is inherently and necessarily personal and outside of the law. Indeed, the very act of killing as a response to insults to the sense of honor is itself regarded as a crime: The threat to social trust is not the provocative conduct, but the disproportional and personal form of retaliation. The answer to the threat of wanton cruelty to avenge insults to someone's honor therefore is not to abdicate insistence on justice or on the preservation of honor, but rather to insist on adherence to justice *under the law* that ensures both personal and societal levels of trust.

If, as we have argued, the essential harm of crime is loss of trust in the offender and in society, understanding the sociobiological underpinnings of trust—the presumption of adherence to reciprocity in others—is an important foundation for the development of a criminal justice system designed to repair the harm of crime. Still, as the science of sociobiology advances and as we become increasingly aware of the instinctual underpinnings of our expectations of reciprocity and reactions to those who betray those expectations, we must recognize that instinct alone can never fully explain human conduct. For one thing, the science of sociobiology (like all sciences) is still a work in progress, and the full story of how humans respond to wrongdoing is yet to be told. We humans may be biological beings, but we are extraordinarily complicated beings, and it should come as no surprise that our individual responses to crime are complex and varied. For many people, for example, the personal revenge motive that "ought" to have been eclipsed by the more impersonal response of official retribution is very much alive. The overwhelming feelings of compassion, mercy, and forgiveness exhibited by some victims may be utterly absent in others. A key lesson we have learned in the social sciences is that, when it comes to explaining human conduct, the best we can do is to identify "factors" rather than "causes" and to speak in terms of probability rather than inevitable outcomes. This is why we can anticipate highly variable reactions to subjective decisions. And it is why we must contain the range of subjective discretion within objective boundaries that reflect a societal-level consensus.

An understanding of the sociobiological foundation of trust is therefore incomplete and should never be thought of as a substitute for the exercise of moral judgment in devising social policy. Because every human attribute is conditioned by culture, so too are our instinctive responses to wrongdoing molded into norms of reciprocity expected of everyone within the cultural unit.[65] We are not the inevitable product of an evolutionary destiny. Our morality is a cultural achievement that cannot be directly inferred from nature.[66] And yet, in conceiving of the fundamental principles of morality, we cannot ignore our *human* nature. If our emotional reactions had evolved differently, our comprehension of moral "principles" would be different as well. And if the capacity for emotional reactions were somehow removed from the human genome, our moral discernment would disappear entirely, and the world of our experience would be a world of mere factuality, without good or evil, right or wrong—a world devoid of value. [67]

It therefore behooves us to understand our human nature and the emotions that are the wellspring of moral discernment to the extent that we can so that the rules of morality we devise may be in harmony with the kind of beings we have evolved to become: *social beings* whose ability to survive and flourish depends on the ability to interact successfully with others. It is no coincidence that the rational principles of harmonious interactions—our morality—make sense to us and promote emotional well-being only when they draw on, and do not contradict, our evolutionary heritage.

Thus, our instincts provide the "raw materials" for the achievement of a socially useful goal: the administration of justice. Criminal justice procedures and policies that thwart our instincts are therefore unlikely to achieve the goals we seek. However, in devising a criminal justice system, we can do more than simply accommodate our desires. We can seek to sublimate our instinctual responses to a higher purpose than mere retaliation for wrongful conduct. Guided by the goal of restoring trust in the offender and in society, we can devise a criminal justice system that promotes genuine healing, forgiveness, and reintegration.

The goal of restoring trust, finally, is not at all a New Age fantasy. It is a timeless, enduring, and fundamental requirement for life in society that is based on the foundation of reciprocity. It not only reflects our evolutionary heritage, but also our highest moral aspirations. As such, it is well suited as a guiding principle for criminal justice policy and practice.

Notes

[1] Packer, "Two Models of the Criminal Process."
[2] Nozick, *Philosophical Explanations.*
[3] O'Manique, *The Origins of Justice,* p. 9.
[4] Johnson, "The Historical Background of Social Darwinism."
[5] Lorenz, *On Aggression*; Ardrey, *The Territorial Imperative.*
[6] Solomon, *A Passion for Justice,* p. 60.
[7] Singer, *The Expanding Circle*, p. 4
[8] Solomon, *supra.*
[9] Fehr & Gachter, "Altruistic Punishment in Humans," p. 137.
[10] Singer, *supra*, pp. 10-11.
[11] De Waal, *Good Natured: The Origins of Right and Wrong in Humans and Other Animals.*
[12] Dawkins, *The Selfish Gene.*
[13] Axelrod, *The Evolution of Cooperation.*
[14] Trivers, "The Evolution of Reciprocal Altruism."
[15] Solomon, *supra, p.* 29.
[16] *Id. p.* 128.
[17] Singer, *supra,* p. 17.
[18] Miller, "Disrespect and the Experience of Injustice," p. 545.
[19] Solomon, *supra*, p. 127.
[20] Walsh, *supra*, p. 853.
[21] *I.e.* Lerner, *The Belief in a Just World.*
[22] *I.e.* Kelln, & Ellard, "An Equity Theory Analysis of the Impact of Forgiveness."
[23] Walsh. "Evolutionary Psychology," p. 851.
[24] Walsh, *supra*, p. 851, *citing* Barkow, *Darwin, Sex and Status*, p. 121.
[25] Singer, *The Expanding Circle*, p. 40.
[26] Walsh, *supra*, p. 851. A good example of this is sexuality. In terms of material costs and benefits, sexuality might appear from the outside as an extraordinary waste of time and effort. To affected individuals, the long-term survival function may not be readily apparent. It is only by virtue of the overwhelming power of our "limbic overrides" that the pursuit of sexual congress becomes, like the pursuit of justice, an irrational obsession whose material pay-off to the "selfish gene" is not realized until long afterward.
[27] Fehr & Gachter, "Altruistic Punishment in Humans;" Boyd, Gintis, Bowles & Richardson, "The Evolution of Strong Reciprocity."
[28] Fehr & Gachter, supra, p. 137.
[29] *Id.*
[30] Solomon, *supra*, p. 246.

[31] That criminal offenses ought to be defined as "willful" violations of trust may appear to be unduly limited, in that the mens rea requirement of the criminal law extends to actions that are not necessarily intentional. While a purely "negligent" act is generally regarded as a civil rather than a criminal matter, harm that results from "reckless" conduct is certainly within the purview of the criminal law. Yet, upon further analysis, even "reckless" conduct can be seen as "willful" in that it is a willful disregard of the duty of care we expect from each other. A person who voluntarily takes actions that expose the public to danger may not intend any specific consequences, but has nonetheless *chosen* to engage in conduct that is likely to cause harm. It is the willful choice of manifestly dangerous conduct that represents a fundamental breach of trust—whether or not that conduct results in any tangible harm. Drunk driving, for example, can be considered a crime in itself, regardless of actual harm—and any actual harm that results from the driver's impaired condition would give rise to criminal as well as civil liability. As fallible human beings we concede the possibility of harms that arise from our mistakes or negligence. Correspondingly, the commission of an act of negligence does not entail a "willful" breach of trust. We may be annoyed—or indeed angered by careless conduct, but only when such conduct is in some sense willful is our resentment aroused—a resentment that is placated by the imposition of some form of punishment, rather than mere payment.

[32] Garvey, "The Moral Emotions of the Criminal Law," p. 105

[33] Murphy, "Forgiveness, Mercy, and the Retributive Emotions," p. 16.

[34] Holmes, *The Common Law*, p. 3

[35] Singer, *supra*, p. 33

[36] Two exceptions to this are religion and political ideology, in which our intuitive moral sentiments may very well give way to the requirements of religious faith or political loyalty. Unconstrained by our instinctual values centering upon reciprocity, our actions may then range from incomprehensible virtue to incomprehensible cruelty.

[37] Holmes, *The Common Law*, p. 3.

[38] Nowak & Sigmund, "Tit for Tat in Heterogeneous Populations."

[39] Ridley, *The Origins of Virtue*, p. 76.

[40] Nowak & Sigmund, "A Strategy of Win-Stay, Lose-Shift."

[41] Wu & Axelrod, "How to Cope With Noise in the Iterated Prisoner's Dilemma."

[42] McCullough, *Beyond Revenge*.

[43] *Id.*, p. 103.

[44] Walsh, *supra*, p. 857.

[45] Singer, *supra*, p. 41.

[46] *Id.* p. 39.

[47] Sampson, Raudenbush, & Earls, "Neighborhoods and Violent Crime."

[48] Jacoby, Susan, *Wild Justice: The Evolution of Revenge*.

[49] Holmes, *supra*, p. 45.

[50] Finckenauer, "Support for Capital Punishment," p. 92; Gardiner, "The Purposes of Criminal Punishment," p. 119.

[51] Tunick, *Punishment: Theory and Practice*, p. 88; Haas, "The Triumph of Vengeance Over Retribution," pp. 132–133; Nozick, *Philosophical Explanations*, pp. 366–374.

[52] Frank, *Passions within Reason: The Strategic Role of the Emotions.*

[53] Psychologist Mona Gustafson-Affinito has made a similar distinction between "vengeance" and "punishment," and regards the former as primarily a non-rational, emotional impulse and to the latter as a rational, problem-solving technique. Gustafson-Affinito, "Forgiveness in Counseling," p. 94.

[54] Notice that "lawful authority" can also be exercised by individuals, such as parents, guardians and teachers. Accordingly, when they "retaliate" against misbehavior, within the scope of their authority, they do so in fulfillment of duty, and the actions are not accompanied by any sense of pleasure in the suffering of the wrongdoer.

[55] De Waal, *Good Natured: The Origins of Right and Wrong in Humans and other Animals*, p. 95.

[56] Durkheim, *The Rules of the Sociological Method*, p. 86.

[57] Seligman, *The Problem of Trust*, p. 43.

[58] Silver, "Friendship and Trust as Moral Ideals," p. 276.

[59] Dimock, *Retributism and Trust*, p. 51.

[60] Mealey, *The Sociobiology of Sociopathy.*

[61] Garvey, *Punishment as Atonement*, p. 1893.

[62] Fukayama, *Trust*, p. 7.

[63] The familiar example of lying to a Nazi search party in order to protect a Jewish refugee is not a contradiction to the claim that lying is universally bad, but rather should be regarded as an instance in which otherwise bad conduct is justifiable. It is equivalent to the justification of self-defense or the use of lethal force in defense of others: the intentional killing of others is wrong, but this wrongful conduct is justified nonetheless by a superseding moral principal:—the defense of innocent life from wrongful actions.

[64] McCullough, *Beyond Revenge*, p. 69.

[65] In classifying those serious violations of the rules of reciprocity we regard as "criminal," we may further distinguish between those violations that immediately and instinctively arouse our resentment (*mala in se*), from those that are merely agreed-upon for public convenience but do not, of themselves, arouse resentment (*mala prohibita*). For *mala in se,* we can presume that all persons recognize their inherent wrongfulness and therefore are justified in applying sanctions for all violations, while for *mala prohibita*, we must insist on adequate public notice, since we cannot presume that a violator was aware of its illegality.

[66] Moore, *Principia Ethica*; Singer, *supra*, p. 80.

[67] Solomon, *True to Our Feelings.*

6

The Pathway Back for Crime Victims

In the discussion so far, I have proposed a sentencing framework that permits restorative justice to function as a comprehensive criminal justice system—one that is applicable to a full range of offenders and offenses. By establishing upper and lower boundaries of sentencing severity that are responsive to the need for community safety and retributive justice, we create a zone of sentencing discretion within which to calibrate criminal sanctions appropriate to the particular needs of the victim, the affected community, and the offender. This framework allows us to exercise an extraordinary degree of creativity and flexibility in order to restore trust *in the offender* without jeopardizing the fundamental values of proportionality, equality of treatment, protection of public safety, and conformity to the rule of law necessary to restore trust *in society*. It therefore helps to resolve one of the two most critical issues facing restorative justice as it attempts to move into the mainstream of criminal justice practice: *reconciling public and private justice.*

This framework for distinguishing between personal and social trust provides a valuable conceptual tool in resolving the other crucial issue for restorative justice as well: *finding a restorative role for punishment.* In this chapter, I will argue that under the overarching goal of restoring trust, the voluntary submission of an offender to a deserved punishment becomes an instrumentality for addressing the material and emotional needs of crime victims as well as the needs of society. Utilizing this goal of restoration helps transform the character of sentencing discretion so that it is no longer confined to the conventional goals of assessing blame and imposing punishment. Finally, the restoration of trust analysis, I will argue, provides valuable insight into the conditions under which emotional recovery can be maximized, and the severity of punishment minimized, in a socially responsible manner.

What Does the Victim Need?

Although the needs of crime victims have often been neglected by the judicial system in the past, the protection of victims' rights has recently emerged as a primary goal of criminal justice. Besides their physical need for safety and the economic need for restitution of their material losses, crime victims endure emotional and psychological losses as a consequence of the crime.[1] Additionally, victims' emotional and psychological losses can be ameliorated or, in fact, compounded by their treatment in the criminal justice system. [2] Emotional reactions reported by victims include anger, anxiety, depression, overall physical distress, resentment, and hostility. [3] Psychological harms to victims include a sense of isolation, loss of faith, shock, enmity, loss of control, self-blame, denigration, and fear.[4] Restorative justice advocates have primarily stressed three vehicles for emotional and psychological recovery: (1) apology, (2) victim participation, and (3) payment of restitution. Whether these three are sufficient to answer the needs of crime victims is a key question that must be addressed before any comprehensive model of restorative justice can be devised. Let us begin with apology.

The central mechanism for emotional and psychological healing cited by virtually all restorative theorists is *apology*. Whether or not apology is relevant to the interests of the state,[5] it is basic to the restorative justice approach to the healing of a victim's emotional losses and is thought to be essential for the successful resolution of a case.[6] Psychologists have noted that an offender's apology should involve not only an admission of responsibility, but also an expression of remorse and shame, a promise to refrain from further violations, and a hope for a renewed relationship with the victim.[7] The messages conveyed by apology are complex and, at times, seemingly contradictory: Apology functions both to convey the acceptance of full responsibility and also to reduce the offender's perceived culpability by explaining motivations. It shows respect for the victim. It denies malicious intent. It affirms the group's norms and may be regarded, by the very act of its offering, as a form of penance.[8] The demonstration of respect inherent in apology is thought to counteract the message of disrespect that often underlies the feeling of injustice, thus lessening the victim's demands both for punishment and for restitution.[9] Incomplete apologies, for example, where there is no acceptance of personal responsibility ("I'm sorry that it happened"), may actually bring about more blame.[10] Although apologies apparently motivated by a desire for leniency are viewed by crime victims as insincere, the sincerity of an apology is made more credible by the commitment to pay restitution.[11]

The healing power of apology has been understood by psychologists in various ways. According to the "attribution theory," crime victims experience a shock to their perception of an orderly world and, in seeking an explanation, they attribute the fault to themselves. The shamefulness of victimization in the eyes of the public and in a victim's own mind is derived from the perception that the victim has failed to manage his or her own affairs competently. [12] The therapeutic effect of apology is therefore in canceling this misconceived attribution of blame.[13] Although punishing the offender may also accomplish this expressive function, the offering of a public apology by the offender is thought to eliminate the necessity for punishment by symbolically restoring the victim's self-esteem.

The attribution theory can be seen as a corollary of the "equity theory" of relationships that attempts to account for a victim's desire to retaliate. In the equity theory, a relationship between people has an expected balance of cause and effect. When one person suffers a loss that is disproportionate to their responsibility for it, an imbalance arises along with a perception of unfairness or injustice. When directed outward, the sense of injustice or unfairness is accompanied by a feeling of resentment.[14] Restoring equity in a relationship means restoring the victim to his or her previous position with respect to the offender who gained an unfair advantage. The greater the inequity, the more distress is felt by the victim, and the harder he or she tries to restore equity.[15] Equity theorists have contended that the resentment and stress experienced by a victim can be appeased either by punishment or by restitution. If the distress stems from inequity, it can be relieved either by increasing the victim's benefits through restitution or by reducing the offender's benefits from the offense by punishment.[16] For this reason, restitution has been regarded by some as an effective sanction, even for violent crimes.[17] Restitution, it has been claimed, was the primary means of reconciling conflicts in early cultures; it was favored as a means of symbolically exacting revenge, "but without the bloody consequences."[18] Payment of restitution has been described as having both a material and nonmaterial benefit to the victim: "The imposition of an obligation to pay compensation is tantamount to inviting the offender to admit to the victim that he or she was in the wrong. Such a gesture can help to restore the victim's shattered sense of justice and feeling of community."[19] Monetary payment alone, for example, through insurance or state-sponsored victims' services, may ameliorate some of the harm associated with victimization, but it does not redress the injury of degradation suffered at the hands of the offender. Therefore, the requirement of restitution is not only a means of material compensation, but also a means of accountability—a symbolic gesture of penance and a corroboration of the sincerity of apology.[20]

Victims who perceive that the offender still has greater benefits or has suffered lesser losses than themselves are the angriest and most distressed.[21] Furthermore, it has been claimed that the equitable balance between a victim and offender involves psychological as well as material gains and losses. These former losses are essentially losses to the sense of equity, self-worth, and social status. Because crime devalues the self-worth and denigrates the status of the victim, proper balance is restored by (1) the offering of an apology by the offender and (2) the communication of condemnation and reproach by society.[22] In this way through expressive acts, rather than through physical punishment, it is believed that the victim is vindicated and the psychological harm of the crime is repaired. The expressive role of apology has also been understood as an act of submission. As an expressive act, the apology acknowledges the validity of the norm that has been violated and expresses the offender's sense of moral inferiority in violating those rules,[23] together with his intention to honor that norm in the future. Beyond this expression of the acceptance of norms, an apology is also an actual act of submission because, through that apology (unlike a mere "account" of the incident), the offender submits to the moral judgment of the victim who is thereby empowered to accept or reject it by granting or withholding forgiveness. Thus, it is up to the victim to determine whether or not to permit the offender back into the "moral community."[24] Apology, then, in which the offender "lays himself completely at the mercy of the victim,"[25] is thought to be the antidote to the victim's disempowerment.[26]

Restorative justice theorists have also contended that the disempowerment, loss of control, and sense of isolation experienced by many victims can be ameliorated by greater involvement and more respectful treatment in the criminal justice system itself. Victims, they have argued, want to be fully informed of the progress of their case, to have their say and their feelings respected, and to participate in decision making.[27] Of course, participation in criminal trials is not regarded as beneficial or stress reducing by those victims who view a criminal trial as the opening of old wounds. This is especially problematic in reviving older cases where victims have long since learned to cope with their losses, but it is also applicable to cases in which the criminal justice process itself is regarded as a type of victimization.[28] Daly, ever the skeptic, wrote that, even in those cases where a victim agrees to participate, the goal of victim-offender encounter in which the victim tells his or her story and the offender responds with empathy and remorse rarely occurs. In her analysis of Australian restorative justice conferences, Daly noted that most offenders were fixated on negotiating a sentence and reported that the victim's story had "little or no affect on them."[29] Yet there is little doubt that offering a victim the choice of participating in the criminal justice system to the degree they feel most comfortable and appropriate is preferable to virtually excluding them from the system, which is what had prevailed until recent years. By enabling the victim to directly confront the offender, express his or her feelings, demand answers to questions, and negotiate an acceptable outcome, the emotional and psychological harm of victimization, it is believed, can be minimized. The primary benefit of victim participation is not so much experienced as an exercise of power, but rather as an opportunity for the victim to receive, firsthand, the offender's apology. Whatever apologies are muttered to the court in the context of a negotiated plea bargain have little likelihood of inducing any sense of satisfaction or closure on the part of the victim because, in that instance, the victim's personhood remains unacknowledged and diminished. As long as the victim is an outsider to the process, the healing power of the offender's apology is never adequately brought to bear on the victim's emotional wounds.

In summary, restorative justice theorists have contended that apology, restitution, personal involvement, and respectful treatment in the court system are effective means of healing the emotional harm of crime by (1) undoing the victim's false attribution of self-blame through apology; (2) readjusting material gains and losses as between the victim and the offender by restitution (augmenting the victim while diminishing the offender) and (3) redressing the loss in status and self-esteem of the victim by the expressive and actual submission inherent in apology, payment of restitution, personal involvement, and respectful treatment. It also operates to facilitate forgiveness by enabling the victim to unburden himself or herself of the feelings of anger and resentment—a topic we will consider in greater depth a bit later.

The restoration of trust perspective is fully in accord with these basic requirements for healing and, further, it helps us understand how the emotional wounds suffered by victims are caused and how they may be repaired. The key to understanding the emotional consequences of crime is a concept we explored at some length in the preceding chapter: *reciprocity*. Humans live in a web of social relations that cohere by the expectation of reciprocity. The presumption of reciprocal treatment by others is, in turn, the essence of trust. When these expectations are betrayed by a criminal act, our orderly world is shattered. We are suddenly and unconsciously awash with emotions that motivate us to respond to this betrayal because, if the betrayal of our expectations of reciprocity is not ameliorated in some manner, it will undermine the foundation of all our social interactions.

Therefore, whatever actions tend to ameliorate the betrayal of trust implicit in crime tend also to diminish those negative reactions that are aroused by crime. *Whatever operates to restore the trust in society and in the offender that was damaged by crime therefore also becomes a modality for emotional restoration.* From this perspective, the mechanisms of healing cited in the restorative justice literature—apology, restitution, personal involvement, and respectful treatment—are all crucially important to the goal of restoring trust and, consequently, to the goal of restoring the emotional well-being of crime victims. But what about punishment: Does it play any constructive role in the inventory of restorative sanctions? Before I examine this issue from the restoration of trust perspective, let us see why this remains a contentious issue within restorative justice advocacy.

Resolving the Debate Over the Role of Punishment in Healing

Although most restorative justice theorists have conceded the necessity for coercion in order to enforce restorative justice requirements and to deal with offenders who refuse to participate in restoration efforts, these limited uses are generally regarded as necessary exceptions to the basic claim that punishment is contradictory to restoration. They have claimed that punishment "does not help the injuries caused by crime and simply creates new injury—now both the victim and the offender are injured,"[30] and that, in order to meet a victim's needs, it is necessary to replace punitive justice with restorative justice.[31] They have asked "How can still more suffering undo the pain of crime?"[32] and claimed that the "personal needs of those offended are not met by revenge, but by addressing the feelings behind the [victim's] anger."[33] For this reason, restorative justice theorists have contended that:

> punishment of the offender is not what victims really want. . . . What victims really want is for the offender to own responsibility for the harm, to shift his or her attitude from disrespect to respect for the victim and the norms of the community, and to feel and express genuine shame, remorse and contrition. . . . They want the public vindication that is achieved through caring and authoritative acknowledgement of their suffering. Punishment does not deliver any of these outcomes.[34]

"Restitution," on the other hand, "serves both the emotional and practical needs of the victim and the idea of social justice—as opposed to punishment, which instead satisfies the rather archaic requirements of retribution".[35] These theorists have seen "no positive value for justice in the very fact of the perpetrator's suffering or sacrifice of well-being."[36] What all these theories have in common is the claim that, whatever benefits punishment may have in maintaining social order, it is not necessary for the restoration of a victim's well-being and, in fact, may be *counterproductive*.[37] Contrary to the goals of reintegration, they claim, punishment induces defiance, denial, and uncooperation.[38] Punishment is believed to impair the desire of offenders to make amends, which is contrary to the goal of restitution and reparation. Punishment induces greater anxiety among victims by making them feel personally responsible for the offender's privations.[39] The restorative justice approach, by contrast, has been claimed to be "justice that promotes healing:"[40]

> Real justice involves much more than the thirst for vengeance. Victims who are absorbed by their hate and obsessed by their desire for vengeance are doomed because they can never regain the peace of mind necessary for a happy existence. Victims who learn how to forgive cope better and heal quicker than the other victims... It is difficult to contrast the humanizing spirit of restorative justice with the brutalizing and demeaning nature of retributive justice or to compare the healing effects of restorative justice with the agonizing and antagonizing outcomes of punitive justice.[41]

If that were the end of the story, we should have to be content with a version of restorative justice that stands as a radical alternative to the conventional system; one that would have little chance of acceptance by those people who regard punishment as a necessary component of justice, especially for serious offenses.

But by no means is this the end of the story because the premise on which it is based—the claim that punishment is either irrelevant or antithetical to healing—lacks a firm empirical foundation. Despite two decades of implementation in programs throughout the world and scores of studies on various aspects of restorative justice programs, not a single study has tested the claim that the restorative justice alternative to punishment is *more conducive* to healing than an approach that includes the use of punishment. While McCold argued that "we now have a growing body of research on programs that everyone agrees are truly restorative, clearly demonstrating their remarkable success at healing and conciliation,"[42] Daly observed that "McCold gives no citations to the research literature."[43] Studies that have focused on victim "satisfaction" have not assessed the victim's emotional and psychological recovery[44] and, more importantly, these studies *have not contrasted the effects of a nonpunitive approach with a traditional sentencing model.*[45] Strang's excellent study of the Reintegrative Shaming Experiments (RISE) Project in Canberra, Australia, relied on by McCullough in *Beyond Revenge* as proof of the therapeutic advantages of forgiveness to crime victims,[46] did not contrast victims' reactions to punitive versus nonpunitive sanctions because the sample frame included only cases that the police were willing to divert from criminal processing altogether.[47] Because the question of punishment was not at issue, Strang's study was evidential of victims' satisfaction with the procedural fairness of the restorative justice approach rather than their greater satisfaction with a nonpunitive alternative. But even in the limited context of victim satisfaction, other researchers have found that victims were the least satisfied of the participants at restorative justice conferences,[48] and that their negative feelings were linked to dissatisfaction with the leniency of the outcome.[49] Despite many claims that punishment is either irrelevant or counterproductive to a victim's recovery, the few studies that have attempted to assess the effect of different sanctions on victim recovery have demonstrated a significant *positive* effect of punishment on the emotional and psychological recovery of crime victims.[50]

While recognizing the value of apology, restitution, and participation toward healing the victim's emotional wounds one must question whether these factors alone are sufficient to that task, especially in the case of serious crime. Critics of a purely nonpunitive approach to restoration have pointed out that, notwithstanding the benefits obtainable to the victim by apology, restitution and participation in the process, exclusive reliance on these modalities fails to address the victim's need for justice. Criminal victimization denigrates the personal autonomy of the victim: "Victimization is being dehumanized."[51] Victims suffer a loss of belief in an orderly world as well as a loss of faith in a just society, and react to these losses of belief by self-blame, depression, and a feeling of helplessness.[52] According to this view, a crime unpunished is a threat to the victim's belief in a just and orderly world, where it makes sense to obey rules and defer gratification because people (generally) get what they deserve.[53] The security in knowing that bad acts are punished and innocent acts are not is restored when a bad act is punished, but it is threatened when bad acts are not punished.[54] If this is so, punishment *will* have a therapeutic affect on victims—irrespective of other means of stress reduction—and the failure to punish will have a deleterious effect on victims irrespective of other sources of stress.[55]

A corollary to the justice motive and equity theory in explaining the role of punishment in the emotional recovery of crime victims is "respect theory."[56] According to this view, the essential harm of a crime, as opposed to a tortious injury, is the contempt expressed in the act by an offender for the victim's self-worth and the value of his or her moral standards. Victims may react to this contempt by withdrawal (manifested affectively by depression and behaviorally by a refusal to cooperate) or by retaliation (manifested by "moralistic anger" and behaviorally by the pursuit of legal—and sometimes extralegal—means of redress).[57] The display of anger by the victim is regarded not only as an outward manifestation of an internal affective state, but also as a sign to others in the social group that the disrespect was unmerited and will not be tolerated.[58] Thus, far from being regarded as an emotional "loss," anger is regarded as a necessary catalyst to action and is therefore an empowering emotion and indicative of self-respect.[59] Moralistic anger, as noted by philosopher Hannah Arendt, motivates the victim to seek punishment "in order to defend the honor of him who was hurt by the offense so that the failure to punish may not cause his degradation."[60] According to this theory, the victim's emotional losses (primarily those related to personal and social humiliation) are therefore healed through retribution while the *absence* of retribution would be the cause of further suffering. To those who have claimed that anger is a "kind of inflammation" that should be unconditionally released by the victim in order to enhance emotional recovery, another researcher responded: "This view of the victim as a diseased person, inflamed by toxic rage, compounds the stigmatizing effect of the original crime."[61]

The therapeutic effect of punishment and the stress associated with the failure to punish is particularly noticeable in serious cases. For these cases, "no amount of therapy or indeed conference discussions, may replace a victim's and community's need to know wrongdoing is punished and that justice is done."[62] Even those who contend that direct victim involvement, apology, and restitution can address all the needs of the victim and the immediate community have made an exception for the most serious cases.[63] However, if restitution and the offering of an apology are insufficient for more serious cases, a non-punitive version of restorative justice theory does not attempt to explain how punishment fulfills the victim's needs in these cases, much less the needs of society. As Ashworth noted, "reconciliation and mediation are unlikely to provide the basis for a theoretically respectable or socially respectable system of dealing with serious crime."[64]

The problem of applying restorative justice to serious crimes is exemplified in the feminist critique of restorative justice. From the feminist perspective, the attempts by the criminal justice system in the past to encourage the preservation of domestic relationships through the conflict resolution model of counseling, restitution, and apology was disadvantageous to women because it encouraged them to find ways to accommodate themselves to an unbalanced situation and manipulated their desire to forgive instead of vindicating their right to be unharmed.[65] "The skill of contrite apology is routinely practiced by abusers in violent intimate relationships. A battered woman herself is also likely to be an expert in apology as a means of appeasing her spouse, of quieting his insecurities. . . . When her apologies are unsuccessful in appeasing his wrath, he beats her."[66] The resurrection of private negotiation in place of prosecutions administered by the state contradicts the advocacy of "zero-tolerance" enforcement policies and mandatory arrest that has been central to feminist demands for reform of domestic violence policy.[67] Feminists have asserted that the physical danger and psychological harm to women associated with domestic violence is not addressed by regarding them as mere "parties to a dispute" and, not only are the family and the community often unable or unwilling to oppose domestic violence, they often are "the primary supports for male control of women."[68] Therefore, the power imbalance implicit in domestic violence is effectively redressed not by referring these cases to mediation, but by mobilizing the state's prosecutorial power.[69] Indeed, victims of domestic violence have reported feeling that the use of restorative justice as an alternative to the state's punitive powers typically employed in violent crimes is a form of "cheap justice"[70] that devalues the seriousness of the offense.[71]

What should be clear from the foregoing is that, while restitution, apology, involvement in decision making, and respectful treatment are all important factors in the restoration of the material and emotional well-being of victims, the role of punishment in the process of repairing the harm suffered by them continues to be a matter of contention within restorative justice advocacy. The resolution of this issue is crucial to the future of restorative justice because, if punishment is proven to be *irrelevant* to healing as many have suggested, restorative justice may very well continue to position itself as a radical alternative to mainstream criminal justice.

On the other hand, if punishment can be shown to play a positive role in the emotional and psychological recovery of victims, the assumed conflict between punishment and restoration would be eliminated. In that case, restorative justice principles could be applied to a variety of cases—to adult as well as juvenile offenders and to violent as well as property offenses—without sacrificing any of its core values. The needs of the individual victim for healing could then be addressed without conflicting with the needs of society for security and the rule of law. Given the importance of this problem to the future of restorative justice, it behooves us to seek an answer to a fundamental question: Can punishment be restorative?

There is an understandable fear that, by acknowledging a positive role of punishment to any extent whatsoever, the integrity of restorative justice will be fatally compromised. This fear, I contend, is not justified. Regarding the fundamental harm of crime as the loss of trust builds on the central restorative justice notion that *restoration*—not merely the imposition of punishment—should be the primary goal of the criminal justice system. To avoid unnecessary ideological disputes, the question of whether punishment can be an instrumentality toward restoration must be treated as an *empirical* question. Looking at this sensitive issue from a social scientific perspective can enable us to deal with it candidly, fearlessly, and with the utmost respect for the diversity of opinions held by the general public for whose benefit, ultimately, restorative justice exists.

The Debate Over Punishment in Restorative Justice

If criminologists are divided over the utility or wisdom of punishment, there is little doubt that punishment has wide public support. Psychologists have noted that retribution is deeply ingrained in human nature and is an omnipresent fact in our social relations. [72] With declining support for rehabilitation, the public's attitude toward punishment became much more strict in the 1990s. [73] Despite rising levels of incarceration, imprisonment was favored by many people for whom the alternatives carried insufficient "penal bite." [74] In numerous public opinion surveys, respondents have expressed a belief that the courts have been too lenient with criminals. [75] And in surveys presenting various criminal scenarios, respondents overwhelmingly favored incarceration as the appropriate form of punishment in most cases. [76]

The prevalence of punitive attitudes by the general public—and victims—has been conceded by restorative justice theorists. "Nearly all citizens at large and crime victims want to see criminals punished." [77] The important question they raise, however, is whether punishment is *all* that the public really wants. Along with their interest in punishment, the public's interest in alternative, nonpunitive solutions has also been recognized. [78] Sessar has disputed the "conventional wisdom"

concerning the public's attitude toward punishment by pointing out that
the public is far more likely to support nonpunitive attitudes when they
are given relevant information about these choices.[79] The public
continues to support attempts at rehabilitation[80] and, despite its concerns
about undue leniency in sentencing, actually displays a more lenient
attitude toward sentencing of drug addicts, muggers, and burglars than
the actual sentences imposed.[81] Other studies have noted that the public,
even those who advocate longer prison terms, preferred public spending
on crime prevention programs rather than prisons,[82] and early
intervention and community corrections as alternatives to prison.[83]

In sum, while the public's support for punishment is well known, its
support for alternatives to punishment and sanctions with a restorative
quality is also strong.[84] But beyond noting the public's interest in
nonpunitive alternatives, many restorative justice advocates, as we have
seen, have questioned the relevance of punishment to the actual needs of
victims. For these theorists, the goals of punishment and restoration are
mutually exclusive. Indeed, restorative justice theory originated as a
response to a criminal justice system that, in abandoning the primacy of
the victim's needs in favor of institutional demands for obedience, "stole
the conflict" from those directly involved in the crime and imposed a
system fixated on the goals of blaming and punishing. [85]

Is punishment relevant to the needs of crime victims? The
restoration of trust analysis, I believe, sheds new light on this crucially
important issue. According to the restoration of trust perspective,
whatever operates to restore trust in the offender and in society also
operates to restore the emotional well-being of the victim who was
harmed by crime. Let us ask: Is the imposition of punishment on a
criminal offender—or the failure to do so—relevant to repairing the
victim's *loss of trust* in the offender and in society? Using this
perspective, it should be readily apparent that imposing or withholding
punishment is not merely relevant, but is instrumental to the goal of
restoring the victim's trust in the offender and in society. On one level,
the imposition of a deserved punishment restores social trust, in that it
provides the necessary means of enforcing the reciprocal altruism on
which we depend for social interactions. On a personal level,
punishment operates to quell the resentment that is aroused by the
offender's betrayal of our presumption of reciprocity (i.e., his betrayal of
trust). The emotional satisfaction experienced by the victim is therefore
not so much a sense of pleasure in seeing others suffer, but a return to a
state of normality that was disturbed by the crime. By the enforcement
of the law, the presumption of trust that underlies social relations can be
resumed.[86] Conversely, the failure to enforce the law compounds the

emotional harm to the victim by undermining his or her faith in an orderly world where it makes sense to engage in social and economic interactions that are based on a presumption of reciprocity. This means that, even in case in which the criminal sanction has little to do with restoring trust *in the offender*, the victim still derives an emotional benefit from the restoration of trust *in society* that is fulfilled by its mandate of administering justice, and suffers a further emotional loss from the failure of society to administer justice in the aftermath of a crime.

This analysis would seem to confirm the position of retributionists, but the restoration of trust analysis permits a much more nuanced view of the role of punishment in the emotional recovery of crime victims. It is a view that, ultimately, enables us to maximize the potential of the criminal sanction to repair the emotional harm of victims and to minimize resort to punishment.

The imposition of some degree of punishment may well be required to restore trust in society, but punishment *alone* is an extraordinarily poor way of restoring trust either in an offender or in society. It is only when coupled with other "indicia" of trust—and, especially, when punishment is voluntarily undertaken in the context of apology—that punishment becomes transformed into an effective instrument of restoring trust both in the offender and in society.

What we wish to restore in the aftermath of crime is the assumption that the world is inhabited by people who are much like ourselves: people with a conscience, with empathy; people who play by the same rules as we do and, if they break those rules, understand the wrong they have committed and accept the agreed-on consequences of their wrongdoing. Everything an offender does to restore his position of trust has a positive emotional effect on the victim by restoring the victim's fundamental presumption of reciprocity in his or her dealings with others. Subscribing to the principle of reciprocity means acknowledging the essential equality of all other members of the moral community (i.e., those who subscribe to the rule of reciprocity) and their mutual protection against domination by others. The expectation of reciprocal treatment—the presumption of trust—is inherent in our nature as social beings and, as such, can be regarded as our natural right. The essence of domination, from this perspective, is the disregard of any requirement of reciprocal treatment of others. It is a disregard and a disrespect of the right of others to expect reciprocal treatment and, accordingly, it is a betrayal of their basic presumption of trust in others.

Someone who commits a crime—not just an accidental harm, but a crime—has broken the bonds of trust we rely on, and, in so doing, has undermined the emotional well-being of the victim. Repairing the loss of trust requires that the offender prove he is responsive to the rules of reciprocity; that he understands these rules, that he agrees to be bound by these rules, and that he is capable of conforming his actions to these rules. Apology indicates both his awareness of the rules and of his moral fault in violating them. Beyond that, remorse indicates his awareness of the pain suffered by the victim, and is therefore a demonstration of empathy. True remorse is based on the awareness of the victim's suffering; it is not simply regret at the suffering that the offender has brought on himself. This expression of empathy is important in restoring trust because the ability to empathize is central to the ability to regulate our conduct so as not to cause others to suffer from our actions. We must somehow put ourselves in their place and inhibit any behavior that, if inflicted on us, would cause us to suffer. Empathizing with the victim therefore operates to restore trust and, correspondingly, to restore the emotional well-being of the victim whose personhood was disrespected by the criminal offense.

All of this can be accomplished by apology and the expression of remorse, but words alone may not suffice. For this reason, the payment of restitution has been regarded as not only a means of repairing material losses, but also as a means of corroborating the sincerity of an offender's remorse. If he is genuinely sorry for what he has done, the least he can do is to "clean up the mess" he has made to the extent that he can.

Although the payment of restitution undoubtedly plays a role in the emotional recovery of a victim as a means of corroborating the offender's sincerity, it may not be obvious whether punishment plays any such role. As many restorative justice advocates have asked: How can the affliction of suffering on the offender operate to "make things right?" The answer, from the restoration of trust perspective, is that punishment operates to heal the emotional harm suffered by a victim to the extent that it operates to restore the victim's trust in the offender and in society. The reciprocity that makes social interaction possible also makes us vulnerable to abuse and exploitation, unless there is a concomitant insistence on enforcement. Those of us who play by the rules, and who benefit from those rules, also submit to the consequences of violating them. Therefore, when an offender has broken the rules, he must remain an untrusted outsider unless he consciously and voluntary submits to the enforcement of those rules. This submission to the agreed-on sanction is a powerful demonstration that the offender "wants in." Unlike the payment of restitution, the offender's submission to punishment does not make things right by repairing material losses, but it does make things right by his acknowledgment of the legitimacy of the rules by which we all live, thereby repudiating the disrespect he has shown to the community and the victim implicit in the criminal act. In this way, the offender helps to mend the web of reciprocity that his crime has disturbed and helps repair the emotional harm suffered by the victim.

The voluntary submission to a deserved sanction also reinforces the restorative function of apology by differentiating apology from mere excuse. Apologies that are used to avoid unpleasant consequences do not operate to restore trust; in fact, they are apt to be regarded as disingenuous and manipulative, and therefore operate to impair trust.

A good example of this is the case of Katherine Ann Powers. After more than 20 years on the run following the murder of a police officer by one of her group of political radicals in the course of a bank robbery, she decided to turn herself in. Waiving her right to a trial, Powers pleaded guilty to manslaughter and was sentenced to a term of 8 to 12 years in prison. When she became eligible for parole, she prepared an eloquent statement of apology in which she accepted full responsibility for the crime, expressed her genuine remorse, and detailed her efforts to change and lead a useful life in society. A *Boston Globe* editorial praised her statement to the parole board as a document that "should be posted in classrooms, government offices, living rooms, boardrooms, hospitals, churches and everywhere people need reminding of their ability to wreak ruin through a single misdeed, and the power of redemption."[87] For Powers, there was something more at stake in this meeting than receiving parole; it presented her with the opportunity to face the family of the victim of the crime and, after so many years, to seek some measure of forgiveness. Yet even after her extraordinary apology, the family of the deceased police officer seemed stony and distant. She searched for something more she could possibly say to bridge the gap that continued to exist between them, but she finally came to see that further words, no matter how heartfelt, were not being perceived by the family as credible because they were stated in the context of a request for lenience from the parole board. Powers determined that:

> It was clear to me from some of the family member's statements to the Parole Board that they didn't really believe what I was saying—because it was attached to my request to be paroled and go home to my family. And it became really clear to me that as long as those two things were joined, the communication that I intended to make was not going to be complete.[88]

Powers therefore decided to do the one thing that might make her words credible and render her plea for forgiveness attainable: She withdrew her application for parole. No, there wasn't a sudden rush of forgiveness from this dramatic turnaround but, for the first time, the victim's family felt that Powers' words were not tainted with self-interest. They respected her for taking responsibility and finally came to believe the sincerity of her apology.

The psychological truth revealed by this encounter is that the acceptance of responsibility for one's actions that is necessary for restoring trust and gaining forgiveness requires acceptance of the consequences for those actions. Apologies that are uttered in the context of avoiding adverse outcomes, no matter how heartfelt, may tend to be regarded as opportunistic. Apologies offered with full awareness of the consequences entailed by admitting liability are respected as truthful and are understood as part of the symbolic act of atonement.[89]

The Critical Nexus of Apology, Restitution, and Punishment

From the restoration of trust perspective, we can see how punishment may play a role not only in addressing the needs of the state, but in addressing the emotional needs of crime victims. Yet it would be a fundamental error to conclude from this that the emotional recovery of victims can be achieved by punishment alone, and the restoration of trust perspective helps us to see why this is so: The mere imposition of punishment on an offender is unlikely to make us trust him. It is just as likely to make us fear and distrust him as ex-offender. The potential ability of punishment to operate as an instrumentality of healing is realized, however, when it is administered *in combination* with all other means of restoring trust, including the expression of apology, the agreement to pay restitution, and the agreement to undergo necessary rehabilitation.[90] It is this nexus of factors that makes each an expression of an offender's desire to make amends and to rejoin the moral community of trustworthy people. Taken alone, the imposition of punishment on an unwilling, recalcitrant, or indifferent offender does little to restore trust and, correspondingly, little to repair the emotional wounds of the victim. The victim may gain some satisfaction in seeing that the offender is punished and that society can be trusted to carry out its pledge of enforcement, but we all know the police cannot be everywhere and that crime cannot be effectively prevented by the threat of official enforcement alone. We must rely on people to desist from crime because they are committed to being members in good standing of the community of law-abiding citizens, and not merely because of the possibility of arrest and conviction.

Just as the nexus of apology, restitution, and voluntary submission to a deserved punishment operates to engender trust, this very context permits us to minimize the imposition of punishment. Intuitively, we demand less punishment for those who strive to restore trust by every means within their power. We feel they simply do not need to be punished further. It may be difficult for a just deserts theorist to explain why an apologetic, remorseful offender should be treated differently from a contemptuous, indifferent offender. But from a restoration of trust perspective, the answer is simple and straightforward: Punishment is only one tool of restoring trust among many and, when trust is restored by other means, resort to its use may be minimized.

Empirical Research

It is unlikely that these disputes concerning the nature of victims' emotional losses and the respective roles of apology, restitution, and retribution in the healing of these losses can be resolved by theoretical analysis alone. What is required is empirical research, which unfortunately has not been convincing to either side. Those few studies that have focused on the issue by surveying responses of crime victims,[91] have encountered similar problems: selection bias resulting from low response rates to questionnaires (typically between 20% to 30%); problems in identifying and standardizing key variables relating to the crime, offender characteristics, and process variables; inability to randomly assign variables, including sentencing options; and difficulties in measuring victims' emotional and psychological reactions.

In reviewing the literature, one researcher concluded that beyond these attempts at empirical research, most theories concerning the therapeutic effects of punishment on the emotional losses of victims are based on anecdotal evidence and still await valid empirical testing.[92] Although restorative justice holds out the promise of more effective healing of victims' emotional losses, empirical support for these claims rests primarily on surveys indicating victim "satisfaction" rather than the measurement of emotional gains and losses.[93] One study of victim's responses to restorative justice programs observed: "Restorative justice is relatively untried and untested-where is the compelling proof that it works?"[94]

Even when attempted, the goal of measuring satisfaction is singularly elusive: "It is virtually impossible to disentangle the multitude of variables which together determine how satisfied people are with any social service."[95] Montado, a leading proponent of the just world theory, claimed to be unaware of any "systematic investigation of the effects court sentences have on victims health and adjustment," although "everyday experiences teach us that unjust sentences or procedures evoke responses of outrage, helplessness or bitterness."[96] In his review of the state of research on the effects of sentencing on victims' emotional well-being, Vidmar noted the large amount of research on the emotional consequences of distributive justice and procedural justice, but lamented that, given the pervasiveness of retribution and revenge as a justice motive, "it is remarkable that so little empirical research has been devoted to these topics."[97]

In view of the paucity of empirical research to date, I undertook a study in 2005 to assess the effect of punishment on victims' emotional and psychological losses using crime scenarios. [98] Specifically, I sought to determine: (1) whether punishment is thought to be a source of improvement to the emotional and psychological well-being of crime victims; (2) whether the failure to impose punishment is thought to be a source of harm to their emotional and psychological well-being; and (3) whether the imposition of punishment, when combined with the offender's apology and court-ordered restitution, is thought to be more beneficial to their emotional and psychological well-being than apology and restitution without punishment.

In this study, over 400 respondents at Rutgers University in New Jersey were asked to gauge their anticipated emotional reactions to a series of crime scenarios involving adult offenders and both property and violent crimes. The respondents included a significant proportion of people who had, in fact, personally been victimized by such crimes. Remarkably, their reported reactions to the crime scenarios were nearly identical with those of the non-victims who could only imagine their reactions to the scenarios, thus corroborating the ability of crime scenarios to replicate real-life encounters. The following scenarios were utilized in this study (see Appendix A for a complete list of scenarios)

On the way to your car, you notice that the passenger side window is broken and the ground is covered with shattered glass. Inside the car, your personal belongings are strewn about—and your radio is gone. Later that week, a 25-year-old man is arrested for breaking into your car and stealing the car radio. He has no prior criminal record. Your total losses (including the radio, damage to the car, and lost time from work) amount to $1,000.

*As you are walking alone in a downtown shopping area at night,
you are grabbed from behind by a man and pushed up against a wall.
He shows you a gun and demands your money. You hand over your
wallet, and he runs around the corner. Later that week, the robber, a
25-year-old man with no prior criminal record, is arrested after he
attempted to use your credit card. Your total losses (including your
wallet and its contents, and lost time from work) amount to $2,000.*

The respondents were first asked to assess their anticipated
emotional reactions (e.g., anger, resentment, and anxiety) to each crime
(See Appendix B). Next, they were asked to assess how their emotional
well-being in the aftermath of the crime might be either improved or
impaired by a number of key factors, including those that have been
cited in the literature as the most important facilitators of emotional
recovery: apology, payment of restitution, and submission to a deserved
punishment. Each of these components is subject to variability in the
real world. Therefore, in order to test the competing claims of their
effectiveness in promoting emotional recovery, an optimal level of
implementation for apology, restitution, and punishment was specified.
Thus, respondents were asked to assess how their emotional recovery, as
a victim, would be *improved* if:

The offender is required to pay for all of my losses,
The offender gives a full and honest apology,
The offender receives a significant punishment,
I am allowed to be involved in the sentencing decision, and
I am treated with respect by the court.

In their answers to these questions, (on a scale of 1-5 from least to
most) each of the factors in the nexus of apology, restitution, and
punishment were reported by respondents to be relevant factors in their
emotional recovery, but payment of restitution and respectful treatment
by the court were thought to be of even greater importance than the
other factors. Apology, by itself, was barely a significant source of
improvement. (See Figure 6.1.)

Figure 6.1. Sources of Improvement to Emotional Recovery of Victims

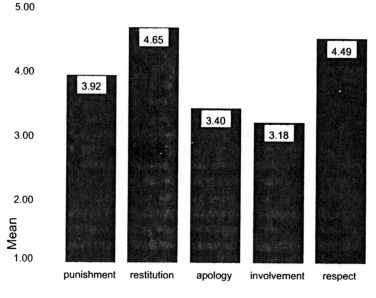

Sources of Improvement

n=336

I then reversed the question and asked respondents to assess the impact of the *absence* of each of these key factors on their emotional recovery. Specifically, the respondents were asked to assess to what extent their emotional recovery, as a victim, would be *impaired* if:

> The offender does not receive any type of punishment (such as imprisonment, fines, or community service),
> The offender does not apologize,
> The offender is not ordered to pay for my losses,
> I am not allowed to be involved in the sentencing decision, and
> I believe I have not been treated with respect by the court.

The results were surprising. As before, punishment, restitution, and apology were determined to be important factors, but now that the respondents were asked to consider the absence of these factors, the prospect of the offender not receiving any degree of punishment was regarded as being by far the most significant source of impairment to their emotional recovery. In other words, the effect of punishment on the emotional recovery of victims was thought to be felt more acutely in its absence than in its presence.

Figure 6.2. Sources of Aggravation to Emotional Recovery of Victims

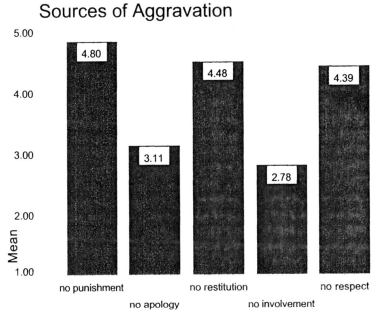

n=336

The next section of the questionnaire focused on the three vital components of recovery—apology, restitution, and punishment—not as individual, isolated factors, but as components in a sentencing "package." Controlling for all other major factors that might promote emotional recovery, such as respectful treatment by the court and involvement in the criminal justice process to the extent desired by the victim, the respondents were asked to assess which combination of apology, restitution, and punishment would have the greatest positive effect on their emotional recovery from the crime. All the possible combinations of apology, restitution, and punishment were presented to the respondents, but my research interest focused on three such combinations:

- Punishment only (without apology or restitution), which I refer to as the "punitive model."
- Apology and restitution only, which I refer to as the restorative justice "non-punitive model" because it excludes the option of punishment, and
- Apology, restitution, and punishment together, which I refer to as the "comprehensive model" because it includes each of the three major components.

Confirming the restorative justice critique of the conventional criminal justice system, the punitive model was found to be less effective in promoting emotional recovery than either the non-punitive or the comprehensive models. (See Figure 6.3.) The punitive model, in fact, was not regarded as conducive to emotional recovery at all by the majority of respondents. However, when the comprehensive and the non-punitive models were compared, the comprehensive model emerged as the unequivocal winner. The results confirmed the power of each of the critical components of healing—apology, restitution, and punishment—and, moreover, confirmed that the nexus of these factors was by far the most powerful agent of emotional recovery.[99]

In summary, these findings suggest not only that punishment was believed to positively benefit the emotional recovery of victims, but also suggest the manner in which this influence might occur. When respondents were asked to assess factors that were likely to *improve* their emotional well-being, punishment was reported to be one such factor, but restitution and respectful treatment were reported to be even more important sources of improvement (Figure 6.1). However, when subjects were asked to assess factors that were likely to *harm* their well-being, the absence of punishment was reported to be by far the most important source of harm (Figure 6.2). These findings suggest that punishment is important to the victim not so much as a means of promoting satisfaction as it is a means of avoiding further distress that would ensue from the failure to punish.

**Figure 6.3. Effect of Sentencing Models on Emotional Recovery of
Victims: Emotional Recovery Index**

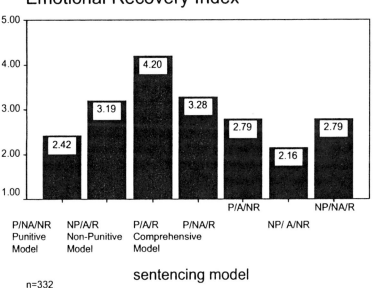

Notes: *P= Punishment; NP= No Punishment; A= Apology; NA= No Apology;
R= Restitution; NR= No Restitution*

These findings also indicate that punishment alone may not bring
about significant improvements to the emotional and psychological
recovery of crime victims. On the contrary, the results from the analysis
of sentencing models indicate that the "punitive model" of punishment
alone is less conducive to emotional recovery than the "non-punitive
model" of apology and restitution without punishment (Figure 6.3).
When punishment was *combined* with apology and restitution, however,
the resulting model was considered to be the most conducive to victim
recovery. Indeed, the "comprehensive model" was the only model that
showed a significant increase in victim recovery for all scenarios. The
expectations of anger, resentment, and insecurity were actually increased

by the punitive model, the "punishment and apology only model," the "apology only model," and the "restitution only model."

Of course, research of this nature cannot be proposed as the final word on the issue of the relevance of punishment to the emotional recovery of crime victims. Besides its limited sample and the inevitable artificiality of the experimental design, this study is also limited with respect to the variables considered.[100] However, the results indicate that, contrary to the often-expressed claim that punishing offenders is irrelevant to the real needs of victims, the public does indeed consider punishment to be relevant to the emotional recovery of victims, both by its presence and its absence. The claim that punishment is the concern of the state rather than the victim is not supported by this study. The respondents to this questionnaire, who were instructed to imagine themselves in the place of crime victims (Appendix B), regarded punishment to be a factor that would promote their emotional recovery: *not alone, but in combination with* an apology regarded as honest, full restitution, respectful treatment by the court, and an opportunity to participate in decision making. [101]

Furthermore, whether or not a victim may gain emotional satisfaction from the offender being punished, this study confirms that the *failure to impose an appropriate punishment* is considered to be a major source of emotional and psychological harm to victims. This tends to corroborate the view that a victim's demand for punishment is more typically a desire to achieve some measure of justice than a desire to get revenge. Although the desire for revenge implies that the victim relishes the suffering of the offender, the desire for obtaining justice can described as a desire for a return to normality or homeostasis.[102] These results are also in accord with prior research that the importance of punishment to the victim is less about achieving satisfaction or "closure" as it is about avoiding the further degradation of the victim's status_both in his or her own eyes and in the eyes of the community—that is entailed in the failure to punish.[103] It is quite possible that, for many crime victims, there can never really be any adequate satisfaction or closure, and that the best the criminal justice system can offer them is the possibility that they will not be further victimized by the experience of injustice.

The importance of this nexus of apology, restitution, and deserved punishment to sentencing theory and practice can also be seen in the third aspect of the questionnaire, in which respondents were asked to assess whether they would be satisfied with a reduction in sentences for defendants who "give a full and honest apology, are ordered to pay for all of their losses, and submit to a significant punishment." For each of the crime scenarios presented in the questionnaire, both for property and violent crimes and for offenders with and without prior convictions, the respondents strongly favored a reduction in their demands for punishment. In other words, just as the nexus of apology, restitution, and punishment operated to improve the victim's emotional recovery, this same combination of factors also operated to reduce their reliance on punishment. This study therefore suggests that, while punishment is regarded as an important element of restoration, the *extent* of punishment can be significantly reduced by maximizing opportunities for apology, restitution and voluntary acceptance of a sentencing by offenders.

According to the non-punitive version of restorative justice, if a victim receives a full and honest apology and restitution for material losses, punishment should no longer matter. But, clearly, it does matter to many, if not most victims. On the other hand, punishment alone, just as some have claimed, is insufficient to satisfy the victims' needs. It is the *combined* effect of apology, restitution, and punishment that best satisfies the victim's material and emotional needs, not merely by an accumulation of additional factors, but by transforming the character of these very factors. Apology as an isolated factor may well be important to the emotional recovery of crime victims but, without requiring payment of restitution and a deserved punishment for the offender, the apology may be viewed as an expedient means of avoiding full accountability. When combined with payment of restitution and submission to a deserved punishment, however, apology becomes credible and therefore becomes relevant to the victim's emotional recovery. Similarly, while payment of restitution is undoubtedly useful to repairing the victim's material losses, mere payment of restitution for a crime, *without* punishment or apology has little relevance to the victim's emotional losses—indeed, it can be seen as an expression of contempt for the victim. At any event, it certainly is a poor means for engendering trust. Finally, punishment, in the absence of apology or restitution, is of little value to the victim. But when coupled with apology and restitution, punishment becomes an expression of atonement that can be of critical importance in addressing the emotional damage to the victim. Finally, if a defendant does all he can to repair the damage that he has caused to the victim and to society, he is doing more than merely serving time—he is taking active steps to repair his standing in the community as a person who, someday, can be trusted as "one of us."

Trust and the Critical Nexus

What conceptually unites the individual components of apology, restitution, and punishment in restoring the well-being of crime victims is the overarching goal of restoring the trust that was destroyed by the crime. Each factor, separately, addresses a separate concern of the victim: *Apology* addresses the victim's need for self-affirmation, *restitution* addresses the victim's need for material compensation, and *punishment* addresses the victim's need for security and justice. But the nexus of these factors addresses the issue of *trust* because they all operate to restore the presumption of reciprocity in dealings with others. Without the unifying concept of trust—the presumption of reciprocity—the extraordinary interdependence of these three factors would not be apparent. The restoration of trust therefore unifies and explains the efficacy of each component in the critical nexus of restoration, and further helps us understand why each component in this nexus is optimized only in combination and not in isolation.

From the personal level of trust, the criminal act engenders a loss of trust in the offender. To regain trust, a victim must have some assurance that the offender is not a continuing threat to his or her personal safety, and also that the offender fully accepts responsibility for the crime and shows genuine contrition. The offender's apology and offer to pay restitution are not necessarily sufficient to achieve these goals, but neither is punishment by itself. As the responses to the questionnaire indicate, the mere imposition of punishment, without apology or restitution, while better than no punishment at all, is not as effective in facilitating the victim's emotional recovery as apology and restitution without punishment. The offender's mere endurance of the hardship of punishment—without accepting responsibility and offering to make amends—has little restorative value. The linkage between restoring trust and restoring the victim's emotional losses is clearly indicated by these results: Punishment that is passively endured is less important to the victim's emotional recovery than punishment that is voluntarily accepted as one's due. Correspondingly, passively endured punishment has little to do with restoring trust. By contrast, the voluntary acceptance of punishment, especially when it is accompanied by a genuine apology and offer of restitution, is simultaneously an instrument for the victim regaining both trust and emotional well-being. In short, the very factors that contribute to the restoration of trust in the offender are precisely those factors that promote the victim's emotional recovery.

Yet the trust analysis, as we have seen, does not end with an examination of the victim's restoration of trust in the offender because crime also affects the victim's trust *in society*. As in the case of the loss of personal trust in the offender, the victim's loss of trust in society is experienced as a distinct emotional loss. The victim, degraded by crime, has an expectation of justice which, if unfulfilled, becomes a source of a deep and enduring humiliation. As the presence or absence of a deserved punishment plays a role in the victim's recovery of trust in society, so does the presence or absence of a deserved punishment play a role in the victim's emotional recovery. In the questionnaire responses, the greatest source of emotional harm to the victim was the absence of a deserved punishment: not the absence of an apology, restitution, involvement or even respectful treatment by the court. The intensification of feelings of resentment, anger, and insecurity brought about by the failure to impose punishment, as seen in the questionnaire, could uncharitably be described as the frustration of the victim's "vindictiveness, " but this characterization fails to convey the true emotional losses suffered. The victim, who has been debased and humiliated by the crime, seeks the support and solidarity with others in the community who share his or her outrage. When the community, in the person of the public prosecutor, declines to prosecute or fails to hold the offender to the consequences of the law, the victim feels betrayed, alienated, and isolated. The contract of mutual obligations that forms the core of civil society has been broken. His or her loss of faith in society creates perhaps an even greater and more persistent emotional loss than the crime itself, for it thereafter puts into question the fundamental guarantee of reciprocity the victim had previously assumed would be respected and enforced.

In sum, the concept of restoring trust helps us understand the linkage each component of the nexus of apology, restitution and punishment—but it is not to be thought of as an abstract philosophical construct. It's more akin to the kind of common sense that informs our ethical judgments. Because of the socio-biological foundation of trust, the application of trust analysis to sentencing issues is not a daunting intellectual challenge, but is immediately and intuitively apparent. We are, in a sense, "hardwired" to assess the key deficiencies in people who we perceive as untrustworthy. In the aftermath of a conviction, we ask: What must this defendant do to regain our trust? Obviously, punishment alone is not going to restore our trust in him if he does not offer a credible apology. Just as obviously, apology alone is not going to make him any more trustworthy if he is unwilling to pay for the victim's losses or to submit to any significant punishment.

And we can go further: Beyond considering apology, restitution, and punishment, we might also ask *what else* the defendant must do in order to regain trust. He may have to agree to a long-term treatment plan. He may have to complete his education. He may have to undergo community supervision. He may even have to move away from his former criminal associates. Whatever those conditions may be, they all a common purpose: to foster the eventual reintegration of the offender into society's web of reciprocal relationships. In order to qualify for this re-inclusion, he must prove that he can be trusted.

The restoration of trust is of great importance to crime victims precisely because, as we have seen, crime is a willful breach of our basic presumption of reciprocity in others—it is a breach of trust—and therefore loss of trust is the essential harm engendered by *crime,* as distinguished from other harms that he or she may suffer. Loss of trust is a harm that cannot be adequately corrected by monetary payment. The victim, in the aftermath of crime, needs reassurance that his or her presumption of reciprocity by others was not just foolishly naive. The victim needs assurance that the world is inhabited by people who subscribe to this pact of reciprocity and who can be trusted to honor its rules with appropriate self-restraint. The presence in the community of people who have deliberately violated these rules is a threat to those assumptions. Therefore, the experience of victimization is a profoundly disorienting event. The victim's emotional losses are deeply related to the subversion of trust occasioned by the crime. Beyond the need to see to it that the rules by which the victim lives are enforced, he or she must reestablish basic trust—the presumption of reciprocity—in mankind. Unless that fundamental presumption is restored, the victim will forever be victimized and continue to live in fear and insecurity. Loss of trust damages her ability to engage freely in economic and social relations and to enjoy the fullness of life. These are the enduring losses of victimization. If restorative justice is to accomplish its goals of repairing the harm of crime, it must enable victims to restore their presumption of trust in their fellow citizen.

The restoration of trust perspective enables us to understand why the *context* of sanctions is so important: It is not punishment *per se* that is important to the victim's emotional well-being, but rather it is the message conveyed by punishment. The message suggested by the mere imposition of suffering on an offender is that people can be trusted only when they are sufficiently fearful of detection and prosecution. But the message conveyed by the offender's voluntary submission to punishment, coupled with a genuine apology and payment of restitution, is that people can be trusted who willingly accept the legitimacy of the rule of reciprocity and do everything in their power to repair the emotional and material harm they have caused.

Resolving the Debate Over Forgiveness

If the severity of punishment can be *reduced* by the demonstration of other indicia of trust, why can't it be eliminated altogether? Many restorative justice advocates have contended that the path to repairing the emotional losses of the victim is achieved by abandoning insistence on punishment and, instead, counseling victims to release their resentment through a voluntary act of forgiveness that short-circuits the conventional demand for retributive justice. By forgiving, they have argued, the victim is able to release the poisonous feelings of anger and resentment. In forgiving, the victim takes charge of his or her own emotional well-being and does not depend on the decision of the offender on whether or not to apologize. Neither does the victim await some illusory satisfaction from seeing the offender suffer through the imposition of punishment. It permits the victim to "move on" and not be caught in the emotional quagmire of victimhood.[104]

Forgiveness, from this perspective, is the explicit renunciation of retribution both as a practice and as a conception of justice.[105] As the very word appears to imply, *forgiveness* is an unconditional gift: the giving of a benefit *before* it is due. It is therefore an altruistic gift, one that is undeserved by offender. Forgiveness, if conceived of as a gratuitous gift by the grace of the victim, requires no reciprocity or mutuality.[106] Transcending the dictates of reciprocity is thought to break the cycle of retribution inherent in *lex talonis*.[107] This is a fundamentally different conception of justice from the familiar pattern of crime and punishment. Here, justice "makes things better, is never satisfied merely with following the rules, however equitable they are, or by asserting one's legal rights, however fair they may be."[108] This conception of justice, indeed, goes beyond forswearing resentment and revenge. It seeks positive beneficence toward the offender, in that it may include "compassion, unconditional worth, generosity, and moral love to which the wrongdoer, by nature of the hurtful action, has no right."[109] For the victim, forgiveness "reopens his heart to take in and reaccept his offender."[110] Furthermore, the act of forgiveness means that the person offended gives up his or her resentment and, by doing so, achieves a degree of tranquility. To the extent that a victim can let go of his or her demands for retributive justice,[111] the possibility of achieving forgiveness and closure is thought to be enhanced. Unilateral forgiveness may initiate repentance in reluctant offenders[112] and, even if he or she fails to repent, unconditional forgiveness is claimed to free the victim of resentment by an internal act of will, without dependence on the offender's decisions.[113] By pursuing the morally "higher ground," the victim denies the lowered status associated with victimization. Forgiveness, it is claimed "elevates the victim to new moral heights, whereas retribution lowers the victim and the State to the same level to which the offender has sunk by his crime."[114]

Restorative justice theorists have generally regarded forgiveness as a means of emotional restoration, although for different reasons. According to the "core sequence theory," the emotional losses of crime expressed as anger, resentment, depression, self-blame, anxiety, and so forth are released in the act of forgiveness.[115] The offering of an apology is a crucial precondition to the offering of forgiveness by the victim. In the core sequence leading to emotional restoration, the offender expresses shame and remorse for his actions, and the victim takes "at least a first step in the forgiveness for the trespass."[116] This sequence may last for only a few seconds, but it offers the key to victim satisfaction.[117] While some restorative justice theorists have taken the view that it is apology alone (the acceptance of responsibility) that triggers forgiveness[118] and others have argued that apology must be linked to the indication of genuine remorse to be effective,[119] there is general agreement that emotional release of victims is accomplished in the act of forgiveness.[120] Victims are believed to desire an apology in order to have the opportunity to forgive "and so to be released of the burden of anger and bitterness resulting from a sense that the emotional hurt is unacknowledged."[121]

The place of justice in forgiveness

Despite these benefits, the conception of forgiveness is not without its problems, however.[122] For one thing, it is by no means clear that apology and restitution are sufficient preconditions for genuine forgiveness. Apology, Duff noted, is more than a communication of responsibility, it is a component of penance.[123] Because of the possibility that apology may be insincere, Duff argues its sincerity must be demonstrated by assuming a burden: "Only if it is burdensome can it serve the role of giving more forceful expression to the apology that's owed."[124] For this reason, he claimed, repentance is necessarily painful.[125] Similarly, pursuant to the equity theory of the victim's emotional losses, it is unlikely that apology and restitution alone are sufficient to restore the moral equilibrium that was disturbed by crime, especially serious crime. Restitution may restore a material imbalance and emotional distress related to material losses, but is irrelevant to the damages that result from the *wrongful* character of crime.[126] The power imbalance created by crime must not simply be acknowledged (i.e., by apology), but redressed by the simultaneous elevation of the victim's status and the lowering of offender's status so that, in both the victim's and the public's view, the offense should be attributed to the bad character of the offender rather than to the weakness of the victim.[127]

Forgiving dangerous offenders, indeed, can be seen as a selfish act, in which the victim, by waving demands for accountability in favor of monetary payment or apology, ignores the needs of the community endangered by crime.[128] Forgiveness is also potentially risky: If no limits are set, an exploitive offender may receive a license to reoffend.[129] This is of particular concern for victims of domestic violence who, by forgiving for the sake of preserving the relationship, may subject themselves to further victimization.[130] The moral virtue of forgiveness that forswears retribution may be evident in minor cases, but can be very problematic in serious cases.[131] Too-easily dispensed forgiveness for offenses against others reveal a fundamental lack of respect for the victim.[132] Then too, the moral resuscitation of the offender may not be achievable by the unilateral forgiveness of the victim. It deprives the offender of the opportunity to earn forgiveness through his acts of apology, contrition, and repentance. As an act of unearned, undeserved charity, unconditional forgiveness places the offender further into moral debt to the victim and to the community, thus compounding his moral exclusion already experienced as a consequence of the crime itself.

While the kind of forgiveness that releases the offender from further consequences without requiring any burden on him has been claimed to be virtuous in that it requires considerable self-control to withstand the urge to retaliate and is not dependent on the offender's decision to repent, [133] others have seen this forgoing of retaliation as a type of moral and psychological weakness.[134] People who tend to forgive without demanding accountability may do so because they are fearful of confrontation or because they want to avoid their own anger.[135] Such willingness to forgive may stem from a desire for ease and comfort and the avoidance of responsibility to the community and to their own self-respect. Under these condition, unilateral forgiveness subdues anger at the cost of accommodating evil: "Slavery, oppression and victimization are made worse, not better, when people are rendered content in their victimization."[136] For this reason, psychologists have been advised to "consider the issue of justice in counseling forgiveness."[137]

Ironically, when forgiveness is dispensed in order to avoid confrontation or when motivated by external pressure from religious imperatives, the letting go of resentment—the one essential and undisputed benefit of forgiveness—is not fully achieved. The ultimate cost of unilateral, self-willed forgiveness is that it may become a hollow semblance of forgiveness, and not genuine forgiveness. It is therefore understandable that those victims whose grant of forgiveness makes no demands on the offender do not tend to experience appreciably warmer feelings toward him.[138] A further cost in advocating such unconditional forgiveness is in neglecting the moral standards and psychological needs of those victims who are unprepared or unwilling to forgive. If forgiveness is thought to be an internal act of will, independent of the actions taken or not taken by the offender, counseling forgiveness in crime victims who not ready to forgive implies an inadequacy on *their part*, and may result in a sense of shame that further impairs their emotional recovery.[139]

This, of course, is not to say that forgiveness is unimportant. On the contrary, it is vitally important to the emotional well-being of both a victim and offender. Advocates of forgiveness often contrast forgiveness with non-forgiveness or, worse, with vengeance,[140] but these are easily defeated "straw men." Important questions involving psychological efficacy and morality can be addressed by distinguishing between *earned forgiveness* that requires positive acts from the offender from *unearned forgiveness* that is achieved unilaterally by the exercise of the victim's will-power. While both earned and unearned forgiveness involve the release of resentment engendered by the crime, this release is achieved by an act of self-will, independent of the actions of the offender in the case of unearned forgiveness but for earned forgiveness, is dependent on the delivery of justice. The psychological issue is whether earned or unearned forgiveness is more conducive to the victim's emotional well-being. And, assuming there are no psychological differences, the next issue is whether earned or unearned forgiveness are both morally defensible responses to crime.

Earned forgiveness involves the release of the victim's resentment, not by relinquishing demands for justice, but by the satisfaction of demands for justice. Earned forgiveness is seen as a culmination of a process, or dialogue, between a victim and offender in which the offender, through apology, remorse, and penance, seeks to be absolved of his moral debt.[141] Against the claim that forgiveness can be achieved by an act of will, independent of the actions of the offender, [142] others caution that those who forgive unilaterally manifest low self-respect [143] and subject themselves to further abuse.[144] The central question for the offender in search of release from his moral debt is this: What can I do to become worthy of the victim's forgiveness? This does not mean that the offender can legitimately demand forgiveness once it is earned. It is a still a gift that can be given or withheld freely. Yet this conception of earned forgiveness implies that the victim is justified in making certain demands on the offender prior to the bestowal of this gift. The primary demands are apology (full acceptance of a responsibility); repayment of losses (insofar as that is possible); and the fulfillment of justice, however this is conceived by the victim, including the acceptance of the victim's right to demand punishment.[145] This view does not insist on the re-definition of acceptance of justice as moral love.[146] Such a concept confuses forgiveness with mercy.[147] It is mercy, not forgiveness, that rejects retribution and renounces punishment in favor of love and exoneration. Forgiveness, by contrast, can come at any time with or without retribution and with or without justice, but can generally be attained

> only after we have worked through a process of addressing the wrong. If we attempt to forgive ourselves or another prematurely...our forgiveness will be incompatible with our self-respect and respect for others. It will therefore be morally inappropriate. Further, it will not be genuine. [148]

Earned forgiveness, unlike unconditional forgiveness, holds out a more realistic possibility of emotional closure on the part of the victim, reintegration of the offender, and respect for individual and communal values. Furthermore, it respects the autonomy of the victim and does not seek to impose moral or religious values that he or she does not hold.[149] As against the examples of all too many "forgiveness counselors," advocates of earned forgiveness do not counsel victims to forgo demands for the imposition of penalties as a consequence of wrongdoing.[150] For this reason, therapists are advised that "those who cannot tolerate punishment as an option" are not qualified to serve as forgiveness counselors.[151]

Legal scholar Stephen Garvey noted that the degradation associated with victimization can result either in an unhealthy inner-directed self-blame or a healthy outer-directed feeling of moral indignation, which insists on preserving a victim's self-worth and is ultimately satisfied not by compensation, counseling, or even by apologies, but by vindication. Following the analysis of Swinburne, Garvey identified the stages necessary for the achievement of genuine forgiveness on the part of victims: repentance, apology, reparation, and penance.[152] In Garvey's view, a criminal act is not simply injurious, it is morally wrongful: "Crime degrades, demeans, diminishes and dishonors the victim, in addition to whatever material damages it may cause."[153]Accordingly, the impulse of the victim to seek retribution in the form of punishment is "our way of censuring or condemning the wrongdoer's wrong, of annulling the false message he implicitly conveys through his wrongdoing, and of vindicating the moral value and standing of the victim."[154] Just as punishment is necessary to vindicate the victim's moral worth, "so too is punishment a necessary part of the process of expiation and atonement."[155] By the acceptance of an appropriate punishment (i.e., penance), an offender may gain the forgiveness of the victim—and the community—that is essential for successful reintegration.[156]

Despite Garvey's analysis of the positive role played by punishment in the process of gaining forgiveness, he believed that such views are incompatible with restorative justice theory. Because of the familiar restorative justice antipathy to punishment, Garvey regarded the goal of restoration to be unattainable merely by restitution, compensation, and community service:

> Restorativism cannot achieve the victim's restoration if it refuses to vindicate the victim's self-worth through punishment. Nor can it restore the offender, who can only atone for his wrong if he willingly submits to punishment. And if neither the victim nor the wrongdoer is restored, then neither is the community of which they are a part. In short, restorativism longs for atonement without punishment, but punishment—tragically—is for us an inescapable part of atonement.[157]

Garvey is correct in his analysis only if punishment is ruled out by restorative justice theorists and practitioners from having any role to play in the restorative process. However, punishment does exist in restorative justice theory and practice as a coercive tool and as an inherent aspect of fines, community service, and interpersonal shaming. Beyond those uses, Garvey's explication of punishment as atonement indicates the possibility of restorative punishment. This possibility was broached by one of the earliest and most ardent advocates of restorative justice, Zehr, who recognized that, if used "in a context where restoration and healing are the goal," "perhaps there are possibilities for 'restorative punishment.'"[158] Zehr cautiously approached this issue, given the real possibility for the destructive uses of punishment, but recognized that a positive, although limited, role could be played by punishment in the restorative process itself:

> The biblical example suggests that the goal, nature and context of punishment is critical. In the biblical context for example, punishment usually is not the end. It aims at liberation and creating shalom. Biblical justice is administered in the context of love. Possibilities for forgiveness and reconciliation are the light at the end of the tunnel.[159]

In sum, those who have proposed that resentment can be eliminated by renouncing demands for justice and peremptorily forgiving the offender are likely to overestimate the ability of human beings to turn off their demand for justice by an act of will. What is worse, regarding victims' desire for justice as an impediment to forgiveness compounds their emotional losses: Not only are they resentful of their treatment by the offender, but they are now made to feel guilty for feeling resentful. Their demands for justice are interpreted as an obstinate "refusal to let go"[160]; a mean-spirited and dysfunctional characteristic that keeps them trapped, in contrast to the healthy "agreeable" and "spiritual" characteristics associated with those who forgive. [161]

Even if it were possible to voluntarily let go of our demands for justice, the moral and psychological consequences of doing so are not particularly desirable. Renouncing demands for justice may mean acquiescing to evil instead of fighting evil and seeking change. In fact, a victim's premature forgiveness perpetuates the wrong. [162] If forgiveness is given in order to relieve the victim's stress, it is a essentially an amoral act that neglects the needs of others in society.

But what if society itself were to change and unconditional forgiveness were to become the rule rather than the exception? For one thing, it is likely that such a society either would cease to exist in short order or would have to be composed of human beings incapable of committing crimes. In *Beyond Revenge*, McCullough invited readers to imagine a "forgiving society" that renounced its insistence on punishing offenders and asked: "What kind of society would you end up with?"[163] It would be, by definition, one in which a person may commit a criminal act with (literally) impunity. While many of us would be bound by conscience or conditioning to honor the code of reciprocity, there would be no protection against those who would take advantage of our vulnerability, and it is precisely in response to this threat that the criminal law exists. As long as the possibility exists for people to deviate from the rules of reciprocity—that is, as long as there is human freedom—the viability of harmonious interaction will continue to rely on the expectation of enforcement rather than the renunciation of enforcement of these rules.

The moral conundrums of forgiveness are not mere abstractions, but are experienced on a visceral level when the intuitive passion for justice is challenged by the ideology of forgiveness. At a small church near Wichita, Kansas, the local pastor imparted a simple message of forgiveness to his young charges:

Holding a stuffed animal and bright yellow toy taxicab, Pastor Michael Clark gathered the children of Christ Lutheran Church around him Sunday morning. He leaned in and told them that the bear and car were two of his favorite toys. Then he asked the children whether anyone had ever taken one of their favorite toys. A few of them nodded. "You want to stay angry," Clark told the children. "But Jesus wants us to let go and forgive."

In the midst of a church tragedy—the arrest Friday of member Dennis Rader—it was clear to adults in the pews that Clark was trying to teach a bigger lesson about forgiveness. [164]

What the congregation had found out two days earlier was that Rader, a former president of the congregation, was identified by the police as the self-styled BTK killer ("Blind, Torture, Kill") who had terrorized their community for over 30 years. Instead of registering disgust and outrage—indeed, instead of trying to retain an open mind about the truth of the charges—the good pastor urged his flock to "let go and forgive." Clearly, the pastor was struggling to do the right thing, but his adherence to the ideology of unconditional forgiveness blinded him to the moral vacuity of his stance, which deprived both himself and his followers with the moral indignation and righteous anger necessary to confront and defeat evil.

Ironically, the quest for serenity at the expense of justice is likely to result in intensified distress. The emotional pain associated with the experience of the injustice is powerful and innate.[165] Once experienced, the possibility of a victim turning off his or her desire for justice through a sheer act of will is unlikely in all but the most trivial offenses. [166]

Furthermore, any reduction in stress that is accomplished by renouncing claims of entitlement to justice comes at the expense of a victim's trust in society. In situations where formal justice is unavailable due to the inadequacy of the legal system, the victim is, perhaps, wise to rid himself or herself of the unrealistic demand for justice. However, by so doing, the victim has lowered the expectation that society can guarantee justice or even his or her safety. The victim is thereby likely to become more guarded and wary in dealings with strangers where there is no expectation of enforcement of the rules of conduct. Forgiveness that arises by removing expectations of justice therefore has a high moral and psychological toll. Forgiveness that grows from the fulfillment of justice, on the other hand, can be seen as an expression of moral strength, psychological well-being, and confidence in the attainability of justice.

These insights also have been corroborated in my own research among university students responding to crime scenarios. Just as I found that the important effects of apology, restitution, and fair punishment on the emotional recovery of crime victims was greatly enhanced when they were combined in a sentencing nexus, so too did this nexus of factors operate to maximize the respondents' willingness to forgive. Respondents were asked to evaluate what effect the various combinations of apology, restitution, and punishment had on their willingness to forgive the offender on a Likert scale of 1 to 5. A score of 1 indicated that their willingness to forgive would *greatly decrease* while a score of 5 indicated that their willingness to forgive would *greatly increase.* The results were highly instructive: the "punitive" model of punishment alone (without apology or restitution) not only failed to increase the respondents' willingness to forgive, it actually *decreased* their willingness to forgive. In other words, the mere imposition of punishment, far from making the respondents more forgiving, made them less forgiving. (See Figure 6.4.) The non-punitive model that consisted of only apology and restitution, but without punishment resulted in a modest increase in willingness to forgive. However, the "comprehensive" model that combined all three factors—a significant punishment, an honest apology, and the requirement for payment of all losses—resulted in a substantial increase in willingness to forgive. Indeed, of all of the various combinations of apology, restitution, and punishment, it was only the combined effect of the three factors that represented a nearly universal positive effect on willingness to forgive.

At this point, it may be useful to compare Figure 6.4 with Figure 6.3 concerning the effect of the various sentencing combinations of apology, restitution, and punishment on the emotional recovery of crime victims. The remarkable correspondence of these two figures is readily apparent. Again, the nexus of apology, restitution, and punishment is found to be most conducive to both the victim's emotional recovery and willingness to forgive. Furthermore, the degree to which each of the three factors—alone or in combination—contributes to the victim's emotional recovery is nearly identical to the effect on their willingness to forgive. In other words, the willingness to forgive is reflective of the state of our emotional recovery. If the ability to forgive were independent of the actions taken by the offender (i.e., if the willingness to forgive would be the same regardless of whether the offender offered an apology, submitted to punishment, or paid restitution), then it might be argued that this unilateral decision "to forgive" constitutes an effective shortcut to emotional well-being because it does not depend on any actions taken or not taken by the offender.

Figure 6.4. Effect of Sentencing Models on Emotional Recovery of Victims: Willingness to Forgive

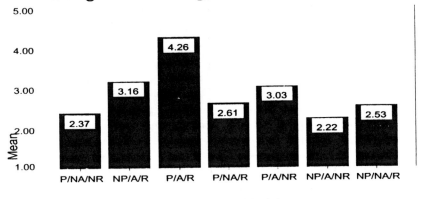

Effect of Sentencing Models on Recovery:

Willingness to Forgive

n=336

Notes: P= Punishment; NP= No Punishment ; A= Apology; NA= No Apology; R= Restitution; NR= No Restitution

But the results of my research show otherwise. Willingness to forgive is indeed reflective of emotional well-being which, in turn, is greatly influenced by the presence or absence of a genuine apology, fair punishment, and adequate restitution. Those who do forgive, despite the absence of those factors found by others to be conducive to such a choice, may very well achieve emotional benefits from their decision to forgive and this is an issue that bears further study. Concomitantly, the emotional toll on victims who are counseled to forgive unconditionally is also worthy of further research. Even assuming, however, that the choice to forgive is, in itself, a factor that promotes emotional well-being (as opposed to being thought of as a *consequence* of emotional well-being), it is apparent from the results that victims are more likely to forgive when they have received a genuine apology and satisfactory restitution, and the offender has received appropriate punishment.

These three factors—alone or, more importantly, in combination—therefore operate simultaneously to maximize both victims' emotional recovery and their willingness to forgive. The factors represent significant conditions under which emotional recovery and forgiveness become more likely to occur.

Earning Forgiveness and Regaining Trust

To better understand whether the bestowal of earned forgiveness or unearned forgiveness is of greater benefit to the victim, we can reframe the issue in the context of regaining trust and ask: Is earned or unearned forgiveness more likely to result in regaining trust in the offender? In this context, it is apparent that any benefits that may be gained by a victim granting unconditional forgiveness have little to do with restoring trust. In forgiveness that is derived from a purely internal, self-willed release of resentment by the victim, nothing the victim does or says is determinative of the victim's decision to forgive. This kind of unearned forgiveness, "does not require that the offender acknowledge the wrong, show remorse or make amends." [167]Here, the victim forgives merely in order to avoid further stress. Bestowal of forgiveness for the purpose of stress reduction is, in fact, a kind of inner-directed, self-administered therapy[168] as opposed to an outer-directed motive to address the source of the victim's feelings of guilt, shame, and exclusion. It is merely a coping mechanism.

Of course, even the non-punitive "purist" version of restorative justice does not advocate wholly unconditional forgiveness.[169] On the contrary, a key function of victim/offender conferencing is to offer the offender the opportunity to apologize and agree to pay restitution as a condition for earning the victim's forgiveness. But, we again ask, is apology and restitution sufficient to earn forgiveness? The answer to this question depends on whether the victim perceives a need for justice. In the ordinary course of life, people are subject to countless harms from others, and for the vast majority of these incidents, apology and, where there is a material loss, monetary payment perfectly suffices to reestablish trust. But occasionally, people are harmed by such grievous and intentional acts that arouse a victim's demands for justice as well. Ought we then to encourage them to relinquish these demands?

Some forgiveness advocates, to be sure, have maintaining that the decision to forgive does not mean the renunciation of demands for justice.[170] However, from the perspective of forgiveness counseling, the victim's demand for justice often impedes her progression toward forgiveness. Accordingly, Worthington has argued that achieving forgiveness is facilitated by narrowing or eliminating the "justice gap" that exists when a victim's expectations exceed the outcomes.[171] That gap, he argues, can be narrowed by "accepting the transgression and moving on," "re-narrating the transgression or the offender's motives" or "appealing to divine justice."[172]

Even assuming that these actions are motivated by genuine religious or ethical convictions and are not mere exercises in self-therapy, it is difficult to see how renouncing entitlement to justice can help restore trust.[173] In dropping demands for justice, the victim decides that the offender is either not morally responsible or is not worth waiting for. The offender will be "forgiven" regardless of what he says or does not say. His words are irrelevant. *He* is irrelevant. The victim is no longer beholden to the offender's decision to apologize because such concerns have been preempted by the victim's desire to forgo further expectations of justice. Therefore, even if the emotional recovery of the victim can be realistically accomplished by the kind of forgiveness that renounces all demands for legal accountability, this kind of forgiveness is not a means of restoring *trust*. On the contrary, it is a means of perpetuating the moral exclusion of the offender: Not only has the offender been excluded by his own criminal actions, he has been discounted as a being subject to moral accountability [174]and has been prevented from earning his way back through atonement for his misconduct.[175] Unearned, unilateral forgiveness that flows from the largesse of the bestower does not, nor is it intended to, restore relations between the victim and the offender. This kind of forgiveness does not operate to restore relationships, but rather is a means to terminate a dysfunctional relationship based on the victim's unfulfillable expectations.[176] Restoration, after all, is not these victims' motive: They simply want to move on.

By contrast, when an offender earns our forgiveness by apology, restitution and voluntary submission to the requirements of law, he redeems himself from social exclusion and resuscitates himself from social death. Just as the criminal conviction labeled the offender as an untrustworthy alien to the moral community, earned forgiveness acknowledges his essential humanity that is not eradicated by his criminal act, for which he remains accountable to the law. When the victim, instead of shunning the offender, insists on the imposition of a deserved sanction, eventual reintegration emerges as a realistic possibility. Whereas the message communicated to those given unconditional forgiveness is that "we release you from any moral obligation," the message of earned forgiveness is "we insist on the fulfillment of your moral obligation." Implied in this message of the fulfillment of the obligation is the possibility that, once the moral obligation is fulfilled, normal relations can be resumed. That is what is meant by "paying one's dues."

In renouncing demands for a deserved punishment under the justification that, ultimately, God alone can judge our actions, we not only abdicate the responsibility to protect ourselves from harm, we abdicate the moral responsibility to create a society with values worth defending. In expecting nothing more than a apology from people who intentionally violate the basic norms of reciprocity, but forgive them anyway, we may well insulate ourselves from the stress of resentment. But in so doing, we consign the offenders to the margins of society. This is not to say that such forgiveness has no role in a restorative criminal justice system. As a mode of self-directed therapy, unconditional forgiveness is clearly preferable to the prolonged harboring of resentment for recalcitrant offenders. When it is clear, but *only* when it is clear, that the victim will not get an apology or payment from the offender, it is simply a matter of self-preservation to drop those demands—then forgive, forget, and move on. Furthermore, when it is clear, but *only* when it is clear, that the victim is not going to get justice (as when the offender cannot be located or is freed on a technicality), the victim may be wise to simply let go.[177] It may be that renunciation of moral demands constitutes a kind of restoration, but it is a very desolate kind indeed. Consider the case of a Holocaust survivor who was willing to forgive the Nazi doctor who conducted cruel experiments on her and her twin sister:

Stossel: "You forgive this doctor?"

Eva K.: "I forgive everybody."

Stossel: "Why?"

Eva K: "A victim feels hurt, hopeless and powerless. A victim never has any choice."

Stossel: "You have a choice. You could be furious."

Eva K: "Will that help me? Will that make my life any better?"[178]

Although it is undoubtedly true that a lifetime of resentment against a long-ago crime may perpetuate a victim's suffering, it is not true that the victim's search for justice is necessarily fruitless nor that, by relinquishing demands for justice, the victim's quality of life will be improved. On the contrary, relinquishing demands for justice in order to release emotional resentment is both morally suspect and psychologically precarious. Would Holocaust survivors be better off if they had waived their demand for justice against Adolph Eichmann or let Klaus Barbie pursue a life of middle-class anonymity in France?[179] Would the world have been better off if the perpetrators of the Holocaust were not held accountable for their crimes against humanity? Of course, we must not condemn Mrs. K. for forgiving this embodiment of human evil. He was dead. There was no possibility of bringing him to justice. And it is precisely under such circumstances that unilateral, self-willed forgiveness emerges as a useful technique for stress reduction. It still does not qualify as a morally appropriate response to wrongdoing but, then again, Mrs. K. did not forgive on the basis of any moral justification whatever. She merely decided that retaining her resentment would not "make her life any better." In fact, she made no evaluation of the conduct she was forgiving. Her forgiveness was entirely indiscriminate: "I forgive everybody."

And that is the essence of unconditional forgiveness: Regardless of an offender's actions, regardless of his acknowledgment of fault, or even his willingness to tell the truth of what occurred, regardless of whether the offender is remorseful, defiant, or contemptuous, he is to be "forgiven." Such a conception of forgiveness strips it of any moral content and becomes, at last, a tool of expediency that ignores the legitimate needs and expectations of the community.[180]

On the other hand, when a person who has committed a crime does all he can reasonably be expected to do to redeem himself in the eyes of the victim and the community, the victim's bestowal of forgiveness is of a fundamentally different character. Here, forgiveness has nothing whatsoever to do with reducing the severity of the punishment. It has nothing to do with the renunciation of demands for justice. The offender is not seeking a way to avoid punishment—he's not looking for a break. What he is seeking through forgiveness is something else entirely: the restoration of his good name. He is seeking the recognition of his status as a human being—a fallible human being to be sure—but a human being nonetheless for whom the possibility of reacceptance by the community remains open. By demonstrating empathy for the victim and willingness to "fess up" to his responsibilities under the law, the offender shows himself to be responsive to the web of reciprocity that binds us. He wants to acknowledge that, while he may have committed a crime, he as a person is not a "criminal." This is a person that asks for forgiveness out of a need for inclusion in the moral community, not as a desire to avoid unpleasant consequences.

It is by the offender acknowledging and accepting the consequences of his criminal act that he assures us he is eligible to rejoin the group. What he has shown by voluntarily accepting the terms of his sentence and by trying to satisfy the legitimate demands of the victim is that he is deeply enmeshed in the reciprocity that requires that the rules of society be adhered to and the value of all humans be respected. The commission of a crime has put the offender's respect for the law and for others very much in question. Indeed, by committing the crime, the offender has indicated a fundamental contempt for the rules of society and for the autonomy of his victim. *But merely punishing such a person will not restore our trust. Forgiving such a person will not restore our trust either.* What we await is a clear demonstration that the offender has renounced this dual contempt for society and the victim. He can do this only when he expresses real remorse, agrees to pay for the material losses, and voluntarily accepts a fair punishment for what he has done. In this way, the offender is offered a pathway back to our forgiveness, to our trust and also to full *reintegration* into our society—a topic we shall turn to next.

Notes

[1] Lurigio & Resick, "Healing the Psychological Wounds of Criminal Victimization," pp. 55–57; Erez, "The Impact of Victimology on Criminal Justice Policy; Carriere *et al.*, "Victim-Offender Negotiations."

[2] Erez & Tontodonato, "Victim Participation in Sentencing;" Young, "A Constitutional Amendment for the Victims of Crime."

[3] Fattah, "Gearing Justice Action to Victim Satisfaction;" Janoff-Bulman & Frieze "A Theoretical Perspective for Understanding Reactions to Victimization."

[4] McCold, "Toward a Holistic Vision of Restorative Juvenile Justice," p. 365. *See also* Weibe, "The Mental Health Implications of Crime Victims' Rights."

[5] Begaric & Amarasekara, "Feeling Sorry? Tell Someone Who Cares."

[6] Strang, *Repair or Revenge: Victims and Restorative Justice*, p. 20.

[7] Petrucci, "Apology in the Criminal Justice Setting," p. 349.

[8] Ohbuchi *et al.* "Apology as Aggression," p. 219

[9] Miller, "The Social Psychology of Punishment Reactions," p. 544; Ohbuchi, Agarie, & Kameda, *supra*; Bennett & Earwaker, "Victims' Responses to Apologies;" Scher & Darley, "How Effective Are the Things People Say to Apologize."

[10] *Id.*, p. 138.

[11] Wagatsuma & Rossett, *supra, p.* 487.

[12] Weiner, *et al.*, "An Attributional Examination of Retributive and Utilitarian Philosophies of Punishment."

[13] Petrucci, *supra*, p. 340.

[14] Shuman & Smith, *Justice and the Prosecution of Old Crimes*, p. 106.

[15] Vidmar, *supra,* pp. 41–42, *56;* Heider, *The Psychology of Interpersonal Relations*, pp. 265–276.

[16] Tontodonato & Erez, "Crime, Punishment and Victim Distress," p. 36.

[17] Weitecamp, "Can Restitution Serve as a Reasonable Alternative to Imprisonment?"

[18] Sessar, "Punitive Attitudes of the Public," p. 290.

[19] Van Dijk, "Ideological Trends within the Victims' Movement," p. 125.

[20] Retzinger & Scheff, *supra*; Shapland, "Victim Assistance and the Criminal Justice System; Wagatsuma & Rossett, *supra.*

[21] Kilpatrick & Otto, "Constitutionally Guaranteed Participation."

[22] Braithwaite & Pettit, *supra,* at p. 91.

[23] Able, *Speaking Respect, Respecting Speech.*

[24] Petrucci, *supra,* p. 352.

[25] Retzinger & Scheff, *supra,* p. 321.

[26] Petrucci, *supra,* p. 352; Enright, "Counseling Within the Forgiveness Triad," p. 109.

[27] Erez & Tontodonato, "Victim Participation in Sentencing," pp. 394–397.

[28] Shuman & Smith, *supra, p.* 102.

[29] Daly, "Restorative Justice: the Real Story," p. 70.

[30] Van Ness & Strong, *Restoring Justice*, 1997 1st Ed., p. 38.

[31] Wright, *Justice for Victims and Offenders*, p. 159–162.

[32] Kaptein, "Against the Pain of Punishment," p. 83.

[33] McCold, "Toward a Holistic Vision of Restorative Juvenile Justice," p. 361.

[34] Acorn, *Compulsory Compassion,* p. 50.

[35] Sessar, *supra,* p. 287–288.

[36] Llewellen & Howse, "Institutions for Restorative Justice in South Africa," p. 376.

[37] For a comprehensive listing as of 2000, see cites collected in Barton, "Empowerment and Retribution," p. 72, at Note 1.

[38] Zehr, *Changing Lenses,* p. 69; Braithwaite, *supra,* pp. 16–21.

[39] Van Dijk, *supra,* p. 126.

[40] Van Ness & Strong, *supra,* p. 37.

[41] Fattah, "Gearing Justice Action to Victim Satisfaction," p. 28.

[42] McCold, "Toward a Holistic Vision of Restorative Juvenile Justice," p. 363.

[43] Daly, "Restorative Justice: The Real Story," p. 67.

[44] Annalise Acorn, a law professor and former-advocate-turned-critic of restorative justice, suggests that some researchers have deliberately avoided putting their claims of "healing" to a test: "restorative justice advocates still hope to craft victim surveys that will yield favourable results so as to justify the allocation of greater resources to restorative justice programs. Though restorative justice promotes itself with the rhetoric of healing, questions about whether victims experienced healing are rarely present on victim satisfaction surveys intended for use in promoting restorative justice" Acorn, *supra,* p. 70.

[45] In 2003, Nugent, Williams and Umbreit performed a comprehensive "meta analysis" of the existing empirical research on the psychological outcomes of restorative justice. Problems of adequate research design

narrowed their focus down to only seven studies, of which all but one—a 1977 mediation project in Brooklyn that predated the development of restorative justice—involved juveniles or youthful offenders. These studies, useful as they are in comparing victim and offender reactions to differing procedures, did not contrast the presence or absence of punishment as a sentencing option. Indeed, the authors' discussion of the victim's belief as to whether the offender was held "accountable," used the concept of accountability solely to indicate whether or not the offender offered an apology. Nugent, Williams & Umbreit, "Participation in Victim-Offender Mediation and the Prevalence and Severity of Subsequent Delinquent Behavior: A Meta-Analysis."

[46] McCullough, *Beyond Revenge*, pp. 175–177

[47] Strang, *Repair or Revenge: Victims and Restorative Justice*, pp. 70–71.

[48] Palk, Hayes, & Prenzler, "Restorative Justice and Community Conferencing;" Miers, Maguire & Goldie, "*An Exploratory Evaluation of Restorative Justice Schemes.*"

[49] Maxwell & Morris, *Family Conferencing and Juvenile Justice: The Way forward or Misplaced Optimism?*

[50] Hammer, *The Effect of Punishment on Crime Victims' Recovery;* Tontodonato & Erez, supra; Orth, "Does Perpetrator Punishment Satisfy Victim's Feelings of Revenge?" "There is a noted paucity of empirical data concerning victim's emotional responses to court procedures and sanctions. Most theories concerning the therapeutic effect of punishment on the emotional losses of victims are based on anecdotal evidence and still await valid empirical testing" (Shuman & Smith, *Justice and the Prosecution of Old Crimes*, p. 103).

[51] Weisstub, "Victims of Crime in the Criminal Justice System," p. 195.

[52] Miller & Vidmar, "Social Psychological Processes Underlying Attitudes Toward Legal Punishment."

[53] Gehm, "The Function of Forgiveness in the Criminal Justice System."

[54] Lerner & Miller, "Just World Research and the Attribution Process."

[55] Shuman & Smith, *supra, p.* 102.

[56] Miller, "Disrespect and the Experience of Injustice."

[57] *Id.*, p. 544.

[58] *Id.*, p. 533.

[59] Neu, "To Understand all is to Forgive all—Or is it?" pp. 21–22.

[60] Arendt, *Eichmann in Jerusalem*, p. 287.

[61] Herman, *supra*, pp. 376-377.

[62] Barton, *supra*, p. 62.

[63] McCold, "Toward a Holistic Vision of Restorative Juvenile Justice," p. 374.

[64] Ashworth, "Some Doubts," p. 289.

[65] Sagrestano, "The Use of Power and Influence in a Gendered World;" Martin, "Retribution Revisited: *A* Reconsideration of Feminist Law Reform Strategies."

[66] Acorn, *supra,* p. 73.

[67] Coker, "Transformative Justice: Anti-Subordination Processes in Cases of Domestic Violence," p. 133.

[68] *Id.* p. 129.

[69] Stubbs, "Domestic Violence and Women's Safety," p. 52.

[70] Coker, *supra*, p. 15.

[71] Wemmers, "Restorative Justice for Victims of Crime," p. 51

[72] Vidmar, *supra*, p. 32.

[73] Kury & Ferdinand, "Public Opinion and Punitively."

[74] Roberts & Hough, "Changing Attitudes to Punishment."

[75] Roberts & Stalans, *Public Opinion, Crime and Criminal Justice.*

[76] Warr, "Public Perceptions and Reactions to Crime," p. 22; Jacobi & Cullen, "The Structure of Punishment Norms."

[77] Umbreit, "Violent Offenders and their Victims," p. 54.

[78] Sessar, "Punitive Attitudes of the Public: Myth and Reality."

[79] *Id.*, p. 297.

[80] Roberts & Hough, "Changing Attitudes to Punishment."

[81] Diamond & Stalans, "The Myth of Judicial Leniency."

[82] Doob, "Transformation Or Punishment?"

[83] Cullen, "Public Support for Correctional Rehabilitation in America."

[84] Flanagan, "Reform Or Punish: Americans' View of the Correctional System."

[85] Bazemore & Walgrave, "Restorative Juvenile Justice: In Search of Fundamentals," p. 46.

[86] Solomon, *A Passion for Justice,* p. 137.

[87] *Cited in* Landman, "Earning Forgiveness: The Story of a Perpetrator, Katherine Ann Power," p. 251.

[88] *Id.*

[89] Robinson, "The Virtues of Restorative Processes," p. 383.

[90] Petrucci, *supra*, p. 357.

[91] See note 50, *supra.*

[92] Shuman & Smith, *supra, p.* 103

[93] Acorn, *supra,* pp. 70-71.

[94] Mika, *et al.* "Listening to Victims," p. 33.

[95] Johnstone, *Restorative Justice: Ideas, Values Debates*, p. 23.

[96] Montado, "Injustice in Harm and Loss," p. 15.

[97] Vidmar, *supra,* p. 33.

[98] London, "The Restoration of Trust."

[99] The major findings include the following results: 1. subjects favored the use of punishment whether the incident was viewed from the individual level or the societal level, for both the property and the violent crime scenarios, involving both first time and repeat offenders; 2. subjects favored the use of punishment for the given scenarios regardless of their agreement with the goals deterrence, incapacitation, rehabilitation, retribution or restorative justice; 3. subjects regarded the imposition of a "significant" punishment to be a source of *improvement* to their well being following the experience of victimization, but less so than the receipt of restitution and respectful treatment by the court; 4. subjects regarded the absence of any punishment to be the most significant source of *impairment* to their well-being following the experience of victimization; 5. subjects regarded the "restorative justice inclusionary" sentencing model of apology, restitution and punishment to be substantially more conducive to their emotional and psychological recovery and their willingness to Forgive than the "retributionist" model of punishment without apology or restitution, or the "restorative justice exclusionary" model of apology and restitution without punishment.; 6. subjects supported a sentence

reduction for offenders who offer an "honest and complete" apology and who are required to pay for all of their losses; 7. whether or not the subject reported to have been a victim of a crime similar to the one depicted in the given scenarios was of no statistical significance in 95% of all questions.

[100] A number of additional salient factors involved in a victim's emotional and psychological recovery were considered in this study: violent vs. non-violent offenses, prior criminal history of the offender, the imposition of punishment, apology, restitution, involvement in the sentencing decision, being given opportunity to express feelings and manner of treatment by the court, age, sex and economic ability and sentencing outlook of victim. however, there are likely to be many more factors affecting the victim's emotional responses, including the respective races of the offender and the victim, the extent of the victim's financial losses, the offender's ability to pay and the victim's perception of the "believability" of the apology.

[101] Since the goal of research was to discern the effects of criminal sanctions on the individual (and, thereby, to test the restorative justice claim that apology and restitution rather than punishment are restorative to the victim), two sets of questionnaires were created. Respondents in one set were instructed to view the scenario as an event that happened to themselves personally, Appendix B, while, in the other, respondents were instructed to view the scenario as an event that they read about in a newspaper article Appendix C. This means of operationalizing the distinction between the individual and the societal levels was chosen in preference to the approach adopted by Oswald *et al.* in which respondents were asked to select whether they were "mainly concerned either with the needs of the victim or those of the offender or those of society as a whole" (Oswald *et al.,*" Lay Perspectives On Criminal Deviance"). In our research, the results indicated no significant difference in responses as to the preferred sanction as between the individual-level questionnaires and the societal -level questionnaires

[102] Vidmar, *supra,* p. 55.

[103] Miller, *supra,* p. 541.

[104] McCullough, "Forgiveness: Who Does It and How Do they Do It?" p. 195.

[105] Worthington, *Dimensions of Forgiveness;* Adams, "Forgiveness: A Christian Model."

[106] Yancey, *What's So Amazing About Grace?*; Enright, Freedman & Rique, Enright, *et al.* "The Psychology of Interpersonal Forgiveness."

[107] Pollard, "Victims and the Criminal Justice System: A New Vision;" Meyer, "Forgiveness and the Public Trust," p. 1527.

[108] Marshall, *Beyond Retribution*, p. 92.

[109] Enright & Fitzgibbons, *Helping Clients Forgive, p.* 29.

[110] Flanagan, "Reform or Punish," p. 11.

[111] McCullough, Sandage & Worthington, *"To Forgive is Human."*

[112] Exline & Baumeister, "Expressing Forgiveness and Repentance."

[113] Diblasio & Proctor, "Therapists and the Clinical use of Forgiveness;" Enright, "Counseling Within the Forgiveness Triad," p. 109.

[114] Fattah, *supra,* p. 28.

[115] Retzinger & Scheff, *supra.*

[116] *Id.,* p. 316–317.

[117] *Id.,* p. 316.

[118] Able, *supra;*   Scheff, *Emotions, the Social Bond and the Human Reality;* Tavuchis, *supra.*

[119] *I.e.,* Goffman, *Relations in Public.*

[120] Tavuchis, *supra,* p. vii.

[121] Strang, *Repair or Revenge,* pp. 20-21.

[122] Gustafson-Affinito, *When to Forgive;* Lamb & Murphy, *Before Forgiving: Cautionary Views of Forgiveness* .

[123] Duff, "Restorative Punishment and Punitive Restoration," p. 88.

[124] *Id.,* p. 94.

[125] *Id.,* p. 96.

[126] Garvey, "Restorative Justice, Punishment and Atonement," p. 1818.

[127] Murphy, "Forgiveness in Counseling;" Miller & Vidmar, "The Social Psychology of Punishment Reactions," p. 156.

[128] *Id.*

[129] Exline & Baumeister, *supra.* p. 148.

[130] Lamb, "Women, Abuse and Forgiveness, " p. 156 ; Gustafson-Affinito, "Caution, Definition and Application," p. 89.

[131] Exline & Baumeister, *supra,* pp. 141–142.

[132] Murphy, "Forgiveness, Mercy and the Retributive Emotions, " p. 6.

[133] Enright, "Counseling Within the Forgiveness Triad," p. 109.

[134] Murphy, *supra,* p. 5.

[135] Lamb, "Women, Abuse and Forgiveness, " pp. 162–164.

[136] Murphy, "Forgiveness in Counseling," p. 46.

[137] Gustafson-Affinito, *supra,* p. 90.

[138] Exline, *et al.* "Forgiveness and Justice," pp. 339-40.

[139] Gustafson-Affinito, *supra,* p. 104.

[140] McCullough, *Beyond Revenge,* pp. 112, 114–115.

[141] Landman, "The Story of a Perpetrator," pp. 235, 237–242.

[142] *See, e.g.* Enright Freedmen & Rique, *supra;* Diblasio & Proctor, "Therapists and the Clinical Use of Forgiveness."

[143] Murphy, "Forgiveness and the Retributive Emotions," p. 5.

[144] Lamb, *supra.* p. 162.

[145] Garvey, "Punishment as Atonement," p. 1823.

[146] See Acorn, *supra,* p. 28.

[147] Murphy, "Forgiveness and the Retributive Emotions," p. 9.

[148] Holmgren, "Forgiveness and Self-Forgiveness," p. 113.

[149] Thomas & Garrod, "Forgiveness After Genocide?" p. 197.

[150] Gustafson-Affinito, *supra,* p. 94.

[151] *Id.,* p. 108.

[152] Garvey, "Punishment as Atonement," p. 1804.

[153] *Id.,* p. 1821.

[154] *Id..*

[155] *Id.,* p. 1823.

[156] *Id.,* pp. 1827-1829.

[157] *Id.,* p. 1844.

[158] Zehr, *Changing Lenses,* p. 210.

[159] *Id.*

[160] Lamb, *supra,* p. 159, *citing* Diblasio.

[161] McCullough, "Forgiveness: Who Does It and How Do they Do It?," p. 195.

[162] Murphy, "Counseling Forgiveness," pp. 46–48.

[163] McCullough, *Beyond Revenge*, p. 180.

[164] Yates, "At Suspect's Church, a Congregation Struggles," p. 1.

[165] Vidmar, "Retribution and Revenge, " pp. 31–33.

[166] An interesting test of the efficacy of forgiveness in promoting mental health was advanced by Enright in his study of incest survivors who were counseled in a program that emphasized forgiveness. (Enright, "Forgiveness is a choice.") Harvard psychologist Judith Lewis Herman has taken issue with his findings and contrasted them with the contrary judgments of other experts in the field of traumatic stress. Herman, "Justice From the Victim's Perspective," p. 576.

[167] Lamb, Women, "Abuse and Forgiveness," p. 157.

[168] Prager, "The Sin of Forgiveness," p. A22. Although advocates of forgiveness in counseling have objected to the characterization of forgiveness as merely a technique of self-help, psychologist Sharon Lamb argues that these objections are disingenuous since the purported psychological benefits of forgiving are the *essential inducements* to forgiveness counseling: " without the self-help argument, they can only persuade a person to forgive because forgiveness is a virtue and because it helps society, but not because it helps the individual." Lamb, *supra*, pp. 157–158. See also Acorn, *supra*, p. 71.

[169] See Umbreit & Armour, *The Paradox of Forgiveness in Restorative Justice*. The authors maintain that restorative justice offers opportunities for bilateral as well as unilateral forgiveness. However, in reviewing research on the conditions that facilitate bilateral forgiveness for both major and minor crimes, they limit the list of conditions to apology, offender remorse and empathy, and do not consider whether the presence or absence of court sanctions has a bearing on the victim's willingness to forgive. *Id*, pp. 496-498.

[170] *See, e.g.* McCullough, *et al.*, "The Psychology of Forgiveness," p. 8: Enright, Freedman & Rique, *supra*, p. 48.

[171] Exline, *et al.*, "Forgiveness and Justice," p. 343.

[172] *Id.*, p. 344.

[173] Gustafson-Affinito, *supra*, p. 88.

[174] *Id.*, p. 101.

[175] Murphy, "Counseling Forgiveness," p. 46.

[176] Lamb, "Women, Abuse and Forgiveness," p. 166.

[177] Gustafson-Affinito, *supra*, p. 95.

[178] Stossel, *Myths, Lies and Downright Stupidity*, pp. 231–232.

[179] See similar discussion in Robinson, "The Virtues of Restorative Processes," p. 381 and Murphy, "Forgiving in Counseling," p. 49.

[180] Another conception of forgiveness attempts to retain the value of pursuing justice by distinguishing between the act and the actor: One can love and forgive the sinner, for example, while hating the sin and insist on legal accountability (Murphy, "Forgiveness, Mercy, and the Retributive Emotions," pp. 6-7). While this approach is preferable to an approach to forgiveness that relinquishes demands for retributive justice, it is not without its own difficulties. Murphy points out that the moral distinction between the "sin and the sinner" is only meaningful when the sinner disassociates himself from the sin by an

explicit renunciation of the sin (*i.e.*, by repentance). Without this dissociation, there is a unity between the sin and the sinner, making it morally unintelligible, Murpy argues, to forgive the sinner without thereby forgiving the sin.

7

The Pathway Back for Offenders

In every society, even those take pride in their modernity, the justice system retains an atmosphere of ritual that is ancient and venerated. The criminal process is not simply a utilitarian means of processing cases; it is a ritualistic "rite of passage" for the accused from one identity to another that is no less significant than a birth, a marriage, or a death. What is involved is the determination of whether or not the accused is to be regarded as one of us: a member of the moral community of trustworthy citizens who share a common commitment to the rules of the group. The process of arresting the suspect and subjecting him to the degradation of handcuffs, fingerprints, mug shots, and imprisonment operates functionally to isolate and identify the accused and guarantee his attendance at trial. But it also operates symbolically to redefine the status of the accused from that of a trustworthy "insider" to an untrustworthy "outsider."

The trial itself is a public spectacle of high drama and ritual significance. The criminal defendant is prominently displayed and the charges against him are invoked with great detail and solemnity. The judge sits in an elevated bench, clothed in ceremonial robes and surrounded by flags, seals, and patriotic murals. The very language of a courtroom (the ancient pronouncements of the bailiff, the deference shown to the judge as "Your Honor"), the gavel, the Bible, the formality of dress, the ritual of standing to address the court, the ceremonial processions, the insistence on absolute quiet all combine to produce an atmosphere of ritual in which the defendant is judged to be worthy or unworthy of inclusion in the community of law-abiding citizens. In view of the devastating impact of the determination of guilt—a determination of the fitness of the individual for life in society as a moral equal—the charges must be sustained by an extraordinarily high level of proof. The ceremonial pronouncement of guilt by the judge or jury is, in itself, a transition from inclusion to exclusion. It is a form of symbolic degradation that strips the offender of his membership in the moral community, much like the stripping of epaulets and the breaking of the sword at a military court-martial. The sentencing hearing continues as a ritual of degradation that reverses the assertion of superiority implicit in the commission of the crime. It is a public demonstration that no one is above the law and that, by disregarding the law, the offender has forfeited his privileged status as a citizen and entitlement to many of the basic rights of citizenship, including, in extreme cases, even the right to life itself.

For the defendant, the pronouncement of a criminal sentence is the key moment in the ritual of exclusion that began with his arrest. It is a moment unlike any other—a moral and psychological turning point for that offender—because it can become the closing of the door to social acceptance or the opening of the door to social rehabilitation. If the offender is merely the passive recipient of a sentence imposed on him by the court, he might understand that sentence as an exercise of official power designed to crush him physically and mentally. Thus, he can look forward only to a lifelong struggle against the society that has determined him to be unworthy. However, if the offender instead understands the sentence as the price he must pay the "going rate" established by the social contract for the offense then the specification of the sentence can represent the conditions to be satisfied in order to quality for readmittance into society.

Unfortunately, the criminal justice system was devised in order to prosecute criminal defendants and not designed to promote their reintegration into the moral community. It evolved over centuries as an exquisite balance between interests: the interest in controlling crime and the interest in protecting the rights of the accused. But today, we are not powerless to redesign the system to accommodate new goals. The system's historical neglect of the needs of crime victims has been fundamentally reformed in recent decades, and it therefore is not beyond the capacity of the criminal justice system to recognize and promote the value of reintegration as a component of every sentence. As much as it requires enforcement of laws in order to survive, society cannot thrive if the direction of criminal justice is exclusively one of social ostracism. While there is an inherent urge to punish an offender, there also is every indication of a similar, counterbalancing urge to reintegrate and forgive that, in many cases, is activated by the offender's demonstration of commitment to the group. The ritual of expulsion can then be turned into a ritual of reintegration by a kind of reciprocal dialogue: The state displays its awesome power to which the offender submits through an act of self-abasement, thus giving rise to a display of generosity and unity once the offender has endured the required hardships. In past eras, this process of transformation was understood in different ways: as a ritual of death and rebirth and, in a religious context, as the expiation of sin through suffering. From the psychological perspective of the modern era, the rite of passage from exclusion to inclusion is understood as a process of interpersonal dynamics in which apology, shame, and remorse demonstrated by the offender are reciprocated by forgiveness and the release of resentment by the victim.[1]

In the final analysis, whether it is understood in mythological, religious, anthropological, or psychological terms, every society must devise both a means of exclusion as well as a means of reinclusion for the vast majority of offenders. By all accounts, however, while we have succeeded in devising an effective means of exclusion through the criminal justice system, we have failed to devise an effective means of reinclusion. Yet, the means of reinclusion are at hand, by using the very same sanctions that promote exclusion. This is because *the criminal sanction is converted into a means of inclusion by its voluntary acceptance by the offender.* It is at the critical junction between the voluntary acceptance and the involuntary imposition of a sentence—a junction that spells the difference between a path to further exclusion and a path to social rehabilitation—that the power of restorative justice as an overarching goal of criminal justice can become instrumental in guiding the direction of the process toward reintegration.

The social cost to an offender by his commission of the crime is expulsion from the moral community, but the possibility must remain open for his reinclusion, subject to certain conditions. What conditions do we, as a society, require for his reentry? At the same time, what must the offender who wants to regain admission to the moral community do to regain the trust of people in his community? The answer, of course, must be the same: Whatever society requires in order to reaccept the offender is exactly what the offender must do to regain the trust that he lost through the commission of the crime. The criminal sentence, if designed as a list of requirements for regaining trust, is actually a *plan for reentry* of the offender, not a destructive weapon to make him suffer.

From the restoration of trust perspective, the task of sentencing reform is one in which the criminal sanction that is part of the process of expelling and excluding offenders can also serve as the means of their eventual reintegration. For every offender, the key question in a restorative system is: What must be done to restore the victim's trust in the offender and in society? Specifying those conditions becomes the terms of the sanction as well as the offender's plan of reentry. Accepting those conditions becomes the offender's path to reentry. Because the sanction will act as a program for personal transformation and reintegration only if voluntarily accepted by the offender, a restorative criminal justice system must make this option attractive to as many defendants as possible. As an all-encompassing goal of sentencing, the restoration of trust can help guide the development of procedures and policies to maximize the probability that an offender will voluntarily accept the terms of his sentence. It will do so by encouraging the active participation of offenders in sentencing negotiations and by offering the possibility of reduced sentences for those who demonstrate genuine remorse, agree to pay for losses, and help design their own program for rehabilitation. In short, the criminal justice process, which must initially function as a ritual of expulsion, either can intensify the offender's social ostracism or become a ritual of transformation from expulsion to reintegration by means of the offender's apology, payment of restitution, and voluntary submission to a deserved punishment.

Reintegration: From Shame to Trust

To understand the procedure features of the restoration of trust approach to offender reintegration, it is useful to contrast our proposal with Braithwaite's justly famous conception of shaming as a component of criminal sanctions. In his seminal work *Crime, Shame and Reintegration*, Braithwaite attempted to chart a new course for criminal justice, one that focuses on the task of reintegration rather than merely assigning blame and imposing punishment. The distinguishing characteristic of crime, as opposed to other types of harmful behavior, Braithwaite contended, is its willful defiance of communal values.[2] The appropriate response to crime therefore is not simply to suppress the behavior by the imposition of punishment, but to take steps to address the offender's disrespect for the rights of others. This can only be done, Braithwaite argued, by community members directly confronting the offender and calling him to task for his disrespect: He must be publicly *shamed*, not merely punished. Braithwaite believed that shaming is more effective than mere punishment because it utilizes the power of social control and also reinforces a positive image of the offender as a person from whom more is expected by the community.

Using this positive approach, that is to say, using the moralizing qualities of social control rather than its repressive qualities,[3] we can expect greater compliance with the law and greater possibilities of reintegration. Braithwaite argued that, while the "uncoupling" of punishment from shame was a necessary step in the evolution of the law, the resulting sanction of state-imposed punishment has been stripped of its expressive power as a means of conveying community disapproval and therefore the state has increased the severity of punishment in order to compensate for the weakening of its power of social control.[4]

Braithwaite thus argued that the time has come to consider *recoupling* shame with punishment—and it is precisely here that the restoration of trust approach would chart a different path to reintegration. There can be little doubt that shaming is a powerful instrument of social control that has been historically removed from the criminal justice system, but the key question for those interested in reforming the system is how shaming can best be incorporated without jeopardizing other values; both those that we wish to preserve and those new restorative values that we wish to introduce. Instead of recoupling informal shaming with the formal criminal sanction, I propose that shaming be introduced into the formal system of criminal justice through victim-offender dialogue: as a stage in the rite of passage from exclusion to inclusion. Braithwaite's proposal for the recoupling of shaming with the formal sanction is a noble effort to humanize the criminal justice system, but it is prone to serious and, I argue, avoidable problems. In order to better understand the proposed use of shaming in the process of offender reintegration, it is necessary to take a closer look at the problems that arise from the merging of shaming with punishment.

1. Application to Noncommunal Societies. Braithwaite noted with approval the use of shaming practices in many countries such as Japan that have low crime rates: "low crime societies are societies where people do not mind their own business, where tolerance of deviance has definite limits, where communities prefer to handle their own crime problems rather than hand them over to professionals."[5] But Braithwaite was careful to note that "shaming is a dangerous game."[6] Shaming can be reintegrative, but it can also be stigmatizing. If handled incorrectly, shaming may be counterproductive by inducing a rejection of the "straight world" in favor of a criminal subculture.[7] Clearly, societies that are socially well integrated have a high degree of social control over their citizens and are therefore more likely to control crime by shaming rituals without resort to the formalities of the law. The superior ability for shaming to function as an instrument for crime control and reintegration, as Braithwaite argued, is principally found in communalistic societies.[8]

The problem for most industrialized societies, however, is whether social shaming can successfully function in non-communalistic settings; especially in urban areas where social anomie is highest and the problem of crime is greatest. It is by virtue of effective social control that shaming can function as a means of crime prevention and reintegration rather than merely as a means of condemnation and exclusion. A society that has a high degree of social integration and cohesion will be able to control crime more effectively by informal means that harness the power of social control than by the mere application of force.[9] In non-communalistic societies, however, the absence of adequate social control is a primary reason for high rates of offending. In these settings, the use of community members to shame an offender into compliance without the use of formal punishments has little chance for succeeding.[10] This is especially so when the offender more closely identifies with a criminal subculture than with the mainstream society.

2. Informal Sanctions and Private Justice. Although Braithwaite insisted that his conception does not amount to a rejection of the rule of law,[11] the reliance on community shaming as the principal means of crime control raises familiar and troublesome problems that have always been associated with privatized justice: the absence of legal standards, the absence of equality of treatment, and, given the subjectivity of judgment, the strong possibility of bias and prejudice toward minorities and those regarded as outsiders. Those with the greatest ties to the community through family, school, business, or religious associations will certainly tend to receive more favorable treatment than others who lack such ties. These problems that are associated with informal justice are especially apparent under Braithwaite's formulation. Because shaming is more effective for offenders who are socially integrated, community members would be fully justified in withholding punishment from insiders who are responsive to shaming while imposing punishment on outsiders who are not so responsive to social shaming. Braithwaite contended that, while the conventional court apparatus would be used to assess guilt, "the court might then throw the responsibility for responding to the problem back to relevant communities of interest creatively assembled in the courtroom by probation professionals."[12] But the problems of subjectivity, inequality, and prejudice are not solved by merely having community members exercise their subjectivity inside the courtroom. Lacking any standards or legal limitations, the presence of community members, however "creatively assembled," would more likely result in the conversion of the chambers into a people's court than the conversion of the community group into an unbiased judicial panel.

3. Informal Sanctions and Personal Autonomy. Besides exacerbating the problems associated with private justice, the use of social shaming by community members also raises another morally vexing problem: the invasion of personal autonomy. This concept sounds highly abstract, but nothing could be more visceral. Braithwaite believed that the uncoupling of shame and punishment within the past several centuries has been mistaken because, without the impact of social condemnation, the mere imposition of punishment is rendered weak and ineffectual. The Anglo-American model of jurisprudence is to blame for this uncoupling, given its insistence on the limitation of the power of the state to control a person's behavior rather than his character, thus preserving the offender's personal autonomy. Braithwaite understood well that recoupling punishment and shame means that the criminal sanctions that he proposed would exceed the boundaries of what would otherwise be permitted in a liberal state, and would extend to a societal condemnation of the offender's character as well as his actions. This is what shaming is all about: It exposes the shortcomings of the offender's character [13] in order to induce a sense of personal failure to live up to the legitimate expectations of others. No doubt, the image of a young person being coaxed into social awareness by his or her friends and family rather than being punished has its charms. But what about an outsider who is Black, Jewish, homeless, a gay man, or a political activist? What happens when that outsider is confronted by a "creatively assembled" group of community members who express their disgust, not merely with his conduct, but with the character of the person himself? Is it really an advance in justice for this group to devise a sentence that will induce shame in the offender?

The issue of civil disobedience illustrates well the disturbing consequences of the criminal justice system's failure to respect the boundaries of personal autonomy. Braithwaite contended that his formulation, which not only permits shame but is *intended* to induce shame, "accommodates civil disobedience better than the traditional theories of sentencing."[14] Would this have been so in the case of a participant in a sit-in at a segregated lunch counter during the civil rights movement? Under the liberal model of jurisprudence, that demonstrator would have been subject to the imposition of a punishment specified by the law, to which the demonstrator would undoubtedly have submitted to in order to expose the moral bankruptcy of the law itself. In submitting to the punishment, the demonstrator would have shown his respect for the legal process, but his *dissent* from the morality of the particular law in question. Because it was his choice to violate the law, he would have willingly paid the price for retaining his freedom of conscience. In Braithwaite's model, however, the demonstrator would have been confronted by "members of the community" whose job have been to make him feel ashamed for his conduct and for himself personally. In order to be effective, these community members would have been drawn from the offender's own family and friends and their mission would have been "to allure and inveigle the citizens to attend to the moral claims of the criminal law, to coax and caress compliance, to reason and remonstrate with him over the harmfulness of his conduct."[15] It is true that the offender would have been "free to reject these attempts to persuade through social disapproval,"[16] but it undoubtedly would have taken a good deal of psychological fortitude to practice civil disobedience at the cost of defying one's family and friends. I wonder what Martin Luther King Jr. would have thought of the state's efforts to enlist the help of members of the African American community during the 1950s who opposed his philosophy of civil disobedience, to "coax and caress" him into compliance with the laws of segregation.

The morally disquieting invasion of autonomy that results from the intercession of personal criticism and social pressure into the criminal justice process is compounded by Braithwaite's notion of proper sentences. The recoupling of crime with shame, which is central to Braithwaite's proposal for a criminological theory based on shaming, embraces the concept that punishment be a public affair designed to communicate "the abhorrence that society extends toward criminal acts."[17] Therefore, the punishment ought to be "visible" and "newsworthy" rather than hidden.[18] The image of a civil rights activist being forced to endure a punishment that expressed the community's abhorrence for his violation of the law hardly recommends the adoption of Braithwaite's proposal to recouple punishment with shame.

This kind of dilemma arises only rarely, of course. Most crimes are actions for which we *ought* to be ashamed. But here too, the problem of undue invasion of personal autonomy is troubling. Shaming, as Braithwaite noted, is a dangerous enterprise because it can result in stigmatization of the offender, thereby obstructing efforts to reintegrate him and promoting his identification with a criminal subgroup.[19]

Indeed, it is precisely by the *uncoupling* of punishment from shame that Western societies have shielded their citizens from the harm that would be caused by the state's use of public humiliation as a means of law enforcement. The price we have paid in uncoupling punishment from shame, to be sure, has been a reduction in the effectiveness of law enforcement. But what we have gained—a shield against intrusions into our personal autonomy—is a value we would be wise to preserve.

4. **Absence of Procedural Protections Against Abuse.** The potential for enormous harm to personal autonomy that is likely to result from the reunification of punishment and shame cannot be prevented by mere warnings against abuse. How, then, can we be sure that the shaming process, which by its nature must be performed by ordinary citizens and not by trained professionals, will result in "good shaming"

and not "bad shaming"? Braithwaite proposed several remedies that he believed would produce shaming that is not oppressive: "Shaming should not be used for criminal behavior that involves no risk of harm to others" and "even when it does harm, the offender should be shamed or punished with dignity rather than stigmatized as a monster or an outcast."[20]

Unfortunately, these precepts offer little assurance to an offender that his case will fall into the reintegrative shaming category and not into the stigmatizing shaming category. First, the requirement that the shaming not be applied to behavior "that risks no harm to other citizens"[21] would not eliminate many cases because every crime, by definition, involves some actual or potential harm to the public welfare. Secondly, the establishment of an ethical mandate that the offender's dignity should be preserved does not create a *safeguard* against abuse. Recall that the purpose of this convocation of citizens is to shame the offender. This is believed to be a justifiable limitation of the offender's autonomy because it does so by "communicating moral claims over which other citizens can reasonably expected to express disgust should we choose to ignore them."[22] Given the delegation of the task of expressing disgust and denouncing the offender to community members, those who are accused of a crime deserve more than verbal assurances that they will be treated with dignity. The examples Braithwaite cited of similar courts in action throughout the world offer little assurance that the dignity of the offender will be respected. Braithwaite referred to shaming practices in ancient Rome in which those who have been wronged "follow their offenders about dressed in mourning clothes and with disheveled hair, sometimes chanting against the person at home or in public places"[23] and in Cuban and Chinese "people's courts" where "ordinary citizens verbally denounce wrongdoing as part of the trial process."[24] Even in the unlikely event that our society could enlist the services of ordinary citizens willing to do such things, this would hardly represent an advance in the humane treatment of offenders.

Braithwaite, again, was acutely aware of the danger that shaming might lapse into stigmatization. The problem is that he did not propose a *mechanism* that would encourage shaming of the reintegrative type while providing adequate safeguards against shaming of the stigmatizing type. In Braithwaite's reference to ceremonies of reacceptance as indicators of whether shaming is reintegrative or stigmatizing, it is not clear whether he was asserting that such ceremonies result in, or result from, reintegrative shaming: "Reintegrative shaming means that expressions of community disapproval, which may range from mild rebuke to degradation ceremonies, are followed by gestures of reacceptance into the community of law abiding citizens."[25] Clearly, if Braithwaite was merely claiming that these ceremonies are indicia of "good shaming," his claim is quite plausible but provides us with no guidance in avoiding the kind of shaming that would result in stigmatization. On the other hand, if Braithwaite was claiming that reacceptance ceremonies are, in themselves, instrumental in making shaming exercises become reintegrative, the claim is far less plausible. Ceremonies of reacceptance have no meaning if they do not derive from genuine reacceptance. If the shaming process itself is stigmatizing, if it causes the offender to retreat into a stance of defiance, what possible good is achieved by enacting a ceremony of reacceptance? In order to assure that the shaming by members of the community would be reintegrative rather than stigmatizing, it is not sufficient to suggest or require that shaming be followed by rituals of reconciliation. That is because rituals that follow a process of stigmatization, regardless of what we initially intend, inevitably become recognized as rituals of social exclusion.

The essential problem of using shaming rituals as an alternative to the conventional process is that it is an example of the larger problem of private justice. Like the silly old nursery rhyme tells us, "when it is good, it is very, very good, but when it is bad it is horrid." The very subjectivity, creativity, and personal intrusiveness that makes shaming a potent agent for change also makes it susceptible to the most flagrant abuses, all in the name of helping the offender.

In summary, Braithwaite's pioneering work helped to focus attention on the inadequacy of the current system to marshal the forces of social control in fashioning criminal sanctions. Yet, troubling problems arise from Braithwaite's proposal to reintroduce informal community shaming as the primary means of addressing crime. Just as in the case of those who advocate the establishment of restorative justice as a new criminal justice paradigm to replace the conventional system, efforts to reform the criminal justice system must avoid substituting one set of problems for another. In the case of Braithwaite's proposals, those problems can be boiled down to two central concerns: to find ways to (1) ensure the achievement of reintegrative rather than stigmatizing shaming and (2) limit the intrusiveness of sanctions into the offender's autonomy without exclusively relying on the goodwill of those who determine criminal sentences.

Several of the principles that I have discussed in the development of the proposed restoration of trust model of restorative justice can help resolve both of these important issues.

Ensuring That Shaming is Reintegrative and Non-stigmatizing

In the context of restoring trust in the offender, shaming functions not as a means of enhancing a criminal sanction, but only as a part of a process in the rite of passage from exclusion to reintegration. Shaming is used as a prod to awareness and not as a psychologically oppressive stigmatizing sanction. Shaming provides a means of expressing a victim's emotional and psychological losses as well as the community's moral condemnation and exclusion, and functions to elicit the offender's remorse, demonstration of empathy, and willingness to accept accountability to make amends. It strips away the offender's defenses and permits him to realize what he has done to isolate himself from the community, and therefore what must be done to regain acceptance. In this way, shaming functions as a means to facilitate the kind of interpersonal dialogue that will result in a restorative sanction, but never as a means of enhancing the sanction to maximize its deterrence or retributive power.

This type of encounter is feasible only in the case of defendants who voluntarily decide to participate. If, at any time, the offender wishes to terminate his encounter with the victim and community representatives, he must be free to do so. This means that reintegrative shaming can never be imposed on the offender, even if it intended to be for "his own good." Once convicted of a crime, the offender may be required to submit to punishment. But he must not be required to submit to social shaming because such a sanction would be counterproductive to the goal of restoring trust in the offender and in society.

Establishing Limits to Invasions of Autonomy

The liberal tradition of uncoupling shame and punishment is a wise social policy against tyranny and must be retained by the law. One way of ensuring that the sanction itself is not unduly oppressive we have seen, is the requirement that any sanction involving social shaming be voluntarily accepted by the defendant. But should an offender who seeks to make amends voluntarily be permitted to agree to a sanction that exposes himself to public shaming? A truly penitent offender might very well be inclined to voluntarily submit to a more personal form of atonement through a criminal sanction, and it a makes sense to permit the parties to devise such creative sanctions—*but within strict limits.* Defining those limits involves the application of Morris's limit-setting principle: Between the level of maximum severity, beyond which a sentence is regarded as undeservedly severe and beneath which it is regarded as undeservedly lenient and insufficiently protective of public safety, the victim and the offender may agree on a sentencing recommendations they believe is appropriate.[26] Furthermore, any sentencing recommendations must be subject to judicial approval. Sentences that do not accord with legislative limitations or that, in the court's opinion, depart from the goal of restoring trust in the offender or in society can be rejected by the exercise of judicial discretion. In this regard, for each recommended sanction coming before the court, a necessary component of judicial approval will be an affirmative answer to the question: Does this sanction operate to promote the trust in the offender and in society? Ideally, sentencing recommendations will result from a personal encounter between the victim and offender and, possibly also, community members, in the course of which the offender will be confronted with the full scope of the harm he has caused and given an opportunity to express remorse and agree on a plan for accountability and reparation. But even in those cases in which either the offender or the victim do not agree to such a dialogue, the goal of restoring individual and societal-level trust can be utilized by the court itself in fashioning a sanction that is within the limitations defined by law to prevent stigmatization and undue intrusiveness.

In summary, the restoration of trust model of sentencing draws on Braithwaite's insights into the power of social shaming to induce repentance and to promote reintegration, but protects against abuses that may arise from shaming. It achieves this protection by (1) utilizing social shaming in the process of the victim-offender encounter rather than as a means of enhancing sanctions; and (2) limiting any sanction that involves social shaming to voluntary agreements, subject to legal boundaries and to judicial approval, guided by the overarching goal of restoring trust.

Devising a Plan for Reentry

By devising sentences with the deliberate intention of setting forth conditions for regaining personal and social trust, we create restorative sanctions that reflect the needs of an individual victim and of society. By voluntarily accepting such a sentence, the offender demonstrates his remorse, his willingness to "make things right," and his desire to regain admittance to the moral community. The entire criminal justice process, under the overall goal of repairing the harm of crime, can therefore be seen as a two-phase ritual. Phase 1 is the *ritual of exclusion* whereby the offender is isolated, suffers a degradation of social status, and is excluded from the moral community. In Phase 2, the ritual of exclusion becomes a *ritual of inclusion* by the offender's act of submission to the group. The conditions of his sanction, devised as conditions for regaining social and personal trust, become in turn, the conditions for his social rehabilitation. The subsequent criminal justice processes—probation and corrections—can therefore function as instrumentalities of reintegration for those offenders who choose the path of reintegration. For those who do not choose this path, whether out of defiance or out of principle, sentencing can remain what it is today: the retributive toll exacted on those who violate the law.

The implications of such a restorative system on probations, corrections and parole will be explored in Chapter 13. But before leaving this section, let us summarize how the victim, the offender, and others involved in the sentencing negotiation may collectively arrive at a restorative sanction—one which, by setting forth reasonable conditions for regaining trust, becomes the offender's plan for reentry into the moral community. At the outset, the objective conditions of trust have already been established by operation of law. Society, through its legislative representatives, has already determined that, for the protection of its citizens, a penalty must be exacted for the commission of the crime. That penalty must be sufficiently harsh to act as a deterrent, but neither so lenient nor so severe as to offend its collective sense of justice. Within these parameters of social trust, the parties to the negotiation are free to consider whatever conditions they believe to be necessary or desirable. This is unlike the establishment of objective conditions of trust, in which lawmakers ask: What must be done in such cases to restore trust in *society*? Instead, the attendees at a sentencing negotiation ask: What must be done to restore trust in *this person*? The victim is likely to seek an agreement for material compensation, but also a demonstration of conscience and empathy in order to establish trust in the offender. The victim wants the offender to fully appreciate the harm he has caused and to show, in words and by deeds, his genuine remorse and commitment to the rule of law. The victim may also want some legal guarantees to ensure his or her own safety such as restrictions on contact or probation supervision that extends over time. Community representatives more likely will take a broader view that attempts to address the causes of the crime and to devise preventive measures against further offending. In this regard, they may consider rehabilitation and counseling, completion of education, and job training. In appropriate cases where there is a history of criminal involvement or of conflict between the victim and offender, the presence of a community representative as well as the family of the victim and the offender can be instrumental in fashioning agreements to desist from harmful contact or to mediate future disputes by a mutually trusted intermediary.

Of course, an offender is not compelled to agree to any of the conditions that are suggested. He is, however, motivated to accept them in view of the likelihood that, if he does so, the victim will reduce his or her insistence on punitivity so that the ultimate sentence will be toward the lower end of the range of sentencing severity established by law. This kind of inducement offered to the offender does not negate the restorative value of voluntary acceptance of the sentence because, by pleading guilty, he already has agreed to be subject to a range of penalties mandated by law. Likewise, the victim retains the ability to insist on recommending more severe penalties within this range if he or she believes that the offender is simply trying to "get off easy." Therefore, while the prospect of obtaining a reduced sentence may motivate the offender to agree to a restorative justice dialogue with the victim and community members, he is also motivated to participate attentively and respectfully and to offer an apology that sounds real because it *is* real.

Another powerful motivation for the offender to voluntarily accept these conditions is (for want of a better term) his *conscience*. In fact, the purpose of an encounter between the victim and offender is to make the offender manifest his conscience. Only if he does so will the possibility of repairing the loss of trust in him become feasible. If the offender's conscience is stirred so that he recognizes and acknowledges his fault and shows remorse for his behavior, it means that he is accepting moral norms and demonstrating respect for the good opinion of the victim and the community as well as a desire to be reaccepted by them. If this desire is strong enough, he will want to show that he willingly submits to the sanction as his just deserts according to the rules of reciprocity. Correspondingly, because the offender has demonstrated conscience, the victim is morally and psychologically inclined to refrain from an unduly vindictive and unreasonably harsh sentence. The provocation of conscience, then, produces both in the offender and in the victim a willingness to fashion a sanction that can be voluntarily accepted as reasonable and deserved.

The result of such combined efforts by a victim and offender, under the guidance of a trained facilitator is a restorative "plan of action" that may include many components. The job of the facilitator requires not only diplomacy and flexibility, but also a strong dose of pragmatism, for every element of the proposed sanction, no matter how good it sounds on paper, must be realistically enforceable. It cannot create conditions that overburden the resources of the probation department. Therefore, an effective mediator will help the parties to devise conditions that satisfy their needs and contain simple and effective methods to monitor and enforce compliance by using the human and institutional resources in the community that are best suited to the job.

Once the sentence is completed, the punishment endured, restitution paid, rehabilitation plans attended, and community supervision ended, the rite of passage from exclusion to inclusion must now be treated with some measure of ceremony. Just as an offender's entry into the criminal justice system was marked with ceremonies of degradation by his arrest, trial, and punishment, now his debt to society must be acknowledged as being "paid in full" if he is to be reaccepted as one of us. At present, no such ceremonies exist. The offender, having been disgraced and rejected by society, merely slinks back into the population, either unnoticed or unwelcomed. But under a system dedicated to the restoration of trust, we can do more—not in all cases, certainly—but much more than we are now doing. For an offender who participated in the stern test of character inherent in the victim-offender encounter, who acknowledged responsibility for his conduct, who participated in the creation of sentencing recommendations that addressed all the reasons why he was distrusted by the victim and the community, and who voluntarily agreed to the terms of his sentence, the successful completion of a restorative criminal sanction should be regarded as a significant accomplishment, and should be promoted as such by the criminal justice system. As in the case of military service, a distinction might be made between those who have completed their term and those who have done so "honorably."

The bonds of trust with the victim, the community, and the larger society that were severed by the offender's criminal act *can be repaired,* although not overnight and, sadly, never completely. But the long and successful history of the human species, despite the inevitability of crime, attests to the power of the social group to heal itself. One reason the contemporary criminal justice system that has evolved to satisfy the interests of the prosecutor and the defense has failed to achieve the goal of repair, is that the determination of a criminal sentence during plea bargaining. Plea bargaining, which accounts for the vast majority of dispositions, is mostly a matter of damage control. There is no effort to devise a restorative solution because the topic simply does not arise. Sentences devised by operation of conventional plea bargaining are typically the result of a mindless marriage of convenience between adversaries. For the most part, a criminal sentence recommendation is determined by the interplay of two factors: the statutory requirements of the offense charged and the probability of conviction. Because both the prosecutor and the defense attorney have an interest in avoiding the humiliation of a defeat, and since the adversary system is a winner-take-all formula, a sentence is devised purely out of considerations of expediency that reflect the minimum the prosecutor will agree to and the maximum that the defense will agree to in order to avoid the risk of either side losing everything at trial. The result is necessarily a compromise, a kind of insurance policy against a catastrophic loss.

Furthermore an apology given in the context of a plea bargain is also a matter of expedience because it is offered in order to fulfill an agreement intended to reduce an offender's exposure to punishment. It is not derived from the experience of a personal encounter with the victim, and often is not even uttered to the victim, but rather to a professional jurist who, after all, holds the only opinion that truly matters to the defendant. The needs of the victim are of little concern because the victim is not a party to the agreement. Whether or not the offender's apology is sincere is hardly ever challenged by the judge who, in the interest of moving the calendar along, is motivated to approve agreements and avoid trials whenever possible. Therefore, even in the case of voluntary agreements, the possibilities of achieving a genuinely restorative disposition within the conventional system are slight because sentences derived from plea bargaining are little more than exercises in risk management by the litigants.

Only in a system that structurally incorporate the participation of victims, offenders, and the relevant community can the development of restorative sanctions become the rule, not the exception. In so doing, the criminal justice process itself can move beyond the pathway of exclusion and become the pathway to reintegration.

Notes

---

[1] Retzinger & Scheff, "Strategy for Community Conferences," pp. 316 -317
[2] Braithwaite, *Crime, Shame and Reintegration*, p. 2.
[3] *Id.*, p. 9.
[4] *Id.*, p. 59.
[5] *Id.*, p. 8.
[6] *Id.*, p. 12.
[7] *Id.*, p. 14.
[8] *Id.*, pp. 12, 84-89.
[9] Robinson, "The Virtues of Restorative Processes," p. 378
[10] Similarly, Braithwaite has us consider family relationships as a counterexample of a successful model of informal justice, (*Crime, Shame and Reintegration*, p. 57). However, the special attributes of family relations underscore their inadequacy to serve as a model of justice for larger social groupings. See pp. 46, 60, 67-69, *supra.*

[11] *Id.,* p. 8.
[12] *Id.,* p. 180.
[13] Garvey, "The Moral Emotions of the Criminal Law," p. 96.
[14] Braithwaite, *supra,* p. 11.
[15] *Id.,* p. 9
[16] *Id.*
[17] *Id.,* pp. 178-179.
[18] *Id.,* p. 178
[19] *Id.,* pp. 13-14.
[20] *Id.,* p. 11.
[21] *Id.*
[22] *Id.,* p. 10.
[23] *Id.,* p. 58
[24] *Id.*
[25] *Id.,* p. 55.
[26] See p. 34, *supra.*

8
Criminal Sentencing
Theory and Policy

In the preceding chapters, I have attempted to develop a "maximalist" approach to restorative justice centered upon the restoration of both personal and social trust. We have seen how this "two level" conception of trust approach enables restorative justice to apply to the widest variety of criminal cases, and how it permits the direct involvement of victims and offenders in fashioning sentencing recommendations without impairing fundamental societal values. In this chapter, we will examine some of the important implications of this approach to criminal justice theory and policy as a basis for the specific reforms and implementation strategies that will be proposed in later chapters.

Major Sentencing Theories: Answers and Anomalies

One of the great ironies of criminology is that, although the ultimate instrumentality of any criminal justice system is the meting out of punishment to offenders, there has been little agreement among theorists as to why we ought to punish at all.

On the surface, there doesn't seem to be anything perplexing about the need to punish criminals. It is, in fact, unthinkable that those who violate society's most fundamental rules of conduct should not have some consequences visited upon them. But should those consequences consist of the deliberate infliction of suffering upon the offender, the deprivation of his liberty, and sometimes even the deprivation of his very life? If we hold it as a value that unnecessary human suffering be reduced, we must question the necessity of the anguish that we justify in the name of the law.

Theories of punishment can be sorted into two groupings: utilitarian and non-utilitarian. These each represent a fundamentally different answer to the same question: Why should we impose a criminal sanction? Utilitarian theorists have agreed that the purpose of any criminal sanction is to prevent crime, although they differ as to the form of the sanction. Deterrence theorists have argued that only by the threat of enduring a harsh punishment will people restrain themselves from reaping the rewards of crime. Rehabilitation theorists have claimed that, for many people, resort to crime stems from a variety of psychological, neurological, or social deficits that must be addressed by appropriate treatment rather than merely by the threat of punishment. Incapacitation theorists have posited that, even if deterrence and rehabilitation fail to prevent future crimes, the one certain way to prevent further occurrences of crime is to render the offender physically incapable of reoffending by imprisonment or other means of "incapacitation."

Non-utilitarian theorists have seen things quite differently. In their view, the justification for a criminal sanction has nothing to do with any socially useful goal. Rather, an appropriate sanction is imposed as a moral imperative: An offender is sanctioned because, and only because, he *deserves* it. Here, the only concern is justice, not utility. Therefore, whether or not a particular sanction operates to prevent crime is irrelevant in determining its merits.

The strengths and weaknesses of these theories have been debated endlessly by both scholars and the public. The major philosophical problem with utilitarian theories is not that they do not produce the results they promise (although empirical support for the efficacy of deterrence, rehabilitation and incapacitation is far from conclusive), but rather that they are not governed by principles of *justice*. Utilitarian sentencing is not guided by what is right, fair, or just. It is guided by what works. Even though utilitarian theorists have presented varied and ingenious means of maximizing the interests of the majority or, more precisely, those who wield power in society, there is no inherent concern in their theories that punishment be proportional to the severity of the offense.[1] There is no principle of justice or humanity that can be appealed to, no moral brakes to the ruthless force of expediency. If crime prevention were the only basis for sentencing, the severity and the duration of sentences would be proportional to their usefulness in preventing crime, not to the blameworthiness of the offense itself. A utilitarian justification for sentencing is scarcely capable of demonstrating any fault, for example, in applying the death sentence for shoplifters in the name of general deterrence, life imprisonment for repeat offenders in the name of incapacitation, or surgical alterations in the name of rehabilitation. In essence, the moral inadequacy of utilitarian theories of criminal sanctions is their failure to honor the personal autonomy and dignity of humans, even those who break the law. What is seems to be lacking in a utilitarian theory of criminal justice, therefore, is the very notion of justice itself.

On the other hand, the non-utilitarian retributionists have seen the infliction of hardship on an offender as a natural and just consequence of wrongdoing. He is punished for a transgression, not in order to achieve a *practical* result, but to achieve a *just* result. This is thought to be a moral response and not the mere urging of a bloodlust for revenge, although some would dignify the atavistic instinct to retaliate as a "theory" of sentencing. At its best, retributive justice is impassive and objective: Punishment is required not by the dictates of human passion, but by the requirements of a universal moral order.

But without resort to utilitarian principles, retributionists have struggled to supply a rational explanation as to why a transgressor should be *punished* instead of merely being *censured*. According to one notable retributionist, the intuitive connection between crime and punishment is reason enough to justify the practice.[2] As the retributionist Duff noted:

> The central objection to all retributionist theories is that they fail... to explain this notion of penal desert, falling back on unexplained intuition or metaphysical mystery-mongering or offering covertly consequentionalist explanations.[3]

The idea that retribution is a kind of "compensation," payable to society, for the harm committed by a transgressor is hardly persuasive. In the first place, the harm to others is notoriously hard to quantify, and harder still to equate with a counterbalancing payment that would disgorge any benefit the offender obtained from the crime. More importantly, even if there were a mechanism for measuring harm so as to provide compensation, it must be borne in mind that compensation is not to be confused with punishment. An act is punitive only when, and to the extent that, it *exceeds* the requirements of fair compensation. Therefore, although it is reasonable, for example, to require a tortfeasor to compensate his victim in order to restore the latter to wholeness insofar as that is possible, retribution requires significantly more for those whose actions are intentionally harmful. It is the increment of hardship beyond that which is necessary for compensation that remains to be justified.

Another non-utilitarian justification for the hardship of punishment is that punishment is necessary to redress an offender's wrongdoing. A variant to this theory is the notion of offsetting the unfair advantages of the social system taken by the transgressor.[4] The problem with this approach is that the harm has already been done and cannot in any meaningful sense be undone by present actions. It is insufficient to say that an offender should not be able to "get away with" his misdeeds. He has already gotten away with it. The question remaining is: What, if any, consequences should be visited on him now? A further justification that retributionists have offered is the claim that the punitive component of sentencing is a necessary part of the expressive power of moral condemnation and an inducement to penance. [5] The proponents of this approach have reasoned that, unless a moral condemnation is accompanied by a tangible and material demonstration of disapproval, the message of condemnation is necessarily weakened. But on examination, this approach is really a form of utilitarianism in that the pain and suffering inflicted on people is justified in terms of the communicative end it aims to achieve. In this case, punishment serves as illumination of text, much like the sculpted expressions of human suffering carved on the portals of Gothic cathedrals help to illustrate the moral teachings of the Bible for the edification of the illiterate masses. If the non-utilitarians base their morality on their refusal to use the suffering of people as means to benefit society as a whole, one can scarcely imagine a more gruesome misuse of human suffering than to punish people in order to teach lessons of morality.

Neither is it sufficient to say that the infliction of pain and suffering is inherently or necessarily related to the pronouncement of a judgment of blameworthiness. True, when delivered in a social context, a pronouncement of blame gives rise to negative social consequences, but it is precisely the social context that makes it so. One can easily imagine a private communication of fault that would engender no public shame. Indeed, public censure is an extremely effective instrument of social control in cohesive societies in which the prospect of social ostracism is far more threatening than any physically uncomfortable sanction. Therefore, even if we accept the notion that justice requires the response of censure to morally blameworthy conduct, we still must account for the *hardship* visited on an offender that is at the heart of punishment.

It would be unfair to require retributionists to justify their claims on utilitarian grounds. Retributionism, after all, is a non-utilitarian theory. Thus, to ask a thoroughgoing retributionist to explain the purpose of punishment begs the question of whether sentencing theory requires a utilitarian justification in the first place. But in the absence of a utilitarian explanation, there ought to be some principled way for non-utilitarians to justify the infliction of punishment (beyond mere censure) on offenders. None, however, appears to be forthcoming.

In recent decades, the old retributionist philosophy has been revived by the "just deserts" school, which has stressed the importance of ensuring the proportionality of a punishment to the blameworthiness of the offense in question, over any practical result that might be obtained.[6] Although this concept of proportionality is a useful antidote to the unbridled discretion employed by the courts in implementing utilitarian sentencing policies, the just deserts school does not offer a convincing explanation for two of the most critical moral questions concerning punishment: (1) Why punish at all? and (2) What are the rational limits to punishment?

As to the first question, the just deserts theory does not offer a new or persuasive argument for a non-utilitarian basis for punishment. It is one thing to say that an offender ought to be punished in proportion to the seriousness of his offense, but quite another to say that the appropriate social response to blameworthy behavior is the infliction of suffering. Why should human suffering be necessary or instrumental to achieve justice? To answer this question, just deserts theorists have inevitably been led to the various arguments offered by the utilitarians: Because people are fallible and prone to pursue their selfish ends at the expense of others, we must impose hard measure (in addition to censure) as a disincentive to the commission of crime.[7] Just deserts advocates have contended that the adoption of punitive measures does not violate their fundamental claim of punishment as being necessarily related to the moral blameworthiness of conduct (rather than any practical end), in that the potentially ruthless measures that could be adopted in the name of crime control would be moderated by the imposition of moral limits to punishment.[8] However, in the absence of demonstrating why punishment—the intentional infliction of suffering—is a "just" desert, it is impossible to establish rational or morally defensible boundaries for its proper application. We can all agree that, in order to be morally justified, such boundaries must exist, but we are at a loss to explain how those boundaries are to be determined. In the absence of such a rational explanation, we are left with tradition and intuition as the only bases for establishing moral limits to the potential excesses of utilitarian applications of punishment – neither of which provide a pathway to moral enlightenment or guidance toward future reforms.

Moreover, the recognition by just deserts theorists that the need for punishment (as opposed to censure) can be derived from a utilitarian model tends to contradict a major premise of the just deserts argument. If the only legitimate reason to punish offenders is derived from a utilitarian concern (i.e., the need to preserve the social order through deterrence or incapacitation), then the reason why criminal offenders are subjected to pain, suffering, or privation is to achieve some useful social end. Quite explicitly, their suffering is justified not on the basis of what they have done, but for the "good" it will do for society sometime in the future. In one stroke, therefore, a theory that draws its moral strength from the insistence on viewing people as ends in themselves and not merely as means for the benefit of others has reversed its moral compass.

Indeed, sentencing based purely on just deserts may well *conflict* with the social goal of controlling crime. The requirement that people must be viewed as ends, and not merely as means, requires that any punishment imposed be calibrated on the basis of the blameworthy conduct itself and not on any future conduct that may be prevented. This emphasis on ensuring proportionality between the punishment and the criminal offense itself means that the neither the offender's character or nor his past conduct may legitimately be considered in determining an appropriate sanction. Because people are judged under the just deserts theory only by the degree of harm inflicted and the degree of culpability of the offender, it could be argued that just deserts theory requires that an experienced criminal be punished no more severely than an infrequent or first-time offender. Worse, it could be argued that, because every factor that makes a person more of a realistic danger to society (e.g., drug or alcohol dependency, psychological impairment, impulsivity, social deprivation, absence of economic alternatives, and incompetent parenting) is also a factor in mitigating culpability to a greater or lesser extent, punishment under the just deserts theory ought to be less severe for those who objectively pose the greatest risk to society. If this argument seems farfetched, readers should be cautioned that a version of this claim has been argued by one of our most noted U.S. criminologists in an attempt to reduce the severity of sentences on socially disadvantaged offenders.[9]

Furthermore, the just deserts theory rejects the notion of disparate treatment for those who may profit from any rehabilitative techniques that actually do work (however few), by regarding state intervention into these matters as being necessarily invasive of an offender's personal autonomy. The state, they have contended, has a right to demand compliance with the law and to punish transgressions, but no right to alter the character of the transgressors. Therefore, rehabilitation, even the most human and the most effective, is viewed as imposing interventions that violate the offender's personal autonomy and that contradict the premise of holding him morally accountable for his misconduct.

It is difficult to assess this review of the just deserts theory without concluding that something of fundamental importance is missing from its analysis. In its zeal to critique utilitarian theories as being amoral, just deserts theory appears to place moral blinders on the community's legitimate need for self-preservation. Security for the life and liberty of members of that community is not a concern that can be casually dismissed as irrelevant to sentencing merely because a criminological theory cannot easily accommodate it.

The problems we see in comparing sentencing theories, in essence, arise from the dilemma of reconciling the goal of establishing justice with the goal of maintaining social order. Some leading theorists have envisioned a hybrid of theories in which just deserts defines the outer "moral" limits of permissible sanctions, within which any and all utilitarian application can be situated.[10] This marriage has dismayed some just deserts theorists as a corruption of proportional sentencing by introducing utilitarian considerations that have nothing to do with blameworthiness.[11] More fundamentally, the hybrid model does not provide a rational explanation for the more basic question: Why is punishment—the intentional infliction of suffering—a morally appropriate response to crime?

In addition to the criticisms of traditional theories noted above, the restorative justice perspective on criminal sanctions raises a fundamentally original challenge to the criminal justice status quo by asking how today's practices can truly repair the harm of crime. The restorative justice notion of viewing crime as harm enables us to critique the existing system from the vantage point of those who suffer from crime: the victim and the community.

From this new perspective, the traditional uses of punishment as a means of crime prevention through deterrence and incapacitation appear shortsighted and, ultimately, ineffective because they neglect the vital role of the community in controlling crime. Adopting important lessons from the Shaw and McKay studies at the University of Chicago [12]and the modern movement toward community-based policing and corrections, restorative justice advocates have stressed that effective crime control is brought about by families and communities—not merely by police. The prevalence of crime in areas of social disorganization, despite the presence of police and the constant threats of harsh criminal sanctions, is vivid testimony to the failure of deterrence as a means of preventing crime. Furthermore, the dehumanization involved in both deterrence and incapacitation is antithetical to the process of offender reintegration.

At the same time that the traditional utilitarian rationales for sentencing tend to neglect the role of communities affected by crime, they are plainly irrelevant to the harm suffered by crime victims. The material and psychological losses resulting from crime are certainly real, but none of the traditional sentencing rationales provide for redress of these injuries. Even rehabilitation, as benevolent as it may hope to be for the improvement of the lives of offenders, ignores the need to improve the lives of victims. The adversary system itself provides no recognition to the victim as an individual stakeholder whose needs are respected and whose participation is required.

Beyond offering a critique of punishment as an effective manner of dealing with crime, many restorative justice advocates have taken issue with the notion that punishment is a morally justifiable response to crime. In their view, the lessons taught by Jesus constitute a rejection of the retributionist ethic of the Old Testament, and offer an opportunity of ending the cycle of violence by showing a different path to healing the harm of crime—the path of forgiveness. This religious insight has opened the door to the exploration of creative alternatives to punishment, but also has operated to limit their political acceptability for use in adult cases and crimes of violence.

This nonpunitive path to restoration is not the path that I advocate. But despite my criticism of the traditional justifications for sentencing, I recognize the exemplary values of proportionality, equality, and social utility that they offer toward the end of crime control. Therefore, rather than offering a radically different concept of criminal justice devoid of the option of punishing offenders, the restoration of trust model, I will argue, focuses on the repair of harm as an overarching goal that not only is compatible with traditional theories, but also helps address many of the important criticisms discussed above.

Compatibility of the Restoration of Trust with Other Sentencing Theories

The restoration of trust approach is not intended as a new theory of sentencing, much less as a replacement "paradigm,"[13] but rather is intended to introduce a new unifying principle. It is a all-inclusive *goal* of sentencing that regards the traditional goals of sentencing (incapacitation, deterrence, rehabilitation, and just deserts) not as isolated or conflicting goals, but as instrumentalities toward the goal of restoration. Therefore, the restoration of trust principle is intended to be compatible with all traditional sentencing theories.

In accordance with deterrence theory, restoration of social trust requires that the state, as guarantor of basic societal relations, must retain the use of punishment as a necessary deterrent to crime. Though we know nothing about a stranger we might encounter, we can base a reasonable degree of trust necessary for social intercourse on the knowledge that we live in a society that enforces the law with appropriately stern measures such as fines, community service, and imprisonment. As we have seen in the chapter on sociobiology,[14] the presumption of trust that is necessary for social cooperation requires the imposition of appropriately severe sanctions for those who violate the basic norms of reciprocity, a concept that is fully consistent with deterrence theory. The failure to enforce laws or the imposition of excessively lenient sanctions undermines the guarantee of social trust.[15] Therefore, even as we would empower victims and offenders to negotiate a sentencing recommendation, the establishment of a mandatory minimum punishment as a requirement for maintaining relations of social trust would operate to constrain excessive leniency.

In accordance with rehabilitation theory, the restoration of trust approach acknowledges that people who are incompetent to manage their affairs and who, by their misconduct, demonstrate a disregard for the rights of others will be reasonably held in distrust. For these people, tangible proof is needed to demonstrate when they have sufficiently overcome their physical, mental, or educational disabilities to qualify for a minimally acceptable life in society without resort to crime. Furthermore, just as empathy-building mechanisms may help to reduce the need for punishment in the process of reestablishing trust, so too can rehabilitation help to reduce the need for punishment. A drug-dependent offender, for example, cannot be reasonably expected to exercise elementary caution or self-control, and so is justifiably distrusted so long as the addiction remains in effect. If we conceive of crime as a willful violation of our presumption of reciprocity in others (i.e., a willful violation of mutual trust), it is likely that, for juvenile offenders, a criminal act manifests a failure of socialization to the norms of reciprocity. For both the drug addict and the juvenile offender, the imposition of punishment, without consideration of further remedial measures, would do little to engender trust. In these and similar cases, the compatibility of rehabilitation with the goal of restoring trust is manifest.

In accordance with incapacitation theory, the duration of incarceration and restrictions on liberty during probation would be regarded as the time necessary for society to reaccept the offender as sufficiently trustworthy to reenter society. Under this view, a period of incapacitation may be justified for more serious offenses, such as violent crimes and repeat offenses, during which time the offender is rendered harmless to others and the public gains the necessary assurances that he has changed sufficiently to be trusted back into society. The restoration of trust approach suggests that locking an offender away or restricting his freedom of movement is justified only when he cannot be reasonably trusted to engage in society freely. For the vast majority of offenders, this requirement of reasonable necessity for incarceration means that other measures not involving physical segregation ought to be considered first and rejected only if found to be inadequate to restore trust in the offender or trust in society. However, when probation fails, or in cases manifesting extreme depravity or recklessness, we may legitimately hold that offender to be so fundamentally untrustworthy as to require his physical removal for a period of time sufficient to assure the public that he has changed and is ready to resume life in society. This theory does not make decisions on the appropriate length of incarceration any less agonizing, but it does establish a basis for rational dialogue. How long should a murderer be incarcerated? Ten years? Twenty years? We know that declarations of personal transformation and rehabilitation are difficult to assess, especially since the defendants in these cases are those whom we would imprison precisely because they have been found to be untrustworthy. The length of incarceration will therefore depend, to some degree, on the ability of prisons to become respected as instruments of transformation rather than mere warehouses (or worse, schools for criminals). Therefore, the restoration of trust approach recognizes the legitimacy of incapacitation, but demands that the period of incapacitation be utilized toward the goal of making the offender more worthy of trust when he "graduates" than when entered prison.

While the determination of an appropriate sentence for a particular offender will be simplified by the establishment of upper and lower limits of sentencing severity, the determination of those limits is no easy task. How long must a person be incarcerated in order for us to be assured that he will not reoffend? How long must a sentence be to deter others from committing the same offense? These questions, although theoretically amenable to empirical research, are unlikely to be resolved scientifically, given the complexity of the problem and the limitations of a social scientific research. It is to be expected therefore that the determination of the upper and lower limits of sentencing will be achieved through the exercise of moral judgment. In this context, the restoration of trust analysis provides some important insights and guidance. As previously noted,[16] in addition to seeking personal safety and compensation for their material losses, victims seek justice, and, for many victims, this means punishing the offender for his crime. However, *only deserved punishment is restorative*: Undeservedly lenient punishment is unrestorative to the victim, and undeservedly harsh punishment is unrestorative to the offender. Therefore, as Dimock has posited, punishment must be proportional to the need to restore conditions of trust.[17] The trust analysis illustrates why this is so: Trust in society is engendered by justice and is jeopardized by criminal sanctions that are considered either cruel or excessively lenient. As a result, the limit-setting principle of restoring trust is in full accordance with the concept of proportionality and the establishment of upper and lower limits of deserved punishment contemplated by the just deserts theory.

Addressing Weaknesses and Enriching Sentencing Theories

By subsuming each of the conventional sentencing theories to the primary goal of restoring trust in an offender and in society, some of their major theoretical weaknesses as independent theories of sentencing can be ameliorated.

Unlike the deterrence and incapacitation theories, a sentencing policy based on the restoration of trust, while accommodating the goal of crime prevention, is necessarily subject to moral constraints. That is because inadequate or excessive sentences are inherently non-restorative both to a victim and to the offender. While embracing the concept of rehabilitation, a trust-based conception of restoration (unlike rehabilitation theory) does not ignore the needs of the victim or the community, nor does it ignore the legitimate desire to hold the offender accountable for the offense. Furthermore, the restoration of trust provides a rationale for limiting the invasiveness of rehabilitative techniques because the utilization of unduly invasive rehabilitation measures would undermine the conditions of trust in society. An Orwellian version of "reforming" criminals might very well reduce crime, but at the cost of eliminating the personal autonomy that is necessary for relations of genuine interpersonal trust and trust in society.

Unlike just deserts theory, a trust-based concept of restoration is not confined to the option of retributory punishment as a legitimate response to crime, but includes punishment as merely one instrumentality among others that may be utilized in pursuit of its fundamental goal: repairing the harm of crime. One important corollary of this concept is that resort to punishment will be minimized as the opportunities to demonstrate trustworthiness (e.g., by expressions of remorse, payment of losses, community supervision, and completion of rehabilitation programs) are maximized. Furthermore, while just deserts theory tends to limit criminal sanctions only to the blameworthiness of a particular criminal episode, the restoration of trust theory would permit a more holistic view of the offender, including his entire criminal history, in fashioning a restorative solution (within, I hasten to add, sentencing boundaries established by law).

As a utilitarian principle, the concept of employing punishment as a means of regaining trust offers an articulable rationale for the "hard treatment" of punishment that has been the source of much consternation among nonutilitarian theorists. While acknowledging the value of punishment in the processes of censure and penance,[18] the restoration of trust approach does not require the view that the imposition of punishment is an essential communicative aspect of censure or a *necessary* inducement to penance, but rather regards punishment as an instrumentality to those desired ends that may be justifiably applied when other means are found to be inadequate. Certainly, in personal relations, the imposition of punishment for transgressions would often communicate the wrong message—a stigmatizing and alienating message—and would as likely induce defensiveness and rejection as it would repentance. A promising area for future research would be to distinguish between those situations in which punishment would result in restorative ends and those that would not. In addition, the expressive theory of punishment, in which punishment is considered a means of penance, does not provide a plausible justification for the use of punishment for those offenders who persist in denying culpability. Duff has contended that the state is justified in imposing punishment on these people nonetheless as a means of focusing their attention an "inducement" to penance.[19] The idea of people being forced to suffer in order to induce moral awareness has a decided medieval ring to it that may strike readers as either remarkably cruel or remarkably naïve but, in any event, far removed from the reactions we might expect from real people in today's world. The restoration of trust analysis helps to "fill in the gaps" of the expressive theory by providing a rationale for the restorative use of punishment in cases of voluntary submission to punishment (through which personal trust in the offender is restored) and also in involuntary cases (through which social trust is restored).

Far from conflicting with traditional sentencing theories, the application of restorative justice as an all-encompassing goal enriches both utilitarian and nonutilitarian theories. By involving the victim, the offender, and the offender's "supporters" (or family) in an effort to devise a restorative solution, deterrence is enhanced by the power of social control. The offender is motivated to comply not merely by the threat of future punishment, but by the far more powerful, more likely, and more immediate threat of forfeiting the love, support, and respect of those closest to him. At the same time, a sanction that results from a dialogue between a victim and offender represents a plan for reintegration that offers a powerful inducement to crime prevention without permanently stigmatizing the offender. It enriches incapacitation theory by placing it within a humane context whereby incapacitation is viewed as a temporary measure—a part of a process designed to eventually restore trust in the offender—rather than as a dehumanizing measure designed to restrain an otherwise uncontrollable beast. It enriches rehabilitation theory by requiring those offenders with certain criminogenic deficiencies (e.g., drug addiction, psychological or neurological problems, or lack of interpersonal or job skills) to address their problems while continuing to insist on acceptance of personal responsibility for their actions, regardless of personal problems. It enriches restitution theory by acknowledging the importance of material compensation, but also recognizing the inadequacy of money—even if it pays for therapy—in dealing with the victim's psychological and emotional losses. If crime is understood to result in a loss of trust, the prospect of repairing the victim's emotional wounds simply by counseling is seen in an altogether new and unflattering light because whatever relief is provided by counseling has nothing to do with restoring trust. It merely converts the victim's insistence on justice and security into personal "problems" that ought to be subdued by will or medication. Also, to the extent that restitution is considered to be the basis of a new approach to criminal sentencing, it may very well result in offering the offender the possibility of paying for his crime as a mere "cost of doing business." In that case, the position of the offender as an outsider to the moral community is concretized rather than ameliorated. The restoration of trust approach would reject this notion of restitution and regard it instead as one instrumentality among others that may be used to repair the victim's looses and also to restore the offender to a position of trust, rather than exclusion.

The goal of restoring trust also enriches retribution theory by explaining the necessity for consideration of prior offenses and by offering an ethical and humane rationale for the suffering that is necessarily involved in punishment. First, because just deserts theory requires that punishment be based on and proportional to the harm and moral fault of the *offense*, it lacks an adequate explanation for differential treatment between offenders based on their history of prior offending or their demonstration of remorse. Neither can it justify the requirement of rehabilitation in addition to the penalty. By contrast, all of these factors—prior history, remorse, and rehabilitation needs—would be extremely relevant to any analysis of trust. Second, the avowedly moralistic, non-utilitarian just deserts theory, while offering an adequate explanation of why sentences must be proportional to blameworthiness, does not adequately explain why the suffering of offenders inherent in punishment is morally required in addition to censure. It must therefore fall back on the utilitarian justification that punishment, besides being the morally appropriate response to wrongdoing, is also a necessary "prudential measure" in order to achieve crime control.[20] Under the restoration of trust model, retribution has a utilitarian function that does not contradict its ethical foundation: It is an essential component of reciprocal altruism and is necessary to maintain relations of trust. The imposition of a deserved punishment correspondingly acts to quell the victim's resentment that arises from the offender's willful violation of trust, and operates to reinforce societal norms of trust in others. The restoration of trust analysis therefore helps to establish the linkage between the criminal sanction as a moral imperative and as a necessary instrumentality to promote the material and emotional well-being of the victim and the economic and social well-being of society.[21]

A Useful Guide for Resolving Sentencing Dilemmas

The restoration of trust model is offered as a means of prioritizing the various diverse and sometimes conflicting sentencing theories through the adoption of a single, overall goal: restoring trust in the offender and in society. It is intended as a useful "rule of thumb" in resolving sentencing dilemmas by the use of a powerful, intuitive, and universal human aptitude. The analysis of restoring trust is especially useful when coupled with the two-level notion of restoring both personal and social trust, whereby subjective considerations relevant to restoring trust in the offender are confined within boundaries representing upper and lower norms of deservedness and protection of public safety, necessary for the preservation of trust in society.

Consider the conflict that often exists between specific and general deterrence in a given situation. A key moral problem that arises is whether it is morally justifiable to require punishment beyond what is necessary to deter an individual offender. The ethical dilemma is typically framed as a choice between the welfare of the individual and the welfare of the public—a zero-sum game in which one side wins and the other loses. The restoration of trust analysis, however, provides a conceptual framework for decision making that avoids the impasses that arise from dichotomous, either-or choices. Because the restoration of trust in society (social trust) requires us to set upper and lower boundaries of severity, it is imperative to first legislatively determine whether any proposed sentencing innovation would be undeservedly severe or undeservedly lenient. We must place an absolute priority on the determination of deserved sentencing because, if we wish this sentencing policy to conform to moral values, no punishment may be imposed that offends the moral standards of excessive severity or undue leniency, regardless of any social or personal benefit that may be intended or achieved. Likewise, the upper and lower limits of sentencing severity would be legislatively determined to protect public safety.

Let us now revisit the question: Is it morally justifiable to require punishment beyond what is necessary to deter an individual offender? Because any sentence falling within the upper and lower boundaries of severity necessary to maintain social trust would be a deserved sentence that sufficiently protects public safety, it would indeed be morally defensible to increase a sentence beyond that which is necessary for the specific deterrence of any one individual so long as the resulting sentence falls within those boundaries. This analysis operates for any such conflict between general and specific deterrence. We can therefore imagine a case in which no formal punishment is required to restore trust in a particular defendant, but in which some level of punishment is nonetheless required to satisfy the minimum concerns of restoring trust in society. Similarly, a greater infliction of punishment may be thought to be necessary in the case of a particularly callous and unrepentant offender, but societal-level notions of deservedness would place absolute limits on this too.

The restoration of trust analysis can be applied to many other theoretical and practical problems in sentencing. For example, is a defendant's expression of remorse relevant to sentencing? From a retributionist point of view, a sentence should be imposed strictly as a consequence of past harmful conduct and therefore any subsequent remedial actions such as the expression of remorse would be deemed irrelevant. This same result would be urged from an entirely different point of view in which a "reward" for remorse might be thought to interfere with the consistency that is believed to be essential for general deterrence to operate. A far different approach has been taken by advocates for rehabilitation who would encourage apology as being essential to reforming an offender. The general public, unburdened by any ideological constraints, has favored sentence reduction for those who accept and express remorse, although they may not have agree on or indeed been cognizant of any rationale. Which opinion shall be used? They all make good sense in their own way, and may be adopted by different judges according to their personal taste, resulting in radically different treatment of similar cases.

The restoration of trust approach, I believe, provides a productive way to reconcile these diverse viewpoints. Under this approach, the expression of remorse would constitute an important instrumentality for restoring trust in an offender and therefore would operate to reduce the demand for punishment, so long as the resulting sanction does not transgress societal-level boundaries of deservedness and utility. This is why the imposition of a less severe sentence for a truly penitent killer (as opposed to a remorseless offender) would indeed be permitted, but not beyond the point where it would be considered insufficiently punitive to satisfy the demands of deserved sentencing or insufficiently protective of the public's right to safety.

Another example of how the restoration of trust model could help resolve contradictions between sentencing theories can be seen in the way it would treat first-time offenders. The idea of reducing punitivity for first-time offenders has intuitive appeal and is an important feature of labeling[22] and rehabilitation theory. Under retribution theory, however, punishment is imposed as a moral consequence of offending and its severity is measured strictly by an evaluation of the harmfulness and blameworthiness of the conduct. Therefore, under this analysis, other instances of misconduct would be considered irrelevant.[23] The same result would also obtain from deterrence theory, although for a different reason. Deterrence theory would tend to regard any concession given to first-time offenders as an impairment to the goal of consistency necessary to convince the public of the futility of attempting to violate the law.

I believe that the tension between these two opposing views on the proper consideration due to prior offenses in determining an appropriate sentence can be resolved by application of the two-level analysis of trust. In this analysis, again, societal-level considerations of deservedness and crime control establish upper and lower boundaries of severity to preserve "social trust," thereby permitting the free operation of subjective considerations such as the desire to rehabilitate an offender and to avoid stigmatization. Assuming the offense is such that social trust does not require the imposition of any mandatory minimum sentence, many first-time offenders may avoid any punishment whatsoever, provided that other indicia of trust are present such as apology, payment of restitution, enrollment in rehabilitation, and community supervision. Furthermore, social policy may actually favor decriminalization altogether for certain cases as a means of advancing the policy of crime control. We can see this today in the policy toward certain drug possession charges in which diversion from the criminal justice system is believed to result in lower recidivism than that which can be achieved through conventional prosecution and punishment. Hence, legislators may choose to eliminate mandatory minimum sentences for cases in which the imposition of punishment is believed to be either unnecessary or counterproductive to the goal of restoring trust in the offender and in society. For these cases, subjective conditions would determine which sanctions, if any, should be imposed, up to the maximum permitted by law.

These examples are among many that demonstrate the practical utility of the restoration of trust analysis in individual sentencing decisions by providing an overarching goal of restoration as well as a framework in which societal concerns of deservedness and crime control act as boundaries for the exercise of individualized sentencing discretion.

Developing a Comprehensive Model of Restorative Justice

The concept of restoring personal and social trust enables the development of a comprehensive model of restorative justice—one that is applicable to a full range of offenses and offenders. By adopting the view that the central contribution of restorative justice is its focus on repairing the harm of crime, we reject the view of restorative justice as a set of unique practices, thus enabling criminal justice planners to consider any number of practices that might achieve the goal of repair. Further, I have argued that, in addition to material losses suffered by a victim, the essential harm of crime that requires repair is loss of trust in the offender and in society. *In all cases, the standard for judging the worth of a practice is the extent to which it can function to repair the harm of crime.*

This comprehensive approach enables restorative justice to bridge the gap between its present niche as a criminal justice "boutique," relevant only to petty, juvenile offenses to the mainstream of criminal justice practice. In bridging this gap, the restoration of trust model offers a number of advantages worthy of consideration.

Contrary to the view that restoration must exist as a radically different criminal justice paradigm that is inapplicable to non-cooperative offenders and serious offenses and that rejects conventional sentencing goals,[24] the goal of restoring trust has no such inherent limitation. For most juvenile cases, the use of punishment might be minimal or ruled out as unnecessary, given the high probability of restoring trust in the offender through personal encounter, apology, and restitution, and indeed may be counterproductive for many offenders. The harm of premature "labeling," especially of juveniles and first-time offenders, is a significant impediment to the restoration of trust in an offender. A policy decision against the use of punishment for certain offenses would also be justifiable if punishing the offender would impair the restoration of personal trust (i.e., by stigmatizing and alienating the offender) without significantly promoting societal trust (i.e., by not being necessary to ensure the public interest in safety or justice). Requiring that a sentence promote social trust would operate to prevent undue leniency that would undermine the credibility of the legal system, but would also place limits on the subjective demands for vengeance that may be sought by unduly vindictive victims and their families.

Similarly, the restoration of trust model is applicable both for cooperative and non-cooperative offenders. Clearly, a system dedicated to restoring trust would favor a cooperative offender by greatly expanding the opportunities for him to acknowledge the suffering of his victim, to admit full responsibility, to devise a plan for repayment and personal rehabilitation, and, not least, to voluntarily submit to a deserved punishment. As for non-cooperative cases, the imposition of punishment would be a necessary means of engendering at least a minimal level of trust. Offenders who show no regard for the needs of the victim or the community by virtue of the severity of their transgression, by their history of repeat offending, or by their refusal to cooperate in the restorative process may nonetheless gain a modicum of trust if they are constrained from further offending by the fear of punishment (deterrence) or the fact of imprisonment (incapacitation). This kind of trust, while certainly better than nothing, is not very much better than nothing. Although renouncing the use of prisons would foolishly expose ourselves and our loved ones to the will of criminals, the kind of security created by deterrence and incapacitation is tissue thin, and it disappears altogether when the shackles are removed and when the offenders' fear of punishment subsides. Sadly, this is just what happens in the conventional system as a general rule but, in a restorative system, resort to involuntary punishment would always be regarded as a failure to be avoided whenever possible. What restorative justice has to offer society, then, is a not the contrast between a system that uses punishment and one that does not, but the contrast between a system directed to the goal of punishing offenders and a system directed to the goal of *restoration*, using punishment only as one of many means to that end. The possibility of restoring personal and social trust therefore exists for both petty and serious offenses, and for cooperative and non-cooperative offenders, by incorporating options for sentencing that are commensurate with the need for restoration.

Finally, because the restoration of trust model is based on a new criminal justice goal rather than any particular procedure, it may be applied in a multitude of different settings, including those in which the parties fail to agree to restorative justice conferencing and those in which there is no identifiable victim. Indeed, there are a vast number of cases involving so-called "victimless crimes" such as drug dealing and prostitution, and crimes affecting the population in aggregate such as tax evasion and environmental offenses, in which victim-offender "encounters" are clearly inapplicable. In these cases, the task of representing the public interest would be assumed by a public prosecutor or community ombudsman, but the key question to be addressed in devising an appropriate sanction would be the same: What must be done in this case to restore trust in this offender and in society? Furthermore, although the restoration of trust model has its greatest impact in uncontested cases—cases in which the offender admits responsibility and agrees to victim-offender restorative justice conference—it can also be used to guide judicial sentencing after determination of guilt in contested cases. Judges, too, need a sensible and morally grounded way to prioritize sentencing considerations. Therefore, even in cases in which the defendant does not concede culpability, the determination of an appropriate sentence may still be guided by the goal of restoring trust in the offender and in society.

Theory Development Under the New Restorative Goal

Although restorative justice cannot entirely replace the current system that employs state prosecution and relies on punishment to compel compliance with behavioral norms, it can replace the *priorities* of the current system so that the goal of restoration may become not simply a new feature of the conventional system, but an "overarching goal of criminal justice"[25] that informs every aspect of the criminal justice system. In this way, it functions as a unifying principle in the development of an integrated theory of criminal sentencing.

The format for an integrated theory of sentencing that includes restoration as an all-encompassing goal is a tantalizing intellectual challenge that is now under way. While a paradigmatic view of restorative justice would hold there to be an irreconcilable conflict between the goals of restorative justice and other sentencing models, an integrative perspective attempts to place the various goals into a rational framework for "an orderly plurality of sentencing goals"[26] in which sentencing discretion is bounded by the rule of law. Fundamental to any such framework is the view that different sentencing goals should be regarded as complementary rather than contradictory insofar as possible.[27] A noteworthy attempt to integrate reparation with the conventional, retributive system was undertaken by Cavadino and Dignan who regarded reparations as a covariant of punishment within an "overall response" rather than as an independent factor that is subservient to the requirement of proportional punishment.[28] The development of such theories can be expected to evolve from critical assessment as well as from empirical testing, but only if paradigmatic discourse is rejected and, along with it, the polarization that promotes theory competition rather than theory integration.[29]

This integrative approach is in contrast to the model of restorative justice as being a radical alternative to the conventional system, but which must rely on the conventional system for hard cases: serious offenses and non-cooperative offenders.[30] Both Braithwaite and McCold held that informal, nonpunitive justice should be the norm and should eventually replace the conventional system altogether. However, since not every offender is amenable to this type of restorative approach (including those whom Braithwaite labeled "sociopaths") the conventional system is seen as a fallback. One way to handle the manifest inadequacy of an informal, nonpunitive system to deal with serious crime and non-cooperative offenders is to utilize a sliding scale of applicability, in which the goals of the conventional system (e.g., deterrence, retribution, and rehabilitation) are placed at one end while the restorative goals of repair and reparation are placed at the other.[31] The result however, is that important restorative values become unavailable to cases that qualify for conventional treatment and, conversely, important societal values such as deserved punishment become unavailable in cases that qualify for restorative justice treatment. In essence, the sliding scale approach embraces a dichotomization of goals, albeit along a continuum.[32] At its extremities, the dichotomization is complete. At the center, the principles for distinguishing between "conventional" and "restorative" policies and practices are cloaked in ambiguity. But unless cases are decided along consistent rational principles, there is a very real danger for the violation of defendants' rights to equality of treatment under the law. On the other hand, if restoration is continued to be viewed as incompatible with retribution, not only will it be inapplicable to the most serious offenses, it may be rejected out of hand for *every* class of offense:

Take away all retributive elements of restorative justice, ..and citizens will be unwilling to use it for any crimes, even minor ones. Demanding that restorative justice reject retribution …will certainly destroy restorative justice altogether. [33]

The restoration of trust approach integrates conventional sentencing theories under the new goal of repairing the harm of crime that applies to *all* cases—not just minor property offenses and cooperative offenders. The keys to this integration are: (1) the recognition that, in the aftermath of crime, both the personal and social dimensions of trust must be repaired; and (2) the "tools" of restoration must include every instrumentality that helps engender trust in the offender and in society, including both conventional modalities (e.g., punishment, community supervision, rehabilitation, and restitution) and nontraditional modalities (e.g., apology, victim-offender dialogue, and other creative sanctions devised to address the particular needs of the victim, the offender, and the community). What is thereby achieved, in Ashworth's memorable phrase, is an "an orderly plurality of sentencing aims" [34] that is applicable to a full range of offenses and offenders.

Reconciling Victim-Centered and Offender-Centered Goals

The appeal of restorative justice to offenders is understandable, given the prospect of reduced punitivity for those willing to engage in victim-offender dialogue. Yet for a criminal justice alternative that offers the victim the prospect of empowerment, emotional healing, and reparation of material loss, it is disconcerting that restorative justice has not been embraced by victims' groups and, in fact, has been regarded by such groups as being "tone deaf to their aspirations."[35]

In one of its earliest appearances, restorative justice developed within the prisoners' rights movements as an alternative to the punitive, stigmatizing, and non-reintegrative features of U.S. penology.[36] Victim satisfaction was not part of the original conception. Indeed, concern for the interests of victims was initially regarded as problematic because their demands were often at odds with the demands of prisoners for penal reform.[37] The perception of undue leniency was at the heart of the uneasy relations between restorative justice and victims' advocacy groups, which often have had a strongly retributional approach to justice.[38]

In an extensive survey of opinion of victims' advocacy groups, widespread dissatisfaction was uncovered concerning restorative justice programs in seven states: "Much of the feedback from the victim community about their experience of justice involves injustice, disrespect, exclusion, lack of empathy, and irrelevance."[39] Specifically, the respondents believed that restorative justice was unresponsive to "the central realities of crime and trauma from a *victim's* point of view"[40] and that it was frustratingly ambiguous about its definition and standards of practices.[41] Moreover, the respondents considered that restorative justice was created primarily for the benefit of offenders in search of reducing punishment and "avoiding responsibility"[42] and that the needs of victims were merely an afterthought.[43] "Where offenders are provided with help to change their lives, but *victims* are not provided help to deal with their trauma, *victims* feel betrayed by the offender orientation of restorative justice."[44] Some respondents reportedly felt they were manipulated into participating by restorative justice "in order to promote and rationalize its agenda"[45] and argued that the characterization of crime as mere interpersonal conflict "trivializes the nature of deep harms and the character of their relationship to the offender."[46] Enticed by the prospect of healing, there was "significant pressure and even coercion to have victims and victim services join the restorative justice bandwagon."[47] Yet despite these promises, "little victim relief" was actually afforded.[48] Without proof of the effectiveness of its programs, the report maintained, "there will continue to be resistance to their blanket implementation and reluctance in the victim community to embrace them."[49]

By not limiting itself to nonpunitive options, a comprehensive model of restorative justice based on the restoration of personal and societal trust makes itself available to a much wider variety of crime victims. However, satisfying the victim's interest in obtaining justice does not mean that the offender's interest in a more humane and reintegrative sentencing policy is disregarded. On the contrary, the proposed comprehensive model of restorative justice, by regarding the restoration of trust as a primary goal, minimizes reliance on punishment and, when punishment is deemed necessary, transforms the character of punishment from that of an instrumentality of stigmatization and exclusion to an instrumentality of atonement and reintegration. The reconciliation between victim-centered goals and offender-centered goals is implicit in the idea that those conditions necessary to restore trust in the offender and in society operate simultaneously to satisfy the victim's emotional and material needs and the offender's goal of reintegration.

Relevance to Reintegration of the Offender

As I have argued throughout, the criminal justice system, while operating as an effective instrument for the social exclusion of the offender, is a poor means for reintegrating the offender back into society. Neither deterrence, incapacitation, nor retribution offers a strategy for reintegration. Even rehabilitation, by itself, is a poor vehicle for genuine reintegration because it neglects the needs of victims and of society for the satisfaction of justice as a precondition for social acceptance. By subsuming each of these traditional goals to the overall goal of restoring trust, however, criminal sentences can be fashioned that attempt to achieve deterrence, incapacitation, restitution, rehabilitation, and retribution not as ends in themselves, but as part of an overall strategy for repairing the harm of crime. Again, using the restoration of trust analysis as a guiding principle for every proposed sentencing option, we ask: What must be done to restore trust both in this offender and in society? From the point of view of the offender, the criminal sentence is transformed from a pronouncement of condemnation and a program for privations and suffering to a plan for reintegration. It might involve an honest and heartfelt apology, an agreement to pay for all losses, a plan for rehabilitation, and, perhaps, the acceptance of a just punishment. It may involve some restrictions on liberty over a period of time to demonstrate real change, but at no time is a sentencing component regarded as a mere infliction of suffering or degradation. Instead, every component of sentencing, even those that involve the deprivation of liberty and the experience of suffering, are part of a plan directed toward the goal of regaining trust.

Let's depart from abstractions for a while and consider this in more personal terms. Suppose you have done something bad: not merely harmful, but actually bad. You fear that this will be the end of whatever life you have made for yourself in the legitimate world. You have become a criminal—an outsider to the moral community. If you feel truly remorseful for what you did and if you want somehow to get back into the good graces of your family, community, and, indeed, the victim of your crime, the restoration of trust analysis forces you (the offender) to ask yourself a hard question: What can I possibly do to enable people to trust me again?

Thinking through what you would be willing to do in order to someday be trusted and reaccepted results in a list of requirements, hardships, and tests that can then be incorporated into a restorative justice sanction: one that respects the needs of the victim and the community and one that constitutes a plan for your eventual reintegration. The potential for the sanction truly achieving these goals of repair and reintegration is undoubtedly increased if you are personally involved in creating the sanction rather than having it imposed on you.

Under a restorative criminal justice system, the participation of the offender in devising an appropriate sentence is not merely a concession to prisoners' rights, but is rather a means by which the goals of sentencing, including the goal of crime control, are enhanced. While the outer boundaries of severity ensure that the resulting sentence conforms to communal standards of deservedness and protection of public safety, the participation of the offender enables him to accept the sentence as deserved, thus making it a means of atonement in addition to being an instrument of retribution. Further, it enables the offender to "buy into" the plan for reparations and rehabilitation and the conditions for reentry, thereby increasing the probability of successful reintegration. For those offenders who yearn for reacceptance by the moral community, a restorative criminal sentence becomes the pathway back.

Guidance in Devising Legislation

The restoration of trust analysis we have used to explore the task of restoring trust in the offender cannot be complete without examining the conditions necessary for restoring trust *in society*. This, however, is the province of the legislature, not the court. In deciding on a sentence appropriate to a given type of crime, the question for lawmakers is not: What must be done to regain trust *in this person*? Instead, it is: What must be done to regain trust *in society* that was damaged by this crime? As discussed previously,[50] for any type of offense, the objective conditions for trust in society include the establishment of sanctions for violations of the law within limits of severity in order to ensure proportionality to the requirements of just deserts and to ensure public safety. Within these limits, subjective considerations may apply freely. The challenge to lawmakers would be to establish a range of penalties: from a "floor" below which a penalty is regarded as undeservedly lenient and of insufficient deterrence value for protecting public safety to a "ceiling" above which a penalty is regarded as undeservedly and unnecessarily harsh. The range should be wide enough to encourage a degree of creativity in fashioning an appropriate sanction, but narrow enough to preserve the values of proportionality and equality of treatment.

Reconciling Restoration with Retribution

The reconciliation of the alleged conflict between restoration and retribution has been an important theme in the discussion thus far, and it has informed the examination of such topics as the origins of restorative justice, the critique of the conventional system, and the role of restoration as an overarching goal of criminal sentencing theory. In addition to the utilitarian function of punishment as the necessary means of ensuring compliance with the law, the emotional and psychological harm to crime victims, I argue, cannot be adequately repaired without the experience of *justice*. Because the imposition of a deserved punishment is overwhelmingly regarded as an important element of justice, a criminal justice system directed toward the goal of repairing the harm of crime is incomplete without the option of retribution.[51] The restoration of trust perspective expands on this analysis by specifying how the victim will "benefit" from the imposition of retribution: (1) by restoring trust in the offender who accepts punishment as his due and (2) by restoring trust in society that has failed to fulfill its mandate to administer justice and to enforce the law. The use of retributive justice therefore is not a necessary evil that is contrary to the goal of restoration, but that is required nonetheless to accommodate the needs of the state. Rather, it is a means used to address the legitimate needs of both the state and the individual crime victim.

One of the key impediments to the acceptance by restorative justice advocates of a constructive, restorative function of punishment is the confusion between vengeance and retribution, both by the members of the general public and by criminologists. Some criminologists have claimed that retribution is equivalen to revenge,[52] but as we have previously noted, crucial differences do exist between the concept of vengeance and the concept of retribution.[53] Vengeance is personal. It is subjective. It derives from feelings of anger and resentment.[54] Because a victim's personhood suffers from the crime, the object of retaliation is the personhood of the offender. The offender is hated and demonized by the victim. Since the victim must demonstrate his or her self-worth through an act of retaliation, the retaliatory act is best performed personally, not through surrogates.[55] A successful act of vengeance, where there is no recourse to law, is a kind of personal warfare. It is risky, it requires courage, and its aim is to defeat, destroy, or harm the offender. In anticipation of the retaliatory act, there is a strengthening of psychological defenses against empathy and a building up of dehumanizing images of the opponent. Vengeance, which aims at the social rehabilitation of the victim, is a kind of public performance that subjects both the victim and the offender to close scrutiny. Will the offender "get away with it" and thus demonstrate his dominance and impunity, or will the victim prevail? In this battle for social standing and personal honor, a successful retaliation is a moral and personal triumph that is experienced as joy in the defeat of the adversary while a failure to retaliate is a humiliating concession to a degraded status. An offender who is defeated by a successful act of retaliation also has a choice either to remain in this degraded condition or to reassert his personhood through his own act of retaliation. This second round of retaliation is not simply injurious to the opponent, it is deliberately harmful because its goal is to defeat or destroy the other party who is now an enemy.

Hence, the cycle of violence continues. The situation worsens when both the "victim" and the "offender" (which, in short order, become interchangeable terms) appeal to clan loyalty for assistance. In many preliterate societies, in fact, clan loyalty is so deeply felt that an insult to any member is automatically regarded as one to everyone in the group.[56] What this means is that the cycle of violence can spin out of control and, instead of being cut short by the death of one of the original participants, it is exacerbated by calls for further vengeance. In the end, the cycle of violence engendered by revenge will be terminated by the subjugation of one party over the other unless there is intercession by an outside agency more powerful than either the victim or the offender and to which both parties have sworn their allegiance. This outside agency is, in essence, the "state" (often personified by a leader) and the power that it exercises is the power of the law. Retribution also seeks retaliation against wrongful actions, but does so within the law: a set of rules administered by the paramount authority.

Unlike the personal, subjective punishment of vengeance, retribution can be defined as "legal punishment,"[57] and it therefore requires a measure of rationality and emotional distance. By imposing sanctions against the violations of rules, retribution seeks to regulate conduct, guarantee safety to its citizens, and uphold the integrity of its values. Its intention is not to demonize or destroy the personhood of the offender, but rather to control and condemn his behavior. Consequently, the imposition of a sanction against wrongdoing is a societal obligation that benefits all. Punishment is imposed as a preventive measure in society to protect the interests of potential crime victims (i.e., everyone in society). An individual crime victim may or may not profit from the suffering caused to the offender by his prosecution and punishment, but the state's primary objective for inflicting retribution is not to satisfy for the victim. Rather, retribution is imposed for the good of others yet unknown.

Furthermore, because retribution, as I use the term, is punishment *within law*, the sanction is not a weapon employed to defeat or harm an adversary, but instead is a measured response to the wrongdoing. Vengeance was rejected by Plato and Aristotle precisely because it was regarded simply as a way of doing harm, not as a way of achieving justice.[58] Retributionism requires a proportional response to crime based on the wrongfulness of the conduct. As Haas described it, vengeance

> is not limited by considerations of desert, proportionality, fairness or equality. Retribution, on the other hand, is a measured infliction of punishment that is imposed by courts and based on careful consideration of the severity of the offense and the offender's blameworthiness and deservedness. It is rooted in the principle of proportionality and the belief that a civilized society must set moral limits on the amount of punishment to be inflicted on wrongdoers.[59]

Retribution is a means for group preservation and not simply for individual preservation. Retributive justice, by removing the controversy from the control of the direct participants, can therefore be regarded as an evolutionary advancement of the justice instinct that compels us to hit back out of an urge for self-preservation.

The distinction between retribution and revenge is also important to the interest of the community in obtaining peace and security. Because it has no internal restraints of proportionality and because its goals are to defeat, destroy, or humiliate, revenge induces retaliation rather than acceptance by the offender. "Successful" consummation of vengeance means submission to the domination of the avenger, not submission to the will of society. Indeed, because vengeance is a private affair, the needs of the society as a whole are irrelevant to the victim and offender. Choices are devised for the convenience of those parties without regard to their effect on others not privy to the dispute. On the other hand, retribution exercised in the name of the law is intended as a means of maintaining order rather than as a means of inflicting damage. By regarding the commission of a crime as a wrong against society, the society asserts its obligation to maintain order. It creates an "objective condition of trust" by enforcing the rules that form the background to the stability and regularity of relationships in society.[60]

Finally, retributive justice, unlike vengeance, is not an unachievable goal that ends up as an obsessional and debilitating fantasy. The administration of justice through law means, at the minimum, that the apparatus of state power is brought into service of a victim to apprehend, prosecute, and sanction the criminal offender. It therefore has a significantly better chance of achieving its kind of justice than the "wild justice" of revenge.[61] Only when recourse to legal justice is unavailable—or unavailing—does vengeance asserts itself as being necessary to redress the harm of crime.[62]

Much of the appeal of antipenal rhetoric, often expressed by restorative justice advocates despite the nearly universal demand for punishing criminals, is based on the moral inadequacies of vengeance rather than on retribution.[63] Criticisms of punishment that appear quite reasonable in the context of punishment as vengeance emerge as quite unreasonable in the context of retributive justice. In the context of vengeance, it is reasonable to claim that punishment does not help the injuries caused by crime, but simply creates new injuries;[64] that the personal needs of a victim are not met by revenge, but by addressing the feelings behind the anger;[65] and that there is no positive role in the very fact that the offender has suffered. Indeed, punishment as vengeance induces defiance and uncooperation, impairs the desire of offenders to make amends, and induces greater anxiety among a victim by making him or her feel personally responsible for the offender's suffering.[66] It is also true, in the context of vengeance, that punishment rather than repairing a victim merely succeeds in damaging the offender in return;[67] that the victim's "fixation on pain infliction is counterproductive to whatever goal is sought"[68] and that "the mechanism of hatred, no matter how justified the moral outrage underlying it, cannot produce well-being....the imposition of pain obviously cannot undo the harm already experienced by the victim."[69]

Each of the above comments makes perfectly good sense and can be corroborated by personal experience, but only as a description of the dysfunctional and morally questionable response of personal vengeance. On the other hand, the logic and intuitive appeal of those comments evaporates in the context of punishment administered *within the law*. In this context, the claim that punishment serves no legitimate needs of a victim is belied by the common experience of crime victims who demand the imposition of a sanction on the offender as a precondition to healing. The claim that the offender's suffering has no positive value is belied by its importance to him in repaying his moral debt, in giving credence to his apology, in demonstrating his remorse, and in affirming the legitimacy of the moral code of his community. The claim that punishment induces defiance on the part of the offender and guilt on the part of the victim (both true in the context of vengeance) ignores the fact that, by placing the dispute within the bounds of the law, state-imposed punishment helps remove the personal animus that produces defiance in the offender and personal responsibility for punishment that produces guilt and anxiety in the victim. Finally, rather than arousing toxic rage, retributive justice permits a victim to rely on the superior power of the state to achieve justice, thereby relieving him or her of personal responsibility for self-help through vengeance. Now, the victim can truly "let go" with confidence and receive the social vindication that is afforded by public prosecution.

In summary, the administration of a retributory sanction by the state as a consequence of crime—rather than the exaction of vengeance by private individual—has a legitimate place in restorative justice theory and practice. The recognition of this legitimate function of punishment as one of several instrumentalities for regaining personal and societal-level trust assists restorative justice in confronting the primary challenges that prevent it from gaining greater application in the real world of criminal justice. It permits restorative justice to accept, without further equivocation and hypocrisy, the uses of punishment that it now routinely employs as a means of enforcing agreements, as a means of achieving accountability to society, and as a means of ensuring community security. Additionally, it allows restorative justice to acknowledge the moral virtue and expressive power of the voluntary submission of an offender to a deserved sentence as an act of penance, demonstrating respect for the victim and for the values of society, thus helping the offender gain readmittance to the moral community.[70]

Reduction in Reliance on Punishment

Guided by the goal of restoring trust, dependence on punishment as a sentencing option can be responsibly reduced:

- Excessively severe sentences are curtailed by the self-limiting principle that only deserved punishments operate to restore trust in the victim, the community, and the offender.
- The victim's demands for punitivity are reduced by maximizing other means of restoring trust (i.e. apology, restitution, rehabilitation, respectful treatment by the court and involvement of the victim, the community, and the offender in devising a restorative sanction)
- By encouraging voluntary submission to punishment rather than the involuntary imposition of punishment, less punishment is needed to make deterrence effective.
- By involving the offender's network of family, friends and sponsors in devising and monitoring restorative sanctions, the

deterrence power of social control increases, thereby reducing the need for formal sanctions.

Many victims may be willing to reduce their demand for punishment if the offender offers what they believe to be a genuine apology and agrees to pay restitution. Because punishment is only one of several components of regaining trust, maximizing other factors in the process of regaining trust minimizes the resort to punishment. Recognizing the validity of punishment as a means of restoring individual and societal trust therefore enables restorative justice to enter the mainstream of criminal justice practice and also permits it to become a significant agent of reform of that mainstream by reducing reliance on punitivity without compromising the goals of public safety or justice.

There appears to be an interactive effect (or "nexus")of apology, of restitution and the voluntary acceptance of punishment, that enhances the power each component as a factor in promoting trust.[71] In the absence of apology and restitution, the demand for more severe punishment can be expected to increase. Lacking evidence of empathy, remorse, responsibility, and respect for the rights of others, a victim will call for more severe punishment in order to achieve a modicum of trust in the offender's desistence from further crime. However, if the offender apologizes, agrees to pay for the victim's expenses, and voluntarily submits to a range of penalties, the process of restoring trust does not rely exclusively on the severity of the punishment.

As a result, if an offender offers a credible apology, agrees to pay restitution, and voluntarily accepts a range of penalties, he can reasonably anticipate a reduction in the severity of the sentence. This format for sentence reduction is consistent with the needs of the victim for justice because he or she is directly involved in devising sentencing recommendations. Furthermore, any recommended sentence reduction is consistent with the needs of society as whole because the upper and lower limits of sentencing discretion within which any reduction in sentencing severity may operate are reflective of society's interest in crime control, maintenance of norms, equality of treatment, and the rule of law. Moreover, the reduction of the victim's demand for punitivity that is expected to accompany the offender's apology and payment of restitution is not only consistent with society's interest in crime control, it is likely to promote greater effectiveness in crime control by increasing the proportion of cases that result in cooperation and acceptance of responsibility over those that result in defiance and rejection.

By utilizing the restoration of trust as an overall goal of sentencing, we can finally place the issue of punishment in a reasonable and humane context. The restoration of trust is not simply another justification or rationalization for punishment. Instead, it replaces punishment as the primary goal of sentencing and regards punishment as simply one means—and not necessarily the most important means—to achieve the goal of restoring trust. The restoration of trust regards punishment unaccompanied by an apology or offer of repayment as the least desirable outcome; yet this is the outcome that is typically produced through the conventional system. We certainly can do better than this, using the same sentencing tools already at hand. It is through its linkage with apology and restitution that the suffering of the offender is transformed from the mere imposition of pain to an expression of remorse and penance, thus opening possibilities for emotional healing for the victim and reintegration for the offender, while reducing the severity of punishment thought to be appropriate.

Reconciliation of Public and Private Justice

To this point in time, restorative justice has largely been conceived as an antidote to the system of state prosecutions in which the needs of victims are ignored. But as we have seen in Chapter 4 the construction of an alternative criminal justice system in which victims are empowered to act as key decision makers introduces a new set of problems: subjectivity, bias, lack of accountability, absence of rules of proportionality and due process of law as well as disregard of the public interest in safety and the maintenance of norms. The procedural framework of bounded discretion in the comprehensive model of restorative justice proposed in this book is designed to accommodate both the public and the private administration of justice by permitting a victim full discretion to negotiate a sentence with the offender within upper and lower limits of severity established by law and to forward the recommended sentence to the judge for final approval in the same manner as sentence negotiations are conducted today between attorneys. This format for accommodating victim-offender negotiations within predetermined limits is analogous to, and illuminated by, the restoration of trust analysis. The upper and lower limits represent the assessment of the minimum and maximum severity of sentences believed to be necessary to restore social trust in society, within which boundaries the victim and offender would explore ways to restore personal trust in the offender himself. In this context, public and private justice are complementary rather than contradictory goals.

Providing a Meaningful Role for Victims Without Compromising the Rule of Law

The criminal law, unlike the civil law of contracts or torts, addresses "those forms of wrongdoing that touch upon public rather than merely private interests."[72] A victim certainly has an interest in the criminal prosecution and is generally acknowledged by a host of legislative reforms to have a number of rights, including the rights to respectful treatment, to be informed of all pertinent facts of the case, to demand compensation for losses, and to be heard concerning the sentencing. But should the right to be heard include the right to exercise sentencing power? Ashworth argued that the retributive function of punishment, a function that is instrumental in promoting restoration for victims, communities, and offenders, requires the exercise of judgment that is dedicated to the public interest in contrast to the non-restorative consequences of personal vengeance. Although victims have an interest in the achievement of retributive justice, they are in no better position to administer or to determine the nature and extent of retributive justice than are other members of society.[73] Further, Ashworth argued, since the quality of retributive justice as administered by the crime victim is inevitably subject to his or her personal biases and prejudices, what is needed to achieve justice is administration by a disinterested tribunal rather than an interested party. Even if the danger of prejudice or bias resulting from the victim's subjectivity were remedied by requiring that all agreements be strictly voluntary, the problems of inequality of treatment, inadequate protection of public safety, and incompetent, biased, or corrupt decision making would still persist. The administration of retributive justice by the victim and offender may therefore be considered of questionable value.

On the other hand, while the administration of sentencing discretion *solely* by the state (whereby the victim is relegated to the status of a witness for the prosecution) may be useful in promoting the social values of crime control, due process protection, proportionality, and the rule of law, it is an imperfect vehicle for achieving restoration for the victim, reintegration for the offender, and peace and security for the community. The conventional system has the advantage over a purely privatized system in protecting the public interest, but *the means by which it administers justice* prevent it from becoming an effective instrument of restoration. In the conventional adversary system, there is no inducement to apology, no disavowal of the moral insult to the victim, and no search for reparative solutions. Passive receipt of punishment is a shallow and limited means of instilling trust in the offender, except for the crudest kind of physical incapacitation and intimidation. It results in a kind of "trust" based on the fear of external force rather than respect for the rights of others. Indeed, because it requires constant vigilance, the application of external force to ensure compliance with the law is better regarded as an indication of *distrust* than of trust.

Therefore, the many advantages of retributive justice over vengeance are undermined by a system in which sentencing discretion is granted either exclusively to victims or exclusively to the state. In order for retributive justice to function as an instrumentality of restoration, what is needed instead is a framework in which the sentencing discretion exercised by both victims and legitimate representatives of the state is *integrated.*

The proposed comprehensive restorative justice model would achieve such integration by permitting a victim and offender to devise sentencing recommendations within sentencing parameters established by law, representing the upper and lower limits of deservedness and public safety. In essence, these negotiated recommendations can be regarded as substitutes for the kind of sentence negotiations now routinely conducted by defense attorneys and prosecutors. Because every sentence falling within those boundaries is deserved, they necessarily adhere to the principle of proportionality.[74] Moreover, since these sentence recommendations are subject to judicial approval, Ashworth's concern that the rule of law in restorative justice proceedings would be compromised by the lack of a disinterested adjudicator is inapplicable. In this way, Ashworth's two major objections to victim involvement in criminal sentencing (a lack of concern for proportionality in sentencing and a lack of neutrality by the decision maker), which both stem from the victim's subjectivity, can be responsibly addressed.

By involving the victim and offender in a search for solutions, the same disposition that might have been arrived at through the conventional adversary system becomes simultaneously an instrumentality for healing the victim's material and emotional losses and also a plan for offender reintegration. If the offender's apology is offered to the victim rather than to a judge, the offender is more likely to empathize with the suffering of the victim and experience genuine remorse for the harm he has inflicted. An apology expressed to the victim personally as well as to the victim's family and the offender's family is likely to be far more personally challenging than an apology to a court official. It subjects the offender to the kind of social shaming that is an essential stage in the process of achieving social reintegration.[75] In this process of shaming, the offender's defensiveness and denials can be penetrated, and he is forced to confront his own failings. By contrast, an apology offered to a disinterested jurist does not compel any such process of self-evaluation, and is done for the sake of expediency—"on advice of counsel"—while permitting the offender to retain his defensiveness.

A victim is no less qualified than is a judge to evaluate the credibility of the offender's apology. The victim has seen the offender "on the street" and is less likely to be deceived as to his account of the incident, together with any excuses offered concerning intention, mistake, desistence from harm, and the like. The victim is often better situated to evaluate many subjective aggravating and mitigating factors that might legitimately influence the severity of the sanction, including the viciousness of the conduct, the degree of hostility exhibited, the apparent influence of alcohol or drugs, the extent of duress, the degree to which the offender was a primary actor or an incidental player, the expression of racial prejudice, and the exploitation of the victim's vulnerability.[76] In private encounters with the victim, the offender is encouraged to "bare his soul" far beyond what may be expected from a brief, scripted dialogue with a judge in the midst of a crowded court calendar.

In sum, the comprehensive restorative justice model would favor involvement of the victim in this evaluative process because, by so doing, the restorative and reintegrative functions of the sanction are maximized. Furthermore, the comprehensive model protects against the potential abuse of the victim's subjectivity by (1) confining the permissible range of sentences to defined boundaries of deservedness, (2) requiring the consent of the offender, and (3) requiring judicial approval of any sentencing recommendations.

More fundamentally, the involvement of victims in sentencing decisions is justifiable because it is not an alternative to judicial sentencing authority, but rather is an alternative to sentencing recommendations by prosecutors and defense attorneys in the context of plea bargains. The participants at a plea-bargaining session are not particularly interested in baring souls or devising creative solutions. They are interested in getting the best possible deal for their respective clients. Getting the best deal typically amounts to little more than assessing the probability of a conviction. Once the deal is made, the appearance before the judge is seldom more than a carefully orchestrated formality designed to memorialize the agreement and to ensure that the defendant has no legal basis to object to it thereafter. For the most part, the victim and community members stand by the wayside and watch as this ritual is played out.

Restorative justice advocates, however divergent their backgrounds and proposals for change, all agree that we can do better than this. Not only are crime victims capable of evaluating the many subjective aggravating and mitigating factors involved in determining a proper sentence, they are, if anything, better qualified than plea bargainers to devise restorative and reintegrative solutions. They, after all, are the ones who have the most to lose in the event the solution ultimately fails.

Moreover, victims are the only participants with moral standing to *forgive*. The comprehensive model of restorative justice that includes punitive sanctions will enable a victim to gain the emotional benefits of receiving an apology while, at the same time, relieving himself or herself, to a large degree, of personal responsibility for sentencing. Because the offender, by entering into a restorative justice sentencing negotiation, has already pleaded guilty and has voluntarily submitted to a range of punishments required by society, the victim can be assured that the basic retributional justice has been accomplished and therefore is largely freed from the emotional stress of insisting on punitive measures. Because the range of deserved sentences has been predetermined by law, the victim is free to exercise forgiveness from a place of genuine compassion instead of moral weakness or disregard for the needs of society. Just as importantly, the act of forgiveness exercised within predetermined boundaries of deservedness can be perceived by others as an act of generosity that is consistent with the victim's self-respect rather than as a form of self-debasement in which the victim fails to insist on the protection of his own rights. In offering victims the opportunity to reduce their demand for punishment and to forgive the offender without thereby renouncing the requirement for basic justice, the restoration of trust approach holds a realistic possibility for genuine healing that could not be reasonably expected in a system in which forgiveness requires the renunciation of demands for retributive justice.

Finally, it must be noted that my proposal to empower the participants at a restorative justice conference with the authority to devise sentencing recommendations is not intended replace negotiations concerning appropriate criminal charges. The initial charges filed against a defendant are often repetitive or unsubstantiated and it is to be expected that the prosecutor's decision to dismiss, consolidate, or downgrade charges to a lesser offense will involve discussions and negotiations with the defense. Only the prosecutor has the authority to dismiss or downgrade charges, and therefore that kind of negotiation would not occur in the context of a restorative justice conference, in which the parties directly involved in the incident attempt to devise sentencing recommendations. As a result, while the restorative justice conference is offered as an alternative to "sentence bargaining" by the prosecution and the defense, it is not intended as an alternative means of negotiating the final charges to which the defendant agrees to plead guilty.

The Restoration of Trust and the State

Much of restorative justice advocacy in the past has concerned itself with denunciations of the state's domination over criminal proceedings. "There is no denying" one author claimed, "the fundamental incompatibility between the State system of doing justice and the principles of restorative justice."[77] By using the state as the offended party, it has been argued, the needs of the actual victims are virtually ignored.[78]

But just as the claims of those who have theorized that the problems plaguing the criminal justice system can be attributed to the "theft" of personal conflicts by the state, and who therefore have conceived of a restorative justice alternate that stands apart from any state-sponsored system of criminal justice,[79] the conception of restoring both personal and social trust necessarily involves the state in establishing and maintaining bonds of trust between its citizens. The agency of the state is required when voluntary associations are found to be inadequate to ensure personal safety, property, and the exercise of liberty. The state not only operates to complement social sanctions, but also to promote the establishment of trust by providing enforcement to breaches of trust. The goal of this delegation of a portion of autonomy is the securing of liberty and personal autonomy as a fundamental value. The ultimate goal in delegating individual coercive power to the state is to ensure the primacy of mutual trust, instead of mutual fear, as the organizing principle of human interaction. In sum, the task of restoring personal and social trust requires the 'good offices" of the state to guarantee security, to ensure protection of constitutional rights, to provide a disinterested trier of facts when the facts are disputed, to establish a range of sanctions in a democratic fashion and to enforce those sanctions fairly and uniformly.

Moreover, the identification of the state as the enemy of restoration fails to account for a victim's need not only for private conflict resolution, but also for public vindication. In her analysis of victims of domestic violence, Herman found that these women did not merely seek material compensation, and neither were they primarily interested in hearing apologies or inflicting punishment on their domestic partners.[80] Material compensation is always necessary, but it is an insufficient response to any victim's psychological and emotional injuries. Apologies are to be encouraged, but victims often suspect them of being the means of manipulation and avoidance of responsibly. Moreover, victims of domestic violence do not necessarily gain any great satisfaction from seeing the offender suffer. What kind of restoration, then, do these victims want? Whether or not they had any desire to reconcile with their partner, Herman found that victims of domestic violence frequently indicated a strong desire to restore their relationship with their community.[81] They want the community to know that they were not at fault and, more importantly, they want a sense of support and solidarity.

In order to vindicate a victim's honor and restore his or her relationship with the community, the offense committed on the victim must not be regarded merely as the victim's private misfortune but as an offense on each citizen. Unlike the approach taken in civil disputes, the state authorities in criminal matters do not stand to the side and feel their duty is discharged by providing a neutral forum; here, they actively take the side of the victim. They prosecute crimes rather than referee disputes. In so doing, they treat the offense as a source of harm to everyone, and not simply the victim's private problem.

In fashioning a new type of criminal justice system focused on the goal of restoration, it therefore is neither necessary nor desirable to reject the use of state prosecutions. Instead, the restoration of trust perspective would refocus and revise the mechanisms of state prosecutions to best achieve the dual goals of restoring trust in the offender and in society.

The Restoration of Trust and Liberal Jurisprudence

The comprehensive model of restorative justice dedicated toward the restoration of personal and social trust entails the establishment of sentencing parameters that operate to curtail the excesses of subjective sentencing decisions and that reflect societal-level interests in public safety and maintenance of norms.[82] Furthermore, the societal-level limitations that establish boundaries of deservedness reflect society's interest in confining the scope of the criminal law to the actions of the offender rather than to his character. From the perspective of regaining social trust, the sole requirement of citizens is conformity of their behavior to the law. The liberal conception of the state envisions the limitation of state power to the regulation of a person's actions—not to their thoughts or beliefs—and, in accordance with retributive justice would justify holding an offender legally accountable for harmful conduct without regard to his personal qualities or his religious, economic or social status. By pleading guilty or having been found guilty, the defendant does not thereby forfeit his right to personal autonomy nor does he consent to being rehabilitatively altered in order to reduce his threat to society. Instead, by pleading guilty or being found guilty, he is simply required to pay the agreed-on price for the crime as specified in the penal code.

The moral advantages of such a system that focuses solely on holding offenders accountable for their behavior, however, must be weighed against its utilitarian disadvantages. As a means of crime control, "paying the price" has limited value. And as a means of restoring trust, it has even less. On the other hand, the utilitarian goals of crime prevention, rehabilitation, and restoration are best achieved by a holistic approach in which the sentence is designed to affect a transformation in the offender himself. In such an approach, the criminal sanction would consist of whatever conditions are necessary to effectuate the desired transformation, no matter how invasive.

A good illustration of the problem of autonomy posed by restorative justice can be seen in the case of apology: How can we retain the restorative features of apology while respecting the personal autonomy of persons accused of crime? However useful apology may be in the reparation of a victim's emotional wounds and in the reintegration of the offender into society, requiring or even encouraging defendants to apologize for their conduct, it has been argued, would extend the reach of the authority of government beyond its legitimate function of controlling harmful behavior and would become intrusive into a person's autonomy.[83] In this view, while the state may impose a penalty on the offender as a means of moral censure, it may not require any particular "attitudinal" response to that criticism because, if it did, the personal autonomy of the subject would be violated.[84] Accordingly, a plan that would offer a tangible reward to those who apologize would thereby operate as an inducement for any person who, rightly or wrongly, is accused of crime to "swallow his dissent." As Christopher Bennett maintained, this would make it "almost impossible for the offender to retain his dignity as an agent whose actions are dictated by his beliefs and values."[85]

This is a fundamental challenge to a sentencing policy that favors apology, a challenge that has been creatively addressed by Bennett. Because he saw great value in apology as a means of repairing the harm suffered by victims and in aiding the process of reintegrating offenders, yet was wary of government intrusion into personal autonomy, Bennett proposed a simple solution: Require apology, but do not require that it be sincere.[86] Of course, sincere apologies are preferable, Bennett argued but, even when they are not sincere, mere ritualistic apologies can satisfy the victim's desire for public vindication and serve as the basis for an offender's "formal" reconciliation with society through the completion of "all that the state can ask of him."[87]

Bennett contended that the performer of a ritualistic apology, having achieved a "limited reconciliation," is therefore "entitled to the goods of full citizenship: it would be illegitimate for (others) to complain about his receiving these despite his false apology."[88] Bennett recognized that, notwithstanding the offender's legal entitlement to full citizenship that arises as a consequence of performing every task required by law, individual members of society might continue to harbor ill feelings toward a truly unrepentant offender who merely satisfied the requirement of apology by rote. Yet even in such cases, Bennett maintained, these morally engaged citizens "ought also to respect his reconciliation with them as a citizen by accepting the restoration to him of full rights of participation in civic life."[89]

Bennett's argument was based on the assumption that the removal of legal barriers to citizenship should also remove social barriers, but that is far from certain. It goes without saying that the removal of legal barriers to citizenship must, of necessity, restore rights of citizenship. The problem is that the restoration of the *full rights* of citizenship does not, by itself, restore to the offender to *full participation* in the life of the community. If the restoration of legal rights would operate automatically to restore full participation in the life of the community, there would be no need to reform the present system because it already establishes a series of preconditions to the restoration of full citizenship. And yet, we know how inadequate that system has proved to be in actually reintegrating offenders into society. Restoration of rights, after all, is not equivalent to the restoration of trust.

In contrast to Bennett's solution of ritualistic apology, the restoration of trust approach offers the possibility of decreased punitivity *only* to those whose apology is regarded as genuine by the close scrutiny of the victim. Under this approach, sham apologies induced by the prospect of leniency gain no advantage to the offender. The question that therefore arises is: Is this consistent with the "liberal" tradition of jurisprudence to base sentencing decisions on the offender's attitude toward the offense as well as on the blameworthiness of the offensive conduct itself?

This opposition between the behavioral limitations of liberal jurisprudence and a more holistic approach to criminal sanctions can be reconciled by a restorative justice system dedicated to the restoration of trust for several reasons. First, under restoration of trust approach, demonstrations of attitudinal change—including apology and the expression of remorse—are never required. The establishment of mandatory punitive sanctions reflects society's legitimate interest in controlling harmful behavior. Society has no right to insist on anything else. It can, however, permit an offender to agree voluntarily to a sanction that does involve greater intrusiveness, as long as the agreed-on sanction does not offend our communal sense of deservedness. Within these boundaries of deservedness, established by law, subjective evaluations may be made—including of the offender's character—but only if the offender, by participating in a personal encounter with the victim, agrees to make such subjective considerations relevant. Just as the offender has the right to keep his personal thoughts to himself and shield them from inspection by the state and the victim, so too may he waive those rights when he believes it is in his best interest to do so. In a similar manner, the offender may refuse to testify at trial and, indeed, refuse to answer any questions that may be incriminating, but also may decide to waive the rights against self-incrimination when it appears in his best interest to do so. This waiver of rights is not the exception, but the general rule, in criminal trial practice. Because a great majority of cases are resolved by voluntary pleas, it is common experience within a system based on the liberal tradition of jurisprudence that defendants will often waive their right to contest the charges as well as their right to demand a trial when it is in their best interest to do so. Similarly, the offender may not be forced to apologize as a result of his criminal conviction. That is because, besides being morally repugnant and legally impermissible, an apology would serve no practical utility. Yet the offender may apologize voluntarily if he believes it is in his interest to do so. As a result, the comprehensive model of restorative justice can maintain adherence to the liberal condition of Anglo-American jurisprudence while permitting voluntary agreements to conditions that would not—and should not—be mandated by law.

Second, while liberal jurisprudence prohibits the consideration of a defendant's character, including his degree of remorse and attitude toward making amends, as a consideration only in determining criminal *culpability*, it does not bar these considerations in criminal *sentencing*. Many personal factors are not relevant to the determination of guilt or innocence, but are highly relevant in devising a sanction intended to accomplish a socially useful objective. Similarly, the restoration of trust approach would permit consideration of the defendant's remorse, his degree of self-reflection, his empathy toward the victim, his willingness to undergo rehabilitation, and many other subjective factors only *after* determination of culpability.

Even among those who regard just deserts as the ultimate moral justification for punishment, it has been conceded that punishment is also morally justifiable as a means of accomplishing a utilitarian goal that is essential for the maintenance of society.[90] Without such a purpose, the infliction of suffering inherent in punishment is evil: It achieves a justifiable moral value only when used as an instrument for a socially desirable goal. If this were not the case, we would be morally justified only in censuring, but not in punishing, wrongdoers. Certainly, a past crime cannot be affected by anything we do afterward. To the extent that we condone the use of punishment to the utilitarian end of controlling crime, it should be employed only to prevent future crimes. Correspondingly, the severity of punishment that is used as a means of preventing crime must be proportional to the danger it seeks to avert, but always within boundaries of just deserts. The determination of an appropriate punishment to serve the purpose of preventing future crime therefore involves a risk assessment. In determining the risk posed by any individual, a number of factors can be regarded as relevant, including, of course, the seriousness of the crime for which the offender is accused, his history of offending and, I submit, his own beliefs as to the wrongfulness of his actions. Inquiring into the offender's attitude toward his offense—whether it is one of defiance, indifference, or remorse—therefore is morally justifiable because it has a significant bearing on the assessment of the risk he poses to society. I hasten to add that, pursuant to the restoration of trust analysis, this kind of utilitarian risk assessment is always within the limits of deservedness and that, as a result, any sentence imposed that abides by these limitations, regardless of the risk presented by the offender, is necessarily a deserved sentence.

Therefore, what is morally objectionable to liberal jurisprudence is not the presence or absence of the offender's remorse as a factor in sentencing but rather the possibility of government using the criminal sanction as a means of coercing an individual into adopting an attitude that contradicts his values and beliefs. The restoration of trust approach is fully in accord with this moral abhorrence of coerced apologies, but rather than abandoning the prospect of encouraging genuine apologies the restoration of trust approach provides the means by which genuine apologies are encouraged and the possibility of coerced and false apologies are minimized. Unlike Bennett's use of Braithwaite's conception of restorative justice as a nonpunitive diversionary alternative,[91] the restoration of trust approach does not automatically reward offenders who apologize by granting them immunity from punishment. The maintenance of societal-level trust requires adherence to minimal and maximum standards of sentencing severity that cannot be avoided by the offering of an apology. Furthermore, the restoration of trust approach offers the possibility of decreased punitivity only to those whose apology is regarded as genuine by the close scrutiny of the victim. Accordingly, the utterance of a false apology offers little, if any advantage. This approach, therefore, offers even more protection against the possibility of an innocent person being induced to offer an apology than the current practice of plea bargaining that does not seek, much less require, the victim's assessment of the sincerity of the apology.

Theory Modification and Testing

The conceptualization of restorative justice as a radically new criminal justice "paradigm," intended to open our minds to new possibilities, ironically became an intellectual straitjacket that constrained scholars to wrestle with contradictions and rationalize preordained conclusions.[92] If, however, it is more modestly regarded as a new and unique criminal justice *goal*, restorative justice becomes open to both theoretical and programmatic development through rational analysis and empirical testing. The restorative justice goal of *repairing the harm of crime* can be used as a yardstick, not only for sentencing practices, but for every criminal justice practice from policing to corrections. In each case, the question is not whether a practice conforms to a given paradigm, but whether it best achieves the goal of repairing the harm of crime to victims, to communities, and to offenders.

A sentencing theory is not a set of *a priori* mandates. Instead, it is a means of expressing our shared, intuitive sense of justice as principles that may be of use in resolving specific problems in a rational manner. When the strict application of these principles leads to a conclusion that contradicts the sense of justice on which the theory is based, it is the theory, and not the sense of justice that requires modification. In the case of the encouragement of apology, we have seen how the strict application of just deserts theory may lead to the remarkable conclusion that the state, for fear of offering any benefits to offenders who sincerely apologize for their criminal actions, can insist only on a ritualistic exercise without requiring sincerity.[93] A sentencing theory that would dictate such a conclusion should not compel us to abandon our intuitive sense of justice because sentencing theories are themselves rational derivatives of our sense of justice. Because the sense of justice demands both that offenders get what they deserve and that those who show remorse for their misconduct be treated differently from those who do not, the inability of just deserts theory to reconcile these goals should not be taken as a critique of the use of apology as a factor in sentencing, but instead as a critique of just deserts theory. The restoration of trust approach is based on the same intuitive justice response as just deserts theory, and, in fact, incorporates the notion of just deserts as a component of trust. However, it also recognizes that a punitive response to offending dictated by just deserts is not the *only* mechanism for restoring trust. In fact, without apology, the imposition of punishment has little effect on the restoration of trust.

In the end, the restoration of trust approach insists that our claims about the needs of victims and community members have a factual foundation. In developing a restorative criminal justice system, rather than assuming or imposing our personal ideological, religious or ethical values on persons affected by crime, we must find out from victims and members of the community what they believe to be necessary to restore trust in the offender and in society in the aftermath of crime. It is on the foundation of these demands that we hope to devise criminal justice sanctions that promote genuine healing and genuine reintegration. The theoretical claims of restorative justice are thereby linked to empirical findings. The major theoretical premise is this: Whatever operates to restore trust in the offender and in society also operates to restore the victim's material and emotional well-being, to promote the safety of the community, and to increase the likelihood of successful reintegration of the offender. The empirical challenge is thus to quantify and to test these claims, to the end that sentencing policy will adopt those policies and practices that work best, without any ideological preconceptions.

Notes

[1] von Hirsch, "Proportionate Sentencing: A Desert Perspective," pp. 118-119.

[2] Moore, "The Moral Worth of Retributionism."

[3] Duff, *Crime and Punishment, cited in* Bilz & Darley, "What's Wrong with Harmless Theories of Punishment?" p. 1222.

[4] Finnis, *Natural Law and Natural Rights*, pp. 263-634.

[5] Duff, "Restorative Punishment and Punitive Restoration," p. 97.

[6] von Hirsch, *Doing Justice; Censure and Sanctions.*

[7] von Hirsch, *Censure and Sanctions,* p. 13

[8] *Id.* p. 13-14

[9] Tonry, *Malign Neglect*, discussed in Chapter 11, *infra.*

[10] Frase, "Limiting Retributionism;" Morris, *The Future of Imprisonment.*

[11] von Hirsch, *Censure and Sanctions,* pp. 55-56
[12] Shaw & McKay, *Juvenile Delinquency and Urban Areas.*
[13] See Chapter 12, *infra.*
[14] See Chapter 5, *infra.*
[15] Dimock, Retributionism and Trust, pp. 51-54.
[16] See Chapter 6, *infra.*
[17] Dimock, *supra,* p. 55.
[18] *I.e.,* Duff, *Punishment, Communication and Community,* von Hirsch, *Censure and Sanction.*
[19] Duff, *Trials and Punishments,* p. 251.
[20] von Hirsch, *Censure and Sanctions,* p. 13.
[21] Fukayama, *Trust,* p. 7.
[22] Becker, *Outsiders.*
[23] Fletcher, *Rethinking Criminal Law*; Bagaric, *Punishment and Sentencing: A Rational Approach.* Other retribution theorists modify this rigorous analysis by regarding the absence of prior criminal involvement as relevant to the issue of "mistake" or immaturity of judgment, and therefore would give a presumptive discount to first offenders, which of course would no longer apply to repeat offenders. Wasik & von Hirsch, "Section 29 Revisited."
[24] See Chapter 12, *infra.*
[25] Van Ness, "New Wine and Old Wineskins," p. 265
[26] Ashworth, "Criminal Justice and Deserved Sentences," p. 352
[27] Bibas & Bierschbach, "Integrating Remorse and Apology Into Criminal Procedure; "Bilz & Darley, "What's Wrong With Harmless Theories of Punishment;" London, "The Restoration of Trust."
[28] Cavadino & Dignan, "Reparation, Retribution and Rights," pp. 244-247
[29] See Chapter 12, *infra.*
[30] McCold, "Toward a Holistic Vision of Restorative Juvenile Justice;" Braithwaite, "Restorative Justice and De-Professionalization;" Robinson, *supra,* p. 388.
[31] See Zehr, *The Little Book of Restorative Justice,* pp. 54-57; Braithwaite, "Restorative Justice and De-Professionalization, p. 29.
[32] Jim Dignan refers to this as a "twin-track" approach rather than an integration of restorative justice and convention strategies. Dignan, "Towards a Systematic Model of Restorative Justice," pp. 145-146.
[33] Bilz & Darley, "What's Wrong With Harmless Theories," p. 1250.
[34] Ashworth, "Criminal Justice and Deserved Sentences," p. 352
[35] Mika, *et al.* "Listening to Victims," p. 40.
[36] Colson, Towards an Understanding of the Origins of Crime.
[37] Zehr, *Changing Lenses,* p. 172.
[38] Buruma, "Doubts on the Upsurge of the Victim's Role in Criminal Law, " p. 2.
[39] Mika, *et al.,* "Listening to Victims," p.35.
[40] *Id.,* p. 33.
[41] *Id.*
[42] *Id.*
[43] *Id.*
[44] *Id.*
[45] *Id.,* p. 34.

[46] *Id.*

[47] *Id.*

[48] *Id.*

[49] *Id.*, p. 34.

[50] See Chapter 4, *supra.*

[51] See Chapter 6, *supra.*

[52] Jacoby, *Wild Justice*, p. 1.

[53] See pp. 73-77, *infra.*

[54] Tunick, *Punishment: Theory and Practice,* p. 88.

[55] Solomon, *A Passion for Justice*, p. 257.

[56] Michalowski, *Order, Law and Crime*, pp. 53-54.

[57] Gibbs, "The Death Penalty: Retribution and Penal Policy," p. 294; von Hirsch, *Doing Justice*, p. 52.

[58] Solomon, *supra,* p. 42.

[59] Haas, "The Triumph of Vengeance over Retribution, " p. 133. This character of proportionality, fairness and equity that distinguishes retribution as a "just"—and not merely a personal, instinctual—response to wrongdoing is emphasized by many contemporary scholars who prefer to use the term "just deserts" when referring to punishment within the law, thereby avoiding any negative connotations that arise from equating retribution with vengeance. See von Hirsch, *Doing Justice*, pp. 45-56.

[60] Dimock, *Retributism and Trust*, p. 51.

[61] Jacoby, *Wild Justice.*

[62] Interestingly, these are also the circumstances in which unconditional forgiveness becomes a morally justifiable option: a paradox well understood by Nietzsche.

[63] Tunick, *supra*, p. 62.

[64] Van Ness & Strong, *supra*, p. 38.

[65] McCold, "Toward a Holistic Vision of Restorative Juvenile Justice," p. 361.

[66] Van Dyke, "Ideological Trends Within the Victims' Movement," p. 126.

[67] Clear, *Harm in American Penology*, p. 132.

[68] Walgrave, "Has Restorative Justice Appropriately Responded to Retribution theory and Impulses?," p. 49.

[69] Clear, *supra*, p. 131.

[70] *See, e.g.* Morris, "Guilt and Punishment," p. 310.

[71] See Chapter 6, *infra.*

[72] Duff, *Punishment, Communication and Community*, pp. 60-62.

[73] Ashworth, "Is Restorative Justice the Way Forward," pp. 169-171.

[74] See Chapter 4, *supra.*

[75] Braithwaite, *Crime, Shame and Reintegration.*

[76] Other, more "objective" sentencing factors would be legislatively pre-determined. These would include factors already specified in the penal code, such as degree of intentionality and harmfulness of the conduct that constitute elements of the offense itself and the offender's criminal history of convictions, but would also include other objective factors such as whether the victim was a police officer or other public official, the use of a prohibited weapon, whether the offense was committed while the offender was on bail, probation or parole;

and whether the offender the offense was part of a planned or organized criminal activity.

[77] Boyes-Watson, "What Are the Implications of the Growing State Involvement in Restorative Justice?" p. 215.

[78] Fattah, "Gearing Justice Action to Victim Satisfaction," p. 17.

[79] *I.e.* McCold, "Paradigm Muddle: the Threat to Restorative Justice Posed by its Merger With Community Justice."

[80] Herman, *supra,* p. 597.

[81] *Id.,* pp. 585 and 598.

[82] *See also* Bargen, "Kids, Cops, Courts, Conferencing and Children's Rights;" Brown, "The Use of Mediation to Resolve Criminal Cases," p. 1247; Delgado, "Goodbye to Hammurabi;" Coker, "Enhancing Autonomy," pp. 38-73.

[83] *Id.* von Hirsch, *Censure and Sanction*, pp. 82-84.

[84] *Id.* p. 83.

[85] Bennett, "Taking the Sincerity out of Saying Sorry," p. 130.

[86] *Id.,* p. 132.

[87] *Id.,* p. 136.

[88] *Id.*

[89] *Id.*

[90] von Hirsch, *Censure and Sanctions*, p. 13.

[91] Bennett, *supra*, p. 129.

[92] See Chapter 12, *infra.*

[93] Bennett, *supra, p.* 132.

9

The Role of the Community

In the preceding chapters, we have examined the importance of victim-offender dialogues in devising sentencing recommendations centered on the goal of restoring trust. But such dialogues are certainly not limited to the participation of the victim and the offender: The option of involving other participants—including members of the community affected by the offense—is available to all restorative justice programs. Some restorative justice advocates, however, have voiced concern that the purity of the original conception of restorative justice would be compromised by incorporating community justice into the restorative justice paradigm, thus interjecting a concern for public safety and demands for law enforcement in an otherwise personal encounter between a victim and offender.[1] Others have cautioned against the parochial and exclusionary quality of community judgments. [2]

In the restorative justice model that I propose, however, the incorporation of community justice does not present a conceptual dilemma because this model is designed to accommodate both individual and societal-level interests. Within this model, the involvement of community representatives is a desirable option whenever it is believed to be useful to the process of restoration, both for the victim and for the offender. For the victim, restoring his or her relation to the community is of fundamental importance in achieving emotional and psychological repair.[3] Thus, the presence of community members in victim-offender negotiations, by demonstrating to the victim that the crime is not merely his or her private misfortune but is an offense to all, is an expression of community solidarity that may aid the victim's psychological and emotional recovery.

For the offender, the participation of community members is important in devising sentencing recommendations that constitute both a criminal sanction and a plan for reintegration. By bringing to the table the persons indirectly involved in the incident, including community members and the offender's network of support, solutions can be devised to prevent future offending, to resolve conflicts, and to establish community peace. These types of proactive solutions do not exceed the scope of actions required for restoration. As we have seen, the commission of a crime necessitates more than material compensation, it requires the restoration of trust. To that end, the victim and members of the community must obtain assurances that the offender's criminal conduct will not continue in the future. To gain such assurances, mere promises to reform are insufficient. A specific, enforceable plan of action must be devised, one that preferably involves the offender and the victim, together with their supporters and mutually trusted persons to act as intermediaries and mentors. Far from impairing the goals of restoration, the involvement of others as resources, monitors, intermediaries, and mentors in an agreement designed to promote the safety and well-being of the victim and the community can be vital to the process of restoration.

The Role of Community in Promoting the Growth of Trust

The importance of involving community members in the process of restoring trust cannot be adequately appreciated unless the role of the community in fostering reciprocal relations of trust is fully recognized. The notion of "trust" itself is a relational concept, and the restoration of trust can be achieved only when the interpersonal conditions that promote or impair the development of trust are addressed in fashioning restorative sentencing recommendations. Before turning to some of the issues associated with the involvement of community members in the criminal justice process, let us explore how social science theorists from a diversity of perspectives have come to understand the relation between community and the growth of trust.

The life of a human being is lived in society, and the richness and well-being of that life is dependent on the ability of its members to act cooperatively in support of their shared objectives.[4] The extent and quality of interactions will produce in its members greater or lesser amounts of "social capital" that enables further enriching contacts. A number of eminent economists have come to realize that the trust that is essential to maintaining norms of social interaction is the foundation of social capital.[5] Putnam maintained that the networks of social interaction made possible by trust enforce the norms of reciprocity and facilitate communication and cooperation. Individual acts within the web of reciprocity, he noted, are seemingly altruistic in the short term in that they benefit others at a cost to the individual, but have a long-term beneficial effect on the individual by benefiting the group as whole and thereby benefiting the social life of each of its participants.[6] Norms of reciprocity are most often enforced on a personal, informal level, but economists have also noted that formal institutions of law enforcement provide an integral backup to personal-level trust and thereby increase the overall accumulation of social capital.[7]

Cooperative behavior, especially outside the circle of intimate family members, involves a certain degree of risk. An individual's willingness to engage in these risky ventures, which are essential to the economic well-being of the group, therefore requires trust. The ability to be trusted by others is equivalent to the ability to enter into a variety of relations that would otherwise be denied to an untrusted person. In this way, the acquisition of trust represents a great economic advantage. It has a value that arises from the person's network of interactions, and that enables the expansion of those interactions. It is like money in the bank: a resource available for the generation of wealth, and therefore rightfully regarded as a real form of "capital." Social capital is the product of a dense network of relations where norms of reciprocity are habitually respected. We can rely on people who are enmeshed in this network—we can trust such people—and it is only by virtue of their involvement in a social network that we can assess their trustworthiness.

Because we are social creatures, the ability to enter into social and economic relations on which our material and emotional well-being depends is closely related to the social capital we have acquired. This social capital, in turn, is very much a function of the observance of the norms of reciprocity in our ever-expanding network of social relations. Therefore, trustworthiness is not a quality of character that can be ascertained merely from an examination of a person's behavior; we must also examine the quality and density of his or her relations to others. In this respect, trustworthiness is fundamentally a social characteristic that arises from the process of socialization. While successful cooperative behavior within the family is strongly—perhaps genetically—rooted in bonds of protectiveness, loyalty, and dependence, it is only through the process of socialization that the norms of reciprocity with others outside the family become internalized. In a very real sense, *reciprocity is developed in community*, and the social capital that is achieved by successful socialization is not just an asset to the individual, but an asset of the entire community. As is well known, however, some communities are much better at providing the conditions for the acquisition of social capital than others. Those that function as an effective environment for the socialization of its members are blessed with a population of citizens that can conduct their affairs under the assumption that the norms of reciprocity will be observed. But in those communities that provide an inadequate environment for socialization, members must endure the ever-present fear of crime, even though they are subject to the same laws and to similar, if not harsher, treatment of offenders through the formal criminal justice system.

The communal impact on socialization and on resulting differences in rates of offending has been major concern of contemporary criminology. Why, indeed, is it that some areas are more afflicted by crime than others? Conventional wisdom would assume that the reason has to do with the presence or absence of poverty. Yet while it is undoubtedly true that there is a linkage between crime and poverty, criminologists have long noted that the fact of economic need, in itself, does not adequately explain why there is a higher crime rate in poorer areas. In the United States, for example, crime has always been greatest in the poorest areas but, ironically, the residents of these communities have almost always come from countries where they were even poorer and yet had far less crime. Newly arrived immigrant groups that initially settled in American urban slums typically experienced greater crime than in their home country from whose poverty they were escaping. What they found in the United States, in fact, were more resources and greater opportunities for advancement, but also a loss of control over their sons and daughters. Traditional patterns of socialization were disrupted in this "new world." The intense social cohesion of the village was replaced by the fragmentation, isolation, and alienation found in a teeming metropolis of transient strangers. A succession of sociological criminologists—from the earliest to the latest—have recognized that the relation between poverty and crime has more to do with the effect of poverty on the strength of social bonds than on a person's "need" to violate the law in order to satisfy their desires. The notion of a person being motivated to commit a crime because of his or her poverty, while possibly accounting for certain thefts under the direst of circumstances, is woefully inadequate in explaining the vast majority of crimes and abuses that afflict the peace and security of inner-city residents. Rather, it is the absence of effective social networks—the absence of dense and powerful bonds of obligation, supervision, accountability, and the social consequences for failing to live up to expectations—that predictably gives rise to higher crime rates both in American inner cities and in inner cities throughout the world. This analysis of the relation between crime and the inadequacy of community resources for socialization has been variously described by criminologists under the heading of "anomie theory,"[8] "social disorganization theory,"[9] "social control theory,"[10] and "collective efficacy theory."[11] What all these theories have in common is the thesis that crime essentially represents a failure of socialization, and that the socialization of individuals is not merely a family matter but necessarily involves the larger community. Somehow, each new member of society who enters the world as a supremely egotistical infant, for whom other humans exist merely as means to satisfy his or her desires, must be reshaped into a self-controlled and responsible adult who conforms to norms of conduct and who respects the rights of others. The formation of such a socialized being is necessarily a communal achievement.

Regardless of a person's social and economic status, it is always tempting to have more—more money, more power, more pleasure—and it therefore is not surprising that people will be motivated to pursue these ends, even if it involves harm to others, as long as there are no adverse consequences in doing so. But we do not see around us a population of egotistical pleasure and power seekers, heedless of their effect on others. Instead, what we typically see is a multitude of socialized beings who exercise self-control and can reasonably be expected to refrain from violent or harmful conduct toward us. We see "socialized beings" with whom we can interact without incapacitating fear. They are, in other words, people we can *trust*.

How does this come about? In the eighteenth century, Beccaria, the first notable criminologist of the Enlightenment, argued that it was the fear of punishment by law that constrained our criminal tendencies.[12] The commission of a crime, in his view, was the result of a rational calculation in which the prospective rewards of the crime were weighed against its likely adverse consequences. The answer to crime, accordingly, was to adopt and publish laws clearly specifying the behavior that would constitute a criminal offense and its associated punishment, coupled with efficient and consistent enforcement. In this way, punishment was not simply the "wages of sin" required by morality, but a utilitarian means of crime prevention through *deterrence*. Yet, upon reflection, this can be only part of story of crime prevention, and rather a small part at that. Life as we know it would be intolerable if the only thing holding people back from robbing us, assaulting us, raping us, or killing us was a concern that they might be caught by the police and eventually punished. This is not to say that a socialized human being conforms to the norms of society merely out of principal. Rather, it is to say that the kinds of consequences that do restrain us from crime are not limited to the threat of legal punishment, and must also include social consequences. Indeed, the punitive "sting" of legal punishment is felt most keenly when it engenders social consequences to the offender such as the potential loss of community standing; the loss of esteem from his friends, relatives, and coworkers; and the loss of his job, income, property, and future prospects. Therefore, even if we were to adopt the logic of deterrence theory, we would acknowledge that deterrence works best when the threat of official sanctions is coupled with the threat of social sanctions and the prospect of social losses. Indeed, deterrence works effectively even in the absence of any formal legal system. Communities exist throughout the world, and have existed since time immemorial, in what we would describe as "undeveloped areas" where there is little or no recourse to a formal system of law enforcement and yet where crime is adequately controlled from within. These places are among the poorest in the world in material terms, yet they are where a dense fabric of social relations ensures that every child is supervised and subject to appropriate discipline, and where the prospect of social disapproval or loss of status is a powerful inducement to conform to the communal norms of reciprocity.

Durkheim, one of the earliest sociologists to address the causes of crime, noted that widespread adherence to norms of behavior is unlikely to occur in areas marked by what he called "anomie," a rapid, sometimes chaotic, change that disrupts traditional social patterns. The concept of social disruption became the central focus of the pioneering work of U.S. criminologists Shaw and McKay in the early twentieth century. Their work, in identifying "social disorganization" as the primary social factor influencing crime rates in U.S. cities, was a welcome antidote to the influence of "biological trait theories" of crime that predominated in the nineteenth century. According to the trait theories, the alarming increase in crime in U.S. cities was attributable to the influx of "criminal types" many of whom were newly arrived immigrants from Ireland, Italy, and Eastern Europe. Of course, these theorists were aware of the fact that there was less crime in the immigrants' home countries, but they argued that the United States' open invitation to the "wretched refuse" of European nations resulted in an influx of the dregs of European society. Curiously, however, within a few generations of life in the United States, these same immigrant groups that were thought to be biologically predisposed to crime were able to escape the urban slums, elevate themselves economically, and settle down to conventional, law-abiding lives. The Irish, for example, who had been depicted in nineteenth-century political cartoons as semi-human misfits and miscreants now had become solidly middle class and, in a few decades, had become a major influence in urban politics and law enforcement. What happened? Their genes remained the same, but their social circumstances had radically changed as they became assimilated into U.S. society. What Shaw and MacKay found in their analysis of crime patterns in Chicago was that the social instability of the "transitional zones"—the inner cities areas in which immigrants initially resided—was the primary culprit in the search for the causes of crime rather than any personal racial or ethnic characteristic of the residents. Furthermore, it wasn't poverty per se that caused crime, but the social conditions of inner-city slums, brought about by poverty and other factors, that mattered. The transience and mobility of tenants living in overcrowded neighborhoods made it impossible to form stable networks of communication, supervision, and accountability. Once settled into stable ethnic neighborhoods around the periphery of these urban transitional zones, communal ties were quickly reestablished and became powerful agencies of socialization. [13] This was the experience for every ethnic group that had to pass through one of the United States' inner cities, all except those for whom the doors of opportunity were closed by racial prejudice. For millions of people of color, entrapped in a U.S. inner city by barriers of discrimination, the chaotic conditions of inner-city life and its inevitable association with crime became an enduring legacy of prejudice.

The influence of the community on crime was brought to a more personal level in Hirschi's theory of "social control."[14] Hirschi's analysis is particular apt in understanding the role of social control in the process of acquiring trust. In addition to the overt forms of social control experienced in the reactions of family, friends, and neighbors who are empowered to reward us by their approval and punish us by their rejection, ridicule, or approbation, every community member has (to a greater or lesser degree) a material and psychological investment in a way of life that would be jeopardized by their misconduct. The socialization process draws us ever deeper into the achievement of social and material advantages—in education, career, marriage, and community life—that we have attained through years of effort and are fearful of forfeiting. At the same time, we "buy into" the prospect of future gains for which we are willing to make great sacrifices and that justify forsaking the prospect of immediate gratification. Weighed against the loss of all that we have attained and the prospect of a better life, any gains that might be achieved by violating the law seem trivial to a person who is sufficiently invested in a "normal" life.

In the context of assessing the risk of forfeiting a good life, the effects of social disorganization, discrimination, and poverty on rates of offending become clear. Children raised in socially disorganized communities have the keen disadvantage of lacking adequate supervision and sources of accountability once they are beyond the orbit of the immediate family. Just as important, those who grow up in poverty and endure the indignity of discrimination often lack a belief in their future possibilities that is strong enough to deter them from spoiling their chances for a better life by the commission of a crime. Without such a powerful inducement to restrain themselves from harmful conduct and to defer gratification, it is little wonder that many of them engage in risky behavior that the rest of us would find "unthinkable": *They just don't seem to care.* We have all encountered people in our lives who seem oblivious to the consequences of their actions, both to others and to themselves. We ask ourselves: Don't they know they could get into trouble? Don't they care?

But that is just the point: Yes, they *do* know that they might get into trouble—and no, they *don't* care very much if they do, because they have a much different assessment of the magnitude of the trouble that would occur if they were caught. The trouble that you and I would do everything in our power to avoid is not so much a fear of the punishment that might result from being arrested but the impact of the arrest itself, not only on what we have already attained in life but also on our future prospects for a better life. For young people who do not believe in such a future for themselves, the risks involved in offending are far less consequential than for a person directed toward what he or she regards as an achievable goal. Tragically, for many young people in U.S. inner cities, the belief in a future life of affluence by the application of hard work, self-control, and the deferral of gratification is subverted by the daily reality of a life inured to poverty and second-class citizenship. The relationship between poverty and crime, from this analysis, is not about a compulsion to commit crime due to economic need, but rather the destructive effect of poverty on a person's motivation to stay out of trouble.

Still, the motivational discouragement of poverty can be counteracted by powerful bonds to others, especially to the family. Even if surrounded by constant reminders of second-class citizenship in this society, a young person may nevertheless absorb the rules of reciprocity by virtue of the strength of his or her association with others in the community. It is through a close network of associations that they will learn to care about their impact on others. Therefore, in the process of socialization, the density and quality of a person's "social bonds"—those of attachment, commitment, involvement, and belief [15]—are crucially important. A person enmeshed in such a network of relations is a person who can be relied on to observe the norms of reciprocity.

Socialization, then, arises *in community*. And the measure of a community's ability to responsibly socialize each new generation of young people is its "collective efficacy." A rich network of associations is necessary for successful socialization, but the mere density of relations alone is not sufficient to engender positive relations of trust. One of the hallmarks of a group's collective efficacy is the willingness of members to intervene to enforce the rules of reciprocity, a characteristic that depends on conditions of mutual trust. It is the linkage between mutual trust and the willingness to intervene for the common good that defines the neighborhood context of collective efficacy.[16] As the Irish philosopher Lecky noted over a century ago, all who are within the "expanding circle" of people in a community exceed their selfish concerns and exercise moral authority for the benefit of all.[17] The efficacy of a group is more than simply that group members share certain values. The effectiveness of maintaining those values comes about by a commitment to enforcing them. Theirs is a *mutual trust* in that it applies not just to people about whom they have specific information, but to everyone within the moral community. It is therefore also a *presumptive trust* that is not initially earned, but which can be severely damaged by a failure to reciprocate, since it rests on the premise that others will not let us down.[18] As in the case of the monkey who, upon failing to reciprocate his grooming "suddenly finds himself without groomers,"[19] in a community manifesting collective efficacy, the identity of a cheater becomes the stuff of widespread gossip. He instantly loses the social capital necessary to enjoy all the benefits of life in society, and becomes the object of derision, ostracism, and social humiliation. It is the communal response to the violations of reciprocity that ultimately deters cheating because, unless that were the case, a cheater could always take advantage of a succession of "suckers" who would give him the advantage of the presumption of reciprocity. Furthermore, unless the intentional violation of the expectations of reciprocity invited a communal response, the continued presumption of reciprocity would exist only for those individuals strong enough to retaliate effectively. There would be no law of the group—only individual relations of power. To permit the extraordinary benefits of communal trust, a communal response against those who violate the presumption of adherence to norms of reciprocity is recognized as a civic duty.

The criminal justice system, in fact, can be regarded as one such communal response to the violation of norms of reciprocity. Within the conventional criminal justice system, the community participates solely through the efforts of the public prosecutor, but in envisioning a criminal justice system oriented toward the larger goal of restoring trust in the offender and in society, the involvement of the community must be seen in a more expansive context. Given the central importance of social relations on the acquisition of trust, it would be unthinkable for a criminal justice system dedicated to the restoration of trust *not* to involve community members in devising restorative sentencing recommendations. As we have seen, the imposition of a punitive sanction as the consequence of wrongdoing, although necessary in many cases, is an inadequate solution to the problem of restoring trust that has been damaged by a crime.[20] For offenders whose social bonds were severed by the commission of the crime, the restoration of trust is a prerequisite to successful readmittance into the community. Therefore, the opinions of members of the community impacted by that offense should be solicited to find out what actions or changes in the offender they would consider to be necessary to restore their trust in this person.

Perhaps more importantly, for those offenders whose criminality can be attributed to the inadequacy of social bonds, the task of restoring trust will necessarily involve both strengthening and expanding the offender's social network. This may be uncharted territory for a criminal justice system that is habituated to the processing of cases from arrest to punishment, but it is one that must occur if we seek a better way toward achieving justice for victims, for offenders, and for the larger community.

Reconciling Restorative Justice with Community Justice

In fashioning a role for community members in the restorative justice process, we must at the outset acknowledge a number of problems inherent in the conception of community involvement. First, it is by no means clear what is meant by the "community" that is affected by a particular offense.[21] What are the community's boundaries: a city, a neighborhood, a block? In using the term "community," we assume a degree of cohesion that may not exist because, within an area, there may be many subgroups coincident with ethnic, social, and class divisions.[22] Second, even if community boundaries are satisfactorily defined, there is the problem of representation. How are these representatives to be determined? How are we to know that they are truly representative?[23] In the conventional criminal justice system, the public is represented by a prosecutor whose position is attained through the political process and who is ultimately accountable to the electorate. By contrast, the process of selecting community representatives is without any public mandate or public accountability. They certainly cannot be representative of everyone; they can represent only a particular subgroup. But which one? It is unlikely that these community representatives will be chosen from the offender's peers. On the contrary, it can be expected that the community representatives will be drawn from the more well-established and well-connected segments of the population.

This raises a third concern: the potential "tyranny" of the status quo. It is almost always to the benefit of the community that interpersonal conflicts be resolved and the status quo be restored, but there is a danger in assuming that the preservation of the status quo is an optimal outcome.[24] Community representatives are likely to consist of members of the majority and therefore would be inclined to favor members of their own social, ethnic, or racial class. Furthermore, it is naïve to assume that community justice is more peaceful and forgiving than conventional justice: Communities can also be punitive and intolerant[25] and community justice may facilitate the abuse of power and the denial of due process.[26] It may tend toward conservative stereotyping of expected behavior.[27] While the community may offer solutions to a problem, it may indeed also be the source of the problem.[28] This is especially problematic in the case of domestic violence cases in which the community may urge parties to reconcile, thereby perpetuating inequalities and old patterns of abuse.[29]

Finally, in contrast to the advantages claimed for "deprofessionalized justice," there are legitimate concerns that community justice can deliver a higher quality of justice than that available under the conventional system. Unlike criminal justice professionals, community representatives are untrained in the law, are subject to no standards of performance, and are accountable to no reviewing authority. Far from being expected to exercise their judgment in a neutral, disinterested manner, they are chosen to attend precisely because they are personally affected by the problem. Without legal constraints and without legal accountability, community justice may well become a law unto itself. Community representatives may be forgiving or unforgiving, tolerant or intolerant, wise or ignorant but, unless some mechanisms are devised to constrain their subjectivity, they will essentially continue to operate outside the rule of law.[30] Community justice without constraints becomes not an alternative form of law, but the absence of law.[31]

As a result, while there are considerable advantages to engaging the help of community members, their influence is not necessarily benign or, indeed, restorative. One solution that can be offered to the problems associated with community justice—lack of definition, lack of legitimate representation, danger of oppression, and uncontrolled subjectivity—is to have the resulting dispositions subject to a judicial review. Although having judicial review as a backup would curtail the more egregious abuses that may occur in community forums, however, it offers no guidance to the participants of these forums. Community justice would then become an arena for unconstrained subjectivity that could affect all cases—not only the flagrant ones that are brought to the attention of the courts.

The restoration of trust approach, by incorporating both an individual and societal level of analysis, permits us to incorporate many of the valuable features of community justice while curtailing its potential for abuse. The same structure that accommodates the subjectivity of victim-offender dialogue is equally applicable to problems that arise from the participation of community members. Because the outer boundaries of sentencing severity that conform to societal-level standards of deservedness and social utility have been established by law, the focus of victim-offender encounters can be on restoring the victim's personal trust in the offender without sacrificing the values of equality, proportionality, and adherence to law. Similarly, the participation of community members can be freely undertaken as long as their discretion is confined to the scope of subjectivity that lies between the upper and lower boundaries of sentencing severity since any sentence falling within the boundaries must be a deserved sentence. As a result, just as in the case of the participation of crime victims, whether or not community members who participate in these dialogues are truly representative of the community, their sentencing recommendations may not be undeservedly harsh or undeservedly lenient. Also, as in the case of crime victims—and unlike the case of the judiciary—we do not require that the judgment of community representatives be "disinterested." In fact, it is by reason of their interest in the matter that they are qualified to engage in this kind of interpersonal dialogue, which is designed to explore and to devise a solution that is restorative *to all who are affected by the crime*. Moreover, the restoration of trust approach, in addition to securing a "zone of subjectivity" within which the parties may devise creative solutions, also requires that this very subjectivity be channeled specifically toward the goal of restoring trust under the guidance of a trained mediator. The resulting dialogue therefore is not an unstructured free-for-all, but a structured format designed to direct the parties toward restorative solutions.

Community participation in sentencing dialogues is problematic only when those dialogues are offered as a radical alternative to the conventional judicial system. In that case, it is a legitimate concern that the participants who wield sentencing power may not be truly representative of the community, that they may not be adequately trained in or accountable to the law, and that their decisions may be influenced by personal interest or, indeed, personal animus. The exercise of such power by the community is, then, hardly distinguishable from "mob rule." But when community participation in sentencing dialogues is incorporated into a process that confines the scope of subjectivity within objective boundaries of deservedness and social utility toward crime prevention, the very subjectivity that would undermine the legitimacy of community justice now becomes a valued source of creativity in devising restorative solutions.

Offenders who already are involved in a supportive network of community relations can certainly benefit from the participation of key persons involved in that network in fashioning restorative solutions. They can also serve as important intermediaries in communicating and monitoring the performance of the offender in fulfilling his obligations. Of course, many offenders lack such a supportive network and it is for such offenders that restorative dialogues can be of inestimable value in strengthening existing relations and in creating new social bonds. For these offenders, the absence of social bonds of commitment, attachment, involvement, and belief underlay their unsuccessful socialization, resulting in a life outside the network of reciprocity enjoyed by the law-abiding community.

But if these bonds are weak or broken, how can they ever be repaired? This question poses a daunting challenge to the criminal justice system, but it is only by posing such a question that we can start to fashion solutions in individual cases. This must begin by involving the right people. As Braithwaite suggests, every offender, no matter how disaffected and alienated, either has or once had someone in his life who cared for him and could be a valuable intermediary, sponsor, mentor, or resource.[32] These people would have much to contribute in devising a restorative solution and in supervising its implementation, and their participation in restorative dialogues would be invaluable. In cases where such personal relations are either insufficient or, indeed, entirely absent, community sponsors can nonetheless be solicited from religious institutions, charitable agencies, and volunteers, including those from nonprofit associations to assist ex-offenders.

Once this new type of "work group" is assembled, the creative work of the restorative justice conference may proceed. Because one of the central concerns of the restoration dialogue is how to restore trust in the offender, the participants will be directed to explore the reasons why the offender, as things stand now, cannot be trusted and what he can do about it. Clearly, the commission of the crime itself is a good reason to be distrusted. But while the crime itself can never be "undone," there are some things the offender can do to repair the resulting loss of trust:

honestly acknowledge responsibility, demonstrate remorse, agree to pay for material losses, and unhesitatingly submit to a sentence he acknowledges to be what he deserves.

Beyond that, the victim and the community may be interested in other reasons why the offender cannot be fully trusted to reenter the community: perhaps he is a loner and unattached to family; perhaps he is unskilled, uneducated, and unemployable; perhaps he has a history of irresponsibility in handling his personal affairs. Whatever the reason, the sources of distrust stemming from the insufficiency of social bonds to the community are a legitimate sources of concern. It is in devising creative and highly individualized proposals to address these concerns that restorative justice can begin to achieve its true potential.

Of course, this work will be highly subjective. Of course, it will depend on the goodwill, creativity, and dedication of the participants and availability of personal and community resources. But by having created a zone of subjectivity wide enough to accommodate such creative, individualized solutions within boundaries that respect legal standards of proportionality, equality of treatment, and deservedness in sentencing, the involvement of community members in sentencing dialogues can be a welcome contribution to the process of restoring trust in the offender and in society.

Notes

[1] McCold, "Paradigm Muddle," pp. 16-17.
[2] *See, e.g.,* Pavlich, "What Are the Dangers as Well as the Promises of Community Involvement?" pp. 176-178.
[3] Herman, "Justice From the Victim's Perspective," pp. 585 and 598.
[4] Putnam, *Making Democracy Work.*
[5] Adler & Kwon, "Social Capital: the Good, the Bad and the Ugly;" Woolcock, " Social Capital and Economic Development;" Nahapitt & Ghosal, "Social Capital, Intellectual Capital, and the Organizational Advantage;" Coleman, "Social Capital in the Creation of Human Capital;" Portes, "Social Capital: Its Origins and Applications in Modern Sociology."
[6] Putnam, *supra,* p. 172.
[7] Levi, "Social and Unsocial Capital," p. 51.
[8] Merton, "Social Structure and Anomie."
[9] Shaw & McKay, *Juvenile Delinquency and Urban Areas*
[10] Hirschi, *Causes of Delinquency,*
[11] Sampson *et al.* "Neighborhoods and Violent Crime."
[12] Beccaria, *On Crimes and Punishments.*
[13] See also modern version of social disorganization theory in Bursik, "Social Disorganization and Theories of Crime and Delinquency: Problems and Prospects."

[14] Hirschi, *supra*, pp. 16-34.

[15] *Id., pp.* 16-26.

[16] Sampson, Raudenbush, & Earls, *supra,* p. 2.

[17] Lecky, *History of European Morals.*

[18] Uslaner, *The Moral Foundations of Trust*, p. 18.

[19] Solomon, *A Passion for Justice,* p. 128

[20] See pp. 104-108, *infra.*

[21] Weisberg, "Restorative Justice and the Danger of 'Community,'" pp. 347, 353 and 358.

[22] Pavovich, *supra,* pp. 176-178.

[23] Ashworth, "Is Restorative Justice the Way Forward," pp. 169-170.

[24] Weisberg, *supra,* p. 370.

[25] Karp & Clear, "Community Justice: A Conceptual Framework," pp. 355-357.

[26] Dignan, *supra*, p. 178.

[27] Weisberg, *supra*, p. 370.

[28] Stubbs, "Domestic Violence and Women's Safety," p. 53.

[29] *Id.* p. 54 ; Crawford, "Introduction, " p. 16.

[30] Delgado, *supra*, pp. 762-770.

[31] Weisberg, *supra*, p. 370.

[32] Braithwaite, "Restorative Justice," pp. 333-334.

10
A Restorative Justice Workshop

Thus far, the discussion in this book has been largely theoretical in nature, and the time has come to try using the restoration of trust approach as a means to help us devise appropriate sanctions.

In the opening chapters, we traced the development of restorative justice from an amalgam of critiques of the prevailing system to a promising new alternative. We then examined several key problems associated with this new vision of criminal justice—the problem of private justice and the problem of punishment—that have severely limited the impact of restorative justice on mainstream criminal justice, and attempted to show how using the restoration of trust as an overarching goal can help resolve those problems. In later chapters, we explored the sociobiology of trust and its relation to reciprocity, the vital precondition for successful cooperative behavior in society, and considered the relation between the restoration of trust and the victim's emotional recovery as well as the offender's hopes for reintegration into the community. And throughout, I have attempted to show how a criminal justice system oriented toward the restoration of trust can be so devised as to accommodate both the individual and the social dimensions of trust, and to permit highly individualized sentencing within boundaries that respect societal interests in security, deserved sentencing, and adherence to the law.

But as important as they are to the fate of restorative justice as a whole, these theoretical developments are only of genuine value if they are truly useful in everyday sentencing decisions. In this regard, the concept of restoring trust must not add to the complexity of sentencing choices that already exists. Instead, by regarding the restoration of trust as an overarching goal of criminal justice policy, we seek to *simplify* the task of devising fair and effective sentences by the adoption of a basic decisional aid in asking: What must be done to restore our trust in this offender and in society?

This approach does not require the decision maker to adopt one or another ideology. It reflects the reality of sentencing decisions of judges and jurists throughout the world who prefer to maintain multiple sentencing goals, but who require a format to guide their intuitions of fairness. Once it is determined that a defendant in a criminal case has violated the law as defined in the criminal code, and once the parameters of sentencing are identified for that particular crime under the terms of the code (i.e., those outer boundaries of severity necessary to preserve trust in society), the restoration of trust analysis provides a basic "rule of thumb" to guide the process of selecting an appropriate sanction. As the defendant (who now can accurately be called the "offender") appears before the judge at sentencing or before the victim at a restorative justice conference the question that must be asked is: What must be done to restore trust in this person?

The focus of this inquiry is different from, but encompasses the assortment of questions that can be derived from conventional sentencing theory: What can we do to deter the defendant from future crime? How long does he need to be incapacitated? What does he need to do to address the problems that contributed to his becoming an offender? Given the facts of this case, what punishment does he deserve? Rather than rejecting any of these concerns, the restoration of trust analysis incorporates them by subsuming each to an overall goal. Adopting this decisional rule does not compel the decision makers to compromise their values or minimize their demands. Rather, it focuses their attention on a goal that encompasses their values and demands. Moreover, this process of focusing on a core goal is guided by the intuitive capacity to seek out sources of distrust, a capacity that is an essential component to our nature as social beings. It therefore can operate as a useful guide for both trained jurists and ordinary participants at restorative justice conferences.

But does the restoration of trust approach *really* offer a practical guide to sentencing decisions? Rather than argue the point, let's see how the application of this approach can help foster creative and restorative sentencing choices in matters that are likely to come before a court. In this chapter, I will present a series of short scenarios of familiar criminal problems. At the end of each scenario, there will be a number of questions for readers to ponder concerning how that case would be handled by the conventional criminal justice system and by several competing alternatives that include the proposed restoration of trust model. I have used these and other scenarios while teaching my courses on sentencing and restorative justice and can attest to the fact that, although individual responses varied, those students who truly plunged into the project were almost always rewarded with new insights into their decision-making process. There are, of course, no right or wrong answers to these problems but, by working through the problems, it is possible to gain a greater appreciation of the effect of differing perspectives on sentencing choices. In so doing, readers will be in a better position to assess whether the adoption of the restoration of trust as an all-encompassing goal is, as I have claimed, a practical, intuitive guide to decision making and a useful means of reconciling competing goals, or whether it is just another well-intentioned but amorphous "New Age" ideal. And further, readers will be able to evaluate whether the outcomes achieved by the application of this approach represent a more comprehensive and just solution to the problems presented than those that would likely result from conventional practices.

On the first day of each class, I distribute a set of scenarios to be considered as well as a standard form of agreement that can be used for both conventional plea bargaining exercises and for restorative justice conferences in order to record the names of the participants and the results of their deliberations. Figure 10.1. The participants decide who shall play one of the various roles specified in the scenarios (prosecutor, defense attorney, defendant, defendant's parents or other family members, victim, store owner, and block association member) as well as a facilitator for the restorative justice conference. The key to the usefulness of this exercise is to make sure that the participants really play the role they are assigned—to try to see things as their character would in that situation. I've found it beneficial to also include a group leader whose job it is to assign tasks and record a summary of the discussions, but who otherwise does not participate in the substance of the discussions. Readers too are encouraged to consider the following scenarios and make note of sentencing options that would likely emerge when the same matter is analyzed from the point of view of different participants.

* * *

Before proceeding to the role-playing scenarios below, participants need to agree on a simplified, standard format (or agenda) for plea bargaining and restorative justice conferencing. It will be the responsibility of the group leader to ensure that this sequence is followed and that everyone has a fair opportunity to speak and respond. Here are two suggested formats for the plea bargaining and the restorative justice alternatives:

Plea Bargaining

1. Discussion of the strengths and weaknesses of both the prosecution and defense.
2. Discussion of the sentences permissible by law for the offense charged.
3. Open discussion of issues relevant to the case.
4. Discussion and drafting of the sentencing agreement. (See Fig 10.1)

Restorative Justice Conferencing

1. Introduction by the facilitator as to the purpose of the meeting: to discuss the case, its impact on the victim and others, and the offender's response; to explore what can be done to repair the harm of the crime; and to devise a restorative solution.
2. Participants introduce themselves briefly.
3. Victim tells his or her "story" and the impact of the crime, followed by similar accounts of others affected by crime.
4. Response from the offender.
5. Open discussion of the causes of the crime, the offender's background, his criminal history, and other topics relevant to the case.
6. Discussion of what can be done to repair the harm of the crime.
7. Drafting of the sentencing agreement.

The results of the deliberations for all cases will be recorded in a form of agreement that identifies the participants and specifies the results.

Figure 10.1. Restorative Justice Workshop Agreement Format

Restorative Justice Workshop Agreement

Problem Number _____ Part _____

Group leader _____

Participants:

Role: _____   Name: _____

Role: _____   Name: _____

Role: _____   Name: _____

Role: _____   Name: _____

Agreement

The undersigned hereby agree to submit the following sentencing recommendations for judicial approval:

The parties further stipulate that, in the event this agreement is not complied with by the defendant, the following shall occur:

Signatures:

Date: _____

Problem 1. Shoplifting by a Homemaker

Michele is a suburban homemaker who stole a jar of aspirin because she had a "splitting headache" and was temporarily short of cash. This, she said, is her second offense. Assume that the penalties for shoplifting (second offense) range from probation only to a maximum of 6 months of imprisonment.

Part 1: Plea Bargain

Imagine the above incident in the context of a conventional plea bargaining conference in your local court.

- Determine who should attend this meeting. Assign roles.
- Summarize what occurs during the conference.
- What is the outcome?

Part 2: Restorative Justice Conference

Imagine the above incident in the context of a restorative justice conference.

- Determine who should attend this meeting. Assign roles.
- Summarize what occurs during the conference.
- What is the outcome?

(General note: After you have completed each exercise, compare your results with the discussion that follows.)

Discussion:
Sentencing recommendations through a plea-bargaining conference.

In a typical plea bargaining, the defendant will agree to plead guilty to the charges if an acceptable sentencing offer is made by the prosecutor. The plea-bargaining conference is attended by the prosecutor (who is interested in protecting the public welfare) and the attorney for the offender (who is interested in getting the best deal for the client). The judge (who is interested in fairness, legality, and efficient case management) decides whether or not to accept the plea agreement.

Within the conventional plea bargaining process, the primary motivating factor in most cases is "damage control." Rather than risk the uncertain outcome of a trial, the parties enter into plea agreements under the belief that it is in their best interest to avoid a catastrophic loss. The plea agreement is hardly ever an optimal outcome for either party and, in many cases, it is not even a desirable outcome, but it is something the parties think they can live with. Each party assesses the strengths and weaknesses of their case and that of their adversary, and applies this assessment to the range of sentences likely to be imposed by the court upon conviction. In many courts, plea bargaining is a routine task of the courtroom work group consisting of the prosecutor and the public defender, together with the judge to whom they are assigned. Over time, the members of the work group develop an ability to quickly evaluate a case in terms of the probability of conviction and to narrow their sentencing expectations to a range that represents the "going rate" for similar cases that have come before the court.

In the case of the shoplifting homemaker, the excuse she offers of having had a splitting headache would likely be ignored as legally irrelevant to the charge and, given the strength of the evidence, there would be no need to explore the motive or any underlying reason for the offense. Instead, the primary issue at hand would be whether the prosecution's sentencing offer fell within the expected going rate for this offense, given the defendant's prior history of offending. Her social status would be considered only in determining the appropriate form of punishment. Depending on her demeanor and her social circumstances, this defendant may very well receive a fine and probation while a lower-class defendant would be likely to receive some jail time or, at the least, a significant amount of community service in addition to probation. It is very unlikely that the reason for this distinction would be discussed.

Here are some examples from the role play in my college classes of sentencing recommendations achieved through plea bargaining for the scenario in Problem 1:

- Fine of $500, 2 days of community service, 6 months probation with "standard conditions" of probation: report to probation office every 2 weeks, no reoffending, urine tests.
- Suspended sentence conditioned on satisfactory completion of probation for 2 years with standard conditions of probation
- Fine of $250, 6 months probation with standard conditions.

Sentencing recommendations through a restorative justice
conference.

The restorative justice conference differs from the conventional plea-bargaining process in a number of ways. First, unlike the case of a plea bargain, in a restorative justice conference the defendant must agree *in advance* to acknowledge full responsibility and plead guilty to the charges. Note that, prior to the restorative justice conference, there may be negotiations between the prosecution and the defense concerning the charges to which the defendant might plead guilty.[1]

Because the defendant has already agreed to plead guilty, he or she cannot enter the restorative justice conference simply to "test the waters" in the hope of obtaining favorable sentencing recommendations because that would undermine the factual honesty and emotional openness sought in personal encounters between the victim and offender. Furthermore, the purpose of the conference is not simply to serve as a forum in which to fashion sentencing recommendations. Instead, the process of the victim-offender encounter itself is intended to offer a pathway toward healing and restoration. Whereas the offender's admission of culpability in a typical plea-bargaining session is put forward in the form of a conditional "proffer" by the defense attorney ("assuming we can arrive at an acceptable plea agreement, my client is prepared to stipulate that. . ."), a restorative justice conference would demand truth-telling as an indispensable first step in the process of restoring trust.

But why would any defendant give up his "bargaining lever" of insisting on a trial by admitting culpability as a condition for entering a restorative justice conference where the sentencing outcome is yet to be determined? The answer to this question will vary with the character and circumstances of the defendant. Some defendants might recognize the futility of winning and the high risk of harsh sentencing if the matter goes to trial. Other defendants, perhaps a majority, might believe that by satisfying the expectations of the victim, they will have the opportunity for greater leniency in such a conference (within the range of sentencing options permitted by law for that offense) than they could expect from a judge or jury. If only in the hope of obtaining leniency, the defendant may therefore be motivated to be factually candid to the victim (who knows the truth of the incident), empathetic of the victim's material and emotional losses, and demonstrate remorse with sufficient sincerity to convince the victim that it is genuine.

A second key difference from conventional plea bargaining is that the participants in a restorative justice conference are *not* the prosecutor, defense attorney, and judge—the familiar members of the courtroom work group who typically engage in plea bargaining on a routine basis. Instead, participants include the defendant, the victim, and other stakeholders who have an interest in the matter, under the guidance of a mediator trained in restorative justice theory and practice. In the case of the shoplifting homemaker, besides the defendant herself, we might expect to be in attendance the store owner or representative to whom the admission of guilt would be directed. Furthermore, some members of the defendant's support network should be there such as a spouse, a parent, a relative, a friend, or a member of the clergy. Having one or more of these people in attendance would help to uncover the reasons for the offense, reasons that undoubtedly go deeper than a momentary "splitting headache." The defendant cannot restore the trust of others unless the reasons for her offense are understood and addressed in the sentencing recommendations.

The following are examples from the role play exercise in my college classes of sentencing recommendations achieved through a restorative justice conference for the scenario in Problem 1:

- Two days of community service, 6 months probation with standard conditions plus psychological counseling and agreement not to enter the store.
- Suspended sentence, 2 years probation with standard conditions plus letter of apology to store owner, volunteer work of any kind at a charity of the defendant's choice for not less than 30 days.

Problem 2. Shoplifting by a Homeless Man

Randall is a homeless man who stole a jar of aspirin because, he said, he had a "splitting headache" and was temporarily short of cash. In fact, outside of panhandling, he has no source of income. This is his second offense. Assume that the penalties for shoplifting (second offense) range from probation only to a maximum of 6 months of imprisonment.

Part 1: Plea Bargain

Imagine the above incident in the context of a conventional plea bargaining conference in your local court.

- Determine who should attend this meeting. Assign roles.
- What is discussed at the conference?

• What is the outcome?

Part 2: Restorative Justice Conference

Imagine the above incident in the context of a restorative justice conference.

• Determine who should attend this meeting. Assign roles.
• What is discussed at the conference?
• What is the outcome?

Discussion:
Sentencing recommendations through a plea-bargaining conference.

Under conventional plea bargaining, the prosecutor and public defender arrive at an acceptable sentence through a process motivated by aversion to the risk of trial. Each side will factor in the probability of success or failure, together with their assessment of the "going rate" for similar offenses, and compare their result with their adversary's offer. If the offer is in line with their expectations, and if the alternate of litigation is too risky, the deal is made.

The key factor in this case is jail time. The prosecutor most likely will want this defendant off the street for a considerable period of time, and is in a good position to take a tough bargaining position. The defense attorney will be happy to take any deal to avoid the seemingly useless exercise of a trial. This is the kind of case that clutters a busy urban court's docket, and the presiding judge will be extremely unhappy if his work group cannot arrive at a "realistic" disposition.

Here are some examples from the role play in my college classes of sentencing recommendations achieved through plea bargaining for the scenario in Problem 2:

• Two months prison, 2 years probation with standard conditions.
• Four months prison, 1 year probation with standard conditions.
• Two weeks prison, 2 years probation, 40 days of community service.

Sentencing recommendations through restorative justice conferencing

Given the goal of restoring trust, there is certainly quite a bit of work to do in this case. There are multiple reasons why the defendant cannot be trusted in the community because he appears to have no viable social network or any legitimate way of making a living. Restoring trust in him will clearly require more than an apology and more than the imposition of a punishment. But what more can be done? Focusing on his apparent lack of ties to the community, we can begin by closely examining whether or not some ties do exist or have existed that can be brought to bear in the conference. Perhaps there is a family member, a relative, or a friend who could be involved; perhaps there still exists some remnant of the life the defendant lived before he became homeless. Whatever associations emerge from this analysis represent opportunities for engaging one or more individuals who could be of help in joining the discussion, in devising a restorative solution, and in monitoring the defendant's performance. If no such persons are found, a volunteer from an appropriate religious or charitable group can be solicited.

Additionally, the restorative justice conference may also involve the attendance of a social worker or a probation officer who is familiar with the range of resources available in the community to deal with the multiple issues that might arise concerning housing, medical and mental health issues, and job training. In Chapter 13, we will comment on some of the options for involving probation officers before and during these conferences. One such option is for the probation department to prepare a type of presentence report on the background and needs of the defendant, together with available community resources and suggested probation conditions for the consideration of the parties at the restorative justice conference. The mediator will also be trained to help the parties understand the report and to incorporate their final recommendations into a written document for submission to the judge.

There is no way of knowing in advance where this discussion will lead but, guided by the objective of restoring trust, the eventual outcome (which is likely to include a plan to address the reasons for the defendant's homelessness and his lack of job skills, and to strengthen whenever ties he may have to people in the community) should be far more effective in restoring trust than the kind of outcomes likely to arise in plea bargaining.

Problem 3. Theft by a Narcotics User

Victor is a longtime narcotics user who has broken into a car and stolen its radio to resell for cash in order to purchase more drugs. This is his second offense. Assume that the penalties for this offense (with one prior conviction) range from probation only to a maximum of 2 years of incarceration.

Part 1: Plea Bargain

Imagine the above incident in the context of a conventional plea-bargaining conference in your local court.

- Determine who should attend this meeting. Assign roles.
- What is discussed at the conference?
- What is the outcome?

Part 2: Restorative Justice Conference

Imagine the above incident in the context of a restorative justice conference.

- Determine who should attend this meeting. Assign roles.
- What is discussed at the conference?
- What is the outcome?

Discussion:
Sentencing recommendations through a plea-bargaining conference

In this case, in addition to the calculations of probable jail time that can be expected in the course of a plea-bargaining conference, the resulting agreement may also include the requirement for entry into a drug rehabilitation program.

Sentencing recommendations through restorative justice conferencing

As in the case of the plea-bargaining conference, the sentencing recommendations from the restorative justice conference will most likely include a rehabilitation program, but the restoration of trust approach will offer a number of key differences. First, the restorative justice conference will be attended by the defendant and may include the victim (if he or she so desires), a member of the community affected by the crime, and a member of the offender's family or other person involved in the offender's social network either past or present. As in the case of the homeless man in Problem 2, if a suitable member of the defendant's social network cannot be located, a volunteer mentor from an appropriate religious or charitable agency can be solicited to attend. Second, the restoration of trust dialogue will place the burden of admitting responsibility directly on the defendant rather than on his attorney. Furthermore, this admission of responsibility will be made directly to the victim—a neighborhood resident who is not only angered by the senseless damage to his property, but who feels personally violated by the crime and insecure about the neighborhood in which he lives. The victim, by attending the conference, seeks answers to his questions, seeks assurances of his future safety, and also seeks reparation for his losses. If a family member of the offender or a close associate within his social network attends the conference, the offender's admission of responsibility will aid his prospect for regaining trust. Finally, although the requirement for a drug rehabilitation program is a probable outcome both from plea bargaining and restorative justice conferencing, the prospect for *successful* rehabilitation will undoubtedly increase if the defendant himself is involved in devising the sentencing recommendations. This is especially so when the decision to enter a rehabilitation program is made in the course of a dialogue in which the defendant accepts responsibility for the crime, publicly acknowledges his drug dependency, and expresses a willingness to change to his family, his friends, and members of the community. This is not a guarantee of success for the rehabilitation program, of course, but its chances of success are higher than if it or a similar program had been accepted in the course of a plea bargain.

Problem 4. Robbery by a Young Man

(This case is adapted from Braithwaite.[2])

Sam, a young man in his early twenties, is arrested for robbery. He knocked down a middle-aged woman and stole her purse. During a police interview, Sam claims that he was a victim of child abuse and has hostile relations with his parents and brother. His grandparents are dead, and his kindly older sister moved out of the house years ago. He is homeless and the only nearby relative is an uncle, George, who he hasn't seen for years. He hated all his teachers (except the hockey coach), and dropped out of school. This is his first offense. Assume that state law authorizes sentencing of 6 months to 5 years of incarceration, except for cases diverted to restorative justice conference, in which sentencing is by the agreement of the victim and the offender.

Part 1: Plea Bargain

Imagine the above incident in the context of a conventional plea-bargaining conference in your local court.

- Determine who should attend this meeting. Assign roles.
- Summarize what occurs during the conference.
- What is the outcome?

Part 2: Restorative Justice Conference Without Punitive Sentencing Guidelines

Imagine the above incident in the context of a restorative justice conference.

- Determine who should attend this meeting. Assign roles.
- Summarize what occurs during the conference.
- What is the outcome?

Discussion

I have adapted Braithwaite's scenario from his important essay, *Restorative Justice and a Better Future*[3] in Problem 4 because it illustrates the differences between conventional sentencing (as in Part 1) and a nonpunitive approach to sentencing (as in Part 2). Following this discussion, in Part 3, I have expanded the options to include a form of restorative justice that would permit the imposition of punishment within legislated sentencing guidelines.

In Braithwaite's commentary, the conventional approach to sentencing would have resulted in a 6-month term of incarceration. Braithwaite went on to envision this young man's descent into a heroin habit that develops during incarceration, followed by a lifetime of crime and drug abuse "until he dies in a gutter, a death no one mourns."[4]

However, things turn out rather differently in the restorative justice alternative depicted by Braithwaite. Sam is alienated from almost all of his family (except his sister and his uncle) and he hated all his teachers. Still, the facilitator persists. "No one ever treated you ok in school?" he asks. As it turns out, there was a hockey coach who acted fairly toward Sam. The sister, Uncle George, and the hockey coach are all tracked down by the facilitator. Together with Sam, the victim, and the victim's daughter, all six assemble at the restorative justice conference. Braithwaite vividly described how the conference proceeds: from Sam's awkward explanations of his offense; to his relatives' shocked, hurt, and disappointed reactions; to the victim's recounting of her suffering; and, finally, Sam's eventual recognition of the magnitude of the harm he has caused. His sister provides the emotional turning point in Sam's transformation from defiance to remorse. Sam expresses contrition and promises to repay the losses, although he has no money now. Sam's sister offers to provide housing (which Uncle George helps to subsidize), the hockey coach offers Sam a job, and, when the conference breaks up, the victim gives Sam a tearful hug and wishes him good luck. In vivid contrast to the young man sentenced to jail for the same offense, Sam goes on to lead a (mostly) law-abiding life. The victim is compensated for her losses and begins to enjoy a sense of security, even during "long walks alone."

The contrast may be a little melodramatic, but Braithwaite aptly depicted the fundamental difference in the character and the objectives of these two different approaches to the same kind of case. The first case is a classic by-product of the assembly-line approach to case administration. The result is obtained swiftly and efficiency, but with little regard to the "collateral damage" done to the human beings affected by the crime: the victim, the offender, and the wider circle of the people who know and care for them. The restorative justice case was handled with far greater care and dedication to those affected by the crime. The process itself was restorative, and the result was restorative. In fact, the result achieved was not even a criminal disposition. Apparently, the parties had agreed to settle their differences out of court and the case pending before Sam was dismissed. Thus, it resulted in a complete restorative justice alternative to the conventional system.

But let's explore this nonpunitive alternative a bit further. We might be satisfied with the quality of justice in the case of Sam, a youthful, first-time offender, but consider: What if this was a second offense, or a third offense? What if the woman was elderly and suffered permanent injuries? What if the victim was black and the offense was racially motivated?

In each of these latter cases, the idea of diverting the matter to a nonpunitive alternative where the outcome would be limited to an apology, a plan for repayment, and perhaps some form of rehabilitation would seem at odds with many victims' conception of justice and, without justice, as we have seen, the emotional recovery of the victim is very much in doubt. It would certainly conflict with societal demands for security because, if an offender who committed a serious crime could avoid punishment by means of a restorative justice diversion, the downside risk of future crime would be unacceptably low.

Suppose, then, that we revise Braithwaite's account of the process and permit the parties to agree on an appropriate punishment. If they fail to agree, of course, the matter is referred back to the court for conventional sentencing. Given this sentencing option, could it not be argued that, as long as the victim and the offender are satisfied with the outcome, their wishes should be respected without further interference by the state?

Actually, there are a number of reasons why the diversion of serious cases such as these to a restorative justice conference would be objectionable, even if punishment were an option for the victim and offender to consider. For one thing, it is unlikely that many offenders would agree on a sentence involving a term of imprisonment if they could get the victim to waive such demands. As a result, the victim would hold the crucial power to either demand or waive the imposition of a punishment. To some, this would represent the triumph of victim empowerment. But let us recall the types of victims, first mentioned in Chapter 4, to whom we would not like to grant sentencing authority:

1. The Overly Forgiving Victim. Mr. Jones is mugged on his way home from the bank by a young man with a lengthy criminal record. At the restorative justice conference, he accepts the offender's apologies and remorse and, believing fully in the power of forgiveness, agrees to drop any demand for incarceration.

2. The Selfish Victim. Mrs. Taylor's house, along with many others on the block, is burglarized by a young man with a lengthy record, and her jewelry is stolen. At the conference, she agrees to drop demands for incarceration if her wedding ring is returned and the defendant agrees to stay away from her house.

3. The Fearful Victim. Mr. Todd's store is robbed by a gang member. He drops demands for imprisonment because he's afraid of retaliation from other gang members.

4. The Favorably Biased Victim. Mr. Reed's car is vandalized by a group of young men. He demands imprisonment—except for the son of his coworker.

5. The Negatively Biased Victim. Mrs. Fisher's car is vandalized by a group of young men. She agrees to probation for the white youths, but insists on a prison term for the two black youths in the group.[5]

As these examples illustrate, the central problem posed by granting sentencing authority to crime victims, with or without the requirement of obtaining the consent of the offender, is that the victim is motivated to pursue purely personal goals, and has no obligation to protect—or even to consider—the public good. Clearly, as in Braithwaite's story of Sam, the participation of victims and others in face-to-face encounters has the potential for yielding restorative outcomes that would be almost impossible to attain (or even imagine) in the context of conventional case administration. But the very subjectivity that makes such creative outcomes feasible renders these kinds of alternatives acceptable *only in those cases where the public interest in safety, equality of treatment, and adherence to minimum standards of deservedness in sentencing are of minimal concern.* These are exactly the kinds of cases that are eligible for restorative justice referral in the vast majority of programs today: juvenile offenders, property crimes, and petty disputes. If restorative justice is to break out of this limited niche and become an important agent for change throughout the mainstream of criminal justice practice, it must offer a responsible means of handling serious crime and addressing societal as well as individual concerns in these cases.

It was precisely to address these societal concerns while, at the same time, permitting those personally interested in a matter to pursue highly individualized, creative, and restorative solutions that the two-level approach to restorative justice, designed to protect both personal and societal trust, has been proposed. In this approach, *every* type of criminal matter can be referred to restorative justice conferencing. There, the parties and their supporters and community members can come together to fashion a plan for restoring trust in the offender to be submitted as a sentencing recommendation, but always within the upper and lower boundaries of sentencing severity that reflect societal values of safety, equality of treatment, and adherence to minimum standards of deservedness in sentencing. So, let's see how the application of this approach might work.

Part 3: Restoration of Trust Conference

Imagine the above incident in the context of a restorative justice conference focused on the *restoration of trust.* Again, assume that state law authorizes sentencing of 6 months to 5 years of incarceration, including cases referred to restorative justice conferences.

- Determine who should attend this meeting. Assign roles.
- Summarize what occurs during the conference.
- What is the outcome?

Discussion

Before examining the differences between this approach and the nonpunitive diversionary approach to restorative justice that has been considered above, I will briefly comment on its distinction from the conventional approach referred to by Braithwaite. He told us little about the process itself, but we can assume it was some form of plea bargaining by the professionals—the prosecutor and the defense attorney—with little if any input from the victim (indeed, in many jurisdictions, the victim may not even have been made aware of any attempts to settle the case until long afterward), and without the personal appearance of anyone at all other than the two attorneys. Further recall that, in Braithwaite's example, the young man received a 6-month jail sentence (the minimum) during which time he developed a drug habit. Eventually, he went on to lead a life of crime and drug abuse that terminated in an early death. By contrast, the restorative justice conference involving Braithwaite's Sam brought to the table not only Sam and his victim, but also the victim's daughter and, after a concerted effort to locate people who could have a positive impact, Sam's sister, his uncle, and his hockey coach, all of whom together worked together to make the conference a transformative experience.

Procedurally, the restoration of trust conference would be identical to Braithwaite's proposal, in that an effort would be made to bring to the table all those who could be instrumental in devising a restorative solution. The conference facilitator would perform the same role of moderator, adviser, and "stage manager" of the event, and would seek to promote open, honest dialogue and to respect the needs of the parties to be heard and understood. Additionally, however, the facilitator would focus the discussion on the effect of the offense on the offender's ability to be trusted by not only by the victim, but also *by society*, and what the offender must do the restore that trust. In the course of this dialogue, it is to be expected that the victims will want to make sure the offender understands the full impact of the crime on their life because, without such understanding, the offender's apology and expressions of remorse will be incomplete. The victims will want to find out if the offender truly empathizes with their suffering because, unless he does, his remorse may be only for his own suffering, not theirs. The victim, the victim's family, and the offender's family will take a careful look at the offender's life to understand why he became willing to violate the basic norms of society. This involves determining what was wrong with his social relations and why he lost concern about planning for a future. The facilitator will lead the participants through an examination of the

offender's background and social ties because the inadequacy of these
social bonds so evident in Sam's case—his homelessness, his alienation
from his family, his lack of education, his lack of marital stability, and
his lack of career—are undoubtedly at the heart of his resorting to crime
to get a few dollars. It would be obvious to everyone in the room that, if
the offender were to be released immediately, he could not be trusted to
conduct himself within the law. On the other hand, it would be equally
apparent to all that merely sending him to jail, without addressing the
sources of distrust, would not make him fit to eventually reenter society.
Therefore, it is to be expected that the reasons why both the victim and
other members of the community are not ready to trust the offender must
be addressed in the sentencing proposal to be submitted to the court.

Despite what we know of the inadequacy of incarceration to deal
with all of these important personal issues, under the restoration of trust
proposal the resulting sentencing recommendations would likely include
a punitive component of some kind, including community service and a
variety of intermediate sanctions that are appropriate to the severity of
the offense. But would the imposition of a punishment be advisable in
such a case as this? Would it be restorative? As in all matters of
sentencing, there cannot possibly be one "correct" answer, but for me,
the answers to these two questions, I submit, are both "yes."

1. Yes, some kind of punishment would be advisable in this case.
Robbery is a violent crime in which an offender is willing to cause great
physical harm and suffering to a vulnerable person. If the law does not
punish such people, then no one is safe except the strong and the
ruthless. Everyone else will live in fear or will so protect themselves
from harm that the scope of their interactions will be greatly restricted.
Robbery can be deadly. A robber has no compunctions about causing
severe injury that may result in death or permanent disability. In Sam's
case, he is fortunate that this victim did not sustain serious injuries, but
what if she did? How would that have changed the nature of what he did
or the threat he presented to the public? What if, following this incident,
Sam was immediately released back to the community and, instead of
forswearing further crimes, he started right in again? Knowing that the
threat of law enforcement was just a "paper tiger," and that with an
apology, a few tears, and an agreement to pay reparations in the future,
all his criminal charges will be dismissed, it might be very difficult for
Sam to resist returning to a life of crime. Of course, Braithwaite might
argue that his program is available only to first-time offenders . If so, it
is unlikely to apply to many people, since those who are charged with a
serious violent crime tend to have a lengthy criminal history. In any

event, it already is common practice in many jurisdictions to give a presumption of non-incarceration to first-time offenders. What would truly be radical in Braithwaite's proposal would be if it also applied to repeat offenders. Braithwaite's non-punitive proposal would be truly innovative if it was intended to apply to repeat offenders, but that is a step he appears unwilling to make take by exempting "incorrigibles" from restorative justice conferencing.[6] But what should we do with them instead? We would have to revert to the conventional system that imposes punishment on offenders because it obviously is necessary to protect the public. In the end, the criminal law is meaningless unless it is backed up by the credible threat of enforcement, and this sobering fact of life is applicable to both conventional and unconventional forms of criminal justice administration.

2. Yes, punishment would be restorative in this case—if not to the victim's trust in the offender, then at least to the victim's trust in society. As I have argued elsewhere in this book, even those who conceive of restorative justice as a nonpunitive alternative to conventional justice have recognized that punishment must nonetheless be imposed in cases involving unresponsive offenders and serious offenses.[7] But in these situations, they have argued, punishment is a necessary evil, a contradiction and impediment to restoration that must be made for the sake of expedience. The restoration of trust proposal does not follow this approach because, in enumerating the ways in which an offender may hope to restore the trust he has forfeited by the commission of a crime, it would include the offender's voluntary decision to "pay his dues" by submitting to a punishment that society, the victim, and, most importantly, the offender himself view as just and deserved. By so doing, the offender indicates that he is willing to abide by the rules that everyone must follow and not seek to avoid them by manipulating the sympathy of his victim.

Proponents of a purely non-punitive version of restorative justice are quite right in regarding the offender's apology and remorse as fundamental to the restoration of the victim's emotional well-being, but they are quite wrong in regarding punishment as being *irrelevant* to this recovery process. When a defendant confesses his errors and expresses remorse in the context of a diversionary program designed to eventually dismiss the pending criminal charges, his words can be seen as mere tactics to gain leniency. But when the defendant, by pleading guilty, waives his right to contest the charges and submits to the range of penalties prescribed by law, his words of apology and expressions of remorse now can be regarded as genuine sttempts at atonement and not simply as strategic means of gaining leniency. When that occurs, the groundwork for restoring trust in the offender has been established. As I have so often stated in this book, *punishment itself is not necessarily restorative of trust in the offender*. But when he accepts it as his due and when, indeed, he has become a participant in determining the sentencing recommendations, the hopes for his eventual restoration to a position of trust are more fully justified than in the alternatives we considered above where there is either a passive imposition of punishment in the course of a plea bargain or a diversion to a nonpunitive offender dialogue.

Problem 5. Your Own Case

In this scenario, you are asked to consider a true-life incident that occurred in which you were involved either directly as the victim or the offender, or indirectly through personal knowledge.
 Now ask:

- How was the matter actually resolved?
- If it was not resolved through the court system, how do you think it would have been resolved in such a setting?
- How might this same case have been resolved in the context of a restorative justice conference designated as a nonpunitive diversionary program?
- How might this same case have been resolved in the context of a restoration of trust conference in which the parties devise a sentencing recommendation within a range of penalties established by law?

Discussion

This is perhaps the best way to compare the conventional model of case processing from the two versions of restorative justice conferencing. As before, this involves an exercise in imagination but, now, the restorative justice possibilities are contrasted with a personal experience of criminal justice. Which outcome best accords with your sense of justice? Which results in a disposition that is most useful to you, to the other parties, and to society? Which outcome has the best prospects for succeeding?

 It is through the process of answering questions such as these that the various theories of sentencing can be put to the test. What will emerge, hopefully, is a vision of criminal justice reform that is worthy of implementation in our own communities and in communities throughout the nation.

Notes

[1] See pp. 195-196, *supra.*
[2] Braithwaite, "Restorative Justice, pp. 326-327.
[3] Braithwaite, "Restorative Justice and a Better Future," pp 9-32.
[4] *Id.,* p. 9.
[5] See pp. 41-42, *supra.*
[6] Braithwaite, "Restorative Justice and De-professionalization," p. 29.
[7] See p. 180, *supra.*

11

Addressing the Concerns
of Minorities

By applying the restoration of trust approach to a variety of crime scenarios, we have been better able to assess its utility in devising sanctions that are restorative for the victim, the offender, and the community. But now let us expand this vision to see how this approach might be applied to important criminal justice issues as well as to individual cases. And certainly, there is no more important criminal justice issues than the rising prison population and the disproportionate incarceration of minorities. Consider the following:

- By 1990, one quarter of all young black men were either in prison, or in jail, or on probation, or paroled, a figure that increased to nearly one third by 1995.[1]
- Under current conditions, over 75 percent of African American men in Washington D.C. can expect to be incarcerated some time in their lives.[2]
- Blacks, who comprise 13% of the U.S. population, make up 50% of the prison population.[3]
- More than one third of all African American men in their twenties are currently under correctional supervision.[4]

Although the differential rates in offending according to race have long been noted, the disparities in rates of incarceration have dramatically increased during the past several decades. This is due in large measure to a change in sentencing policy that, ironically, was designed to *reduce* racial disparities in sentencing. Given the extraordinarily broad sentencing discretion granted to both federal and state judges by indeterminate sentencing that prevailed before 1980, the likelihood always existed for favoritism by (typically) white affluent judges against (typically) poor black defendants. It was therefore believed by many sentencing reformers that the best way to ensure that a criminal sanction is "color blind" was the creation of uniform sentencing standards based on the philosophy of just deserts that focuses on the seriousness of the crime and the criminal history of the offender, without regard to the offender's personal characteristics. At the same time as minorities and liberals sought to rein in sentencing discretion as a means of curtailing racism, conservatives sought to restrain the discretion of the judiciary that, in their opinion, had become far too activist and uncontrolled. These conservative legislators increasingly saw rehabilitation and social welfare programs as ineffectual means of combating the growing problem of law and order, and therefore also embraced the moralistic philosophy of just deserts that reflected their value for personal responsibility. As a result, both liberals and conservatives came to agree on the need for restraints on judicial discretion by the adoption of the just deserts rationale, albeit for vastly different reasons.

The adoption of just deserts as a favorite sentencing policy was implemented in the federal government and in many states not only by the adoption of sentencing guidelines that focused on the severity of the offense and the offender's criminal history, but also by the enactment of mandatory sentencing laws such as for gun possession or for drug dealing. While the primary goal of these laws was the restriction of judicial discretion according to moral principles of proportionality, they were quickly put to the service of a politically more compelling goal: the "war on crime" and, in particular, the war on drugs. Here too, minority community leaders were early supporters of stricter measures. Life in U.S. inner cities had become increasingly intolerable as crime rates soared during the 1970s and reached epidemic proportions with the introduction of crack cocaine in the 1980s. Bipartisan support for a series of tough crime and drug control legislation resulted in the passage of laws calling for radical increases in penalties, many with mandatory incarceration features targeting violent crime and drug dealing. The result, predictably, was an unprecedented increase in incarceration rates. From 1972 to 1998, the prison population grew nearly 500 percent.[5] From 1980 to 1992, the chances of receiving a prison term for a drug arrest increased by 447 percent.[6] The political leaders of the minority community, who had earlier embraced the idea of sentencing guidelines to control racial bias in sentencing, and who sought a powerful remedy to the explosion of crimes and drugs in their communities, now realized that the net result of their efforts was a generation of young black men behind bars.

Was it worth it? Many were convinced that the significant drop in crime during the late 1990s had little to do with the recently adopted "get-tough" programs.[7] Criminologists have long maintained that violent crime is never significantly deterred by marginal increases in punishment. [8] As for drug offenses, the arrest and removal of one low-level drug dealer is rapidly replaced by another, and any decline in the rate of violent offending is more attributable to the establishment agreed-on territories than to any changes in sentencing policies. Furthermore, despite any gains in security, the adoption of strict sentencing guidelines failed to achieve the one thing that it was supposed to accomplish: the reduction in sentencing disparities along racial lines. Eliminating the possibility of judges considering the circumstances of an offender's life may have deprived black offenders from the possible benefit of judges having some empathy for their personal plight.

In the aftermath of the dramatic expansion of incarceration rates in the United States, particularly among minorities, a number of reforms were suggested to reduce the overall punitivity of the criminal justice system, including the elimination of mandatory prison terms for drug and weapons charges and the revocation of "three strikes and you're out" legislation. These proposed reforms have not met with great success throughout the United States, despite the enormous financial burden imposed on taxpayers and the devastating effect of such large-scale incarceration on minority populations. But even if these reforms were enacted and an overall reduction in punitivity were to be achieved, the racial divide in sentencing that, more and more, looks like a twenty-first-century version of legal segregation, will continue.

One thing is clear: The elimination of subjectivity in sentencing, and its replacement with mandatory sentencing based on objective criteria, did not end or even reduce sentencing disparities across racial lines. Many scholars, both liberal and conservative, were obligated to conclude that the standardization of sentences according to just deserts criteria of crime severity and criminal history has no prospect of minimizing racial disparities in sentencing because the persistently high crime rate of blacks has always been associated with poverty, unemployment, urban overcrowding, inferior education, and a host of social disadvantages uniquely suffered by people of color in this country. A societal response to this problem that is limited to the imposition of increasingly more severe punishment, instead of addressing those conditions associated with high rates of offending, will increase the suffering, alienation, and social disruption of the black community without significantly ensuring community safety. Criminal sentences are already severe enough to deter those of us with a "stake in conformity." But those who are undeterred by these penalties today are unlikely to change their ways merely by ratcheting up their severity. Moreover, even without increasing the severity of sentencing, the goal of uniformity of treatment solely predicated on the characteristics of the crime, without taking into consideration the circumstances of the offender, is destined to result in vast sentencing inequalities between the socially advantaged and the socially disadvantaged.

The challenge to sentencing theorists and reformers troubled by the disparities in sentencing along racial lines was how to reintroduce subjectivity in order to humanize the decision-making process and to permit a more "holistic" view of the offender without thereby infecting the process with the racial bias that previously existed when subjectivity in sentencing was the norm. One such proposal to reintroduce a measure of subjectivity in sentencing was presented by the acclaimed criminologist Michael Tonry in *Malign Neglect*. To address the problem of sentencing disparities, Tonry asked: "How can we change criminal justice policies so that it will be less destructive of the lives of black Americans and more restorative of the life chances of disadvantaged blacks?"[9] If we ought to base sentencing strictly on "moral blameworthiness" instead of the unproven empirical claims of utilitarian theories, Tonry argued, why limit consideration of the morality of conduct to the seriousness of the crime? Because we already gauge the morality of criminal conduct by examining the offender's mental competency, intentionality, and motivation for the action in establishing the legal "elements" of the offense as well as in establishing legal justifications (such as self-defense), affirmative defenses (such as insanity), and aggravation and mitigation factors, why not make a comprehensive examination of *all* of the factors bearing on the offender's moral culpability? Citing Walker, Tonry noted that "a system of punishment truly premised on notions of social culpability and morally deserved punishments would take account of all the particulars of an offender's life."[10]

Tonry therefore proposed that, in addition to measures designed to reduce the overall severity of punishment, the scope of judicial discretion should be expanded to enable judges "to lower sentences in particular cases to take account of the offender's circumstances. In criminal law jargon, informal mitigation should be encouraged."[11] Tonry understood that this proposal would reverse the trend of sentencing policies: "It requires rejection of the just deserts as an overarching rationale for sentencing and the system of rigid sentencing guidelines based on that rationale" because such a rationale and guidelines based on just deserts "generally forbid[s] judges to mitigate sentences to take account of the offender's background and personal circumstances."[12]

Tonry's proposal for a more individualized approach to sentencing bears close scrutiny because it demonstrates an awareness of the need for criminal justice policies to be responsive to the needs of the people affected by crime, and not simply to abstract principles of equality that may not be applicable to an unjust society. It represents a marked improvement over a system that claims to be based on the morality of strict retribution but that, given the reality of life in U.S. inner cities, operates to inflict needlessly cruel punishment on a foreseeably large proportion of the minority population. Tonry's moral argument in favor of the consideration of social adversity in mitigating sentencing is that those whose chances in life have been diminished by forces beyond their control are *less blameworthy* for their resulting misconduct than those who suffered no such disadvantages. Given the temptations of crime, Tonry asked: "Should the criminal law blame a disadvantaged youth for succumbing to all but overwhelming temptation?"[13] And since, from the retributionist perspective, wrongdoers who give in to great pressure are less blameworthy than wrongdoers "who face no pressure at all,"[14] it is not morally wrong to "sympathize with the pressure he was under and try, for his sake and ours, to help him resist temptation next time."[15]

Tonry's proposal for a "social adversity" ground for mitigation of sentences, although not intended as a restorative justice innovation, raises some important moral problems that should be considered in the development of restorative justice as a means of reducing racial disparities in sentencing. However laudatory the goal of reducing punitivity to socially disadvantaged persons may be, those very factors that make a crime an overwhelming "temptation" to those who are socially disadvantaged and those factors that make for greater "pressure" to commit criminal acts render a person a greater danger to the community. The problems that afflict U.S. inner cities—poverty, unemployment, overcrowding, bad housing, and poor education—are the same risk factors that render a person more likely to become involved in crime. In other words, reducing the severity of punishment because of a person's exposure to social adversity means reducing the severity of punishment for *those who pose the greatest risks to the community.* Indeed, a policy that rewards those exposed to various forms of social dysfunction, all of which predictably contribute to higher rates of offending runs the risk of *greater* victimization to members of a minority community that already suffers levels of victimization that would be unimaginable in any white community. The numbers tell a story of devastated and devalued lives:

- Homicide represents a leading cause of death among black males from age 15 through 34.[16]
- Of the major racial groups in the U.S., African Americans are the most likely to be victimized by crime—especially violent crime.[17]
- From 1976 to 2005, 93% of black victims were killed by blacks. [18]
- Blacks, who constitute about 12% of the nation's population, represent half of its homicide victims.[19]
- Between 2001 and 2005, about 35% of all violent crime against blacks involved offenders with a weapon.[20]
- The number of African American males who died from injury by firearms in 1997 was 46.1 per 100,000, compared to 18.1 per 100,000 for white males.[21]

Beyond these numbers is the daily life experience of millions of black men, women, and children who live their lives amid chronic insecurity. Whether or not they are the direct victims of crime, the psychological toll on everyone who lives in a high-crime area is incalculable. How does one measure the anxiety of a mother as she sends her children off to school? How does one measure the concern that your son or daughter will be lured into a youth gang or will be tempted by drugs? What effect do these temptations have on the ability of minority youths to concentrate their energies and ambitions on academic success? Unfortunately, to white Americans, these injuries, both physical and psychological, that are suffered by minorities as a direct or indirect consequence of crime are largely hidden. The reality of this country is that, despite our efforts to combat racism, we still live in a racially segregated society. Therefore, white Americans have little, if any, contact with black victims and have little ability to assess the psychological consequences of crime on the lives of ordinary black people. And what is true for the typical white American is also true for the typical member of the criminal system, for whom the modern inner city is still regarded, in the words of novelist James Baldwin, as "another country."[22]

In fashioning an effective and moral response to the devastating toll on members of the black community, it is not enough to "sympathize with the pressure [the offender] was under and try for his sake and for ours to help him resist the temptation next time."[23] We must also extend some sympathy for the plight of the victim, and make sure that there will be no "next time." The black victim, every bit as much as the white victim, deserves protection and deserves justice; neither of which is advanced by offering sentence reductions to those whose personal histories have rendered them the gravest and most foreseeable risk to their neighbors. Holding black offenders *less* to account by virtue of their disadvantages perpetuates discrimination by regarding them as correspondingly less capable of resisting temptation and exercising self-control, and by devaluing the lives of black victims.

And, indeed, the devaluation of black victims has long been noted. During the era of legal segregation, crimes against blacks, whether committed by blacks or whites, were virtually *ignored*. Scholars have analyzed the leniency shown toward victimizers of blacks both as a function of the majority's contempt for the life of black victims and as a corresponding paternalism that views blacks as having "diminished responsibility for their actions, resulting in more lenient sentences."[24] Modern versions of paternalism, outlined by Kleck, have the same theme of diminished responsibility by black offenders: the sociology-based tolerance of criminality in which the forces of poverty and racism and the resulting black subculture are seen as mitigating factors ("their crimes are due to factors beyond their control and are at least to be expected").[25]

When blacks are entrusted with positions of responsibility in the criminal justice system, however, the paternalism and devaluation experienced by minorities tends to evaporate. Black police officers are not less willing to arrest black offenders—in fact there is some evidence that black officers may be more inclined to arrest black suspects based upon the requests of black victims.[26] Correspondingly, black judges, who unlike their white counterparts, are less likely to excuse black offenders on the ground of sociological forces "beyond their control" or feel obligated to provide compensation for historical mistreatment,[27] are found to be as harsh or harsher on black defendants than white judges.[28] And just as the forcefulness of black police officers is regarded positively by the black community, the stricter sentencing practices of many black judges is seen by many in the minority community as evidence of greater sensitivity to the needs of black victims.[29] Blacks, of course, are no less interested in protecting themselves against the ravages of crime, regardless of the race of their victimizers than are whites. The vast majority of African Americans are law-abiding people whose major complaint is the *lack* of adequate police protection. Indeed, it has been claimed by Harvard scholar Randall Kennedy that "African Americans desire more rather than less prosecution and punishment for all types of criminals"[30] and that "deliberately withholding protection against criminality…is one of the most destructive forms of oppression that has been visited upon African Americans."[31]

Although the answer to the problem of disparate sentencing cannot be solved by imposing rigid rules of proportionality, the reintroduction of sentencing discretion with the intention of permitting greater leniency for offenders from socially disadvantaged backgrounds merely reinforces the kind of attitudes that have devaluated black victims and that have patronized the entire black community by collectively holding its members to a lower standard of moral accountability. Even a kindly disposed judge who sympathizes with the pressures and the temptations differentially experienced by disadvantaged offenders, might not recognize the racism implied in reducing the sentences for those crimes that appear to be "everyday occurrences" in the inner cities while insisting on stricter accountabilities for those who venture into white communities.

Implicit in the moral argument in favor of sentence reductions for the socially disadvantaged is a theory of criminality that assumes that the social conditions associated with high crime rates in the inner cities somehow "impels" a person toward crime. The inner-city resident is believed to be subjected to temptations and pressures that would result in higher rates of offending by anyone—black or white—who is exposed to such conditions. Because of the differential exposure to these sources of motivation, it is argued, the society that creates or permits such differences should make allowances for their predictable reactions by reducing the severity of sanctions.[32]

What is absent from this analysis is an important body of research that attributes different rates of offending to different levels of social control rather than different levels of motivation. From this perspective, poverty, unemployment, and poor schools do not *impel* a person to crime by making crime more tempting or by inducing greater pressure. Instead, all of these factors make it less likely that a person will be enmeshed in a network of family, school, community, and career that *restrains* people from crime far more effectively than the threat of law enforcement. Indeed, it is because of the failure of ordinary social controls to restrain potentially harmful conduct that society resorts to the heavy-handed instrument of law enforcement. Therefore, the notion of reducing the threat of punishment to those who are the least constrained by social control makes little sense, either morally or practically. From the standpoint of community safety, these are the people who require more diligent law enforcement, not less. From the standpoint of morality, it mocks the efforts of those who try to live by the rules and those who try to instill respect for those rules in their children. Social policy, one would think, should operate to encourage everything that makes a person less likely to live a life of crime: staying in school, honoring parental obligations, getting a job. This type of encouragement is not achieved by offering sentence reductions to those who, by the failure of socialization, are most likely to victimize others. In summary, while it is necessary to reform the policy of just deserts that requires strict proportionality in sentencing, the proposal to replace it with a system that encourages sentencing reductions for the socially disadvantaged is unlikely to improve the lives of inner-city residents.

Reducing Sentencing Severity

The restoration of trust approach offers an alternative to the just deserts model of strict proportionality in sentencing. This new approach offers the possibility of significant decreases in sentencing severity by encouraging the sentencing authorities to take a more holistic view of the offender, but within boundaries that respect the right of the minority community members to be protected from crime. The result, I argue, is substantial reductions in sentencing severity to black offenders without devaluing the dignity of black victims:

1. **The application of the principle of restoring trust reduces reliance on punishment.** I adopt the premise that the strict application of rules of proportionality in sentencing cannot, by itself, ameliorate sentencing disparities along socioeconomic lines, and therefore acknowledge the need to include other, more subjective criteria in sentencing rather than exclusive reliance on the severity and blameworthiness of the offender's actions. But instead of granting more favorable treatment to those whose social conditions put them at the gravest risk to public safety, the restoration of trust approach would grant sentencing concessions *to those who demonstrate trustworthiness by their voluntary actions.*

Because the overall goal is to restore trust, punishment is less necessary for those who prove their trustworthiness by other means. Those means may include agreeing to meet with the victim to hear his or her story, demonstrating empathy, offering a genuine apology, offering to repay losses, and voluntarily submitting to a deserved punishment. Under this principle, we should expect substantial reductions in the demands of the victim and community members for punishment. Those who accept responsibility for their actions prove themselves to be more worthy of trust than those who deny responsibility for their behavior, and thus require less punishment as a condition for reentry into society.

2. **The restoration of trust approach empowers, rather than devalues, the black victim.** A key moral problem of the proposal for

sentencing concessions to the socially disadvantaged is that it perpetuates a long history of devaluation of black victims. By holding the most disadvantaged offenders to a lower standard of morality, the message to the black victim is: "You don't count. You might have suffered a loss by the crime, but just consider what the offender had to go through in his life!" This condescending and patronizing attitude to persons of color can best be appreciated by others if the social disadvantage mitigation were used in a case involving a violent crime committed upon yourself or your family by a member of your own racial or ethnic group. If the judge in such a case determined that the offender should receive a reduced sentence because of "the pressure he was under" or the "overwhelming temptation" offered to him by victimizing you, given his social disadvantages, both you (the victim) *and* the offender would be morally disparaged. The restoration of trust model rejects this point of view of the offender's accountability. Indeed, it is the acknowledgment of the offender's moral accountability and not the justification or rationalization of conduct that deserves our encouragement.

Reducing Sentencing Disparities

Because maximizing other means of restoring trust has the effect of reducing reliance on punitively, the adoption of the restoration of trust model offers the prospect of significant reductions in *overall* punitivity. But will this reduction in punitivity also reduce sentencing *disparities* between blacks and those of other races? No one can answer this with any certainty. Perhaps it is good enough to have reasonable confidence that the utility of the restoration of trust model will operate to reduce the severity of sentencing in general. Yet there are good reasons to believe that the adoption of the restoration of trust model will also operate to reduce racial disparities for a full spectrum of offenses:

1. **"Leveling the playing field" by focusing on the defendant's desire to regain trust.** Within the conventional criminal justice system, any policy of granting sentence reductions to those who are most responsive to social control would operate to further alienate and compound the disadvantages suffered by those subject to the least social control. In the context of a restorative justice system designed toward the goal of regaining trust, however, while the absence of social control will continue to operate as a disability, it is not an inescapable or uncorrectable disability. A central mission of restorative justice is to involve the victim, the offender, and their family, friends, and

community members in an effort to design creative restorative solutions. The function of the restorative justice conference is to build on whatever level of social control exists to promote greater trust in the offender. To a large extent, therefore, the prospect of regaining trust depends on the desire of the offender to reform and to be regarded as a good and trustworthy person. It is not being unduly naïve, I hope, to assume that this desire is not dependent on affluence or social class. It is quite likely that an attitude of defiance and rejection of social control is as prevalent among privileged offenders as it is in underprivileged offenders. In essence, it is not so much the *availability* of social controls such as family, school, and career that denotes trustworthiness in an individual, but the person's *receptivity* to these controls. As a result, the use of the restoration of trust model as source of guidance offers the possibility of sentence reduction based more on the offender's expressed desire to reconnect with his community than his past exposure to social control. Consequently, the use of this approach for disadvantaged offenders offers the promise not only of a reduction in overall punitivity but also a reduction in sentencing disparities. Although we may despair about the chances of ever eliminating economic and social disparities, we can reasonably expect the narrowing of sentencing disparities if sentence reductions are granted to those who manifest a genuine desire to reconnect with their community, regardless of the level of available community resources.

2. Favoring treatment over punishment in drug-related offenses. Since the largest proportion of the increase in incarceration during the 1980s and 1990s was due to drug-related offenses, racial disparities that stem from drug-related cases, whether due to disparate rates of drug use or disparate sentencing severity, can be reduced by favoring treatment over punishment whenever possible. The priority for drug treatment follows from the premise that sentencing should be guided by the goal of restoring trust. Punishment is useless in the process of restoring trust in a drug addict because the problem of *drug dependence* is not treatable by the threat or use of punishment. It also makes sense to reward those who voluntarily submit to drug rehabilitation, who complete the program, and who stay clean. And whatever operates to reduce the severity of incarceration for drug-related offenses reduces racial disparities in sentencing.

3. Enhancing prospects for crime prevention. To the extent that disparities in sentencing are based on differential rates of offending, the restoration of trust model offers a number of significant advantages over both the just deserts model of proportionality and the subjective approach that favors sentencing concessions to offenders who have had social disadvantages. The primary reason why just deserts could not close the racial gap in sentencing is because it is merely reflective of differential patterns of offending. Furthermore, the proposal to close this gap by reducing the sentences of the socially disadvantaged, as I have argued, comes at an intolerable cost to the safety of the black community by offering less deterrence to those who pose the greatest risk.

The restoration of trust model, on the other hand, may very well operate to reduce the black-white gap, not by reducing the power of deterrence, but by actually *enhancing its effectiveness* through the combined power of legal sanctions and social sanctions. Restoring trust means restoring social networks, and the enmeshment of a person in a web of social relations is the basis of social control. The result of a successful restorative justice conference is not simply a negotiated sentence; it is a plan that is individualized to the needs and expectations of the victim and the community as well as to the capabilities and commitments of the offender. It is not a "one-shot deal" or a sudden emotional epiphany that showers the offender with love and forgiveness. It is an agreement—a contract—that, if followed, will enable the offender to attend to his responsibilities and, in the end, will permit him to reenter the moral community as an equal. When restorative agreements are devised, as they must be, with the full cooperation of the offender (or, in the case of juveniles, with the offender's family), the result is more likely to be reintegrative rather than stigmatizing.

The payoffs for this approach are not only the increase in victim satisfaction and the increase in possibilities for reintegration, but also the increase in the power of deterrence. This is so because it is only when the potential re-offender is involved in a social network of love, support, supervision, expectations, and scrutiny that the true power of deterrence is mobilized. Everyone is a potential offender, but those who are not restrained by the fear of disappointing the expectations of people on whom they depend cannot be trusted to conform to community norms of behavior. Building a criminal justice system based on the restoration of trust thus holds out the promise of achieving higher levels of crime control than can be expected from a system that merely punishes, stigmatizes, and represses.

This is particularly important in the case of juveniles and youthful offenders. According to labeling theory, the early contact between a young offender and the authorities is crucial in determining the subsequent direction of the young person's life. If a youthful offender is processed through the formal system criminal justice, whatever good may be achieved in terms of deterring him from further crime is undermined by his designation as being a "delinquent." Once officially declared to be a delinquent, a youthful offender will often spend the rest of his life playing out that role. Alienated and rejected from the community, he thus finds social acceptance within a criminal subculture. But if a purely punitive approach is counterproductive to crime control for youthful offenders, a permissive approach is not much better. Tolerance of youth crime in the inner cities is patronizing to the offender, disrespectful to the victim, and likely to result in greater recidivism because it turns the criminal justice system into a sham—a paper tiger that sounds frightening, but has no claws. An encounter with a criminal justice system that appears fearsome, but turns out to be a charade, neutralizes the power of deterrence and paves the way for future offending.

A justice system process based on the restoration of trust, however, rather than resorting to the stigmatizing effect of punishment on the one hand or well-intentioned but ineffectual leniency on the other, attempts to solve the problem of delinquency in youthful offenders by a kind of "full court press" that involves the victim, the offender, their families, members of the community, and others involved in the young person's life. The idea is to strip away the offender's defenses, make him take responsibility for his actions, and engage him in devising an overall plan to restore trust. Obviously, this effort will cost money, but far less than the amount currently spent on corrections. Society is perfectly willing to spend billions on the incarceration of healthy young men and women who should be working in society and paying taxes. Let's assume that there is enough money to bring the necessary people together and to provide a forum under the guidance of a restorative justice mediator in which to collectively devise an individualized plan for the youthful offender. If such a program is adopted for an offender's *first* encounter with the criminal justice system, it is difficult to imagine how this approach would not reduce the likelihood of his continued involvement in crime. Because the most salient predictor of criminality in any one person is the age of his earliest involvement in crime, the extent to which the system can make a powerful, effective restorative and reintegrative response to early offending can offer the prospect of significant reductions in subsequent rates of offending.

But the true potential of restorative justice to affect crime rates goes much further because restorative justice is not simply an approach to *criminal justice sentencing*. It is a new way of envisioning *criminal justice policy*, and therefore extends to every aspect of the criminal justice system. It helps to guide the policies and practices of policing, prosecution, corrections, and probation toward the goal of repairing harm and restoring trust. In so doing, it encourages active participation of the community in solving problems and designing and implementing restorative solutions. A criminal justice system that is dedicated to the goal of restoring personal and social trust will tend to engender greater levels of community support for law enforcement, *without which crime control cannot succeed.* By increasing community cooperation, the effectiveness of law enforcement is greatly enhanced and, as every student of deterrence theory is well aware, the resulting increase in the certainty of apprehension and conviction will greatly reduce the need for more severe sentences. Indeed, the alienation and resentment felt by the minority community toward the police is in itself a reason for high rates of offending in the inner cities. If members of this community believe that a call to 911 will be a waste of time or, worse, an encounter with a disrespectful, contemptuous, or ineffectual police officer, why bother? If some kids are out on the street making trouble, experience has taught these residents that calling the police will do nothing to stop them. And so the kids will continue to misbehave with impunity. Why? It's not because those kids are "bad," it's because so many of them believe—*quite correctly!*—that they can get away with it. Conversely, when it is made very clear to them that they will not get away with it, that the adults in the community will intervene whenever it's necessary, these same kids will start behaving themselves. And that, after all, is what we mean by effective deterrence. Therefore, the task of building a cooperative relationship between the community and the police is not just a matter of public relations, *it is necessary for effective crime control.* By its insistence on mutual respect at all levels, the restorative justice trust model can help shape the development of that relationship.

In summary, the adoption of well-funded restorative justice programs in the inner cities offers a realistic possibility for reducing sentencing disparities by directly addressing some of the primary reason for those disparities, and it can do so humanely and without neglecting the legitimate needs and expectations of victims and other community residents.

This is not to suggest that the adoption of the restoration of trust approach is a panacea for all social ills. Obviously, it is not. So long as there is poverty and discrimination in the inner cities, a disproportionate share of the our population will be involved in crime—both as offenders and as victims. It is therefore incumbent on us to work for a more just and prosperous society. But while we work toward the elimination of poverty and discrimination, we must also help to preserve the safety and security of minorities *right now.* Reorienting the criminal justice system toward the goal of restoring trust aims to do just that—not by increasing resort to incarceration under the theory of just deserts nor by granting sentence reductions to the socially disadvantaged, but instead by expanding the opportunities for effective social control, effective deterrence, and effective policing that will protect the lives and respect the rights of all inner-city residents.

Notes

[1] Tonry, *Malign Neglect*, p. vii ; Mauer, *Race to Incarcerate*, pp. 124-125.
[2] Braman, "Families and Incarceration,"   p. 117.
[3] Bureau of Justice Statistics, *Prison Inmates at Midyear* 2007, p. 7.
[4] Clear, Cole & Reisig, *American Corrections*, p. 478.
[5] Mauer, *The Race to Incarcerate*, p. 1.
[6] Beck & Gilliard, *Prisoners in 1994*, p. 13.
[7] *Id.* Bowling, "The Rise and Fall of New York Murder," pp. 531-554; Eck & Maguire, "Have Changes in Policing Reduced Violent Crime?" p. 235.
[8] Tonry, *Malign Neglect*, p. 18.
[9] *Id.*, p. 79.
[10] *Id.*, p. 45.
[11] *Id.*, p. 126
[12] *Id.*, p. 127
[13] *Id.*, p. 135.
[14] *Id.*, p. 151.
[15] *Id.*, p. 163.
[16] National Vital Statistics Reports, Vol. 47, No. 19, Centers for Disease Control and Prevention, National Center for Health Statistics, June 30, 1999.
[17] Walker, Spohn & Delone, *The Color of Justice*, 2nd Ed. p. 29.
[18] Harrell, *Black Victims of Violent Crime,* p. 3.
[19] Uniform Crime Reports, Supplementary Homicide Report), Table One.; Http://Www.Fbi.Gov/Ucr/05cius/offenses/Expanded_Information/Murder_Hom icide.Html
[20] Harrell, *supra*, p. 6
[21] National Vital Statistics Reports, Vol. 47, No. 19, Centers for Disease Control and Prevention, National Center for Health Statistics, June 30, 1999.
[22] Baldwin, *Another Country.*
[23] Tonry, *supra*, p. 163.
[24] Kleck, "Racial Discrimination in Criminal Sentencing," p. 800.
[25] *Id.*
[26] Black, "The Manners and Customs of the Police," p. 108.
[27] Kleck, *supra*, p. 800.
[28] Walker, Spohn, & Delone, *supra*, p. 212-213.
[29] Spohn, "The Sentencing Decisions of Black and White Judges," p. 1213.
[30] Kennedy, *Race, Crime and Law*, pp. 305-306.
[31] *Id.*, p. 29.
[32] Tonry, *supra,* p. 163.

12
Problems in Paradigms

(Reader's advisory: For the criminal justice practitioner, to whom the internal divisions within restorative justice must appear to be a "weird interfaith squabble,"[1] I would recommend bypassing this chapter and proceeding directly to the policy and practice reforms specified in the following two chapters. For everyone else—and, in particular, those readers already involved in the restorative justice movement—I would urge you not to proceed to the practical applications in the next chapters without first considering the problems created by the rhetoric of "paradigms;" problems that have caused unnecessary divisions among too many people in search of a "better way" for criminal justice This chapter is offered in the spirit of dissolving those divisions and opening up genuine dialogue among restorative justice advocates.)

I am well aware that much of the foregoing analysis of the need to extend the reach of restorative justice—especially my insistence on the incorporation of punishment as a valid sentencing alternative—will be rejected by some restorative justice "purists" as a corruption of the original vision. Restorative justice was conceived, after all, as a new criminal justice paradigm: a fully-fledged alternative to the conventional system that is obsessed with blame and punishment. In the eyes of these "defenders of the faith," my attempts at creating a maximalist model for restorative justice will have so far exceeded the boundaries of the original paradigm that it cannot be considered a true restorative model at all.

To these charges from the restorative justice purists among us, I must respectfully dissent. Restorative justice has something wonderful and important to contribute—a way to transform the practice of criminal justice in our country. But this cannot and will not happen as long as it is regarded as a fundamentally new paradigm that is inherently irreconcilable with "conventional" criminal justice values. By rejecting the artificial divisiveness that arises from paradigm discourse and, instead, by regarding the central contribution of restorative justice—*repairing the harm of crime*—as a wholly new and original criminal justice *goal*, the potential of restorative justice to transform every aspect of the criminal justice system, I believe, can proceed in an atmosphere that fosters open dialogue, that is responsive to empirical research and that encourages program innovation with no allegiance other than to the best interests of those who are harmed by crime. [2]

The notion of restorative justice as a new *paradigm* and not simply a new theory is principally attributed to the work of Howard Zehr, and has been a standard feature of the restorative justice literature since he published *Changing Lenses* in 1990. Zehr conceived of restorative justice as a fundamentally different approach to crime and justice, whose mission could not be accomplished by simply tinkering with the existing system. Instead, Zehr challenged his readers to look at the problem of crime without the baggage of preconceptions carried over from the traditional system. He invited a new generation to become, like himself, visionaries of a "better way." By promoting restorative justice as a new paradigm,[3] Zehr positioned restorative justice as something quite exceptional in the ever-crowded marketplace of ideas. What ensued was an outpouring of enthusiasm from a multitude of scholars and practitioners who saw in restorative justice a radical alternative to the "obedience through punishment paradigm," and advanced it as a model that would eventually replace the conventional approach to criminal justice.[4]

But what has been achieved by promoting restorative justice as a new paradigm has come at a considerable cost. To understand this cost, it is necessary to understand what is intended by the expression "paradigm." Modern usage of this term can be traced to the work of Thomas Kuhn who coined the term "paradigm shift" to describe a new way of formulating a problem.[5] As Kuhn explained it, once in a very great while, an intellectual discovery is made that is so thoroughly original and that is such a radical departure from previous understanding that it provides us with more than just new *information* about the world; it shows us a completely new way of *seeing* the world. Copernicus's conception of the motion of the planets, for example, did not just add a new feature to the earth-centered view; it replaced it entirely. In order to understand any one feature of a new paradigm, it is necessary to adopt the new perspective; otherwise, the new feature would simply be incomprehensible. Correspondingly, understanding the new paradigm opens up a new world of previously invisible insights, connections, and patterns that instantly become recognizable. But because different paradigms involve different viewpoints or frameworks of explanation, they exist as separate, closed systems. They are, as Kuhn described it, "incommensurable" with each other. Their features therefore cannot be merged, balanced, or reconciled. Kuhn's work gained wide acceptance both by scholars and by the general public, and his paradigm terminology came into common parlance for a bewildering variety of innovations.[6] Not content to advocate mere reform, theorists, academics, and policy analysts offered up "revolutionary" alternatives to the welfare paradigm, the health care paradigm, the political paradigm, the education paradigm, and, inevitably, to the "criminal justice paradigm."

If the only danger posed by applying paradigm terminology to the newly emerging conception of restorative justice was rhetorical excess, the harm could have been corrected easily by the use of more modest language. The problem, however, was that the proselytizers of restorative justice, perhaps unaware of the profligate use of paradigm terminology in virtually every field of human activity, took the notion of restorative justice as a paradigm shift quite seriously. They fully embraced the idea that restorative justice constituted a radically new way of seeing the problem of crime, and not just a new approach to an old problem. In so doing, they unwittingly created dilemmas that derived more from the attributes of paradigms than from any inherent feature of a theory of criminal justice centered on the goal of repairing harm.

The Creation of Dichotomies

A paradigm shift is, essentially, an all-or-nothing proposition. One system is superseded by another; one worldview is superseded by another. If one paradigm is counterpoised against another, every element of one replaces every element of the other: it is not possible to pick and choose elements of one or the other that we might wish to retain. The tendency to dichotomize between self-contained systems, however useful in highlighting true innovations, has the unfortunate tendency to reject both the truly useful and important features of the disfavored paradigm, together with its objectionable features (i.e., it "throws the baby out with the bathwater"). The implication for restorative justice is that values that have evolved within the traditional criminal justice system, however desirable, and the means employed to achieve those goals, however useful, must be rejected in favor of the alternatives embodied in the new paradigm. Conceptualizing restorative justice as a new paradigm fosters the rejection of ideas as being contradictory instead of promoting the evaluation of ideas as being potentially complementary.

Elaborate diagrams have been devised to distinguish the characteristics of the old and the new paradigms.[7] According to one restorative justice advocate, restoration is to be favored even at the expense of traditional notions of justice: restorative justice "makes things better, is never satisfied merely with following the rules, however equitable they are, or by asserting one's legal rights, however fair they may be."[8] In the interest of promoting personal, face-to-face dialogue instead of public adjudication, restorative justice advocates have minimized concern for due process protections for the accused and the values of proportionality, equality of treatment, and adherence to the rule of law.[9] Since the new paradigm "includes only the elements of the restorative paradigm without elements of the obedience (retribution/deterrence) and treatment paradigms,"[10] the restorative justice paradigm, some advocates contend, rejects the concept of crime prevention through deterrence and incapacitation[11] and even rehabilitation.[12]

Conversely, since the elements of a paradigm form an indissoluble whole, acceptance of the paradigm leads to the uncritical acceptance of even its most questionable features. Any departure from the original conception raises the possibility of compromises in which restorative justice risks "losing its soul."[13] And so, for example, because the involvement of the victim in face-to-face dialogues with the offender is regarded by some as a procedural requirement,[14] and an essential element of healing,[15] it is thought to be a fundamental part of the restorative justice paradigm[16] despite the fact that, for many victims, direct involvement with the offender would be emotionally traumatic.[17] For others, the restorative justice paradigm is claimed to include a constellation of ethical values, such as the elimination of the distinction between crimes and civil wrongs[18] and the acceptance of an economic theory in which wealth is distributed on the basis of need rather than merit,[19] which many who might otherwise welcome the introduction of restorative values into the criminal justice system would find questionable.

The Debate Becomes Ideological

A new paradigm is not merely a new explanation of facts; it is a new way of envisioning those facts. To use Zehr's metaphor, it is a "new lens."[20] While having a new paradigm influences our understanding of the facts, the converse is not true: New facts do not change the paradigm. New facts do not change the lens. Instead of being modified by factual "anomalies," paradigms are *challenged* by these inconsistencies. Facts that do not fit neatly within the paradigm undermine its utility, and an accumulation of inconsistent facts leads to the development of competing paradigms. Those having a personal interest in the preservation of a particular paradigm therefore cannot be neutral in the evaluation of data because the public awareness of inconsistent data will determine the fate of the paradigm. In this manner, the development of a new paradigm takes on the character of an ideology.[21]

Unhappily, the ideological character of discourse concerning restorative justice has manifested itself all too often, and is unlikely to abate as long as restorative justice advocates insist on regarding it as a paradigm. Ideologies are self-contained systems of ideas that aspire to intellectual rigor. At their core, they contain fundamental principles that become the basis for differentiation from other ideologies as well as the standards for judging the acceptability of practices within that ideology. The set of agreed-on principals of an ideology constitutes an orthodoxy, without which the ideology would lose its focus, its identity, and, indeed, its "soul." Defenders of an ideology therefore must regard every attempt at reform with suspicion, regardless of its apparent utility. The dichotomizing tendency of the paradigmatic approach to restorative justice thus inhibits its ability to function as an agent of reform. It not only dismisses the capacity of the existing system to meaningfully reform its own practices,[22] but actually *discourages* reform efforts. Those restorative justice advocates who prefer reform over revolution are denounced as corrupters of the "original vision" while those within the conventional system who seek to adopt restorative practices are thought to co-opt restorative justice programs to their own ends,[23] a process that amounts to "the hijacking of restorative justice."[24]

Furthermore, unlike the development of social scientific theories, in which empirical challenges to core principals are welcomed as a necessary step in theory evolution, empirical challenges to any of the core principals of an ideology represent a threat to its very existence. One telling example of the ideological tendency of restorative justice is its claims concerning its unique method of healing the victim's emotional and psychological wounds without retribution for the crime. There can scarcely be a more central claim than this because "healing is what is on offer for the victim. Indeed, 'healing' is probably the most emotionally powerful word in the restorative justice vocabulary."[25] Time after time, restorative justice theorists have put forward the notion that punishing offenders accomplishes nothing for the victim, but only adds more harm than pain in the world, [26] while offering restorative justice as "the justice that promotes healing."[27]

And yet, as we have seen, despite two decades of implementation in programs throughout the world and scores of studies on various aspects of restorative justice programs, not a single empirical study has verified the claim that the restorative justice alternative to punishment is more conducive to healing than an approach that includes the use of punishment.[28] In the absence of empirical proof, the central claim of restorative justice rests on the foundation of belief: "The acknowledgement of the wrong and the active participation in the reparation of harm is *believed to be* the most direct way to healing for all those affected by a specific crime" (emphasis added).[29] A revolutionary new theory that rejects the use of punishment specifically because it does not promote healing and offers the promise of a non-punitive system of "justice that promotes healing" must do more than base its core challenge to the conventional system on anecdotal evidence or mere belief.

In secular terms, because the paradigm model induces categorical divisions between incommensurable viewpoints, restorative justice is not simply a theory of criminal justice, it is "the restorative justice movement"[30] which requires ideological conformity to "correct thinking."[31] It therefore rejects attempts to achieve balance or accommodation with other goals, however desirable, as a form of co-optation which "should lead to increasing caution about the dangers of compromise."[32] This view of efforts at compromise as acts of betrayal has produced a series of attacks and counterattacks that seem rather as a "weird interfaith squabble in an obscure religious sect"[33] than as a rational debate. A good example of the kind of ideological infighting that results from the view of restorative justice as a new paradigm can be seen in the debate over the inclusion of community justice within restorative justice. To an outsider to this controversy, the issue under consideration must seem fairly innocuous: To what extent should restorative justice consider the needs of the community in solving problems and preventing crime? Since restorative justice theorists have universally recognized that crime is harmful to communities as well as to individual victims,[34] the participation of community representation at restorative justice conferences would not appear to be especially problematic. And yet, an entire issue of the *Contemporary Justice Review*, a leading academic journal of restorative justice research, was devoted to airing the attack by Paul McCold, a leading advocate of restorative justice "purism"[35] against those who would incorporate community justice goals into the restorative justice paradigm.[36] Incorporating community justice concepts into restorative justice theory, McCold claimed, "risks washing away the bold steps of the pioneers of restorative justice in a wave of muddle."[37] Once formulated as a clash of paradigms, the idea of accommodating a wider range of values is regarded as an attack on the integrity of the "purist" vision: "The effort to merge the two distinct paradigms . . . has been shown to pose serious threats to the future of the restorative justice paradigm."[38]

Another telling example of the ideological tendency of the paradigmatic approach that impairs the integrity of restorative justice scholarship can be seen in the historical and anthropological claims put forth concerning its origins. Although restorative justice is advanced as a new paradigm, a central historical contention of its advocates is that the adoption of the restorative justice paradigm represents a return to humanity's earliest experience of justice: a form of justice that has been usurped in modern times by the rise of the state. In this version of history, parties to conflicts in the past are imagined to have achieved justice by conflict resolution and restitution instead of retribution.[39] In introducing readers to the emerging field of restorative justice, Braithwaite boldly asserted "Restorative justice has been the dominant model of criminal justice throughout most of human history for all the world's peoples."[40] Such claims as these, however, are disputed by both historians and anthropologists who have asserted that all known human societies, both primitive and modern, have incorporated a variety of retributive features as well as reparative features, and that "the alleged near-universality of restorative justice-style dispute settlement is quickly refuted by any serious look at the literature of legal anthropology."[41] Attempts to support these claims by references to Hoebel's classic work on primitive justice have been cited as "either grossly overstated or flatly contradicted" by Hoebel's writings.[42]

This tendency to mythologize the origin of restorative justice and to pronounce grandiose and unsupported claims, such as the notion that restorative justice has been "the dominant model of criminal justice throughout most of human history for all of human society,"[43] or that "restorative justice has existed since humans began forming communities"[44] would be incomprehensible were it not for the ideological character of restorative justice advocacy. As Crawford noted, the idealized origin myth of restorative justice is a form of "willful nostalgia" that "collapses diversity and irons over important contradictory evidence and countervailing developments for the sake of a coherent 'story.'"[45] Daly, although clearly unhappy with the misuse of historical claims by restorative justice advocates, generously concluded that "I do not see bad faith at work here. Rather, advocates are trying to move an idea into the political and policy arena and this may necessitate having to utilize a simple contrast of the good and the bad justice, along with an origin myth of how it all came to be."[46] In Daly's view, the harm of misrepresenting historical fact is mitigated by the goal of the misrepresentation—to "move an idea." Yet it is precisely *because* the misrepresentation arose from ideological motives that the misuse of historical scholarship is so objectionable.

The pity is that resort to biased research would be altogether unnecessary if restorative justice were not so insistent on promoting itself as a new paradigm. As a new approach to criminal justice, its merits can be evaluated exclusively on the basis of its morality and utility. Its *age* should be entirely irrelevant. For an ideology, however, the function of an origin myth is clear: It posits a vision of original purity that has subsequently become corrupted. In so doing, it privileges a certain viewpoint and, correspondingly, de-legitimizes competing ideas.[47] In the service of the restorative justice paradigm, the origin myth becomes a tool of advocacy, a way to move an idea, and must therefore be deeply troubling to those who view the study of history as a search for truth rather than as a means of promoting an ideology.

To sum up, the dichotomizing tendency of viewing restorative justice as a new paradigm in contrast to the traditional criminal justice model gives rise to a multitude of dilemmas that impair its theoretical and programmatic development, that introduce an unfortunate ideological character to academic discourse, and that impose a particular mechanism of healing and a particular conception of justice that may have little to do with the real needs and expectations of crime victims. These consequences arise not from any inherent feature of restorative justice itself, but rather to the all-or-nothing quality of paradigm discourse that compels it to reject features of the old system regardless of their merit and to maintain adherence to every feature of the new system without regard to their utility.

The claim advanced by many restorative justice theorists is that restorative justice represents a new paradigm, replacing a state-control model that relies on punishment to compel obedience with a privatized model that relies on cooperation.[48] But this claim is undermined by the inevitable reliance of a "pure" form of restorative justice on the conventional system to achieve the essential goal of ensuring public safety as well as its own unique goal of restoration, much less those goals of the conventional system for which it offers no alternative solutions such as due process rights of the accused, proportionality in sentencing, equality of treatment, and the adjudication of contested cases. This necessary reliance on the conventional system disqualifies it as a new criminal justice "paradigm" in the Kuhnian sense. It is, in short, only a new paradigm in a rhetorical sense—a way to move an idea. But as we have seen, this particular marketing strategy has come at a considerable cost.

Let's therefore take the sage advice of colleagues in other fields who, at first bedazzled by paradigm terminology, now counsel to "Eschew That Paradigm. Drop the Jargon."[49] Many conflicts, contradictions, and dysfunctions that adhere to the notion of paradigms can be avoided by another kind of paradigm shift: rejecting the rhetoric of paradigms and paradigm shifts altogether. By stripping away its self-promotion as a new criminal justice paradigm and, instead, understanding the central contribution of restorative justice—*repairing the harm of crime*—as a wholly new and original criminal justice *goal*, the vast potential for restorative justice to transform criminal justice theory and practice can begin to be fulfilled.

In truth, nobody "owns" restorative justice. The original visionaries of restorative justice have bequeathed to the world a wonderful gift: an idea to transform criminal justice as we know it. The true beneficiaries of this gift are neither the theorists nor the criminal justice practitioners, but rather those who suffer from the trauma of crime. The challenge to restorative justice theory and practice is to develop a criminal justice system that is more effective, fair, and humane in order to address the needs of victims and communities, without preconceptions as to what they "really need" and without limitation to those practices that conform to a favored paradigm.

Notes

[1] Bazemore & Schiff, "Paradigm Muddle Or Paradigm Paralysis?" p. 51.

[2] A full treatment of the arguments in this chapter are presented in my article, "Paradigms Lost: Repairing the Harm of Paradigm Discourse in Restorative Justice."

[3] Zehr, *Changing Lenses*, pp. 83-94.

[4] Braithwaite, "A Future Where Punishment Is Marginalized," pp. 1729, 1749; McCold, "Paradigm Muddle," p. 14; Zehr, *Changing Lenses*, pp. 211-214.

[5] Kuhn, *The Structure of Scientific Revolutions*.

[6] *See, e.g.* Berghel, H. & Sallach, D. (2004) "A Paradigm Shift in Computing and IT Education." *Communications of the ACM*, 47(6), 83-88; Blackburn, T. & Sloviter, R. (2003). "Epilepsy, Parkinson's Disease, Migraine and Brain Plasticity—The Next Paradigm Shift?" *Current Opinion in Pharmacology*, 3 (1), 3; Blair, E. (1995) "Achieving a Total Safety Paradigm Through Authentic Caring." *Professional Safety*, 41 (5), 24; Bull, A., Ward, A. (2000). "Search and Discovery Strategies for Biotechnology: the Paradigm Shift." *Microbiology & Molecular Biology Reviews*, 64 (3), 573; Cantor, G. (1972). "Use of a Conflict Paradigm to Study Race Awareness in Children."

Child Development, 43(4), 1437-1442; Carlton, W. (1999). "School Readiness: the Need for a Paradigm Shift." *School Psychology Review*, 28 (3), 338-352; Castilla, J. & Defeo, O. (2005). "Paradigm Shifts Needed for World Fisheries." *Science*, 309 (5739); 1324-1325; Corley, L. (2002). "Radical Paradigm Shifts in Evo–Devo." *Trends in Ecology & Evolution*, 17 (12), 544; English, M. *et al.* (2002). "A Paradigm Shift in Irrigation Management." *Journal of Irrigation & Drainage Engineering*, 128 (5), 267; Eoyang, E. (2003). "Teaching English as Culture: Paradigm Shifts in Postcolonial Discourse." Sage Publications Inc., 50 (2), 3-17; Field-Fote, E. (2003). "Quantification of Functional Behavior in Humans and Animals: Time for a Paradigm Shift." *Journal of Rehabilitation Research & Development*, 40 (4), 19-24; Franco, E. (2003). "Are We Ready for a Paradigm Change in Cervical Cancer Screening?" *Lancet*, 362 (9399), 1866-1867; Friedman, M. (1998). "Coping With Consumer Fraud: the Need for a Paradigm Shift." *Journal of Consumer Affairs*, 32 (1), 1-13; Gallagher, E. (2002). "Leadership: A Paradigm Shift." *Management in Education*, 16 (3), 24-29; Galvin, J. (1994). "From the Humanity of Christ to the Jesus of History: A Paradigm Shift in Catholic Christology." *Theological Studies*, 55 (2), 252-274; Garman, T. (1998). "Consumer Educators, Now Is the Time for a Paradigm Shift." *Consumer Interests Annual*, 44, 48-56; Green, p. (2003). "Welcoming a Paradigm Shift in Neuropsychology." *Archives of Clinical Neuropsychology*, 18 (6), 625; Hampel, G. *et al.* (2005) "The New Paradigm for Wireless Network Optimization: A Synergy of Automated Processes and Human Intervention." *Communications Magazine*, 43: 3; Jeffcoate, W. (2005). "The Roper Management of Diabetic Foot Ulcers: Time for a Paradigm Shift." *Diabetic Medicine*, 21 (8), 809-809; Jo, S. & Shim, S. (2005). "Paradigm Shift of Employee Communication: the Effect of Management Communication On Trusting Relationships." *Public Relations Review*, 31 (2), 277-280; Kaushik, V. & Gudgeon, C. (2003). "Caesarean for Breech: A Paradigm Shift?" *Australian & New Zealand Journal of Obstetrics & Gynaecology*, 43 (4), 298-301; Kusumi, a. *et al.* (2005). "Paradigm Shift of the Plasma Membrane Concept From the Two-Dimensional Continuum Fluid to the Partitioned Fluid: High-Speed Single-Molecule Tracking of Membrane Molecules." *Annual Review of Biophysics & Biomolecular Structure*, 34 (1), 351-387; La Sorte, M. (1972). "Replication as a Verification Technique in Survey Research: A Paradigm." *Sociological Quarterly*, 13(2), 218-227; Liu, J. (2003). "Menopausal Hormone therapy: A Paradigm Shift?" *Fertility & Sterility*, 80 (3), 494; Lloyd, B., Lloyd, R. (1971). "Paradigms and Reading Flexibility." *Education*, 92 (1), 57; Mariner, W. (2001). "Slouching Toward Managed Care Liability: Reflections On Doctrinal Boundaries, Paradigm Shifts, and Incremental Reform." *Journal of Law, Medicine & Ethics*, 29   3/4, 253; Marshall J., *et al.* (2004). "Discussion of 'A Paradigm Shift in Irrigation Management.'" *Journal of Irrigation & Drainage Engineering*, 130 (1), 96-98; McNamara, T. (2003). "Tearing Us Apart Again: the Paradigm Wars and the Search for Validity." *Eurosla Yearbook*, 3, 229-238; Meckstroth, E. (1992). "Paradigm Shifts Into Giftedness." *Roeper Review*, 15 (2), 91; Mohan, C. (2003). "Raja: A Paradigm Shift Toward South Asia?" *Washington Quarterly*, 26 (1), 141-155; Moos, R., Finney, J & Cronkite, R. (1980) "The Need for a Paradigm Shift in Evaluations of Treatment Outcome: Extrapolations From the Rand Research." *British Journal of Addiction*, 75 (4), 347-350; Morris, M.

(1998). "The Paradigm Shift to Communication and the Eclipse of the Object."
South Atlantic Quarterly, 96 (4), 755-788; Ovadia, M. (2002). "A Paradigm
Shift in Myocardial Stunning." *Journal of the American College of
Cardiology*, 39 (10), 1710; Piko, B. & Kopp, M. (2004). "Paradigm Shifts in
Medical and Dental Education: Behavioural Sciences and Behavioural
Medicine." *European Journal of Dental Education*, February, 2004
Supplement 1 (8), 25-31; Pledger, C. (2004). "Disability Paradigm Shift."
American Psychologist, 59 (4), 275-276; Reschly, D. (2004). "Commentary:
Paradigm Shift, Outcomes Criteria, and Behavioral Interventions: Foundations
for the Future of School Psychology." *School Psychology Review*, 2004, 33 (
3), 408-416; Ross, L. (2002). "Genetic Exceptionalism vs. Paradigm Shift:
Lessons From HIV." *Journal of Law, Medicine & Ethics*, 29 (2), 141; Roy, H.
(1997). "Hyperplastic Polyps and Colon Cancer: Hype Or Paradigm Shift?"
American Journal of Gastroenterology, 97 (6), 1293; Savino, R & Ciliberto, G.
(2004). "A Paradigm Shift for Perythropoietin: No Longer a Specialized Growth
Factor, But Rather an All-Purpose T -Protective Agent." *Cell Death &
Differentiation*, July Supplement 1 (11), S2-S4; Scavo, C. & Shi, Y. (2000).
"Administration: The Role of Information Technology in the Reinventing
Government Paradigm-Normative Predicates and Practical Challenges." *Social
Science Computer Review*, 18 (2), 166-179; Settergren, G. (2003). "Brain
Death: an Important Paradigm Shift in the 20th Century." *Acta
Anaesthesiologica Scandinavica*, 47 (9), 1053; Smith, M. & Schnell, D. (2001).
"Peroxisomal Protein Import: the Paradigm Shifts." *Cell*, 105 (3), 293; Stanney,
K., *et al.*s. (2004). "A Paradigm Shift in Interactive Computing: Deriving
Multimodal Design Principles form Behavioral and Neurological Foundations. "
International Journal of Human-Computer Interaction, 17 (2), 229-257; Stuart,
R. (2005). "Treatment for Partner Abuse: Time for a Paradigm Shift."
Professional Psychology: Research & Practice, 36 (3) 254-263; Sutherland, I.
(2004). "Paradigm Shift: the Challenge to Graphic Design Education and
Professional Practice in Post-Apartheid South Africa." *Design*, 20 (2), 51-60;
Tannenbaum, J. (2002). "The Paradigm Shift Toward Animal Happiness."
Society, 39 (6), 24-36; Van Roggen, L. (2002). "A Fleeting Paradigms in
Dielectrics and Electrical Insulation." *Transactions On Dielectrics & Electrical
Insulation*, 9 (5), 638; Weinstein, R. (1972). "Patients' Perceptions of Mental
Illness Paradigms for Analysis." *Journal of Health & Social Behavior*, 13 (1),
38-47.
    [7] McCold, "Paradigm Muddle," pp. 18-19.
    [8] Marshall, *Beyond Retribution*, p. 92.
    [9] Delgado, "Goodbye to Hammurabi."
    [10] McCold, "Toward a Holistic Vision of Restorative Justice," p. 358.
    [11] Wright, *Justice for Victims and Offenders*; Umbreit, Coats & Kalanj,
Victim Meets Offender; Zehr, *Changing Lenses*.
    [12] McCold, "Toward a Holistic Vision of Restorative Justice," p. 358.
    [13] Umbreit, "Avoiding the Marginalization and 'McDonaldization' of
Victim-Offender Mediation," p. 214.
    [14] Marshall, "The Evolution of Restorative Justice," p. 37.
    [15] Retzinger & Scheff, "Strategy for Community Conferences," pp. 316-
317.
    [16] McCold, "Toward a Holistic Vision of Restorative Justice," p. 373.

[17] Shuman & Smith, *Justice and the Prosecution of Old Crimes, p.* 102.
[18] Fattah, "Gearing Justice Action to Victim Satisfaction," p. 21
[19] Sullivan & Tifft, *supra*, pp. 99-118
[20] Zehr, *supra*, p. 175.
[21] Thorne, "The Problematic Allure of the Binary," pp. 123-125.
[22] Groenhuijsen, "Victim's Rights and Restorative Justice," p. 75
[23] Sullivan & Tifft, *Restorative Justice: Healing the Foundations of Our Everyday Lives*, p. 55; Fattah, *supra*, p. 26
[24] Roberts & Peters, "How Restorative Justice is Able to Transcend Prison Walls," p. 116.
[25] Acorn, *Compulsory Compassion,* p. 71.
[26] Van Ness & Strong, *Restoring Justice*, p. 38. Kaptein, "Against the Pain of Punishment," p. 83 McCold; "Toward a Holistic Vision," p. 361.
[27] Van Ness & Strong, *supra*, p. 31; Sharpe, *Restorative Justice: A Vision for Healing and Change*, pp. 8-9; Consedine, *Restorative Justice: Healing the Effects of Crime.*
[28] See pp. 99-100, *infra.*
[29] McCold, "Toward a Holistic Vision of Restorative Justice," p. 373
[30] Sullivan & Tifft, *Restorative Justice,* p. 55
[31] McCold, "Toward a Holistic Vision of Restorative Justice," p. 358.
[32] Fattah, *supra*, p. 26.
[33] Bazemore & Schiff, "Paradigm Muddle or Paradigm Paralysis?" p. 51.
[34] Zehr, *Changing Lenses*, pp. 95-126; Van Ness & Strong, *supra*, pp. 32-36; Crawford, "The State, Community and Restorative Justice," p. 118.
[35] McCold, "Toward a Holistic Vision of Restorative Justice," pp. 372-373.
[36] McCold, Paradigm Muddle, pp. 3-36.
[37] *Id.,* p. 29.
[38] *Id.,* p. 28.
[39] Consedine, *Restorative Justice: Healing the Effects of Crime;* Weitecamp, "The History of Restorative Justice," pp. 81-83.
[40] Braithwaite, "Assessing Optimistic and Pessimistic Accounts," p. 2. This claim is repeated in Braithwaite, "Restorative Justice," p. 323.
[41] Bottoms, "Some Sociological Reflections on Restorative Justice," p. 88.
[42] Sylvester, "Myth in Restorative Justice History," p. 502.
[43] Braithwaite, "Assessing Optimistic and Pessimistic Accounts," p. 2.
[44] Weitecamp, "The History of Restorative Justice," p. 81.
[45] Crawford, "The State, Community and Restorative Justice," p. 109.
[46] Daly, "Restorative Justice: The Real Story," p. 63.
[47] There is a psychological defense in much of paradigm discourse that also operates to exempt itself from criticism and de-legitimize opposing viewpoints. Those who remain mired in the old paradigm of criminal justice, one may claim, "just don't get it" and so are in no position to understand, much less judge, the features of the new paradigm. See Chapter 4, *supra.*
[48] Fattah, *supra*; McCold, "Paradigm Muddle," p. 14; McCold, "Toward a Holistic Vision," p. 382
[49] Theibert, "Manager's Journal: Eschew That Paradigm. Drop the Jargon."

13
Toward Criminal Justice Reforms

Restorative justice can fulfill its potential for fundamental change when criminal justice policies and practices are guided by the goal of repairing the harm of crime. Regarded as a new criminal justice goal rather than a specific set of practices, restorative justice is capable of a multitude of applications in different settings.

Let's take a look at some of the possibilities that emerge from a simple "thought experiment." Let's examine some of the main features of criminal justice system, from policy to practice, in the areas of policing, adjunction, sentencing, probation and corrections, and ask ourselves if any changes can be made that would actively facilitate the restoration of trust in the offender and in society. What follows are the results of my own exploration of these issues. As such, they are certainly not intended to be the "last word" on any issue I have covered. Instead, I hope it will help to stir your own imagination as to restorative possibilities that emerge almost everywhere you look when you are guided by the goal of restoring trust in the offender and in society. Ultimately, the development of our ideas and innovations depends on the creativity and insight of practitioners and the political will to reform, together with the accumulation of careful empirical evaluations of what works and what does not.

Policy Guidelines

In devising specific reforms, here are some guiding principles to be utilized, all of which can be encompassed by a standard benchmark in evaluating practices: Does it enhance or impair the restoration of trust in the offender and in society?

- Does it promote the respectful treatment of stakeholders?
- Does it create opportunities for greater involvement of stakeholders?

- Does it maximize opportunities for apology?
- Does it involve the offender in planning sentencing recommendations?
- Does it help us solve problems—not just "process cases"?
- Does it require new measures for evaluating programs and personnel?

1. Use of a standard benchmark in evaluating practices: Does it enhance or impair the restoration of trust in the offender and in society?

The adoption of the trust model of restorative justice means that, in addition to any other values we wish to promote, *every* proposed policy and practice should actively facilitate the restoration of trust in the offender and in society. The goal of restoring trust, as I have maintained throughout, is not a substitute for other criminal justice goals, but should be thought of as an overarching goal that incorporates and prioritizes them. It is a goal that is consistent with the societal goals of crime control and the protection of due process rights, but also one that makes additional demands on the system so that the needs of victims and the needs of the immediate community do not remain neglected.

In evaluating and developing criminal justice policy and practices, the restoration of trust model requires that provisions be made for the restoration of both social and personal trust. This is the key to the design of criminal justice policies that will accommodate the use of informal, personalized procedures in a socially responsible manner.

2. Does it promote the respectful treatment of stakeholders?

Restoring trust also involves an awareness that the manner in which the work is done—the respect, competency, consideration, and integrity with which it is done—is itself a critical factor in engendering trust. Even if we changed nothing at all about existing criminal justice programs and practices, we would significantly enhance their ability to repair the harm of crime if we demanded respectful treatment of victims, community members, and offenders, and utilized appropriate performance standards to motivate criminal justice professionals to adhere to these standards.

The achievement of justice is not simply the result of a process, but is an inherent aspect of the process itself. Respectful treatment offers no adversarial advantage to either party to a proceeding. As criminal justice professionals, we cannot guarantee a favorable outcome to any party, but we can guarantee a fair and respectful process. This is something entirely within our power. In my own experience as a trial court judge, I have noted that most defendants (or, at least, those many who actually committed the crime) will maturely accept a guilty verdict when they are treated respectfully throughout the process. They understand that judges are not gods who can peer into people's souls and ascertain the truth, and that every trial involves considerable risk. When the evidence has been presented fairly, when they have been given a full opportunity to be heard, and when their testimony has been conscientiously evaluated, unsuccessful defendants can still be satisfied that the legal process was essentially fair.

3. Does it create opportunities for greater involvement of stakeholders?

Involving the stakeholders in the criminal justice process has been an essential value of restorative justice advocacy from the beginning, primarily as a reaction to the alienation and frustration experienced by many victims within the traditional criminal justice system. The advantages offered by direct involvement to a victim and offender are impressive: greater completion of restitution, greater satisfaction of the parties, reduced fear, and even, it is claimed, reduced recidivism.[1] Restorative justice advocacy concerning victims' rights, offenders' rights, and community rights has resulted in calls for a return to informal procedures to resolve cases; to "reprivatize" a conflict resolution that has been "stolen" by criminal justice professionals.[2] As we have seen, however, the model of privatized justice has a number of regrettable features that impair the fair administration of justice.[3] Under the restoration of trust analysis, the involvement of stakeholders is not regarded as a panacea or a radical alternative to a failed system. Instead, as with any procedural innovation, it is understood as a possible *instrumentality* toward the restoration of trust in the offender and in society. From this perspective, the possibility of involving the victim and offender in face-to-face dialogue is desirable in many cases because it presents the opportunity for those victims who choose to participate to move beyond his or her distrust in the offender and in society. The victim can express his or her feelings and attempt to elicit an emotional response from the offender: Does he empathize with the victim's suffering? Does he show genuine remorse? Does he demonstrate a commitment to repayment, to community standards of conduct, and to a plan for change? Fundamentally, all of these questions are variants on one single question: Can this person be trusted? Without understanding the victim's losses, without empathy, without remorse, and without demonstration of a commitment to repayment and change, the offender has no opportunity to prove that he can be trusted and the victim has no reason to trust him. Personal involvement is therefore potentially an important means of restoring trust for those victims who wish to become personally involved. The same type of analysis would be applicable to the many cases in which the victim *does not* wish to become involved or, indeed, to those cases, such as environmental crimes, in which there is no identifiable victim, by its use in judicial sentencing.

4. Does it maximize opportunities for apology?

The restoration of trust analysis makes us aware that creating opportunities for apology is not an ancillary goal of criminal justice, but an essential goal. Under the conventional system, apology is of value only as a confirmation of legal responsibility. It helps the case processing "machine" to move efficiently by providing evidence useful for a prompt conviction. By contrast, under the restoration of trust model, the loss of trust that is regarded as the essential crime of harm cannot be adequately remedied within a context in which the accused is expected and counseled to refrain from the acceptance of personal responsibility, as is typically the case in the conventional adversary system.

We must acknowledge, however, that a policy of encouraging defendants to accept personal responsibility for the commission of a crime raises the possibility of compromising the rights of the accused to demand a trial and to refrain from self-incriminating testimony. To answer these concerns, I maintain that, since the restoration of trust model encompasses the goal of restoring trust *in society* as well as in the individual defendant, the legal system must maintain all essential protections for the rights of the accused. Our collective trust in society would be diminished if any of these rights were not protected. Under the restoration of trust model, the right to contest charges will remain inviolate. What will change—and should change—is the manner in which *uncontested* cases are handled. Because the vast majority of cases that are now processed through the conventional system are resolved through voluntary pleas, the encouragement of apology would affect the manner in which such pleas are made: not through a formulaic procedure before a disinterested judge, but through interpersonal dialogue in which the offender admits responsibility directly to the victim. It is only in the context of a face-to face encounter with the person harmed that apology has real meaning.[4] Just as we have evolved exquisite mechanisms for detecting cheaters who violate the rules of reciprocity,[5] so have we developed the ability to avoid detection by the masking and feigning of emotions that express guilt, shame, anxiety, and empathy. The victim, who has seen the offender "in the street," is certainly capable and motivated to ascertain whether the offender's story is accurate and his apology is genuine. The victim, not the judge, is the one who benefits most by the offender's personal and painful admission of responsibility. Therefore, whenever possible, the offender's apology ought to be made directly to those victims who choose to participate in face-to-face encounters.

5. Does it involvement the offender in planning sentencing recommendations?

Although limitations are necessarily imposed on the range of permissible sanctions for any given offense, the direct involvement of the offender that is encouraged under the restoration of trust analysis offers the opportunity for him to "buy into" the plan, thus enhancing the chances for successful completion. Under the restoration of trust model, the involvement of the offender in planning the sentencing recommendations also has an expressive value. It means that the offender not only accepts the responsibility for committing the offense, but also accepts its costs. It therefore indicates his acceptance of the legitimacy of the social contract and his desire for re-inclusion in the moral community. His willingness to undergo rehabilitation, for example, demonstrates his commitment to change. Court-ordered rehabilitation, by contrast, has little chance for success if the offender does not believe it is necessary and beneficial. Of course, having the offender participate in his own plan of rehabilitation does not ensure success, but does make the attainment of success more feasible. Offenders who passively endure punishment do nothing to counteract the assertion of contempt for the law inherent in their crime. Involving the offender in planning a sanction, however, converts the sanction from a mere instrument of punishment to an instrumentality for the restoration of trust.

6. Does it help us solve problems—not just "process cases"?

Criminal justice professionals at every level are driven by the needs of the system. At one end is a mass of unresolved cases: crimes for which the perpetrator has not been adjudicated and sanctioned. These are open cases, and the goal of the conventional system is to close them as expeditiously as possible.

Restorative justice is not satisfied with merely "closing out" cases because, at the end of a case, we must ask: What has been done to repair the harm of crime? The restoration of trust analysis refines this audacious new approach a step further by asking: Now that the case is closed, what has been done *to restore trust in the offender and in society*? By requiring criminal justice professionals to consider the implications of what they do upon the prospects for restoring personal and social trust, the possibility emerges for the systematic recognition and reward of positive results and also the recognition and discouragement of negative results. In this way, every case presents the opportunity for criminal justice practitioners to employ their professional skills, their diligence and their creativity to the task of restoration – a task that is hardly ever considered in our haste to "close out" cases.

7. Does it require new measures for evaluating programs and personnel?

The criminal justice system is, and ever shall be, an immense government bureaucracy. Every worker fits within a hierarchy of supervision intended to conform his or her behavior to the expectations of supervisors. The adoption of any reform results in a change of expectations, and those changes must be communicated clearly. But communication is not enough. Training is not enough. The day-to-day business of a bureaucracy requires that changes of expectations be reflected in specific, measurable performance requirements. This poses some unique challenges for the implementation of the restoration of trust model because, in contrast to conventional case processing, it places a high value on the respectful treatment of all participants and its ability to address the needs of victims and the community. Therefore, in addition to the many performance measures typically utilized in the conventional system, such as the extent of case backlogs (a measure of efficiency) and rates of recidivism (a measure of crime control), we would also add qualitative evaluations by the participants in the process. We want to know if they were satisfied with the way in which they were treated, whether their questions were answered, whether they had an opportunity to be heard, and whether their experience enhanced or detracted from their respect for the system of justice and their sense of personal safety. These qualitative evaluations provide invaluable feedback to criminal justice workers and provide necessary information for their evaluation by supervisors. Clearly, no professional enjoys the prospect of criticism, yet there can be little doubt that the mere existence of such feedback is an important motivational tool. If we expect more from the justice system than simply efficiency in processing cases, these new expectations require innovative and useful outcome measures.

With these policy guidelines in mind, let us now proceed to a number of specific practical applications. For each example, readers are encouraged to consider whether the application would be feasible in their jurisdiction and whether other alternatives could be devised that would enhance the opportunities for restoring personal and social trust.

Settings and Limitations

The goal of restoring trust in the offender and in society is intended to be applicable to every case within the criminal justice system. The restoration of trust approach is clearly appropriate for juvenile matters, as are most other restorative justice formats. But beyond those limited uses, since there are no inherent limitations to non-punitive sanctions, there is no reason that the restoration of trust approach could not also be utilized for adult offenders and serious offenses. For each type of offense, a victim and offender would be free to negotiate sentencing recommendations within boundaries of sentencing severity established by law. Victim-offender dialogues conducted to create sentencing recommendations would operate exclusively in uncontested cases (i.e., those in which criminal liability is conceded by the defendant), but the restoration of trust analysis could be utilized in both uncontested and contested cases. During the trial of a contested case, the traditional adversary model would be employed without alteration. At the completion of the trial, however, if the defendant is convicted, the restoration of trust approach could be utilized as a guide for the judge in selecting appropriate sanctions.

Let us take a closer look at three types of cases that demonstrate the versatility of the restoration of trust approach in contrast to both the conventional system and a nonpunitive version of restorative justice: domestic violence, priest sex abuse cases and violent crime.

Domestic Violence

Restorative justice, as presently construed, has had an uneasy relationship with advocates for victims of domestic violence. The approach of peacemaking, reconciliation, and conflict resolution that is offered as an alternative to the conventional approach of arrest and prosecution of criminal defendants has little appeal for those who remember the time, not very long ago, when domestic violence was considered a private matter between partners that was best dealt with by counseling and cooling-off periods. Rather than treat wife beaters as common criminals, the law tended to avoid criminal procedures altogether, steering the couple toward special domestic relations courts. This attitude underwent a fundamental change in the 1980s, and the idea of now reprivatizing domestic violence by way of adopting non-punitive and conciliatory restorative justice techniques is regarded by many women's advocates as regressive.[6] Some victims of domestic violence, however, are uncomfortable with the new get-tough policy of mandatory arrest and prosecution of their domestic partners and would prefer to have the alternative of mediation available.[7] The restoration of trust model offers a way out of this dilemma because it enables parties to discuss and negotiate what they consider to be an appropriate sanction within boundaries established by law that ensure maintenance of social values of justice and public safety. If both parties freely and voluntarily agree to meet, present and former domestic partners could therefore decide on sentencing recommendations that neither would exceed the maximum nor fail to comply with the minimum level of severity required by law. The existence of a mandatory minimum sentence frees the victim of domestic violence from the guilt that may be associated with demanding criminal punishment for an intimate relation, which is often exacerbated by entreaties from friends and family members. Realistically, this will not prevent many victims of domestic violence from effectively dismissing criminal charges by their refusal to cooperate at trial. But offering them a forum in which to resolve their domestic issues and the possibility of reduced punitivity to their partners may encourage more victims to maintain cooperation in the prosecution of these cases.

The problem of choosing between informal, nonpunitive dispute resolution on the one hand and criminal prosecution of domestic violence on the other is, in fact, only one manifestation of a major issue that has impeded the development of restorative justice: the problem of private justice that may impair the public good. Accordingly, the solution to this underlying problem that is offered by the restoration of trust model is also applicable to domestic violence cases. Because the restoration of trust requires both the restoration of personal trust and the restoration of social trust, personal and informal procedures applicable to the restoration of individual trust must always be confined within boundaries that represent societal-level standards of public safety and just deserts. Private justice, in short, can be accommodated in domestic violence cases when it is mutually desired, but cannot contradict the requirements of public justice.

Clergy Sex Abuse Cases

Cases involving allegations of sexual abuse by priests might appear to be just the kind of cases that would benefit from a restorative approach. Instead, they pose a significant challenge to restorative justice theory and practice. In the past, these cases were addressed by spiritual and psychological counseling, with a high priority placed on the bestowal of forgiveness and healing, but hardly ever by criminal prosecution. To some extent, the decision to keep sex abuse cases "in house" was a means of damage control so that the misdeeds of a few would not impair public respect for the institution of the Roman Catholic Church itself. Viewed in a more positive manner, the decision to regard these allegations as internal matters reflected a religious perspective that placed a high value on forgiveness, compassion, and mercy rather than criminal prosecution.

The sex abuse scandals of the 1980s and 1990s put a halt to such thinking. Instead of fostering forgiveness and healing, the policy of dealing with sex abuse claims by private, secret agreements was now understood to be the source of lasting psychological trauma to victims and the perpetuation of abuse by church officials. In the midst of this crisis that threatened the financial ruin of the Roman Catholic Church and the alienation of many of its members, the church at various times offered the possibility of utilizing restorative justice as a means of resolving sex abuse claims. But by now, the public was in no mood for confidential meetings and non-punitive measures. The restorative justice approach that was offered by the church was really nothing new. In fact, it was the very approach that victims had come to regard as the church's way of sweeping an ugly problem under the rug.

The restoration of trust approach suffers from no such infirmities because it is dedicated to repairing the very thing that victims of the clergy sex abuse and the general public have most grievously lost in these cases. For each of these cases, the restoration of trust approach compels the parties and the criminal justice professionals to squarely face the question: What must be done to restore trust—in this offender, in the church, and in society? Persons who violate the law are held to standards of deserved sentencing and deterrence established by law and, within those boundaries, all affected parties can confer to create an individualized sentencing recommendations. It also provides a forum in which the parties, *if they choose,* can deal with each other on a personal basis for the purpose of healing and reestablishing trust to fullest extent possible, while adhering to mandatory sentencing policies required by law. The restoration of trust model does not pretend to offer a specific solution to each of these difficult problems, but it does offer a framework for analysis on which an informed and morally grounded consensus may be built.

Violent Crime

When restorative justice was first posed as a nonpunitive alternative to conventional criminal justice, its eventual use in cases of serious crimes was not a realistic possibility. Serious crime in fact posed a major theoretical, moral, and practical dilemma for restorative justice advocates because, if restorative justice could not be used to protect people from serious crime and provide adequate justice in such cases, it had to ultimately rely on the conventional system to achieve these very goals. In that case, it could only function as a diversionary strategy for juvenile and petty offending rather than a "new paradigm" intended to replace the conventional criminal justice system.

But the restoration of trust model, as I have argued, is not intended to replace the conventional system, but rather serves to reorder its *priorities* under a new, all-encompassing goal. Accordingly, all the instrumentalities of the conventional system, rather than being rejected out of hand, are critically evaluated by a single test: Does this operate to promote or to impair the restoration of trust? As we have seen, deserved punishment is regarded by the public and by crime victims as a necessary aspect of justice and therefore its presence or absence is highly relevant to the emotional recovery of crime victims.[8] Correspondingly, the victim's restoration of trust in society is harmed by the perceived failure to impose a sentence that she believes to be required. The victim's faith in the orderliness of society is shattered when the rules are flouted and no ill consequences attached to violations.[9] The restoration of the victim's trust in society—her basic presumption of reciprocity in others—may require the imposition of an appropriately severe punishment. Any version of restorative justice that does not accommodate this sentencing option is, and must remain unsuitable for violent crimes.

But while the imposition of a criminal sanction criminal sanction may help restore trust in society, is it possible to restore *trust in the offender* for the most serious of crimes? My belief is that this, too, is possible in many cases or, at the very least is far more likely to be so than under the existing system. If the offender acknowledges his wrongdoing, demonstrates genuine remorse for his actions, readily accepts a long-term prison sentence as his due, and devotes his life to reform and to counseling others to refrain from crime, the foundations are prepared for his reacceptance by the community and even, perhaps, by the victim. If a pathway back is possible in such cases—however long and however arduous it may be—then the possibility emerges for restoring trust for a multitude of offenders who otherwise might face a lifetime of rejection, alienation, and eventual reinvolvement in crime.

But what about the most serious of crime? What about rape? What about murder? Is there any value in providing opportunities for the offender—even murderers—to become re-accepted as human beings?

Let's pause to think this one through. Imagine the worst. Imagine a homicide—but now it's not just some item in the newspaper. Imagine the victim is your own son or daughter. There probably are some saintly people out there who could overcome their grief and their rage upon hearing this and be able to see the offender not as an inhuman beast but as a fallible human being. I certainly would not be one of those. If given the opportunity, I could imagine myself killing him with my own hands. And yet even I could imagine that sometime in the distant future, I get a letter from a man in prison. In it, he tells me the whole story of how it happened when he himself was young, how ashamed he is at his crime, how he has grieved for my loss, how he has willingly accepted a life behind bars as his deserved punishment—and will continue to do so until the day he dies. In the letter he does not ask for mercy or even for forgiveness. He simply wants me to know that the person who killed my child is an eternally remorseful human being. Would I forgive such a person? Honestly, I don't know if I could. But, even so, I could not help being moved by his letter and I could not help acknowledging, for once, his humanity. Would this make the pain go away? Of course not—it would in fact revive the agony that always lay beneath the surface of daily life. But would it be *restorative*? Yes—in a strange way, I think it would, especially if contrasted with the icy silence victims and their families routinely encounter today.

No, I think it would not be a vain effort or a quixotic delusion to imagine the goal of restoring trust applied to the most serious cases. If we provide the tools necessary to achieve real justice and the opportunities for offenders demonstrating their underlying humanity, the bonds of social trust and personal trust can only be enhanced. When this happens, and to whatever degree it happens, we all benefit—victims, communities and offenders too.

Applications to Policing

The evolution of policing in the United States involved two fundamental crises, both of which was occasioned by the public's lost of trust. In the first such crisis, the system of political patronage of the nineteenth century that dictated the hiring practices, duties, and ethics of police officers was unmasked as blatantly corrupt. Police officers owed their livelihoods to party bosses who demanded only their political loyalty and ability to get out the vote in their district. Education, expertise, motivation, and character meant nothing without the pledge of political loyalty. [10]The result was a system that favored the well-connected "in's" and ignored the rest. It was against this model of politicized policing that the great reforms of the early twentieth century were instituted.[11] Now, instead of the local cop as surrogate for the political ward healers, the reformers envisioned a new type of officer: educated, professional, and removed from personal and political involvement. Indeed, the professional model of policing encouraged the periodic rotation of officers to different districts precisely in order to discourage familiarity with community members. Two technological innovations completed the transition away from the personal involvement of police officers: the automobile and the telephone. With these two devices, the day of the cop walking the beat was over. Officers would now stay in the station house or their squad cars and respond to 911 calls on as needed basis.

But this move toward professionalization, taken in response to the public's distrust of the former politicized model, went much too far in isolating the police from the life of the community. With the rapid changes in the ethnic composition of U.S. inner cities, the police were increasingly seen by racial minorities as an occupying army, a force of oppression rather than a service organization for the protection of the people.[12] Tragically, it was in the areas with the greatest need for effective policing that distrust of police was at its most intense. The time had come for another fundamental change in order for the police to regain the trust of the population it served. What ensued were a host of proposals for change, each designed to transform the image of the police from that of oppressor to problem solver. This has not been easy to accomplish, however. After a long history of abuse and neglect, why should the minority community trust the police now?

The application of the restoration of trust analysis to contemporary policing should be readily apparent. Trust is essential in order to obtain the active cooperation of the community, without whose support there can be no effective crime control. The strategy of community policing that has become one of the most significant policy innovations in recent decades is predicated on the understanding that the police, by themselves, can never have sufficient resources to control crime. The only practical way to do so is through a partnership with the citizens. This partnership, in turn, is impossible without trust.

Lest the restoration of trust approach be regarded as a soft response to crime, note that the primary responsibility of the police is the preservation of social trust. Social trust is the indispensable background of enforceable, mutual obligations that permit citizens to conduct every type of social and economic transaction without fear. It is the guarantee of the expectations of reciprocity, without which life truly becomes "nasty, brutal and short." To accomplish this mission, the police must be reliable, fair, and effective enforcers of the law. Several principles emerge from these requirements, all directed toward the preservation of trust in society:

- The measure of success in policing is effectiveness, not "toughness." A police force that is fearsome and intimidating, but does not adequately detect and prevent crime, is a failure.
- Effectiveness depends on the ability of the police to engage the support of the community.
- To engage the support of the community, the police must be respected by community members. In order for the police to be respected, they must show respect for community members, *including criminal suspects.*

A good example of how effective policing depends on community support can be seen in the case of neighborhood drug dealing. This is an open and notorious activity in almost every community in which it flourishes. It is, after all, conducted in open "markets" in order to attract customers, in plain view of mothers, fathers, and children. So why don't residents of the community do something about it? In my own experience, as a judge and prosecutor but, more importantly, as a community activist in a neighborhood that had experienced a significant crime problem, the answer is simple: Many neighborhood residents do not trust the police. Some residents, of course, are fearful of reprisals that might ensue from giving information and offering testimony at trial. Yet despite assurances of confidentiality and anonymity, they still refuse to cooperate because they do not trust the assurances. Others do not wish to contact the police because they believe it is simply a waste of time. Inner-city residents are accustomed to the police arriving too late, if at all, and achieving nothing. On these occasions, the police are prone to wax eloquent about what they cannot do, blaming lack of an adequate work force or legal "handcuffs." Their intervention typically results in nothing more than a meaningless report rather than any significant action. Other community residents are wary of police encounters of any sort because of the distrust and contempt that has been shown for them in the past. For many police officers who count the hours to their retirement pension, the greatest source of discomfort is not the offender, *but the complainant*. While the offender wants nothing more than to avoid involving the police in his affairs, the complainant is the one who makes an officer's life uncomfortable by insisting on action, diligence, and results. It is for the benefit of the complainant that time must be spent generating long and useless reports. No wonder, then, that citizens who request police assistance in solving difficult community problems, such as gangs and drug dealers, are regarded as pests by many police officers. Often, those with the most important information to share have no confidence that police intervention will do any good, and have ample reason to believe that it will be degrading and harmful to seek their assistance.

The restoration of trust approach provides a framework for creative solutions to these issues. Restoring trust involves restoring trust *in society* and to that end, the process of law enforcement itself must be perceived by community members as being fair and respectful. As in the case of adjudication, even though the results of policing cannot be guaranteed, the fairness of the process is certainly within our power. Restoring social trust requires from the police:

• Respectful treatment of complainants.
• Active efforts at problem solving.
• Adequate police resources.
• Cooperation with neighborhood organizations.
• Encouragement of community feedback.
• Rewarding police personnel on the basis of qualitative assessments.

The goal of conventional policing, following the professional model of Volmer and Wilson, is to achieve crime prevention and maintenance of order through the apprehension of offenders.[13] In essence, the function of traditional policing was to feed new cases into the system. What eventually happened to those cases thereafter was of no particular relevance to the police. Of course, to the victim, the community, and, of course, the offender and his or her family, what happens after arrest is of greatest consequence. The victim needs compensation and justice, the community needs safety, and the offender needs to become reintegrated back into the community. But many "professional" police officers were indifferent to all that: after the arrest, their job, except for the paperwork, was essentially over. The restoration of trust model demands more. It demands answers to important questions: How is the victim to be made whole? How is the community to be assured that the problems caused by this offender are resolved? How is the offender to learn from this experience and eventually be accepted back into society?

The police cannot answer all of these important questions, but they can provide necessary information and resources when each of these questions is eventually considered by other criminal justice practitioners down the line (prosecutors, defense attorneys, mediators, probation workers, corrections workers) and also, as we would propose, by the victim and offender themselves in the course of planning an appropriate sentencing recommendation. As in the case of the conventional system, from the very first encounter between the police and the criminal defendant, the police assume responsibility for the collection of incriminating evidence. Under a system dedicated to the restoration of trust, this requirement of evidence collection and presentation would continue, but it would be supplemented by the requirement to collect other relevant "evidence" as well—information concerning the causes and context of the offense, the extent of the harm to the victim and the community, and likely sources of remediation.

Just as police training now includes instruction about the relevance of certain types of evidence in relation to the legal requirements for conviction, under the restoration of trust model it would inform officers about the relevance of information necessary for the planning of reparations; not simply for exceptional cases, but routinely, and in every case.

Below are five examples of the kinds of information that would be useful to the restoration of trust model:

1. Identification of Stakeholders. In order to repair the harm of crime, police officers should attempt to identify those who have been directly harmed and also those whose safety has been placed at risk by the criminal conduct, including neighborhood residents and business owners.

2. Identification of Criminal and Noncriminal Associates. Although a criminal case concerns a specific individual charged with an offense, he rarely acts alone. Whether or not his associates are charged with an offense, they may play an important role in devising a solution, especially if this is an ongoing problem or if there is a threat of retaliation.

3. Identification of Trusted Intermediaries. Even though the victim and the community understandably may harbor doubts about the trustworthiness of the offender, they may yet gain a measure of reassurance that the terms of any proposed plan for remediation will be implemented if the offender can produce a trustworthy intermediary. The intermediary may be a parent, a friend, a member of the clergy, or, indeed, anyone who is trusted by both the victim and the offender. The presence of such a person at the restorative justice conference can help facilitate candid communication at the meeting itself and can help provide a safe and reliable conduit for future communications

4. Placing the Problem in Context. Devising a realistic solution involves an understanding of the scope of the problem manifested in the crime itself. Is it an ongoing problem? Are others involved? Are the victim and his or her associates also involved? Police officers often have creative ideas about the source of the problem and possible solutions, yet this vital knowledge is hardly ever encouraged within conventional policing. By contrast, the restoration of trust model would welcome such information because the goal of policing is not simply to supply new cases to the criminal justice system, but to restore community trust. This means that a core function of policing will involve an active search for solutions to ongoing problems.

5. Treatment of the Accused Offender. Finally, the restoration of trust approach requires the *respectful treatment* by the police of the accused because we seek the eventual reintegration of the offender back into the community. Respectful treatment does not mean that the offender's misconduct is to be ignored, excused, or minimized. On the contrary, it means that, although the offender's conduct is condemned, the intrinsic worth of the offender *as a person* does not need to be degraded. In essence, the police should deal forcibly with those who violate the law, but must never forget that these offenders are our sons and daughters. The philosophy of "tough love"—condemning the sin while loving the sinner—not only facilitates the restoration of trust in the offender, but also benefits the restoration of trust in society by enhancing community respect and support for the police. A police force that deals with offenders forcefully, but respectfully, is not soft on crime. On the contrary, it can accomplish the mission of crime control far beyond the capabilities of a police force that relies on intimidation to achieve its goals.

Adjudication

Although restorative justice advocates have often spoken in favor of the need to create a de-professionalized alternative to the criminal justice system,[14] the restoration of trust model requires no such drastic measures. Rather than attempt to eliminate criminal justice professionals, the restoration of trust model challenges us to reexamine the roles and obligations of practitioners so that their work may result in the achievement of greater, rather than less, trust in society and in the offender.

Under the restoration of trust model, little change can be expected in the handling of *contested* cases. Prosecutors would continue to prepare their cases as if they were to be tried in court and would continue to dismiss unsupported allegations. In so doing, rigorous standards of proof would be maintained and the constitutional rights of the accused would be protected. Defense attorneys would continue to strategize ways to avoid or minimize adverse consequences to their clients. Persons accused of crimes require nothing less than zealous advocacy on their behalf. Still, in criticizing the role of attorneys in the criminal justice system, some restorative justice advocates apparently have neglected the fact that some people accused of crime may actually be innocent, and that even those who are factually guilty have rights to a fair trial that are worth defending. Braithwaite, for example, in explaining why he would bar lawyers from restorative justice conferences, argued that lawyers "invite people who as witnesses can inflict maximum damage to the other side" while restorative justice "facilitators empower stakeholders, both victims and offenders, to invite people who will provide maximum support for their own side."[15]

In the real world of criminal law practice, of course, few cases are brought to trial. The vast majority are settled by mutual agreement. Ironically, while criminal justice professionals receive extensive training for trials, which rarely occur, they receive almost no training for negotiations, which routinely occur. For noncontested cases, the restoration of trust approach would indeed envision face-to-face dialogue between victims and offenders whenever it is mutually agreed to do so, but this does not mean that the function of the prosecutor and the defense attorney should therefore be eliminated.

The prosecution and defense would continue to prepare their cases as under the conventional system, and would be expected to negotiate the final charges to which the defendant will plead after evaluating the available evidence, the legal requirements for the charges, and the intangible risks of litigation. Before a case would be ready for victim-offender dialogue, the parameters of the negotiations need to be established: What charges can be considered? What charges are to be dropped, consolidated, or reduced for lack of sufficient evidence or legal justification? These are questions that require legal expertise, and it would be unconscionable to assume that ordinary victims and offenders are suitably qualified. They are, however, fully qualified to speak the truth to each other, to evaluate the sincerity of each other's expressions, and to consider what must be done—and what they are willing to do—to regain trust. While some restorative justice critics of the adversary system believe that the involvement of lawyers is an impediment to restoration and that it discourages candor and induces defensiveness, the right to counsel offers the parties the assurance that their rights will be protected.[16] Regardless of how neutral and unbiased a mediator may be, the parties need assurance that the process fully protects their rights and that the choices they make are truly in their best interests.

Contrary to the view that in restorative justice conferencing, "experts in substantive criminal law are not needed because [under a restorative justice system] crime is not viewed as breaching state laws but as violating community norms,"[17] I contend that the knowledge of the law is a *prerequisite* for the fair administration of restorative justice. This follows from my rejection of the idea that restorative justice should concern itself with "conflict resolution" rather than with law enforcement. If parties were free to negotiate deals based solely on their personal preferences, without regard to the requirements of law, the public would never be assured of the reliability and enforceability of mutual obligations. Consequently, restorative justice would fail as a means of promoting social trust in society.

Should attorneys be permitted to attend the restorative justice conference itself? The restoration of trust model does not mandate any particular procedural rule, so local courts would be free to design their programs as they see fit. While attorneys are trained to zealously protect their client's interests, it does not follow that they represent a threat to a system that envisions a prominent role for negotiations rather than adversarial confrontation. On the contrary, they can be of great use in facilitating negotiations. In my own experience, prosecutors and defense attorneys both share an aversion to taking unnecessary risks. Once a case has been adequately prepared, it is the universal practice of both sides to evaluate the probability of success and failure and to consider the alternative of settlement. It is at this point that lawyers for the defense and the prosecution abruptly and seamlessly change their focus from combat to compromise. The parties themselves are often too emotionally involved and too eager for a fight to consider compromising their claims. Criminal defendants who are factually guilty of their charges typically have told so many lies to themselves and their supporters that they find it almost impossible to suddenly reverse course and admit the truth. Their attorney, however, can see through all the posturing and recognize the truth for what it is. Furthermore, it is because of his or her expertise, experience, and legally protected power as an advocate that the attorney can counsel the client as to the range of probable outcomes and the desirability of the offer. The attorney, far from being an obstructionist, becomes a facilitator of compromise. Compromise is nothing new for attorneys—it is a standard aspect of the practice of law.

In a restorative justice system, such as I propose, that offers the prospect of a tangible benefit to those who admit responsibility and agree to a face-to-face dialogue with the victim, the defendant needs assurance that he can profit from such a dialogue only if he ceases his defensiveness and denial. A professional mediator may attempt to make such assurances to the defendant, but a defendant facing serious charges would most likely wish to hear these assurances from his own attorney before committing himself to "telling all."

Other Participants

The restoration of trust approach does not mandate either who is required or who is prohibited at restorative justice dialogues. Given the broad range of applications to a wide variety of offenses and offenders, a diversity of procedural rules is to be expected. However, certain features of the restoration of trust analysis suggest possibilities worth considering. First, the core encounter between a victim and offender ought to be preserved and the opportunity for personal, candid discussions ought to be maximized. Therefore, the number of participants should be restricted to some degree in order to ensure intimacy. Beyond the victim-offender core encounter, it would be desirable to engage those directly affected by the crime and those most likely to participate in the plan for restoration. Under the restoration of trust model in which adherence to societal standards of deservedness and public safety are predetermined through upper and lower boundaries of sentencing severity, the need for guardians of the "public interest" to be present at the victim-offender dialogue is eliminated. On the other hand, those community members who are actually impacted by the offense or who can be instrumental in providing a solution should be invited either as direct participants or (as in the case of attorneys) as consultants.

Any person who might qualify as the offender's "sponsor"—someone who is capable of being trusted by both the offender and the victim—would be a most welcome participant. Aside from the context of victim-offender restorative justice conferencing, the presence of trusted intermediaries is often essential for many forms of conflict resolution. In traditional societies and in well-integrated modern communities, mutually trusted individuals are often called on to communicate with the parties in situations where the emotions, pride, and self-interests of the parties make direct communication between the victim and offender all but impossible. In the case of juveniles, this role is often assumed by their parents who act not only as responsible conduits for information, but also as guardians and monitors who can ensure compliance with any agreement that may be made for restitution or desistence from further harmful actions. Likewise, tapping into the offender's social network is a means by which the highly effective force of social control becomes available to the process of restoring trust.

Family loyalties, on the other hand, are sometimes the *cause* of conflicts, of which an individual crime may be only a specific instance. Here, too, the restoration of trust approach would envision the need for family participation in an attempt to go beyond processing an individual case and proceed toward the goal of solving the larger problem. Undoubtedly, this would make extraordinary demands on the skills and patience of the restorative justice mediator [18] but this type of engagement of affected parties is to be encouraged rather than avoided. The criminal case, then, offers the opportunity to explore and devise solutions to underlying grievances and ongoing conflicts. If, indeed, the family is the source of the problem, attempts to address these issues communally, although involving great patience and effort, would appear to be more productive than merely focusing on the assessment of blame for one criminal episode.

Offenders who are fortunate enough to be enmeshed in a network of community relations are more likely to be trusted than socially isolated offenders precisely due to the social control to which they are beholden. Therefore, the participation of key members of this network can only enhance the prospects for the offender regaining the community's trust. Unfortunately, a central reason why some people tend to engage in crime is the *absence* of social bonds. Unconstrained by family, community, educational, marital, or occupational influences, they tend to act selfishly, impulsively, and with less regard for long-term consequences than those more "embedded" members of society who are continually adjusting their actions to conform to the expectations of others. For good reason, these alienated loners are regarded as untrustworthy, and so the prospect of them regaining the community's trust in the aftermath of crime would not seem altogether promising. Yet what are the alternatives? Should we reconcile ourselves to the fact that a socially isolated offender, as an untrustworthy outlaw, must be subjected to a criminal sentence designed either to "teach him a lesson" or to incapacitate him for as long as possible?

The restoration of trust approach would suggest that because a solely punitive sanction has such a negligible effect on restoring trust, every effort ought to be made to engage whatever social connections exist between the offender and the " moral community" of law-abiding citizens. In the life of almost every offender, there is likely to be least one person who could supply this link: someone who could be trusted as an intermediary and, optimally, as a mentor or guardian. The search for such persons should constitute an essential task for any restorative justice system and should begin at the earliest opportunity. Investigating, soliciting, and supporting the participation of such potential mentors not only helps to achieve the central goal of restoration for the victim and the community (by increasing levels of trust and improving the likelihood of compliance) and the offender (by reducing the victim's demand for punishment and enhancing the prospect of successful reintegration), but also helps to strengthen the bonds of social control that already exist. In those cases where no such mentor or intermediary can be located, a vacuum exists that may be filled, nonetheless, by charitable volunteers. Religious organizations or nonprofit associations of ex-offenders, for example, might play a key role in providing a reliable "friend to the friendless."

All these are mere possibilities to be considered in crafting a form of restorative justice conference suited to the needs and wishes of the locality. For every proposed innovation, the central test remains the same: Will this advance or detract from the restoration of trust in the offender and in society?

Mediators

If restorative justice, as it has sometimes been claimed, represents a new way of conceiving of justice—a form of justice that rejects retribution in favor of forgiveness[19]—it is easy to see why restorative justice mediators may find themselves assuming the role of proselytizers for this new kind of justice.[20] The danger of this tendency, however, should be readily apparent. For many victims, insistence on unconditional forgiveness is neither morally desirable nor emotionally feasible and, in fact, may compound the harms they suffered as a consequence of crime by adding to it the harm of guilt as well as resentment toward a system that shows little respect for their moral values. The restoration of trust approach, however, does not pretend to offer a new definition of justice. Instead, it seeks to repair the essential harm of crime suffered by victims, regardless of their differing views on punishment, accountability, and forgiveness. Under this approach, the mediator must be sensitive to the needs and expectations of the parties themselves, rather than imposing his or her own values on them. The mediator need not steer the parties toward or away from a particular sanction but, instead, can guide them toward a thoughtful consideration of alternatives and resources. The results of their agreement will then be transmitted to the judge as sentencing recommendations.

The mediator also functions as a kind of "stage manager" for the successful unfolding of a restorative justice conference. Through training and experience, the mediator learns to anticipate the necessary stages that the parties must go through in order to progress from their initial intransigence, denial, or timidity toward greater openness and candor. The restoration of trust is understood to be a process that cannot be rushed. While encouraging emotional breakthroughs, the mediator must also realize the pitfalls of sudden euphoria and inform the parties that restoring trust is a long-term effort that requires verification over time, despite the magnanimity of spirit that hopefully is attained at the conference. Promises must be specified, they must be reduced to writing, and suitable enforcement measures must be established if the restorative justice conference is to have lasting value.[21]

Above all, the mediator must provide a neutral, congenial, and "safe" environment so that the parties can gain maximum benefit from a personal encounter. The experienced mediator may indicate a variety of options that the parties may not have previously considered, and encourage the kind of creativity needed for effective and highly individualized plans for restoration embodied in the sentencing recommendations. By establishing the groundwork for this level of communication and cooperation, the skilled mediator advances the restoration of trust in many ways: by facilitating the expression of genuine empathy by the offender; by encouraging the offender to participate in devising sentencing recommendations, thereby increasing the likelihood of compliance; and by engaging the support of the family, friends, and supporters of both the victim and the offender. Under these circumstances, the victim may be able to recognize the humanity of the offender and thus become open to the possibility of forgiveness—a kind of forgiveness that emerges in the course of honest and open dialogue rather than through any pressure brought to bear by a mediator, however well intentioned he or she may be.

Sentencing "Discounts"

One of the interesting implications of the restoration of trust analysis is that, because the severity of punishment demanded in any given case is understood as being only one of several means of restoring trust in the offender, the perceived necessity for punishment decreases as other non-punitive means of restoring of trust increase. Let's consider two offenders who have committed identical offenses. Offender A refuses to accept responsibility, shows no empathy for the victim or remorse for his action, and undertakes no plan for restitution or participation in rehabilitation but plans to passively endure the punishment that is imposed on him. But Offender B accepts responsibility, expresses empathy and remorse, agrees to make restitution and undergo rehabilitation, and readily agrees to and acknowledges the legitimacy of any punishment he may endure. The punishment regarded as appropriate for Offender A can be expected to be much greater than the punishment believed to be necessary or appropriate for Offender B. The latter offender does not seem to need or deserve the same level of punishment as the former, despite the fact that he has committed an identical offense with the same criminal intent. We know this conclusion intuitively—some people just need more punishment than others—but the restoration of trust analysis provides a credible explanation for why this so: Punishment is simply one means of ensuring trust in the offender among others, and therefore the offender who demonstrates all the other earmarks of trust does not need to be punished severely in order to restore the trust that was damaged by crime. Conversely, those who manifest no signs of trustworthiness must correspondingly be punished more severely before we can trust their ability to desist from crime.

In view of the societal preference for offenders who accept responsibility which, I argue, is essential for the restoration of trust, the question arises as to whether a sentencing "discount" should be offered to those defendants who admit criminal responsibility and therefore qualify for victim-offender restorative justice conferencing. But looked at from another perspective, any benefit offered to those who are willing to accept responsibility may be seen as a *penalty* to others accused of crime who maintain their innocence and insist on a trial. There is a further concern that, if the inducement to admit responsibility is sufficiently great, persons wrongfully accused of crime might enter guilty pleas out of sheer expediency. In light of the great value to the victim, to society, and ultimately to the offender himself, we would do well to offer a sentence reduction as an inducement to the acceptance of responsibility, but we must be careful to do so without thereby inducing false confessions or penalizing those who exercise their right to trial.[22]

In answer to the concern of false confessions, it must be remembered that the process of dialogue is by no means a guarantee of leniency. For one thing, an offender cannot avoid the imposition of a punishment that falls within the upper and lower limits established by law. Furthermore, the restorative justice conference requires the offender to subject himself to close scrutiny as to his candor in explaining his conduct and his sincerity in offering an apology, expressing remorse, and agreeing to terms of restitution. It is exceedingly unlikely that an innocent person can expect to convince the victim of his sincerity and remorse for a crime he has never committed. The more serious objection to sentence reductions for those who admit responsibility is that it operates to *penalize* those who would exercise their right to trial. This argument has little moral weight for those who are factually guilty, but who have reason to believe that they may nonetheless prevail at trial because of the weaknesses of the prosecution's case. All they have given up is their chance to avoid "beating the system." For those who justify the defense of the factually guilty as a means of keeping the prosecution "honest," the use of sentencing reductions as an inducement to plead guilty would not forfeit their ability to challenge procedural irregularities because they could still be remedied by pretrial motions. The more critical moral problem in offering a sentencing discount for those who admit criminal liability concerns those who are *factually innocent* because, if they are convicted after trial, they might suffer a greater penalty than those who had admitted their involvement and thereby benefited from a reduction in sentencing severity. In such cases, not only is the defendant wrongfully convicted, but his sentence is apt to be more severe than that of a person whose guilt is readily apparent.

The answer to this dilemma, I would argue, is that, rather than eliminate the advantages gained from offering sentencing reductions to those who admit responsibility, the rights of those who seek to challenge the charges at trial should be *augmented*. This can be done by permitting into evidence a defendant's refusal to accept the possibility of a sentencing discount in exchange for an admission of responsibility and by adopting a specific jury instruction permitting the jury to draw a favorable inference of the defendant's credibility from his refusal to accept the discount. By giving the defendant this powerful evidentiary tool, any disadvantage of rejecting the sentencing reduction offer is offset by the advantage gained in reducing the risks inevitably encountered in a criminal trial.

Confidentiality of Statements Made During Victim-Offender Encounter Sessions

Under the conventional system, defendants (usually on advice of counsel) are disinclined to "tell all." There is simply no advantage to it. But the restoration of trust model would encourage the parties to change that mindset in order to achieve the full advantages of the restorative justice conference. The goal is for the dialogue to result in a meeting of the minds, not only with respect to a truthful recounting of the crime and its emotional and psychological effects, but also with respect to a plan for remediation and recommended sanctions. If no agreement is reached, however, should the parties' statements made during the conference be available for subsequent use in criminal and civil proceedings? The position of the American Bar Association is that, in order to encourage candor during the sessions, the defendant's decision to waive his Fifth Amendment rights should be limited to its use during those sessions, and subsequent use of statements would be barred in any civil or criminal proceeding.[23] This is analogous to the rule of evidence rendering inadmissible statements made in the course of settlement negotiations. The reasoning behind this rule is that, while such statements would ordinarily be admissible as relevant, material, and highly probative of the truth, they are nonetheless held inadmissible in order to encourage candor and to advance the social policy favoring attempts at informal, out-of-court settlements whenever possible.

Under the restoration of trust analysis, however, the adoption of a similar policy of shielding statements made by the parties in the course of victim-offender dialogue against further use would appear to be both unwise and unnecessary. The strength of the offender's acceptance of responsibility and expression of remorse derives precisely from the adverse consequences that flow from such statements. By accepting responsibility and by acknowledging the extent of the losses suffered by the victim and the community, he forfeits his ability to assert any claim or defense that would limit his civil or criminal liability. This awareness of the consequences of his statements makes them credible and serves as the basis for the restoration of trust in him by the victim and by the community. Recall the case of Kathryn Ann Powers, whose heart-rending expression of contrition meant little to the family of her victim until she abruptly changed course at her parole hearing and dropped her request for early release.[24] It was only then that her words resonated with the family and she could finally obtain the acknowledgment of her humanity that she had long sought.

Accordingly, in victim-offender conferences, the very candor that is hoped to be achieved by an evidentiary rule of confidentiality[25] is vitiated by the distrust with which such testimony may be regarded by the victim when it is shielded from any subsequent use. If the offender who stands to gain the possibility of a sentence reduction by telling all can retract those statements if no agreement is reached, his statements would be of little value in the process of regaining trust.

In the final analysis, the success of victim-offender dialogue does not appear to be advanced by the adoption of rules of confidentiality. The prospect of obtaining a significant sentence reduction through victim-offender negotiations should be inducement enough for offenders to honestly relate the full extent of their crime, to accept responsibility, and to demonstrate remorse. Offenders should be concerned about whether their statements are regarded by the victim as credible. To use the restorative justice conference as a way to "test the waters," to obtain the best deal possible, and to withdraw admissions of liability if the offender doesn't get what he wishes is wholly contrary to the goal of restoring trust.

Devising an Appropriate Sentence Recommendation

Throughout earlier chapters, and particularly in Chapter 8, the primary focus has been on the implications to sentencing theory and practice that can be derived from the restoration of trust model. Rather than repeat that analysis, a few points are worth considering now before we proceed to other criminal procedure applications:

- Encouragement of Creative and Individualized Sentencing.
- Application to Judicial Sentencing.
- Arousing Empathy.
- Minimizing Resort to Punishment.
- Mandatory Minimum Sentences.
- Policy on First-Time Offenders.
- "Net Widening"

Encouragement of Creative and Individualized Sentencing

At the restorative justice conference, the participants need not concern themselves with the effect of their sentencing recommendation on society. This is not because those considerations are irrelevant, but because the needs of society as a whole have already been taken into account by the legislature in fashioning the upper and lower limits of severity permissible for any sentence. Therefore, the parties can focus all their attention on one problem: *restoring trust in the offender*. They can proceed to ask some simple and powerful questions: Why, exactly don't I trust this person? What must he do to change this perception so that he may be reaccepted into the community?

The mediator (or "facilitator") has an important role in helping the victim analyze the reasons for his or her distrust. If the victim's distrust is based on superficial appearances or, indeed, on his or her own prejudices, the victim would be encouraged to go beyond these preconceptions and explore the real basis of those concerns and use them alone to construct a recommended plan of remediation. If the offender does not seem honest or his apology does not seem sincere, perhaps a more probing series of questions will penetrate his defenses or unmask his deceptions. If the offender seems likely to reoffend, perhaps this is due to his lack of marketable skills, or involvement with delinquent peers, or drug dependency. Perhaps, despite the offender's genuine desire to change, the victim needs more tangible proof of change in the offender over time in order to believe that his commitment to change is genuine. Ideally, each of these concerns will to the end that a sentencing recommendation will contain a plan for remediation for those factors that impede our trust in the offender.

Application to Judicial Sentencing

Obviously, not every victim and not every offender would choose to go through all of this. It is difficult to speculate on the proportion of victims and offenders who would want to get so deeply involved. For the many cases in which victim-offender dialogues are not undertaken, the restoration of trust analysis would still remain applicable to judicial sentencing. In those proceedings, the exercise of subjective discretion is vested in a criminal justice professional, but this does not mean that the soul of restorative justice is thereby forfeited. It means, instead, that the principle of restoring trust becomes available as a "judicial guide to the perplexed." Speaking from personal experience, judges also need a way to reconcile the often-conflicting goals of sentencing policy as well as to base their ultimate decision on a foundation that is legally sound and that accords with their common sense and moral values. In our proposed model, because each of these concerns is encompassed by the overarching goal of restoring trust, a path to a comprehensive solution that subsumes all these important values may be found by asking: What must be done in this case to restore trust in the offender and in society?

Arousing Empathy

The restoration of trust model also suggests possibilities for creative sentencing based on the examination of those factors that might operate to enhance trust, including many that are not predicted from conventional sentencing theory. So, for example, an offender may be regarded as untrustworthy because he does not appear to adequately understand or empathize with the suffering of his victim. Victims have a tremendous interest in telling their story and making sure the offender comprehends the full impact of their loss. This fundamental desire has no favored position in the conventional sentencing theories of retribution, deterrence, or incapacitation. Even rehabilitation theory would tend to view the lack of empathy as a deficiency that could be addressed in subsequent counseling and the need of the victim to communicate his loss as ancillary to the goal of rehabilitating offenders. Restitution theory (insofar as it constitutes a theory of sentencing) would recognize the value in specifying the victim's emotional losses, but would fail to recognize empathy as a form of remediation.

By contrast, the victim's desire to tell her story and to elicit empathy for the full extent of her emotional losses are central features in the process of reestablishing of trust. For the victim, the crime represents a fundamental assault on her assumptions of fair play and reciprocity in society. The victim must be assured that people in the community are responsive to feelings of guilt and shame because, without the assumption of moral conscience in others, the trauma of a specific crime could well become the basis of a lasting and pervasive sense of insecurity. As a basic component of reciprocity, the offender must demonstrate his awareness of the effect of his crime on others. Without an understanding of the harm that he has caused, the offender will continue to live in an egotistical world of pleasure seeking and domination, The only antidote would be incapacitation or the infliction of such punishment as to persuade him to refrain from crime merely because of the fear of being caught. Empathy, in short, is of central importance to the restoration of trust in the offender, and creative sanctions specifically designed to induce empathy are logical outgrowths of the restoration of trust analysis even though they would be irrelevant to and disregarded by conventional sentencing theories. These creative sanctions might include hospital visits, encounter sessions with other victims and victims' groups, and the encouragement of letter writing and individual projects to make amends to crime victims.

Since these empathy-inducing measures designed to restore personal trust in the offender would necessarily exist within boundaries that respect the needs of society for deserved sentences and crime control, they can in no sense be regarded as soft alternatives to the rigors of prison. If a prison sentence is deemed necessary for a given offense, the voluntary participation of an inmate in an empathy-inducing program within prison is likely to result in greater, not less security to the community when he is ultimately released.

Minimizing Resort to Punishment

As I have previously argued, the restoration of trust approach does not reject the use of punishment, but would operate to minimize its use.[26] It therefore fully accords with other sentencing philosophies that reject the infliction of pain and suffering on a human being unless it is necessary and minimized whenever possible. From a utilitarian perspective, punishment should never exceed that which is necessary to accomplish the goal of crime prevention. And also from a non-utilitarian perspective, punishment should never exceed that which is necessary to achieve justice.[27] The restoration of trust model incorporates both the utilitarian and nonutilitarian perspectives by the recognition of both societal and individual levels of trust.

The net result is that the restoration of trust approach, like other sentencing philosophies, regards the minimization of punishment as a desirable goal but, in addition, it specifies a socially responsible means by which this can be achieved. Under the restoration of trust approach, punishment is not regarded as the antithesis of restoration (a familiar, but unfortunate, claim of many restorative justice advocates), but as a potential instrumentality of restoration; one that exists alongside many others. Punishment is seen as part of a restorative nexus inclusive of all other means of restoration such as apology, remorse, restitution, the passage of time, the presence of mentors, and the completion of a program of rehabilitation. These components are all indicia of trust. Furthermore, the restorative potential of punishment is understood as being maximized by its relation to these other indicia of trust. Punishment by itself, for example, is regarded as less effective toward the goal of restoring trust than punishment that is coupled with remorse (i.e., punishment that is voluntarily accepted as one's due). Hence, as I have stresed throughout, the severity of punishment is minimized when other indicia of trust are maximized. Because punishment is to be used only when necessary, the restoration of trust approach suggests that every attempt be made to employ non-punitive means of engendering trust before devising an appropriate punishment for any given individual. In this manner, we can minimize unnecessary suffering and unnecessary costs while maintaining the standards of deservedness and crime prevention required for the preservation of social trust in society.

Mandatory Minimum Sentences

While most restorative justice advocates would insist on the creation of *maximum limits* on sentencing severity to confine the retributive tendencies of victims or community representatives, some (even among those who recognize the necessity of punishment) would object to the establishment of *minimal limitations*. If a victim and offender agree to dispense with the necessity for punishment, they argue, why second-guess their judgment? We can well imagine many cases, such as those involving first offenders, in which the imposition of punishment would be antithetical to restoration by unnecessarily labeling the offender a "criminal" or inducing defensiveness and denial when what we seek is candor and the acceptance of personal responsibility. Furthermore, as Braithwaite argued, given the goal of restoration for the victim, the victim should be offered the opportunity for achieving the "grace" that comes from forgiveness:

> Upper limits against the imposition of disproportionately high punishments can and should be part of a synthesis of just deserts and restorative justice. But lower limits are a roadblock to victims being able to get the grace of mercy when this is what they see as important to their own healing.[28]

> I do not believe there is any such thing as a disproportionately low sanction, as a matter of justice versus mercy.[29]

Why, then, must the victim unwillingly execute the power to inflict retribution when what he or she really wants is the power to exercise mercy?

If the restoration of trust approach were concerned only with the restoration of personal trust (trust in the offender), then we would readily adopt Braithwaite's point of view and permit the waiver of penalties whenever it serves the interests of the victim as well as the offender. But the restoration of trust approach is more comprehensive than that. It recognizes the legitimate need for society to maintain its standards of deserved sentencing and crime control *irrespective of their applicability to any one case*. This may appear unreasonably harsh, but the implications for ignoring the needs of society are far worse. Granting a victim the right to attain grace through the exercise of mercy (here understood as the renunciation of demands for punishment) means the abandonment of the rule of law.[30] The concept of "law" means that it is universal, enforceable, and not subject to dissolution by the will of any one person, whether it is a judge, a jury member, or a crime victim. The one exception to this concept of the supremacy of law is the extraordinary power of pardon granted to the chief executive. But that is a highly public act that subjects the executive to public accountability through the political process. In the case of a victim's desire to negate the power of law by asserting the power to bestow mercy, there is no corresponding mechanism of public accountability. Every victim, if given this power, would be a law unto himself or herself, and could safely and with utter impunity ignore the moral standards of society and its need to maintain public safety.

There are wiser means of helping victims deal with their emotional losses than by granting them the power to nullify the law. For one thing, restorative justice conferences need not include the option of recommending a sentence for those victims who are uncomfortable exercising such power, however limited. Victims who object to the imposition of even a mandatory minimum may nonetheless profit from a restorative justice conference conducted solely for establishing a dialogue with the offender or in order to establish reasonable terms of restitution. In cases in which punishment is deemed to be inappropriate, prosecutorial discretion may be exercised to divert matters away from formal prosecution altogether. In addition, the legislature may reject the imposition of a mandatory minimum punishment as being unnecessary, or, indeed, counterproductive in many cases. This is seen today with respect to petty offenses, juvenile offenses, first-time offenders, and drug possession charges. Therefore, it is only with respect to more serious offenses and repeat offenders—cases in which the legislature may be expected to impose mandatory minimum punishments—that the issue arises concerning the waiver of penalties for exceptionally meritorious offenders.

But even in these unusual situations, in which the application of the minimum standards of severity imposed by the legislature might be regarded as unnecessary or unfair for certain offenders, the law could easily accommodate a reconciliation of private and public justice by permitting exceptions to mandatory sentencing guidelines in exceptional circumstances. There is nothing particularly novel in this formulation. It is a standard component of state and federal sentencing guidelines.[31] Instead of giving victims carte blanche authority to ignore any standards imposed by law in their quest to attain grace, a more sensible procedure would be for the participants of a restorative justice conference to request that the court approve a recommended sentence that varies from the guidelines. Such a procedure would ensure protection of the public interest by requiring notice and by offering all interested parties the opportunity to address the court. It would require the parties to the proposal to specify the reasons for departure from the guidelines in order to expose any venality, corruption, collusion, or intimidation. The power of accepting or rejecting sentencing recommendations would remain with a neutral judicial officer who is accountable to reviewing courts for the exercise of sound judgment. Excluded from the reasons for accepting a departure for sentencing guidelines would be a victim's desire for the attainment of grace as well as a judge's personal desire to attain grace as a justification for abnegating the requirements of law. The governing principle for departures from mandatory guidelines, either under restorative justice or a conventional system, is whether such action is in the interest of justice and not whether it is in the interest of any one party to the proceedings to attain the benefits of beatitude.

Policy on First-Time Offenders

From the restoration of trust perspective, first-time offenders *should* be treated differently from repeat offenders, but not merely by diversion or dismissal of charges to avoid labeling or even by encouraging rehabilitation in lieu of punishment. The first offense presents the best opportunity to accomplish the essential mission of restorative justice. It is a decisive moment in the offender's life that should not be squandered by merely giving offenders a "second chance."

A first-time offender typically enters the criminal justice system with great trepidation, if not abject terror. After all the lectures about the consequences of crime, he is finally caught, removed from his parents and friends, and now awaits his fate. But if instead of receiving the kind of sentence he has been led to believe is the inevitable consequence of wrongdoing, the court gives him "second chance" because it is his first offense, the message of deterrence is fatally compromised. The once-dreaded system is now seen as a paper tiger whose snarl will never again appear so fearsome.[32] This is a disaster both in terms of the goal of restoring trust in the offender because he has less fear of arrest and punishment, but also in terms of the goal of restoring trust in society because the message conveyed by dismissing criminal charges is that the system does not back up its threats with credible actions. The victim, meanwhile, is left with the sobering impression that the system is more interested in the emotional well-being of criminals than of the innocent persons they prey upon.

The restoration of trust approach also recognizes the desirability of avoiding criminal labels since labeling person as a criminal or a delinquent may be an impediment to restoring trust in the offender. But instead of merely dismissing charges, our approach would use the occasion of a first-time arrest to intensify all available means to bring the offender "back into the fold." One imagines a virtual swarm of activity involving as many people as possible as mentors, advisors, intermediaries, problem solvers, and monitors, and to construct a plan for restoration that is comprehensive, individualized, and enforceable. This extraordinary effort should be made for first-time offenders because this is the time in their life when significant change is most likely to occur.

"Net Widening"

Subjecting first-time offenders to this "swarm" of interventions raises the possibility of "net widening": the more conditions that are placed on a person and the closer we monitor compliance with those conditions, the more likely it is that violations will be detected and prosecuted. A simple offense (say, shoplifting) could give rise to a multitude of conditions in sentencing, each representing the potential for further court involvement. And so, as these conditions multiply, the net is widened. But is such net widening truly *undesirable*? From the perspective of restoring trust, I would argue that it is, instead, desirable. After all, our intent is not simply to process a case, but to solve a problem. If a person engages in conduct forbidden by the criminal law, a serious problem immediately arises. He has placed himself outside of the moral community, and we are fully justified in trying to find out why he has done so. It may be something trivial—a momentary lapse of judgment, perhaps. On the other hand, it may be symptomatic of a deeper, more intractable pathology that is the result of abuse, neglect, or association with delinquent peers. It compels us, along with the offender himself, to explore the reasons for his initial involvement and to establish reasonable conditions of probation in light of what we have found, together with an effective method for monitoring compliance. But if an offender whose initial sentence was partially suspended by placing him on probation, again transgresses the fundamental rules of behavior specified in the criminal law or if he significantly violates the terms of probation he has agreed to, we will have every right to insist on appropriately severe sanctions up to, but never exceeding, the original sentence.

Probation and Parole

The restoration of trust model provides probation workers with a mission that goes far beyond the bureaucratic task of monitoring compliance with court-imposed rules. It therefore holds the prospect of engaging their energies and creativity and enabling them to achieve greater job satisfaction as criminal justice professionals.[33] Because probation plays a central role in the process of restoring trust, both in the offender and in society, the entire system benefits from the enhanced involvement and dedication of probation workers.

The process begins when the probation worker performs a comprehensive profile and risk assessment of the defendant. This is not just a routine background check because, in both bail and sentencing decisions, we are interested in knowing whether this person can be trusted and, if not, what can be done about it. In addition to the offender's overt antisocial behavior in the form of criminal history, there are any number of reasons to regard him as insufficiently untrustworthy to permit immediate, unconditional reentry into the community. These can include drug addiction, lack of employable skills, mental health issues, involvement in a criminal subculture, absence of social controls, lack of remorse or empathy, and so forth—each of which must be addressed in divising the eventual sanction. Although probation workers do not have the authority to impose sanctions, they do have the authority and the expertise necessary to *advise* the key decision makers.

The first use of probation assessments typically occurs at pretrial hearings in relation to bail setting or eligibility to diversionary programs. The bail decision is particularly relevant to the issue of restoring trust because it essentially involves the question: Can this person be trusted to return to court on his own volition? We want to know whether his ties to the community are such that he will not be tempted to flee. We want to know whether he has betrayed the trust of the court previously by skipping bail. As in the case of the criminal sanction, incarceration is seen as a last resort when the other indicia of trustworthiness are found to be insufficient. Similarly, the prosecution uses the pretrial assessment to determine whether the case is eligible for diversion. In this case, the issue is whether the societal concerns of deserved punishment and crime control, both essential elements of social trust, would be advanced or impaired by diverting the case away from formal prosecution. In some cases, diversion may be favored because society's interest in crime control is believed to be *hindered* by formal prosecution and *advanced* by informal conflict resolution or rehabilitation. In many courts, for example, including the municipal court in which I served, parties to neighborhood disputes are often encouraged to resolve their differences through informal mediation. For these cases, resort to formal prosecution is wasteful, costly, humiliating, ineffective, and, for some individuals, counterproductive. These people don't need a criminal record; they need a sensible solution to their problem. Still, not all minor disputes should be handled informally. Permitting members of a criminal subculture to dismiss charges against each other, for example, would harm rather than improve the restoration of trust in society. Therefore, in deciding whether to divert a given case away from formal prosecution, both the individual and social dimensions of trust must be considered.

Probation assessment reports also may be used by the prosecution in determining whether a particular case is eligible for restorative justice conferencing. Although it is anticipated that a majority of cases will be eligible (subject, of course, to the voluntary participation of both the victim and the offender), there may be certain cases in which the prosecution nonetheless desires to retain control over sentencing for a variety of reasons, including the potential for corruption or collusion among the participants and the existence of plea agreements and grants of immunity requiring cooperation in subsequent investigations. Finally, for cases that are referred to restorative justice conferencing, the probation assessment report is useful in informing the parties and the mediator as to all of those risk factors that may be considered in fashioning an appropriate sentencing recommendation.

For the offender, the restoration of trust approach permits him to understand the successful completion of probation as his *personal mission*. It is a challenging and difficult mission, perhaps, but an honorable mission worthy of his best efforts because the ultimate goal is to restore both his privileges as a citizen and his good name as a member of the community. By contrast, the conventional system of probation is but a personal burden—often a humiliating burden—that communicates a message of distrust and exclusion by society. In the conventional system, the only reason to comply with probation is fear of adverse consequences for not doing so. The probationer's tasks are to "go through the motions," to avoid detection of violations, and, essentially, to "get it over with." The restoration of trust approach would make probation more intensive and intrusive by virtue of the involvement of the offender's support network, but this is just the kind of involvement that is a necessary for restoring trust in this person and permitting him reentry into the community as an equal.

An offender's eventual reentry into society is the culmination of a process that began by devising strategies for restoring trust: accepting responsibility, agreeing to pay restitution, submitting to a deserved punishment, and undergoing a period of supervision to monitor compliance. The satisfaction of the conditions of probation thus marks a transition in the life of the offender. It is a rite of passage that is no less significant than his initial entry into the criminal justice system. Yet while the rite of passage *into the criminal justice system* is marked with ostentatious ceremonies reflecting the power and majesty of the law, the rite of passage *back into society* is strangely devoid of ceremony. Under the conventional case-processing model, the end of probation is simply the termination of a case —the closing of a file. Under the restoration of trust model, the completion of probation would be regarded as a very significant accomplishment worthy of ceremony. The efforts of the criminal justice planners, the administrators, the community members, the sponsors, the victims, and, not least, the hard work and commitment of the probationer himself should be appropriately acknowledged. The purpose of this ceremony marking the completion of probation is to certify the results of probation, possibly in the form of an "honorable discharge" indicating that the probationer successfully completed his program without any infractions, that he fulfilled his requirements for repaying losses, and that he completed all educational and rehabilitation requirements. Such a certificate would aid his prospects for employment and help restore his relations with his family and neighbors.

Of course, the past cannot be entirely forgotten, and, depending on the offense, the offender can expect to be informally "on probation" for years to come. But among the members of the public, a substantial number can be found who will understand the value of a person who has faced up to his responsibilities, who has compensated the victim, who has received his just deserts required by law, and who has tried to the best of his ability to reform and to make amends. These people have earned a second chance to live a decent life in society. For them, restoring trust is not an exercise of naïveté, but an exercise of faith in the human capacity for change and redemption.

Corrections

The prospect of transforming criminals into law-abiding citizens has been so alluring to moralists, philosophers, politicians, theologians, social activists, and "social engineers" over the ages but, at the same time, the success rate of their proposals has been so dismal that the history of corrections has seemed at times like a procession of failed panaceas. The restoration of trust approach, however, is not proposed as another corrections "theory du jour," but as a way of prioritizing goals, assessing the quality of practices, and providing guidance and motivation for corrections workers. Under this guiding principle, every aspect of corrections can be analyzed in terms of its tendency to promote or detract from the restoration of trust in the offender and in society.

At the outset, we should take note of the irony involved in introducing the notion of "trust" into the field of corrections. The corrections system, for the most part, is about prisons, and prisons are the ultimate expression of society's *distrust* in some of its members. Yet it is in the prison setting that the issue of regaining trust is of uppermost concern. A term of imprisonment represents a transitional period from exclusion to inclusion. With rare exceptions, these inmates will return to their communities, and so we must ask: Can we now trust them? From the perspective of the community in which the offender will return, what happens inside prison is far less important than what will happen afterward when the inmate is released. It is therefore remarkable that, despite society's keen interest in the issue of offender reentry, and despite the colossal resources allocated to corrections, so little of these resources, so little planning, and so little creativity are allocated to addressing the issue of reentry. Under the restoration of trust approach, however, successful reintegration of the offender is a central concern of corrections. A number of principles can be derived from this restorative and reintegrative approach to corrections:

1. Tough Love. It is essential that the offender be treated as a human being; a *flawed* human being, no doubt, but a human being nonetheless. He deserves to be punished for his misconduct because that is the price that must be paid for violation of the terms of the social contract, but punishment need not be degrading or humiliating in order to be effective.

As I noted in the case of policing,[34] lest these cautions about demeaning punishment appear naïve or "soft on crime," let us be clear that the primary function of prison is, in fact, to impose *punishment*, and punishment necessarily involves suffering. If punishment is considered to be a disincentive to violations of the law and justifiably painful consequence of wrongdoing, we may ask: What is objectionable about *degrading and humiliating* punishment? In addition to the philosophic objections offered by other sentencing theories,[35] the restoration of trust approach provides its own simple solution to this question: While deserved punishment is justifiable because it is an instrumentality of restoring trust, *degrading and humiliating punishment is antithetical to the restoration of trust.* It not only impairs the restoration of trust in the offender, but also impairs the restoration of trust in society because social trust is based on society's basic commitment to principles of fairness and adherence to the law, not to the exercise of raw power. Actions that are motivated by malice may engender fear, but they do not engender trust. Effective enforcement of the law is enforcement that is consistent, swift, and efficient, but also *fair.* It holds each of us to a single standard of conduct regardless of our individual backgrounds, values, vices, and virtues.[36] Furthermore, since the associated purpose of corrections is to reform the offender, it is abundantly clear that behavior modification is unlikely to occur under conditions that impel defiance and rejection. Therefore, even in the absence of humanitarian considerations, the *usefulness* of degradation as a means of reforming behavior is of dubious value. Those who learn to conform their behavior in prison solely out of fear of harsh consequences are unlikely to maintain their good behavior upon release to their community when those strictures are removed. In short, prisons can and should be tough in order to restore trust in society, but they impair that trust when they inflict needless cruelty and humiliation.

2. Reentry Planning Must Be an Ongoing Effort. Reentry planning must inform every aspect of corrections. A term of imprisonment presents an opportunity for both the corrections staff and the offender to examine each of the sources of distrust in the offender: drug addiction, lack of job competency, lack of social skills, lack of empathy for the suffering of crime victims, lack of remorse for the offense, or a combination of these. Having a person under the controlled environment of prison presents opportunities for change, especially for those individuals who were involved in devising the terms of their own sentence. Even for those whose prison sentence was imposed on them against their will, the restoration of trust approach would require prison officials to make available rehabilitation programs, including those programs designed to elicit empathy for the suffering of victims, the acceptance of responsibility for harm, and, perhaps, the expression of remorse. Regardless of the recalcitrance of the offender during the adjudication phase, the door must always be open to his eventual acceptance of responsibility. From the point of view of conventional corrections practices, whether or not an offender "owns up" to his responsibilities is of no great importance. The goal is to have prisoners do their time without causing trouble. Whether inmates remain in denial or express remorse is typically regarded as their own business.

The restoration of trust approach would suggest otherwise. Perhaps as a consequence of the adversary system that not only fails to encourage candor, but actively discourages it, or perhaps as a consequence of our natural aversion to painful self-examination, prison inmates have a pronounced tendency toward denial. Many of them, ever since their arrest, have been so preoccupied with the task of denying criminal liability—to the police, to their families, to their attorneys, to the jury—that it may be unrealistic to expect them to suddenly reverse course in prison. And this is even more difficult when they are surrounded by other prisoners who blame everyone and everything for their predicament except, of course, themselves. This hardened attitude of denial is fundamentally at odds with the goal of restoring trust. Of course, criminal defendants, even after conviction, have an absolute right to maintain their innocence and nothing can or should be done to impair that right. Nonetheless, the restoration of trust approach would have us carefully consider ways in which even these recalcitrant offenders can be offered opportunities to acknowledge the truth of what occurred, to empathize with the suffering of their victims, and to express remorse for their actions. No one should ever be forced to do these things, but the door must remain open to inmates who wish to drop sham excuses, assume responsibility for their actions, and try to make amends. Guided by the goal of restoring trust, we can offer expanded opportunities for inmates to face the truth about themselves in a responsible manner as a first step toward committing themselves to a new way of life.

   3. Utilizing the Restoration of Trust Approach to Improve Morale and Upgrade Performance of Corrections Workers. For many years, corrections officers occupied the lowest rungs of the criminal justice status hierarchy. They were regarded as strong-backed, insensitive brutes who knew how to handle inmates, but little more. This stereotype has changed considerably within the past several decades. As compensation levels have grown, there has been a corresponding elevation in educational standards and selectivity. The need for intelligent, well-trained corrections officers has never been greater, especially now that an alarmingly large proportion of our citizens are, or someday will be, behind bars. Yet we cannot hope to retain the best of these officers in the corrections system nor can we provide millions of people—mostly young, mostly poor, mostly minorities—with a realistic opportunity for change as long as prisons continue to function essentially as warehouses of human beings. It is stultifying and demoralizing to corrections personnel and dehumanizing to the inmates. The alternative approach advanced here is *to envision corrections as an* *essential part of the process of restoring trust.* Every aspect of corrections must be measured by the same standard: Does this help or hinder the restoration of trust in the offender and in society? As in the case of probation workers, the restoration of trust model enables corrections officers to take pride in their work by directing their efforts toward an honorable ideal. This is particularly important for minority corrections officers. They know there are far too many men and women of color behind bars, and they are acutely aware of its impact on their families and the community. The restoration of trust model permits these minority corrections officers to serve as dignified role models, to encourage young people to participate in restorative justice programs, and to work toward rehabilitation and successful reintegration into the community.

It makes sense to expend efforts toward the restoration trust in the offender because if the offender buys into the process—by accepting responsibility, demonstrating remorse, acknowledging the deservedness of his sentence, undergoing rehabilitation, working off his restitution debt, and agreeing to post-release conditions—there are positive benefits not only to the offender but also to the victim, the immediate community, and to the larger society. But do note the use of a key word in the previous sentence: "if." *If* the offender does not buy into this process, and *if* he is not cooperative, we must then fall back on the conventional strategy of punishment and incapacitation as the only means available to restore trust: trust in society (through the demonstration of the power and consistency of the law), but also, to a lesser extent, trust in the offender (through the crude behavioral conditioning of pain infliction and by physical separation from society). The role of corrections officers in relation to non-cooperative offenders, unfortunately, must be less personally fulfilling than their role with respect to cooperative offenders, but it may be imbued with dignity and purpose nonetheless. Even for the population of uncooperative offenders, corrections officers can serve as a symbol of fairness and professionalism. And they can still exercise the kind of "tough love" that maintains rigorously high standards, but never forgets that behind those bars is a human being for whom this period of imprisonment is regrettably necessary for the long-term process of restoring trust. If imprisonment is understood to be a necessary phase in the process of restoring trust in society and the offender, we can expect more corrections officers to take pride in their work, even when dealing with the toughest cases.

As with every other aspect of the criminal justice system, the successful implementation of these programs will ultimately depend on the skill, dedication, and professionalism of the workers who make it happen. One of the key benefits of establishing the restoration of trust as a primary criminal justice goal, however, is its ability to direct the efforts of corrections officers toward a positive, honorable goal: not just imposing hardships on offenders under their supervision, but restoring trust in them.

* * *

In this chapter, I have suggested a number of possible changes we can make to the criminal justice system that would actively facilitate the restoration of trust in the offender and in society. But the suggestions I have made should just be a starting point for your own explorations of restorative possibilities. The fact that you have ventured this far into a book about criminal justice reform indicates that you are not willing to accept "business as usual" but are interested in a better way of achieving criminal justice.

Guided by the principle of restoring trust in the aftermath of crime, I am confident that you too will envision a host of possibilities for reform in your own area of practice and expertise. If so, my advice to you is this: take the next step and try to make it happen. Don't wait for restorative justice to finally make the transition from the margin to the mainstream of criminal justice practice. When those of us who dream of a "better way" start acting on those dreams in the areas of practice we know best, the transition to the mainstream becomes a reality.

Notes

[1] Maxwell & Morris, "Restorative Justice and Reoffending," p. 261.
[2] Christie, "Conflicts as Property."
[3] See Chapter 4, *supra.*
[4] Petrucci, "Apology in the Criminal Justice Setting," p. 343.
[5] See Chapter 5, *supra.*
[6] *See* pp. 102, 196-197, *supra.*
[7] *See, e.g.,* Stubbs, "Domestic Violence and Women's Safety," pp. 51 and 57; Coker, "Transformative Justice: Anti-Subordination Processes in Cases of Domestic Violence," p. 133.
[8] See Chapter 6, *supra.*
[9] Lerner & Miller, "Just World Research and the Attribution Process."
[10] Walker & Katz, *The Police in America,* (5th Ed.), pp. 30-31.
[11] Walker, *A Critical History of Police Reform,* pp. 61-66.
[12] Kerner Commission, *Report of the National Advisory Commission On Civil Disorders.*

[13] Wilson, *Police Administration.*

[14] Olson & Dzur, "Reconstructing Professional Roles in Restorative Justice Programs," pp. 63-64.

[15] Braithwaite, "Restorative Justice and De-Professionalization," p. 28.

[16] Olson & Dzur, *supra*, p. 75.

[17] *Id.,* p. 63.

[18] I use the term "mediator" with some misgivings because it may connote a search for some "middle ground" between the positions of the victim and the offender. While seeking a compromise may be desirable in civil cases, it is morally repugnant in criminal cases which involve an innocent victim and a culpable offender. Perhaps a better term might be a restorative justice "facilitator", but this seems a bit awkward and bureaucratic. In the end, I settled upon the use of the term "mediator" because it readily distinguishes this role from that of a participant, an advocate or an adjudicator.

[19] See Acorn, *supra*, p. 28.

[20] Mika, *et al. supra*, p. 34.

[21] Levrant, *et al. supra.*, pp. 22-23.

[22] Bibas & Bierschbach, "Integrating Remorse and Apology into Criminal Procedure."

[23] "The statements made by victims and offenders and documents and other materials produced during the mediation/dialogue process are inadmissible in criminal or civil court proceedings." ABA House of Delegates, Victim-Offender Mediation/Dialogue Programs, Par. 8. (August, 1994).

[24] See pp. 107-108, *supra.*

[25] Ikpa, "Balancing Restorative Justice Principles and Due Process Rights," ("Establishing a privilege for statements made in the course of a restorative conference not only preserves offenders' rights against self-incrimination and double jeopardy, but will allow the offender to be more open in his communications." p. 324).

[26] See pp. 105, 109, 171, *supra.*

[27] Hart, *Punishment and Responsibility.*

[28] Braithwaite, "Holism, Justice and Atonement," p. 391.

[29] Braithwaite, "Thinking Harder About Democratizing Social Control," p. 205.

[30] Murphy, "Forgiveness, Mercy and the Retributive Emotions," p. 10. Accordingly, "the judge who is influenced simply by the plight of the offender before him may lose sight of the fact that his job is to uphold the entire system of justice that protects the security of all citizens," *Id.,* p. 11.

[31] *See, e.g.* 18 U.S.C. 3553(B)(1).

[32] See p. 241, *supra.*

[33] Umbreit & Carey, "Restorative Justice: Implications for Organizational Change," pp. 48-49.

[34] See p. 285, *supra.*

[35] *See, e.g.* von Hirsch, *Censure and Sanction*, pp. 83-84.

[36] Roscoe Pound, *The Ideal Element in Law.*

14
Conclusion:
The Pathway Ahead

Restorative justice is a bold and thought-provoking innovation that has engaged the energies and excited the hopes of criminal justice reformers throughout the world over the last several decades. And yet, while it has achieved outstanding results in thousands of programs, it has remained a marginal development because it has failed to articulate a theory and set of practice applicable to serious crimes and adult offenders. Unless it can do so, it may very well remain on the sidelines, "doomed to irrelevance and marginality."[1]

In attempting to bridge the divide that separates restorative justice from the mainstream of criminal justice practice, we must first abandon the illusory choice between a purist and a maximalist version of restorative justice, and focus instead on the core values of restorative justice that may be applicable not merely to the easy cases that we always have handled through conciliation and diversion, but also to the hard cases that now fill the nation's prisons and that are most in need of fundamental reform.

We need an end to the marginality of restorative justice, an end to dysfunctional hyperbole, and, candidly, an end to hypocrisy. We must stop using restorative justice as a way of promoting political and religious agendas. We must stop romanticizing a utopian past uncorrupted by the state and deal honestly and pragmatically with crime as it exists in today's society. By stripping away our ideological agendas and romantic illusions, we can focus on the unique and original contribution that restorative justice has to offer; the innovation that every restorative justice advocate regardless of his or her ideological "baggage" can agree on: establishing the *repair of harm* as the overarching goal of criminal justice policy and practice. This is precisely how restorative justice is different from conventional justice: *it's about restoration.* Identifying the specific mechanisms of restoration and the policies that best advance restoration are all secondary considerations.

First, we must be committed to the goal of restoration, and, second, we must decide how to achieve it.

Throughout this book, I have invited a closer look at the all-encompassing goal of repair by asking: What is the essential harm of crime that must be repaired? In addition to the material losses that require monetary compensation, there are nonmaterial losses. What exactly is it that is damaged by crime: our peace of mind, our security, our faith in society, our relationship to others? I believe that all of these losses are involved and, further, that they have a common nexus in a concept that draws on our instinctual responses to justice and injustice. In the English language, we call this concept *"trust"* but, in every language, a special term is devised for the quality we expect and require from everyone with whom we interact. It is a quality without which cooperative interaction cannot exist. Just as trust is a fundamental quality to life in society, actions that destroy trust are fundamental threats to society. Restoring trust in the aftermath of crime, I argue, is not simply a tangential value that might or might not be achieved in a criminal case. The maintenance of trust as well as the loss and restoration of trust are central concerns of organized life and are fundamentally implicated in every criminal case. While there are many actions that another person can do to harm us physically or emotionally, only those that constitute a deliberate violation of our basic expectations of adherence to norms of reciprocity—in other words, deliberate *breaches of trust*—do we characterize as "criminal acts" that must be suppressed by a collective response.

Every culture and every subculture, including criminal subcultures, require reciprocity among their members and have mechanisms for identifying and sanctioning those who willfully fail to satisfy our reasonable expectations of reciprocity (i.e., those who betray our trust). Trust, therefore, far from being a rare or ideal quality is commonplace; so much so, that it is *presumed* to exist in our fellow man unless something tangible is done to impair it. Nevertheless, despite its central importance in maintaining human relationships, trust, once damaged, is not beyond repair. In the personal and social relationships of every age and every society, the loss and repair of trust has been and is now an ongoing human activity. It may be a difficult, costly, and lengthy process, but *trust is restorable*: if not for every offender, then at least for the victim's trust in society that was damaged by the crime. As criminal justice practitioners and theorists, it behooves us to understand how this happens so that those mechanisms of restoration can be incorporated into the way that we deal with criminal cases.

It is precisely because trust is so central to social interactions that, as opposed to other desirable goals such as love, respect, compassion, and honor, it's loss can be regarded as the central, nonmaterial harm of crime that must be addressed by the criminal justice system. All of these other qualities are important, but none of them is a prerequisite for life in society. Furthermore, trust is not a vague, subjective "feel good" term with little utility to the real world of crime and criminal justice. Because of its linkage to a genetic strategy for successful social interaction and its associated affective responses, the discernment of trust (like the discernment of justice) is a potent, innate human ability, which probably existed before there was such a thing as law. Despite deep philosophical and political divisions over the causes of crime and the appropriate means to address them, the goal of restoring trust is a theme that unites the diverse perspectives of victims, community members, persons accused of crime (whether guilty or innocent), police officers, litigators, judges, probation workers, and corrections workers. It is a necessary goal, an honorable goal, and, for those willing to take the necessary steps, an achievable goal.

Among offenders who seek to restore their membership in the moral community and who are willing to pay the price—by offering an apology, paying for losses, voluntarily submitting to a deserved punishment, and passing the test of time—the goal of restoring trust that was damaged by their offense is realistically achievable in many cases: not all, certainly, but far more so than under the conventional system. And while we cannot expect any significant restoration of trust in offenders who refuse to participate in this effort, the imposition of sanctions that reflect society's demand for deserved punishment and deterrence helps restore the societal dimension of trust that was damaged by the offense.

Incorporating the individual and the societal dimensions of trust into the restoration of trust model is the key to reconciling public and private justice. It is the basis for restorative justice expanding into the mainstream of criminal justice practice and applying to the widest variety of criminal matters-—juvenile and adult, petty and serious, property and violent crime. It can do so without losing its soul because the soul of restorative justice is not a set of procedures, but a new criminal justice goal: *repairing the harm of crime.* This is precisely the focus of the restoration of trust model. Focusing on the goal of restoring personal and social trust thus bridges the gap between private justice and public justice, and moreover, it does so without sacrificing the important corollary values associated with restorative justice advocacy:

- Direct involvement of the victim and the offender in face-to-face dialogue.
- Offering the victim an opportunity to express his or her loss.
- Offering the offender an opportunity to apologize and to express remorse.
- Widening the circle of stakeholders.
- Involving the offender in devising sentencing recommendations.
- Minimizing resort to punishment.
- Providing genuine repair for the material and emotional harm to the victim.
- Requiring full accountability for the offender's actions.
- Providing offenders a pathway back to reacceptance by the community.
- Providing opportunities for genuine forgiveness.
- Solving problems rather than simply processing cases.
- Transforming relationships.

Direct involvement of the victim and the offender in face-to-face dialogue is favored whenever it is mutually agreeable to the parties. This is not because of any ideological claim that it restores to the parties the conflict that was "stolen by the state," but because face-to-face dialogue is a mechanism that effectively advances the goal of restoring trust. *It provides the means by which the victim can tell his or her story so that the full extent of this loss is appreciated.* These encounters also provide forums within which the offender's empathy can be aroused, expressed and meaningfully evaluated.

The offender is offered the opportunity to apologize and to express remorse, not as a punitive, shaming ritual, but as a critical first step toward regaining trust. An offender who passively submits to punishment without apologizing provides no evidence that he is committed to be bound by the rules of reciprocity. But an offender who apologizes and voluntarily submits to a punishment he regards as deserved is one who demonstrates a desire to return to the good graces of society. The apology negates his contempt for the rules of reciprocity implicit in the crime, thereby helping to restore trust in the offender personally and also the victim's trust in society that was shattered by the crime.

The widening of the circle of stakeholders to include family, supporters, persons affected by the crime, and intermediaries is favored not because it harkens back to a romanticized tribal past, but because their involvement is of practical value in the process of restoring trust. By contrast, cases that are processed routinely through the system for the convenience of criminal justice professionals manifest little regard to the effects of these decisions on the victim and the community. Opportunities for restoration, healing, and reintegration are thereby squandered in the shortsighted effort to "close a file," "move a calendar" or "eliminate backlog."

The restoration of trust model also recognizes the value of *involving the offender in devising sentencing recommendations*, not out of antipathy toward state prosecution, but because the personal involvement of the offender enhances the effectiveness of the resulting sanction. When an offender buys into his sanction, it becomes a vehicle for expressing remorse. It facilitates the repair of the victim's emotional losses because it explicitly negates the contempt shown toward the victim. It enhances the prospect for successful completion of restitution and also repairs the victim's nonmaterial losses by verifying the credibility of the offender's apology. In the aftermath of crime, words of apology are important, but words alone are not enough to restore trust because they can easily be interpreted as excuses. There must be a cost attached if the apology is to be considered genuine by the victim and his or her family. In every case, the same question arises for the offender: What can I possibly do to earn my way back into the public's trust? Whatever sanction is devised, its restorative power is greatly enhanced if the offender participates in devising it. At that point, it is not simply a punishment, it is a pathway back.

Viewed in the context of restoring trust, the contentious issue of the role of punishment in restorative justice can be treated with candor and, I suggest, can be the basis of significant agreement among both purists and maximalists. As we have seen, even the purists who declaim against the use of punishment concede a role for it nonetheless when necessary for public safety or in the interest of justice.[2] Their legitimate goal is therefore not for the elimination of punishment, but for the elimination of unnecessary punishment and *minimizing resort to punishment*. The restoration of trust approach fully accords with this goal and, in addition, offers a socially responsible basis for minimizing punishment together with a practical plan for doing so. Under the restoration of trust analysis, punishment, like every other component of criminal justice practice, is evaluated according to its ability to promote or impair trust. Punishment thus understood (especially if voluntarily accepted), operates as a potential means of restoring trust, along with such other means as apology, payment of restitution, completion of rehabilitation, and monitored performance over time in the community. Accordingly, as other indicia of trust are increased, the severity of punishment regarded as appropriate is correspondingly decreased. Under the restoration of trust analysis, this reduction in severity can be extended even further by bringing to bear many other such indicia of trust. The offender, in short, is motivated to do everything possible to demonstrate responsibility, empathy, and a willingness to change. If this results in a less severe sentence than one given to an offender who shows no remorse, no empathy and no willingness to change, who would regard this difference in treatment as unjust?

Ultimately, the value of any proposal for conceptualizing restorative justice lies in the benefits that can be obtained by the key stakeholders in any criminal case: the victim, the community, the offender, and the larger society. For the victim, the restoration of trust approach offers the prospect of *genuine repair for the material and emotional harm.* The establishment of sentencing parameters consistent with societal interests in deservedness and crime control supports the victim's desire for justice, for vindication of honor, and for the restoration of his or her fundamental presumptions of trust in others. The victim needs to know that he or she lives in a world populated by people with a conscience who are responsive to the suffering of others and not just by people who desist from crime only by the possibility of arrest. Besides telling his or her story, the victim needs to ask questions and receive answers, and to elicit shame, remorse, and signs of empathy from the offender. This is not so much to restore any preexisting relationship between the victim and offender as it is to restore the victim's faith in a world so that they may "regain the sense of personal autonomy and order that is essential to wholeness."[3]

For the community, the restoration of trust offers the prospect of involvement in problem solving toward the goal of achieving safety and resolving ongoing conflicts. For the offender, the restoration of trust approach enhances the likelihood of regaining acceptance into the moral community of law-abiding people by the demonstration of accountability both for the material losses and the moral transgressions involved in the crime. It offers the kind of *full accountability for the offender's actions* that we expect from criminal defendants, by accepting both the responsibility for the repayment of losses and the consequences of violating the basic rules of conduct that make life in society possible. It gives the offender a *pathway back to reacceptance by the community*: a way to pay his dues, to reconstruct his personal honor, and, perhaps, to gain forgiveness from the people he hurt. The forgiveness that the offender seeks is not the automatic, reflexive kind that merely serves a victim's need to rid himself or herself of unwanted stress, but *the opportunity for genuine forgiveness* that acknowledges the moral worth of the offender's attempt to set things right.

Although it encompasses the goal of restoring relationships, the restoration of trust cannot be only about restoring the status quo. For one thing, many criminal cases involve no prior relationship between the parties. And, as we have seen, even where there is a prior relationship, the relationship itself may be the source of the problem that resulted in the crime.[4] The restoration sought by victims of an abusive or imbalanced relationship is not the resumption of past inequalities, but the restoration of their right to fair treatment by others. Restorative justice is about *solving problems rather than simply processing cases*, including problems caused by abusive relationships. For this reason, the restoration of trust approach offers the prospect of dealing responsibly with intra-family and domestic violence, for which the return to the status quo is neither feasible nor desirable. For these and other cases, the restoration of trust means *transforming relationships* rather than restoring the status quo.

It is in the victim's hope of restoring trust in society that we see a desire to restore an original position that was disturbed by the crime: a basic presumption that others will comply with rules of reciprocity. In many cases, the victim, whose faith in the expectation of fair treatment by others has been undermined, needs his relation to society to be restored far more than his relation to the offender. The system we design for the benefit of victims must never neglect the need to repair the fundamental harm of crime: the loss of trust in humankind. Yet as devastating as this loss may be in the aftermath of crime, it is only deepened when the system itself fails to fulfill the victim's expectations of justice. Crime is traumatic, but it is not wholly unanticipated. We create a criminal justice system and spend billions to maintain it because we intend to use it. Our sense of order in society is interrupted by crime, but it is eventually restored when the rule of law asserts its supremacy. However, if the justice system *itself* fails the victim because it is unresponsive, neglectful, or abusive, the victim's trust in society that was initially damaged by the crime may now suffer a blow from which there can be no full recovery. Harmed by the crime, the victim now is betrayed by society.

Although most restorative justice advocacy has rightfully emphasized the value of restitution and the healing power of the personal encounter, the task of repairing emotional and psychological harm to the victim requires that due consideration be made to the restoration of *trust in society*. This is the critical background trust—the assumption of regularity—that permits members of society to interact without fear of coercion or deception. No system can claim to be fully restorative to the emotional and psychological harm suffered by victims without addressing the need to restore both the individual and societal dimensions of trust.

Implementation in the Real World

The restoration of trust approach does not pretend to answer every criminal justice problem, but it does provide a valuable tool of problem solving by helping us focus on what matters most to victims, neighbors, offenders, and members of the general public. In the hands of a criminal justice theorist, student, or practitioner who is in search of a better way, the concept of restoring trust is an idea-generating tool—a "heuristic device"—for envisioning significant reforms. But visions of a better way are not enough; they must be capable of implementation in the real world or they will be destined to remain tantalizing, but unrealizable, ideals. Unhappily, it is because restorative justice has failed to present, in Ashworth's words, a "theoretically respectable or socially acceptable system" to deal with serious crime [5] that restorative justice remains to this day a fascinating, but marginal, development. The potential of restorative justice to reform criminal justice as we know it has thereby been squandered by those who remain fixated on the notion that restorative justice is, and must remain, an entirely new paradigm with fundamentally different values than those addressed by conventional justice. In Chapter 12, I attempted to show the unintended harm that has resulted from paradigm discourse: how it has created false and intractable dichotomies, how it has delegitimized opposing viewpoints, how it has discouraged open inquiries, and how it has imposed a concept of justice that has little to do with the real needs and expectations of crime victims. Once free of the intellectual shackles of paradigm discourse and unburdened by the ideological baggage with which it has become associated, the prospect of restorative justice becoming a major influence on criminal justice policy becomes a socially acceptable and politically achievable goal.

The public can be counted on to support criminal justice reform, but never at the expense of its security.[6] The continued insistence by many restorative justice advocates to eliminate retributive justice altogether "erodes its ability to appeal across political lines."[7] The restoration of trust approach helps restorative justice overcome its marginality by presenting a way to enhance rather than oppose conventional criminal justice values, many of which represent the highest and most fundamental ideals of this civilization: due process of law, equality of treatment, proportionality in sentencing, and, not least, the right of its citizens to safety in their homes and in their persons. In so doing, it has the potential to appeal to a broad spectrum of political positions and constituencies, from conservative to liberal.

For conservatives, the restoration of trust model need not represent a "soft" response to crime because the fundamental societal values of deserved sanctions and effective deterrence are preserved by legislatively mandated sentencing boundaries. These boundaries could be as "soft" or as "hard" as the legislative process determines. In this regard, the challenge to conservatives would be no different from the challenge they face today, a challenge also faced by liberals: convincing a majority of voters to adopt their standards of sentencing severity. The restoration of trust approach also supports the value of accountability that is typically associated with conservatives, but goes beyond the mere semblance of accountability achieved through passive submission to punishment on the one hand and mere apology and restitution on the other.

The restoration of trust approach also helps make the liberal goal of rehabilitation politically acceptable to conservatives by reframing its function. For conservatives, the essential problem of rehabilitation is neither its inconsistent record of effectiveness nor its high cost. If cost and effectiveness were all that mattered, conservatives would never tolerate the vast sums that are spent today in the name of deterrence. Rather, conservatives tend to be wary of excuses for misconduct and are apt to regard such misbehavior as the offender's choice. Regardless of the unhappy circumstances of an offender's life, conservatives believe that he is still capable of making moral choices. From this perspective, having the government assume responsibility for initiating programs such as anger management, child rearing, and interpersonal skills has fostered a culture of dependency and made us regard criminals as society's victims rather than its victimizers. Furthermore, while society is justified in imposing consequences on those who violate the law, conservatives maintain that it has no business tinkering with the inner workings of the offender's character. To them, that is not part of the deal implicit in the social contract and is a deviation from the legitimate goal of law enforcement: protecting us from the harmful conduct of others rather than protecting us from our own failings.

The restoration of trust model provides a rationale for rehabilitation that does not conflict with the conservative perspective. First, rehabilitation is seen neither as a substitute for retribution nor an alternative vision of criminal justice. The restoration of trust model requires the consideration of the needs of society, including the need for deserved sanctions and crime deterrence, and these needs are not satisfied by rehabilitation alone. Second, under the restoration of trust analysis, rehabilitation, rather than being a substitute for accountability to the law, is *coupled* with legal accountability. Trust in the offender is engendered from multiple sources: acceptance of responsibility, agreeing to pay for losses, voluntary submission to a deserved punishment, and voluntarily entering a program designed to address any deficiency that impairs his ability to be treated as a functioning member of society. A person addicted to drugs, for example, cannot be fully trusted to engage in the daily life of society without resort to crime. It is therefore fair to expect this person to undergo rehabilitation before we fully reaccept him into the social order. Society has no right to impose these conditions on the offender, but it does have a right to consider his amenability to reforming himself during its evaluation of any appropriate sentence. The offender is therefore encouraged to fully own up to his offense and assume personal responsibility for its punitive consequences, for the payment of restitution, and for addressing his personal deficiencies so that he can again become a functioning member of society. What is thereby achieved is full accountability; indeed, the kind of accountability that engenders trust.

For liberals, the restoration of trust model offers the realistic possibility of humanizing the criminal justice system without sacrificing fundamental societal values. It offers a way to address the needs of victims, community members, and offenders far beyond the artificial limitations imposed by conventional justice practice. It offers a way to minimize reliance on punishment, but not by offering up a utopian vision of recompense and forgiveness as a radical alternative to conventional notions of justice.[8] Instead, under the restoration of trust model, punishment is viewed as one of several potent mechanisms for restoring trust and, to the extent that other non-punitive factors are increased, reliance on punishment is correspondingly decreased. In the end, the goal is not the elimination of punishment, but the use of punishment only when necessary, a principle that can be accepted by both liberals and conservatives alike.

In order for restorative justice to win support from the electorate, it must first be embraced by the very groups that it purportedly serves: victims and offenders. Unfortunately, while offenders have every reason to accept an alternative that offers the prospect of reduced punitivity and greater opportunities for reintegration, the victims' rights community has thus far been wary of restorative justice initiatives. For a criminal justice alternative that has been offered as a means of victim empowerment and a pathway to healing, the feedback from victims' groups that complains of its "injustice, disrespect, exclusion, lack of empathy, and irrelevance"[9] to victims must be more than a devastating rebuke to restorative justice advocates. It must be the occasion to reevaluate its core mission.

Against this background of wariness that separates restorative justice from its most vital constituency, the restoration of trust approach offers a way to responsibly and effectively address the needs of crime victims as well as offenders. It does not impose an ideological agenda on victims and insists on criminal justice reforms that are responsive to their actual needs and demands for empowerment, for reparation, for healing, for security, and for justice.

The restoration of trust model also offers the prospect of dealing effectively, fairly, and compassionately with crime in the minority community. With alarmingly high rates of incarceration, and equally alarming rates of victimization, the minority community is torn between abhorrence of and dependence on law enforcement. Standard solutions offered by liberals and conservatives alike have proven ineffective. Liberals who have long advocated for the rights of the accused have paid scant attention to the rights of minorities to live their lives without the fear of crime. Conservatives who have always promoted tough law-and-order measures have failed to win the support of the black community, without whose active cooperation crime control cannot be achieved.

Even though the restoration of trust approach cannot provide an instant solution to these difficult problems, it can provide a format for problem solving that can engage the imagination and political will of the minority community. Under the restoration of trust analysis, the criminal justice system exists not merely to assign blame and to punish offenders, but to repair the harm of crime to the victim, to the community, and also to the offender. In recognition of the need to establish and maintain trust in society, law enforcement consequently must be powerful—*but trust is not engendered by power alone.* The restoration of trust requires fairness and respectful treatment of the accused, with a kind of tough love that deals firmly with offenders without forgetting that they are our children. This is the kind of law enforcement demanded by minorities. The restoration of trust model, while not relinquishing the use of punishment when necessary, provides a realistic method of reducing reliance on punishment in dealing with offenders. More importantly, it channels criminal justice policy and practice toward the goals of restoration and reintegration. In fashioning a criminal sanction, we therefore ask: What must be done to restore trust in this offender and in society? In so doing, the criminal sanction becomes more than simply a punishment. It becomes a pathway back to a useful life in the community.

This is a vision of criminal justice that offers the possibility of significant reform for every aspect of criminal justice under the guiding principle of restoring trust in the offender and in society. Yet it need not remain simply a vision because, as I have maintained, it holds out the realistic possibility of political support from a diversity of constituencies: liberal and conservative, majority and minority. Furthermore, because it is applicable to a full range of offenses, it offers the possibility that restorative justice can finally emerge from its seclusion and become a significant operating principle in the criminal justice mainstream.

Through the pages of this book, I have invited readers to brainstorm along with me while exploring the many implications of a conception of restorative justice based on restoring trust in the offender and in society. Having engaged in the field of criminal justice for many years as an attorney, as a judge, and as a professor, I am very aware of the diversity and complexity of criminal justice practice in this country. Therefore, even as I have indicated my own views of how the restoration of trust model could be implemented in a variety of settings, I urge readers to consider how this approach may be best utilized in your own area and within the scope of your own expertise. What I offer is not an answer to every problem and not a checklist of procedural reforms, but *a way of solving problems* and *a way of envisioning reforms*. Guided by the overall goal of restoring trust in the aftermath of crime, we will be able to summon the creative energies, the practical judgment, and the political will to transform the way that we administer criminal justice in this country.

Notes

[1] Dignan, "Restorative Justice and the Law," p. 179.

[2] See pp. 18, 98, 180, *supra*.

[3] Zehr, "Justice as Restoration," p. 76.

[4] Coker, "Transformative Justice: Anti-Subordination Processes in Cases of Domestic Violence," p. 129; Murphy, "Counseling Forgiveness," p. 46.

[5] Ashworth, "Some Doubts About Restorative Justice," p. 298.

[6] Groenhuijsen, "Victim's Rights and Restorative Justice," pp. 76-78.

[7] Bilz & Darley, What's Wrong with Harmless theories of Punishment,   p. 1249.

[8] Robinson, in approving the restorative processes but rejecting restorative "justice" goes so far as to characterize the non-punitive form of the restorative justice as an "anti-justice view." Robinson, "The Virtues of Restorative Processes," p. 378.

[9] Mika, *et al.*, "Listening to Victims," p. 35.

Appendix A:
Scenarios Utilized in This Study

A. Individual-Level Scenarios (respondent as victim)

1. Minor offense—no prior convictions

Imagine <u>you are the victim</u> of the following crime:

> *On the way to your car, you notice that the passenger side window is broken and the ground is covered with shattered glass. Inside the car, your personal belongings are strewn about—and your radio is gone.*
>
> *Later that week, a 25-year-old man is arrested for breaking into your car and stealing the car radio. He has no prior criminal record. Your total losses (including the radio, damage to the car, and lost time from work) amount to $1,000.*

2. Minor offense—one prior conviction

Imagine <u>you are the victim</u> of the following crime:

> *On the way to your car, you notice that the passenger side window is broken and the ground is covered with shattered glass. Inside the car, your personal belongings are strewn about—and your radio is gone.*
>
> *Later that week, a 25-year-old man is arrested for breaking into your car and stealing the car radio. He has a record of one prior conviction for a similar offense. Your total losses (including the radio, damage to the car, and lost time from work) amount to $1,000.*

3. Serious offense—no prior convictions

Imagine <u>you are the victim</u> of the following crime:

As you are walking alone in a downtown shopping area at night, you are grabbed from behind by a man and pushed up against a wall. He shows you a gun and demands your money. You hand over your wallet, and he runs around the corner. Later that week, the robber, a 25-year-old man with no prior criminal record, is arrested after he attempted to use your credit card. Your total losses (including your wallet and its contents, and lost time from work) amount to $2,000.

4. Serious offense—one prior conviction

Imagine <u>you are the victim</u> of the following crime:

As you are walking alone in a downtown shopping area at night, you are grabbed from behind by a man and pushed up against a wall. He shows you a gun and demands your money. You hand over your wallet, and he runs around the corner. Later that week, the robber, a 25-year-old man with a record of one conviction for a similar offense, is arrested after he attempted to use your credit card. Your total losses (including your wallet and its contents, and lost time from work) amount to $2,000.

B. Societal-Level Scenarios (respondent as nonvictim)

1. Minor offense—no prior convictions

Imagine <u>you read about</u> the following crime in a newspaper:

A 25-year-old man is arrested for breaking into a car and stealing the car radio. He has no prior criminal record. The victim's total losses (including the radio, damage to the car, and lost time from work) amount to $1,000.

2. Serious offense—no prior convictions

Imagine <u>you read about</u> the following crime in a newspaper:

A 25-year-old man is arrested for robbing a college student with the use of a gun. He has a record of one prior conviction for a similar offense. The victim's total losses (including a wallet and its contents, and lost time from work) amount to $2,000.

Appendix B:
Sample Questionnaire
(Individual Level)

Three important notes before you begin:

1. Your scores

Relax. This is a survey—not a test. You won't receive a grade. (We won't even know your name!) There is no "right" or "wrong" answer to any question. We just want to know your <u>opinions</u> on several important criminal justice issues so that we can have a better idea of what most people think.

2. Definitions

For the purposes of this survey, please assume that when we use the word "punishment," we include <u>any type of penalty, such as:</u>

- Incarceration. (imprisonment), or
- Fines. (penalty payments to the government), or
- Community service. (court-ordered work without pay)

But our use of the term "punishment" does not include such options as:

- Rehabilitation. (programs that address offender's problems such as drug use, mental health or lack of education) or
- Restitution. (payments to the victim to his or her losses).

If you took this survey before—stop!

You may have taken this survey in another class. Of so, please don't take it again. It will make a mess of our data analysis. Please take the alternate exercise provided by your instructor instead.

Ok—now begin!

On a scale of 1-5, how much do you agree or disagree with the following statements?

1.....................2.....................3....................4..........................5

strongly disagree   strongly agree

Circle one choice

1.   Criminal sentences should set an example that will
influence other people not to commit the same offense.   1   2   3   4   5

2.   Unless offenders receive a prison sentence, they will
continue to pose a threat to society.   1   2   3   4   5

3.   Criminal sentences should involve a punishment
the offender deserves.   1   2   3   4   5

4.   Justice is achieved when the offender is punished.   1   2   3   4   5

5.   It is more important for the offender to repair
the harm caused by this crime than for the offender

to be punished.   1   2   3   4   5

6.   It is an important function of the criminal justice system

to try to reform the offender.   1   2   3   4   5

7.   The criminal justice process can only be
thought of as a success if the victim is satisfied

with the outcome of this case.   1   2   3   4   5

330

SECTION II

Imagine you are the victim of the following crime:

As you are walking alone in a downtown shopping area at night, you are grabbed from behind my a man
and pushed up against a wall. He shows you a gun, and demands your money. You give over your wallet- and he
runs around the corner. Later that week, the robber, a 25-year-old man with a record of one conviction for a
similar offense, is arrested after he attempted to use your credit card. Your total losses.. (including your wallet and
its contents, and lost time from work), amount to $1,000.00.

On a scale of 1-5, how much do you agree or disagree with the following statements?

1....................2....................3....................4....................5

strongly disagree   strongly agree

                                                      Circle one choice

8.   The sentence in this case should include
an order to pay for victim's losses   1   2   3   4   5

9. The sentence in this case should include payment of a fine   1   2   3   4   5

10. The sentence in this case should include community service   1   2   3   4   5

11. The sentence in this case should include imprisonment   1   2   3   4   5

12. The sentence in this case should include
some type of punishment   1   2   3   4   5

On a scale of 1-5, how much do you agree or disagree with the following statements?

1.....................2.....................3.....................4.........................5

strongly disagree   strongly agree

As a victim of this crime, I will probably feel:

	Circle one choice				
13. Angry	1	2	3	4	5
14. Resentful	1	2	3	4	5
15. Insecure	1	2	3	4	5
16. Depressed		1	2	3	4	5
17. Nervous		1	2	3	4	5

18. If there are other words you would use to describe the way you'd probably feel, write them here:

_____

_____

Again, imagining yourself to be the victim of this crime,

on a scale of 1-5, how much do you agree or disagree with the following statements?

1.....................2.....................3.....................4.........................5

332

As a victim of this crime, I am likely to feel <u>better</u> if:

Circle one choice

19. the offender is required to pay for all of my losses   1   2   3   4   5

20. the offender gives a full and honest apology   1   2   3   4   5

21. the offender receives a significant punishment   1   2   3   4   5

22. I am allowed to be involved in the sentencing decision   1   2   3   4   5

23. I have been treated with respect by the court   1   2   3   4   5

1....................2....................3....................4....................5

strongly disagree   strongly agree

As a victim of this crime, I am likely to feel <u>worse</u> if:

Circle one choice

24. the offender does not receive any type of punishment

(such as imprisonment, fines or community service)   1   2   3   4   5

25. the offender does not apologize   1   2   3   4   5

26. the offender is not ordered to pay for my losses   1   2   3   4   5

27. I am not allowed to be involved in the sentencing decision   1   2   3   4   5

28. I believe I have not been treated with respect by the court   1   2   3   4   5

SECTION III . (Read this carefully!)

It is now the day of the court hearing. Instead of having a trial, the defendant intends to plead guilty to the charges. All along, you have been treated with respect by the court. Also, you have been permitted to participate in this case as much- or as little- as you wanted, including the <u>option</u> to meet with the offender under supervision to express your feelings, ask questions and try to agree on what should be done in this case.

334

29. Given what you know about this case and your own personality, do you think you would chose to participate in such a meeting?

Yes = 1

No = 2   1   2   3

Uncertain = 3

For all the following questions, if you answered "Yes" to q. 29 above,

 assume that you went to the meeting.

If you answered "No" or "Uncertain" to this question,

 assume that you did not meet with the offender.

A. If this offender:

1.   receives a significant punishment, but
2.   gives no apology and
3.   is not required to pay for your losses,

what effect . (if any) do you believe this will have on the following reactions:

1....................2......................3.....................4..........................5

greatly decrease   greatly increase

Circle one choice

30. your anger   1   2   3   4   5

31. your resentment   1   2   3   4   5

32. your feelings of insecurity   1   2   3   4   5

33. your willingness to forgive   1   2   3   4   5

B. If this offender:

1.   Does not receive any type of punishment, but
2.   gives a full and honest apology, but
3.   is required to pay for all of your losses,
<u>what effect</u> . (if any) do you believe this will have on the following reactions:

1................2...................3....................4........................5

greatly decrease   greatly increase

Circle one choice

34. your anger   1   2   3   4   5

35. your resentment   1   2   3   4   5

36. your feelings of insecurity   1   2   3   4   5

37. your willingness to forgive   1   2   3   4   5

C. If this offender:

1.   receives a significant punishment,
2.   gives a full an honest apology, and
3.   is required to pay for all of your losses,
<u>what effect</u> . (if any) do you believe this will have on the following reactions:

1................2...................3....................4........................5

greatly decrease   greatly increase

38. your anger   1   2   3   4   5

39. your resentment   1   2   3   4   5

40. your feelings of insecurity   1   2   3   4   5

41. your willingness to forgive   1   2   3   4   5

On a scale of 1-5, how much do you agree or disagree with the following statements?

1................2.......................3...................4.......................5

strongly disagree   strongly agree

50. I would be satisfied with <u>less punishment</u> if this offender: Circle one choice

1.   gives a full and honest apology, and
2.   is required to pay for all of my losses.   1   2   3   4   5

Finally, please answer the following questions about yourself:

Circle one choice

51. My gender is

     male= 1; female= 2   1   2

52. My age is

    16-19 = 1

20- 23 = 2

24-30 = 3

31- 35= 4

over 35= 5   1   2   3   4   5

53. My household income is

0 - $20,000   = 1

$21,000 - 40,000   = 2

$41,000 - 70,000   = 3

above $70,000   = 4   1   2   3   4

54. My race/ethnicity is

            White= 1
            Hispanic= 2
African-American = 3

Asian = 4

Other/no response= 5   1   2   3   4   5

55. How religious would you say are?

    Very religious   = 1

    Somewhat religious = 2

    Not religious   = 3

    Other/No response = 4   1   2   3   4

56. My permanent residence is:

in the city   = 1

in the suburbs   = 2

in the country   = 3

outside the US   = 4   1   2   3   4

57. Have you ever personally been a victim of the kind of crime that was

described earlier in this survey . (an automobile break-in)?

yes = 1

no = 2

Other/no response = 3   1   2   3

Appendix C:
Sample Questionnaire (Societal Level)

On a scale of 1-5, how much do you agree or disagree with the following statements?

1........................2.......................3.................... ....4 5

strongly agree   strongly disagree

Circle one choice

1.   "Criminal sentences should set an example that will
influence other people not to commit the same offense."   1....2....3....4....5

2.   "Unless offenders receive a prison sentence, they will
continue to pose a threat to society."   1....2...3 ...4 ...5

3.   "Criminal sentences should involve a punishment
the offender deserves."   1....2....3....4....5

4.   "Justice is achieved when the offender is punished."
                                                                  1....2....3....4....5

5.   "It is more important for the offender to repair
the harm caused by this crime than for the offender

to be punished.   1...2...3....4 ...5

6.   "It is an important function of the criminal justice system

to try to reform the offender."   1....2....3....4....5

7.   "The criminal justice process can only be
thought of as a success if the victim is satisfied

with the outcome of this case."   1....2....3....4....5

Section II

A.   Imagine you read about the following crime in a newspaper:

A 25-year-old man is arrested for breaking into a car and stealing the car radio. He has no

prior criminal record. The victim's total losses,. (including the radio, damage to the car and lost time

from work), amount to $2,000.00.

On a scale of 1-5, how much do you agree or disagree with the following statements?

1..........................2........................3.............................4.........................5

strongly agree   strongly disagree

9. The sentence in this case should include an order to pay

restitution. (compensation for victim's losses)   1....2...3....4....5

10. The sentence in this case should include payment of a fine   1....2...3....4....5

11. The sentence in this case should include community service   1....2...3....4....5

342

12. The sentence in this case should include incarceration   1....2....3....4....5

13.   The sentence in this case should include   1....2....3....4....5
       some form of punishment

B.   *Consider the same offense. (auto break-in), with the following difference: the* offender *has a record of one prior conviction for a similar offense.*

On a scale of 1-5, how much do you agree or disagree with the following statements?

1..........................2..........................3..........................4..........................5

strongly agree   strongly disagree

                                                            Circle one choice

14. The sentence in this case should include an order to pay

    restitution. (compensation for victim's losses)   1....2....3....4....5

15. The sentence in this case should include payment of a fine   1....2....3....4....5

16. The sentence in this case should include community service   1....2....3....4....5

17. The sentence in this case should include incarceration   1....2....3....4....5

18.   The sentence in this case should include   1....2....3....4....5
       some form of punishment

343

Section III

A.   Imagine you read about the following crime in a newspaper:

A 25-year-old man is arrested for robbery of a college student with the use of a gun. He has a record of one prior conviction for a similar offense. The victim's total losses,. (including a wallet and its contents, and lost time from work), amount to $2,000.00.

On a scale of 1-5, how much do you agree or disagree with the following statements?

1...................2.....................3...........................4.....................5

strongly agree   stronglydisagree

19. The sentence in this case should include an order to pay
      restitution. (compensation for victim's losses)   1....2....3....4....5

20 The sentence in this case should include payment of a fine   1....2....3....4....5

21. The sentence in this case should include community service   1....2....3....4....5

22. The sentence in this case should include incarceration   1....2....3....4....5

23 The sentence in this case should include   1....2....3....4....5
      some form of punishment

344

B. Consider the same offense. (armed robbery), with the following difference: the offender has no record of prior convictions for similar offenses.

On a scale of 1-5, how much do you agree or disagree with the following statements?

1........................2........................3............................4........................5

strongly agree   strongly disagree

                                                          Circle one choice

24. The sentence in this case should include an order to pay

    restitution. (compensation for victim's losses)   1....2....3....4....5

25. The sentence in this case should include payment of a fine   1....2....3....4....5

26. The sentence in this case should include community service   1....2....3....4....5

27. The sentence in this case should include incarceration   1....2....3....4....5

28 The sentence in this case should include   1....2....3....4....5

    some form of punishment

(questions 29- 35, demographic questions. See Appendix B. Sample Questionnaire (Individual

Level)

Bibliography

Abel, Charles and Marsh, Frank. *Punishment as Restitution: A Restitution-Based Approach to Crime and the Criminal.* Westport, CT: Greenwood Press, 1984.

Achilles, Mary. "Will Restorative Justice Live Up to its Promise to Victims?" In H. Zehr and B. Toews (eds.), *Critical Issues in Restorative Justice.* Monsey, NY: Criminal Justice Press, 2004.

Acorn, Annalise. *Compulsory Compassion: A Critique of Restorative Justice.* Vancouver, British Columbia, Canada: UBC Press, 2004.

Adams, Marilyn. "Forgiveness: A Christian Model." *Faith and Philosophy* 8 (1991): 277–304.

Adler, Paul S. and Kwon, Seok-Woo. "Social Capital: The Good, the Bad and the Ugly." In E. Lesser (ed.), *Knowledge and Social Capital: Foundations and Application.* Portsmouth, NH: Butterworth-Heinemann, 2000.

Aguirre, Adalberto and Baker, David. "Racial Discrimination in the Imposition of the Death Penalty." *Criminal Justice Abstracts* 22, no. 1 (1990): 135–153.

Alder, Christine and Wundersitz, Joy (eds.) *Family Conferencing and Juvenile Justice: The Way Forward or Misplaced Optimism?* Canberra, Australia: Australian Institute of Criminology, 1994.

Allard, Pierre and Northey, Wayne. "Christianity: The Rediscovery of Restorative Justice." In M. Hadley (ed.), *The Spiritual Roots of Restorative Justice.* Albany: State University of New York Press, 2001.

American Bar Association, House of Delegates, Victim-Offender Mediation/Dialogue Programs, August, 1994. Par. 8. Http://Www.Vorp.Com/Articles/Abaendors.Html

Analects of Confucius 15:23. Http://Members.Aol.Com/Porchfour/Religion/Golden.Htm

Appelgate, Brandon, Cullen, Francis, Turner, Michael, and Sundt, Jody. "Assessing Public Support for Three-Strikes-You're Out Laws: Global Versus Specific Attitudes." *Crime and Delinquency* 42, no. 4 (1996): 517-34.

Ardrey, Robert. *The Territorial Imperative.* New York: Atheneum, 1966.

Arendt, Hannah. *Eichmann in Jerusalem.* New York: Viking Press, 1964.

Ashworth, Andrew. "Criminal Justice and Deserved Sentences." *Criminal Law Review* 36 (1989): 340-355.

Ashworth, Andrew. "Some Doubts About Restorative Justice." *Criminal Law Forum* 4, no. 2 (1993): 277–299.

Ashworth, Andrew. "Responsibilities, Rights and Restorative Justice." *British Journal of Criminology* 42 (2002): 578–595.

Ashworth, Andrew. "Is Restorative Justice the Way Forward for Criminal Justice?" In E. McLaughlin, R. Fergusson, G. Hughes, and L. Westmoreland, (eds.), *Restorative Justice: Critical Issues*. London, England: Sage, 2003.

Atkinson, Paul. "Some Perils of Paradigms." *Qualitative Health Research* 5 (1995): 117–124.

Axelrod, Robert. *The Evolution of Cooperation*. New York, NY: Basic Books, 1984.

Bagaric, Mirko. *Punishment and Sentencing: A Rational Approach*. Sydney: Cavendish Publishing, 2001

Baldwin, James. *Another Country*. New York, NY: Vintage Press, 1960.

Bandes, Susan. "When Victims Seek Closure: Forgiveness, Vengeance and the Role of Government." *Fordham Urban Law Journal* 27 (2000): 1599–1606.

Bargen, Jenny. "Kids, Cops, Courts, Conferencing and Children's Rights: A Note on Perspectives." *Australian Journal of Human Rights* 2 no. 2 (1996): 209–228.

Barkow, Jerome. *Darwin Sex and Status: Biological Approaches to Mind and Culture*. Toronto: University of Toronto Press, 1989.

Barnett, Randy. "Restitution: A New Paradigm of Criminal Justice." *Ethics* 87 (1977): 279–301.

Barnett, Randy. "Assessing the Criminal: Restitution, Retribution and the Legal Process." In R. Barnett and J. Hagel, (eds.) *Assessing the Criminal*. Cambridge, MA: Ballinger, 1977.

Barton, Charles. "Empowerment and Retribution in Criminal Justice." In H. Strang and J. Braithwaite, (eds.). *Restorative Justice: Philosophy to Practice*. Hants, England: Dartmouth, 2000.

Barton, Charles. *Restorative Justice: The Empowerment Model*. Sydney, New South Wales, Australia: Hawkins Press, 2003.

Bazemore, Gordon. "After Shaming, Whither Reintegration: Restorative Justice and Relational Rehabilitation." In G. Bazemore and L. Walgrave, (eds.), *Restorative Juvenile Justice: Repairing the Harm of Youth Crime*. Monsey, NY: Criminal Justice Press, 1999: 155–195.

Bazemore, Gordon. "Rock and Roll, Restorative Justice and the Continuum of the Real World: A Response to 'Purism' in Operationalizing Restorative Justice." *Contemporary Justice Review* 3 (2000): 459–477.

Bazemore, Gordon and Schiff, Mara. "Paradigm Muddle or Paradigm Paralysis? The Wide and Narrow Paths to Restorative Justice Reform or, a Little Confusion May be a Good Thing." *Contemporary Justice Review* 7, (2004): 37–57.

Bazemore, Gordon and Walgrave, Lode. "Restorative Juvenile Justice: in Search of Fundamentals and An Outline for Systemic Reform." In G. Bazemore and L. Walgrave, (eds.), *Restorative Juvenile Justice: Repairing the Harm of Youth Crime*. Monsey, NY: Criminal Justice Press, 1999.

Bazemore, Gordon and Walgrave, Lode. "Reflections on the Future of Restorative Justice for Juveniles." In G. Bazemore and L. Walgrave, (eds.), *Restorative Juvenile Justice: Repairing the Harm of Youth Crime*. Monsey, NY: Criminal Justice Press, 1999.

Beck, Allen and Gilliard, Darrell, *Prisoners in 1994.* Washington, D.C.: Bureau of Justice Statistics, 1995
Becker, Howard. *Outsiders.* New York: Free Press, 1963 (Revised, 1973).
Bennett, Christopher. "Taking the Sincerity Out of Saying Sorry: Restorative Justice as Ritual." *Journal of Applied Philosophy 23* (2006): 127–143.
Begaric, Mirko and Amarasekara, Kumar. "Feeling Sorry?- Tell Someone Who Cares: The Irrelevance of Remorse in Sentencing." *The Howard Journal* 40, no. 4 (2001): 364-376.
Bennett, Mark and Earwaker, Deborah. "Victims' Responses to Apologies: The Effect of Offender Responsibility and Offense Severity." *The Journal of Social Psychology* 13, no. 4 (1994): 457–464.
Bernstein, Ilene, Kelly, William and Doyle, Patricia. "Societal Reaction to Deviants: The Case of Criminal Defendants." *American Sociological Review* 42 (1977):743–795.
Bianchi, Herman. *Justice as Sanctuary: Toward a new System of Crime Control.* Bloomington: Indiana University Press, 1994.
Bianchi, Herman and Van Swaaningen, Rene. *Abolitionism: Toward a Non-Repressive Approach to Crime.* Amsterdam: Free University Press, 1986.
Bibas, Stephanos and Bierschbach, Richard. "Integrating Remorse and Apology into Criminal Procedure." *Yale Law Journal* 114 (2004): 85–148.
Bilz, Kenworthy and Darley, John. "What's Wrong With Harmless Theories of Punishment?" *Chicago-Kent Law Review* 79 (2004): 1215–1235.
Binmore, Ken. *Natural Justice.* New York, NY: Oxford University Press, 2005.
Black, Donald. "The Social Organization of Arrest." In *The Manners and Customs of the Police,* D. Black, (ed.) New York: Academic Press, 1980.
Blumstein, Alfred. Cohen, Jacqueline and Nagin, Daniel (eds). *Deterrence and incapacitation: Estimating the Effects of Criminal Sanctions on Crime Rates, Report of the Panel of Deterrence and Incapacitation,* Washington, D.C.: National Academy of Sciences, 1978.
Bottoms, Anthony. "Some Sociological Reflections on Restorative Justice." In A. Von Hirsch, J. Roberts, A. E. Bottoms, K. Roach, and M. Schiff, (eds.), *Restorative Justice and Criminal Justice: Competing or Reconcilable Paradigms?* Oxford, England: Hart, 2003: 79–11.
Boudreaux, Paul. "*Booth V. Maryland* and the Individual Vengeance Rationale for Criminal Punishment." *Journal of Criminal Law and Criminology* 80 (1989):177–190.
Bowles, Samuel and Gintis, Herbert. "The Evolution of Strong Reciprocity: Cooperation in Heterogeneous Populations." *Theoretical Population Biology* 65, no. 17 (2004).
Bowling, Benjamin. "The Rise and Fall of New York Murder: Zero Tolerance or Crack's Decline?" *British Journal of Criminology* 39 (1999): 531–54.
Boyes-Watson, Carolyn. "What Are the Implications of the Growing State Involvement in Restorative Justice?" In H. Zehr and B. Toews (eds.), *Critical Issues in Restorative Justice.* Monsey, NY: Criminal Justice Press, 2004.
Braithwaite, John. *Crime, Shame and Reintegration.* Cambridge, England: Cambridge University Press, 1989.
Braithwaite, John. "Thinking Harder About Democratizing Social Control." In Alder, Christine and Wundersitz, Joy, (eds.). *Family Conferencing and*

Juvenile Justice: The Way Forward or Misplaced Optimism? Canberra, Australia: Australian Institute of Criminology, 1994: 199–216.

Braithwaite, John. "Restorative Justice and a Better Future." *Dalhousie Review* 76 (1996): 9–32.

Braithwaite, John. "A Future where Punishment is Marginalized: Realistic or Utopian?" *UCLA Law Review* 46 (1999):1717–1750.

Braithwaite, John. "Restorative Justice: Assessing Optimistic and Pessimistic Accounts." In M. Tonry, (ed.), *Crime and Justice: A Review of Research* (Vol. 25). Chicago, IL: University of Chicago Press, 1999: 1–127.

Braithwaite, John. "Restorative Justice." In M. Tonry, (ed.), *The Handbook of Crime and Punishment.* New York: Oxford University Press, 2000: 323–344.

Braithwaite, John. *Restorative Justice and Responsive Regulation.* Cambridge, England: Oxford University Press, 2002.

Braithwaite, John. "Holism, Justice and Atonement." *Utah Law Review* 1 (2003): 391–412.

Braithwaite, John. "Restorative Justice and De-Professionalization." *The Good Society* 13, no. 1 (2004): 28–31.

Braithwaite, John and Parker, Christine. "Restorative Justice is Republican Justice." In G. Bazemore and L. Walgrave, (eds.), *Restorative Juvenile Justice: Repairing the Harm of Youth Crime.* Monsey, NY: Criminal Justice Press, 1999.

Braithwaite, John and Pettit, Philip. *Not Just Deserts: A Republican Theory of Criminal Justice.* Oxford, UK: Oxford University Press, 2002.

Braithwaite, John and Strang, Heather. "Connecting Philosophy and Practice in Restorative Justice." In H. Strang and J. Braithwaite (eds.), *Restorative Justice, from Philosophy to Practice.* Hants, England: Dartmouth, 2000.

Braman, David. "Families and Incarceration." In M. Mauer. and M. Chesney-Lind , (eds.). *Invisible Punishment.* New York: The New Press, 2002.

Brown, Jennifer. "The Use of Mediation to Resolve Criminal Cases: A Procedural Critique." *Emory Law Journal* 43 (1994): 1247–1309.

Brunk, Conrad. "Restorative Justice and the Philosophic Theories of Criminal Punishment." In M. Hadley, (ed.), *The Spiritual Roots of Restorative Justice.* Albany: State University of New York Press, 2001: 31–56.

Bureau of Justice Statistics. Http://Www.Ojp.Usdoj.Gov/Bjs/Homicide/ Race.Htm. (2007).

Bursik, Robert. "Social Disorganization and Theories of Crime and Delinquency: Problems and Prospects." *Criminology* 26 (1988):519–551.

Buruma, Ybo. "Doubts on the Upsurge of the Victim's Role in Criminal Law." In H. Kaptein and M. Malsch, (eds.), *Crime, Victims and Justice: Essays on Principles and Practice.* Aldershot, England: Ashgate, 2004: 1–15.

Bush, Darren. "Law and Economics of Restorative Justice: Why Restorative Justice cannot and should not be Solely About Restoration." Utah Law Review 1 (2003):429–469.

Cardenas, Juan. "The Crime Victim and the Prosecutorial Process." *Harvard Journal of Law and Public Policy* 9 (1986): 357–98.

Carlsmith, Kevin, Darley, John and Robinson, Paul. "Why Do We Punish? Deterrence and Just Deserts as Motives for Punishment." *Journal of Personality and Social Psychology* 83 (2002): 284–299.

Carriere, Rafaela, Malsch, Marijka, Vermunt, Riel, and DeKeijser, Jan. "An Exploratory Study on Different Damage Types and Compensation." *International Review of Victimology* 5 (1998): 221–234.

Cavadino, Michael, and Dignan, James. "Reparation, Retribution and Rights." *International Review of Victimology* 4 (1997): 233–253.

Christie, Nils. "Conflicts as Property." *British Journal of Criminology* 17 (1977): 1–15.

Christie, Nils. *Limits to Pain.* Oxford: Martin Robinson, 1982.

Clark, James. "Black-On-Black Violence." *Society* 33, no. 5 (1996): 46–50.

Clark, Ramsey. *Crime in America: Observations on its Nature, Causes, Prevention and Control.* New York, NY: Simon and Schuster, 1970.

Clear, Todd. *Harm in American Penology.* Albany: State University of New York Press, 1994.

Clear, Todd, Cole, George and Reisig, Michael. *American Corrections,* (7th ed.) Belmonte, CA: Thomson Wadsworth, 2006.

Clear, Todd and Karp, David. *The Community Justice Ideal.* Boulder, CO: Westview Press, 1999.

Cohen, Jon. "The March of Paradigms." *Science* 283 (1999): 5410.

Cohn, Michael. "Don't Talk to Me About Paradigms." *Computerworld* 27 (1993): 24–37.

Coker, Diana. "Enhancing Autonomy for Battered Women: Lessons from Navaho Peacemaking." *UCLA Law Review* 47 (1999): 1–111.

Coker, Donna. "Transformative Justice: Anti-Subordination Processes in Cases of Domestic Violence." In H. Strang and J. Braithwaite, (eds.), *Restorative Justice and Family Violence.* Cambridge, England: Cambridge University Press, 2002: 128–152.

Coleman, James. "Social Capital in the Creation of Human Capital." *American Journal of Sociology* 94 (1988): S95–S120

Colson, Charles. "Towards An Understanding of the origins of Crime." In J. Stott and N. Miller, (eds.), *Crime and the Responsible Community: A Christian Contribution to the Debate about Criminal Justice.* London: Hodder and Stoughton, 1980.

Colson, Charles and Benson, Daniel. "Restitution as An Alternative to Imprisonment."*Detroit College of Law Review* 2 (1980): 523–598.

Consedine, Jim. *Restorative Justice: Healing the Effects of Crime.* Lyttleton, New Zealand: Ploughshares, 1995.

Cragg, Wesley. *The Practice of Punishment: Towards a Theory of Restorative Justice.* New York, NY: Routledge, 1992.

Crawford, Adam. "Introduction. " In A. Crawford and J. Goodey, (eds.), *Integrating a Victim Perspective into the Criminal Justice System : International Debates.* Aldershot, UK: Ashgate Publishing, 2000.

Crawford, Adam. "The State, Community and Restorative Justice: Heresy, Nostalgia and Butterfly Collecting." In L. Walgrave, (ed.), *Restorative Justice and the Law.* Cullompton, England: Willan, 2002.

Crawford, Adam and Clear, Todd. "Community Justice: Transforming Communities Through Restorative Justice." In G. Bazemore and M. Schiff (eds.), *Restorative Community Justice.* Cincinnati, OH: Anderson, 2000: 127–149.

Cullen, Francis, Pealer, Jennifer, Fisher, Bonnie, Applegate, Brandon and Santana, Shannon. "Public Support for Correctional Rehabilitation in

America: Change or Consistency?" In J. Roberts and M. Hough, (eds.), *Changing Attitudes to Punishment: Public Opinion, Crime and Justice.* Cullompton, Devon, UK: Willan Publishing, 2002.

Curtis- Fawley, Sarah and Daly, Kathleen. "Gendered Violence and Restorative Justice: The Views of Victim Advocates." *Violence Against Women* 11, no. 5 (2005): 603–638.

Daly, Kathleen "Revisiting the Relationship Between Retributive and Restorative Justice." In H. Strang and J. Braithwaite , (eds.) *Restorative Justice, from Philosophy to Practice.* Hants, England: Dartmouth, 2000.

Daly, Kathleen. "Restorative Justice: the Real Story." *Punishment and Society* 4 (2002): 55–79.

Daly, Kathleen. "Mind the Gap: Restorative Justice in Theory and Practice." In A. Von Hirsch, J. Roberts, A. E. Bottoms, K. Roach, and M. Schiff , (eds.), *Restorative Justice and Criminal Justice: Competing or Reconcilable Paradigms?* Oxford, England: Hart, 2003.

Darwin, Charles. *The Descent of Man and Selection in Relation to Sex.* New York: Appleton, 1871.

Davenport, Donna. "The Functions of Anger and Forgiveness: Guidelines for Psychotherapy With Victims." *Psychotherapy* 28 (1991):140–144.

Davis, Gwynn. *Making Amends: Mediation and Reparation in Criminal Justice.* London, England: Routledge, 1992.

Dawkins, Richard. *The Selfish Gene.* Oxford, England: Oxford University Press, 1976.

Delgado, Richard. "Goodbye to Hammurabi: Analyzing the Atavitistic Appeal of Restorative Justice." *Stanford Law Review 52* (2000) : 751–771.

De Waal, Frans. *The Ape and the Sushi Master.* New York, NY: Basic Books, 2001.

De Waal, Frans. *Tree of Origin: What Primate Behavior Can Tell Us About Human Social Evolution.* Cambridge, MA: Harvard University Press, 2001.

De Waal, Frans, *Good Natured: the Origins of Right and Wrong in Humans and Other Animals.* London: Harvard University Press, 1996.

Diamond, Shari and Stalans, Loretta. "The Myth of Judicial Leniency in Sentencing." *Behavioral Sciences and the Law* 7, no. 1 (1989): 73–89.

Diblasio, Frederick. "The Use of Decision-Based Forgiveness Intervention within Intergenerational Family Therapy." *Journal of Family Therapy* 20 (1998):77–94.

Diblasio, Frederick and Proctor, Judith. "Therapists and the Clinical Use of Forgiveness." *American Journal of Family Therapy* 21 (1993):175–184.

Dignan, Jim. "Restorative Justice and the Law: The Case for an Integrated, Systematic Approach." In L. Walgrave, (ed.), *Restorative Justice and the Law.* Cullompton, England: Willan, 2002.

Dignan, Jim. "Toward a Systematic Model of Restorative Justice: Reflections on the Concept, its Context and the need for clear Constraints." In A. Von Hirsch, J. Roberts, A. E. Bottoms, K. Roach, and M. Schiff, (eds.), *Restorative Justice and Criminal Justice: Competing or Reconcilable Paradigms?* Oxford, England: Hart, 2003: 135–156.

Dimock, Susan. Retributivism and Trust. *Law and Philosophy* 16 (1997): 37–62.

Doble, John and Klein, Josh. *Punishing Criminals: The Public's View.* New York, NY: Edna McConnell Clark Foundation, 1989.

Dodig-Crankovic, Gordana. "Shifting the Paradigm of Philosophy of Science: Philosophy of Information and a New Renaissance." *Minds and Machines* 13 (2003):521–536.

Dollard, John. *Caste and Class in a Southern Town.* New Haven, CT: Yale University Press, 1937.

Doob, Anthony. "Transformation or Punishment? Understanding Public Views of What Should be Accomplished in Sentencing." *Canadian Journal of Criminology* 42, no. 3 (2000): 323–341.

Duff, R. A. *Trials and Punishments.* Cambridge, UK: Cambridge University Press, 1986.

Duff, R. A. *Punishment, Communication and Community.* New York, NY: Oxford University Press, 2001.

Duff, R. A. "Restorative Punishment and Punitive Restoration. " In L. Walgrave, (ed.), *Restorative Justice and the Law.* Cullompton, England: Willan, 2002: 82–100.

Duff, R. A. "Restoration and Retribution." In A. Von Hirsch, J. Roberts, A. E. Bottoms, K. Roach, and M. Schiff, (eds.), *Restorative Justice and Criminal Justice: Competing or Reconcilable Paradigms?* Oxford, England: Hart, 2003.

Durkheim, Emile. *The Rules of the Sociological Method.* S. Lukes, (ed.). New York: Free Press, 1982.

Dutton, Donald and Lake, Robert. "Threat of Own Prejudice and Reverse Discrimination in Interracial Situations." *Journal of Personality and Social Psychology* 28 (1973): 94–100.

Dzur, Albert and Olson, Susan. "The Value of Community Participation in Restorative Justice." *Journal of Social Philosophy,* 35 (2004): 91–107.

Dzur, Albert, and Wertheimer, Alan. "Forgiveness and Public Deliberation: The Practice of Restorative Justice." *Criminal Justice Ethics* 22 (2002): 3–20.

Eck, John and Maguire, Edward. "Have Changes in Policing Reduced Violent Crime? An Assessment of the Evidence." In A. Blumstein and J. Wallman, (eds.), *The Crime Drop in America.* Cambridge, UK: University of Cambridge Press, 2000.

Effrat, Andrew. "Power to the Paradigms: An Editorial Introduction." *Sociological Inquiry,* 42, nos. 3–4 (1972):3–33.

Elias, Robert. *The Politics of Victimization: Victims, Victimology and Human Rights.* New York, NY: Oxford University Press, 1986.

Elias, Robert. "Which Victim Movement? The Politics of Victim Policy." In A. Lurigio, (ed.), *Victims of Crime: Problems, Policies, and Programs.* Newbury Park, CA: Sage, 1990.

Enright, Robert. "Counseling Within the Forgiveness Triad: On Forgiving, Receiving Forgiveness and Self-Forgiveness." *Counseling and Values,* 40, no. 2, (1996): 107–126.

Enright, Robert and Fitzgibbons, Richard. *Helping Clients Forgive: An Empirical Guide for Resolving Anger and Restoring Hope.* Washington, DC: American Psychological Association, 2000.

Enright, Robert, Freedman, Suzanne and Rique, Julio. "The Psychology of Interpersonal Forgiveness." In R. Enright and J. North, (eds.), *Exploring Forgiveness.* Madison: University of Wisconsin Press, 1998: 46–63.

Erez, Edna."The Impact of Victimology on Criminal Justice Policy." *Criminal Justice Policy Review* 3 (1989): 236–256.

Erez, Edna, Roeger, L. and Morgan, F. "Victim Harm, Impact Statements and Victim Satisfaction." *International Review of Victimology* 1 (1997): 37–60.

Erez, Edna and Tontodonato, Pamela. "Victim Participation in Sentencing and Satisfaction with Justice." *Justice Quarterly* 9 (1992): 393–417.

Etizioni, Amatai. *The Spirit of Community: Rights, Responsibilities and the Communitarian Agenda.* London: Fontana Press, 1995.

Exline, Julie and Baumeister, Roy. "Expressing Forgiveness and Repentance: Benefits and Barriers." In M. McCullough, K. Pargament, and C. Thoresen, (eds.), *Forgiveness: Theory, Research, and Practice.* New York: Guilford, 2000:133–155.

Exline, Julie, Worthington, Everett, Hill, Peter and McCullough, Michael. "Forgiveness and Justice: A Research Agenda for Social and Personality Psychology."*Personality and Social Psychology Review* 7, no. 4 (2003): 337–348.

Fatic, Aleksandar. *Punishment and Restorative Crime-Handling: A Social Theory of Trust.* Aldershot, England: Avebury Press, 1995.

Fattah, Ezzat. "Gearing Justice Action to Victim Satisfaction: Contrasting Two Justice Philosophies: Retribution and Redress." In H. Kaptein and M. Malsch (eds.), *Crime, Victims and Justice: Essays on Principles and Practice.* Aldershot, England: Ashgate, 2004.

Fehr, Ernst and Gachter, Simon. "Altruistic Punishment in Humans." *Nature* 415 (2002): 137–140.

Feld, Barry. "Rehabilitation, Retribution and Restorative Justice: Alternative Conceptions of Juvenile Justice." In G. Bazemore and L. Walgrave, (eds.), *Restorative Juvenile Justice: Repairing the Harm of Youth Crime.* Monsey, NY: Criminal Justice Press, 1999: 17–44.

Finckenauer, James. "Death Penalty Support." *Justice Quarterly* 5 (1988): 88–99.

Finnis, John, *Natural Law and Natural Rights.* Oxford, UK: Clarendon Press, 1980.

Flanagan, Timothy. "Reform or Punish: Americans' View of the Correctional System." In T. Flanagan and D. Longmire, (eds.), *Americans View Crime and Justice.* Thousand Oaks, CA: Sage, 1996.

Fletcher, George. *Rethinking Criminal Law.* Boston, MA: Little, Brown and Company, 1976.

Frank, Robert. *Passions Within Reason. the Strategic Role of the Emotions.* New York: W. W. Norton and Company, 1988.

Frankel, Marvin. *Criminal Sentences: Law Without Order.* New York: Hill and Wang, 1972.

Frase, Richard. "Limiting Retributionism." In M. Tonry, (ed.) *The Future of Imprisonment.* New York: Oxford University Press, 2004: 85–111.

Gardiner, Gerald. "The Purposes of Criminal Punishment." *Modern Law Review* 21 (1958).

Garfinkel, Harold. "Research Notes on Inter and Intra Racial Homicides." *Social Forces* 27 (1949): 369–381.

Garvey, Stephen. "Punishment as Atonement." *UCLA Law Review* 46 (1999):1801–1858.

Garvey, Stephen. "The Moral Emotions of the Criminal Law." *Quinnipiac Law Review* 22 (2003): 89–108.

Garvey, Stephen. "Restorative Justice, Punishment and Atonement." *Utah Law Review* 1 (2003): 303–317.

Gehm, John. "The Function of Forgiveness in the Criminal Justice System." In H. Messmer, and H. Otto, (eds.), *Restorative Justice on Trial.* Dordrecht, the Netherlands: Kluwer, 1992: 551–557.

Gibbs, Jack. "The Death Penalty: Retribution and Penal Policy." *Journal of Criminal Law and Criminology* 69 (1978): 291–299.

Goffman, Erving. *Relations in Public: Microstudies of the Public Order.* New York: Basic Books, 1971.

Gottfredson, Michael, and Hirschi, Travis. *A General Theory of Crime.* Stanford, CA: Stanford University Press, 1990.

Griffiths, Curt and Hamilton, Ron. "Sanctioning and Healing: Restorative Justice in Canadian Aboriginal Communities." In B. Galaway and J. Hudson, (eds.), *Restorative Justice: International Perspectives.* Monsey, NY: Criminal Justice Press, 1996.

Groenhuijsen, Marc. "Victim's Rights and Restorative Justice: Piecemeal Reform of the Criminal Justice System or a Change of Paradigm?" In H. Kaptein and M. Malsch, (eds.), *Crime, Victims and Justice.* Aldershot, England: Ashgate, 2004.

Gustafson-Affinito, Mona. *When to Forgive: A Healing Guide.* Oakland, CA: New Harbinger Publications, 1999.

Haaken, Janice. "The Good, the Bad, and the Ugly: Psychoanalytic and Cultural Perspectives on Forgiveness." In S. Lamb and J. G. Murphy, (eds.), *Before Forgiving: Cautionary Views of Forgiveness in Psychotherapy.* New York, NY: Oxford University Press, 2002: 172–191.

Haas, Kenneth. "The Triumph of Vengeance Over Retribution: The United States Supreme Court and the Death Penalty. " *Crime, Law and Social Change* 21, no. 1. (1994):127–154.

Haber, Joram. *Forgiveness.* Savage, MD: Rowman and Littlefield, 1991.

Hadley, Michael. *The Spiritual Roots of Restorative Justice.* Albany: State University of New York Press, 2001.

Hammer, Joel. *The Effect of Punishment on Crime Victims' Recovery and Perceived Fairness Equity and Process Control.* Unpublished Doctoral Dissertation. New York City: New School for Social Research, 1989.

Harrell, Erika. *Black Victims of Violent Crime.* Washington, D.C.: US Department of Justice, Bureau of Justice Statistics United States, 2007.

Hart, H. L. A. *Punishment and Responsibility: Essays in the Philosophy of Law.* Oxford, England: Oxford University Press, 1968.

Haueser, Marc. *Moral Minds: How Nature Designed Our Universal Sense of Right and Wrong.* New York, NY: HarperCollins, 2006.

Heider, Fritz. *The Psychology of Interpersonal Relations.* New York: Wiley, 1958.

Held, Virginia. "Moral Subjects: The Natural and the Normative." *Proceedings and Addresses of the American Philosophical Association,* 76, no. 2 (2002): 7–24.

Hepburn, John. "Race and the Decision to Arrest: An Analysis of Warrant Issues." *Journal of Research and Crime and Delinquency* 15 (1978): 54–73.

Herman, Judith. "Justice from the Victim's Perspective." *Violence Against Women* 11 (2005): 571–602.

Hirschi, Travis. *Causes of Delinquency*. Berkeley, CA: University of California Press, 1969.

Hobbes, Thomas. *Leviathan*. C. Macpherson, (ed.). London: Penguin Classics, 1986. Original work published 1651

Holmes, Oliver Wendell. *The Common Law*. Boston, MA: Little, Brown, 1881.

Hume, David. A *Treatise on Human Nature* (2nd ed.). L. Selby-Rigg, (ed.). Oxford, England: Clarendon Press, 1978. Original work published 1785.

Immarigeon, Russ. "What Is the Place of Punishment and Incarceration in Restorative Justice?" in H. Zehr and B. Toews, (eds.), *Critical Issues in Restorative Justice*. Monsey, NY: Criminal Justice Press, 2004: 143–154.

Immerwahr, John. "Crime and Punishment: A New Look." *Responsive Community* 3 (1993):58–60

Ikpa, Tina. "Balancing Restorative Justice Principles and Due Process Rights in order to Reform the Criminal Justice System." *Journal of Law and Policy* 24 (2007): 301–325.

Jacoby, Joseph and Cullen, Francis. "The Structure of Punishment Norms: Applying the Rossi-Berk Model." *Journal of Criminal Law and Criminology*, 89 (1998): 245–313.

Jacoby, Susan, *Wild Justice*, New York: Harper and Row, 1983.

Janoff-Bulman, Ronnie and Frieze, Irene. "A Theoretical Perspective for Understanding Reactions to Victimization." *Journal of Social Issues*, 39, no. 2 (1983): 1–17.

Johnson, D. Paul. "The Historical Background of Social Darwinism" in D. Paul Johnson, (ed.), *Contemporary Sociological Theory*. Berlin: Springer (2008).

Johnson, Guy B. "The Negro and Crime." *Annals of the American Academy*, 217 (1949): 93–104.

Johnstone, Gerry. *Restorative Justice: Ideas, Values Debates*. Cullompton, Devon, UK: Willan Publishing, 2002.

Kaptein, Hendrik. "Against the Pain of Punishment: Retribution as Reparation Through Penal Servitude." In H. Kapstein and M. Malsch, (eds.). Aldershot, England: Ashgate, 2004.

Karmen, Andrew. *Crime Victims: An Introduction to Victimology* (2nd ed.). Wadsworth Publishing, Belmont, CA, 1990.

Karp, David, and Clear, Todd. "Community Justice: A Conceptual Framework." In *Criminal Justice 2000: Boundary Change in Criminal Justice Organizations, Vol. 2*, 2000: 223–268.

Kelln, Brad and Ellard, John. "An Equity Theory Analysis of the Impact of Forgiveness and Retribution on Transgressor Compliance." *Personality and Social Psychology Bulletin*, 25 (1999): 864–872.

Kennedy, Randall. *Race, Crime, and Law*. New York: Vintage Books, 1997.

Kerner Commission, *Report of the National Advisory Commission on Civil Disorders*. Washington: U.S. Government Printing Office, 1968.

Kirkpatrick, Dean and Otto, Randy. "Constitutionally Guaranteed Participation in Criminal Proceedings for Victims: Potential Effects on Psychological Functioning." *Wayne Law Review* (1987): 7–28.

Kleck, Gary. "Racial Discrimination in Criminal Sentencing: A Critical Evaluation of the Evidence With Additional Data on the Death Penalty." *American Sociological Review* 46 (1981): 783–805.

Knack, Steven and Keefer, Phillip. "Does Social Capital Have An Economic Payoff? A Cross-Country Investigation." *Quarterly Journal of Economics* 112 (1997): 1251–1288.

Kuhn, Thomas. *The Structure of Scientific Revolutions.* Chicago, IL: University of Chicago Press, 1962.

Kurki, Leena. "Restorative and Community Justice in the United States." In M. Tonry, (ed.), *Crime and Justice: A Review of Research.* Chicago: University of Chicago Press, 2000.

Kury, Helmut and Ferdinand, Theodore. "Public Opinion and Punitively." *International Journal of Law and Psychiatry* 22 (1999): 373–392.

Lamb, Sharon. "Women, Abuse and Forgiveness: A Special Case." In S. Lamb and J. Murphy, (eds.). *Before Forgiving: Cautionary Views of Forgiveness in Psychotherapy.* New York: Oxford University Press, 2002.

Landman, Janet. "Earning Forgiveness: The Story of a Perpetrator, Katherine Ann Power." In S. Lamb and J. G. Murphy, (eds.), *Before Forgiving: Cautionary Views of Forgiveness in Psychotherapy.* New York, NY: Oxford University Press, 2002.

Lecky, William. E. H. *History of European Morals from Augustus to Charlemagne.* New York, NY: George Braziller, 1955.

Lerner, Melvin. *The Belief in a Just World.* New York, NY: Plenum, 1980.

Lerner, Melvin and Miller, Dale. "Just World Research and the Attribution Process: Looking Back and Looking Ahead." *Psychological Bulletin* 85 (1976): 1030–1151.

Levi, Margaret. "Social and Unsocial Capital: A Review Essay of Robert Putnam's *Making Democracy Work.*" *Politics and Society* 24 (1996): 46–55

Levrant, Sharon. Cullen, Francis, Fulton, Betsy, and Wozniak, John. "Reconsidering Restorative Justice: The Corruption of Benevolence Revisited." *Crime and Delinquency* 54 (1999): 3–27

Lipton, Douglas, Martinson, Robert and Wilks, Judith. *The Effectiveness of Correctional Treatment: A Survey of Treatment Evaluation Studies.* New York, NY: Praeger, 1974.

Llewellen, Jennifer and Howse, Robert. "Institutions for Restorative Justice in South Africa Truth and Reconciliation Commission." *University of Toronto Law Journal* 49 (1999): 355–388.

London, Ross. "The Restoration of Trust: Bringing Restorative Justice from the Margins to the Mainstream." *Criminal Justice Studies* 16 (2003): 175–195.

London, Ross. "The Role of Punishment in the Emotional Recovery of Crime Victims." *Restorative Directions Journal* 2 (2006): 95–128,

Lorenz, Konrad. *On Aggression.* New York: Harcourt, Brace and World, Inc., 1966.

Lurigio, Arthur and Resick, Patricia. "Healing the Psychological Wounds of Criminal Victimization." In A.J. Lurigio, W. Skogan and R. Davis, (eds.). *Victims of Crime: Problems, Policy and Programs.* Newberry, CA: Sage, 1990: 50–68.

McGuire, Meredith. "Words of Power: Personal Empowerment and Healing." *Culture, Medicine and Psychiatry* 7 (1983):221–240.

Mann, Coramae Richey. *Unequal Justice.* Bloomington: Indiana University Press, 1993.

Marshall, Christopher. *Beyond Retribution: A New Testament Vision for Justice, Crime and Punishment.* Grand Rapids, MI: Eerdmans, 2001.

Marshall, Tony. "The Evolution of Restorative Justice." *British and European Journal on Criminal Policy and Research* 4 (1996): 21–43.

Martin, Dianne. "Retribution Revisited: A Reconsideration of Feminist Law Reform Strategies." *Osgoode Law Journal,* 36 (1998): 151–188.

Mauer, Marc. *Americans Behind Bars: The International Use of Incarceration.* Washington, DC: The Sentencing Project, 1994 and 1997.

Maxwell, Gabrielle, and Morris, Allison. "The New Zealand Model of Family Group Conferences." In C. Alder and J. Wundersitz, (eds.), *Family Conferencing and Juvenile Justice: The Way Forward or Misplaced Optimism?* Canberra: Australian Institute of Criminology, 1994.

Maxwell, Gabrielle, and Morris, Allison. "Restorative Justice and Reoffending." In H. Strang and J. Braithwaite, (eds.). *Restorative Justice: from Philosophy to Practice.* Aldershot: Ashgate/Dartmouth, 2000: 93–103.

Maxwell, Gabrielle and Morris, Allison. "Family Group Conferences and Reoffending." In A. Morris and G. Maxwell, (eds.). *Restorative Justice for Juveniles: Conferencing, Mediation and Circles.* Oxford, UK: Hart Publishing, 2001.

McCold, Paul. "Restorative Justice and the Role of the Community." In B. Galaway and J. Hudson, (eds.), *Restorative Justice: International Perspectives.* Monsey, NY: Criminal Justice Press, 1996.

McCold, Paul. "Toward a Holistic Vision of Restorative Juvenile Justice: A Reply to the Maximalist Model." *Contemporary Justice Review* 3 (2000): 357–414.

McCold, Paul. " Paradigm Muddle: The Threat to Restorative Justice Posed by its Merger with Community Justice." *Contemporary Justice Review* 7 (2004):15–35.

McCullough, Michael. "Forgiveness: Who Does it and How do they do it?" *Current Directions in Psychological Science,* 10, no. 6 (2001):194–197.

McCullough, Michael. *Beyond Revenge: The Evolution of the Forgiveness Instinct.* San Francisco, CA : John Wiley & Sons, 2008.

McCullough, Michael, Pargament, Kenneth and Thoresen Carl, "The Psychology of Forgiveness." In M. McCullough, K. Pargament, and C. Thoresen, (eds.), *Forgiveness: Theory, Research, and Practice.* New York: Guilford, 2000: 1–14.

McCullough, Michael, Sandage, Steven and Worthington Everett. *To Forgive Is Human: How to Put Your Past in the Past.* Downer's Grove, IL: Interuniversity Press, 1997.

McCullough, Michael and Worthington, Everett. "Encouraging Clients to Forgive People Who Have Hurt Them: Review, Critique and Research Prospectus." *Journal of Psychology and Theology* 22 (1994):3–20.

McCullough, Michael and Worthington, Everett. "Religion and the Forgiving Personality." *Journal of Personality* 67 (1999):1141–1164.

McDonald, William. *Criminal Justice and the Victim.* Beverly Hills, CA: Sage, 1976.

McHugh, Gerald. *Christian Faith and Criminal Justice: Toward a Christian Response to Crime and Punishment.* New York, NY: Paulist Press, 1978.

McNamara, Tim. "Tearing Us Apart Again: The Paradigm Wars and the Search for Validity." *Eurosla Yearbook* 3 (2003): 229–238

Mealey, Linda. "The Sociobiology of Sociopathy: An Integrated Evolutionary Model." *Behavioral and Brain Sciences* 18, no. 3 (1995): 523–559.

Merton, Robert. "Social Structure and Anomie." *American Sociological Review* 3 (1938): 672–682.

Meyer, Linda. "Forgiveness and the Public Trust." *Fordham Urban Law Journal* 27 (2000): 1515–1540.

Michalowski, Raymond. *Order, Law, and Crime.* New York: Random House, 1985.

Miers, David, Maguire, Mike, and Goldie, Sheila. *An Exploratory Evaluation of Restorative Justice Schemes.* London, England: Home Office, 2001.

Mika, Harry, Achilles, Mary, Halbert, Ellen, Amstutz, Lorraine, and Zehr, Howard. "Listening to Victims: A Critique of Restorative Justice Policy and Practice in the United States." *Federal Probation* 68 (2004):32–38.

Miller, Dale. "Disrespect and the Experience of Injustice." *Annual Review of Psychology* 52 (2001): 527–553.

Miller, Dale and Vidmar, Neil. "The Social Psychology of Punishment Reactions." In M. Lerner and S. Lerner, (eds.), *The Justice Motive in Social Behavior.* New York: Plenum Press, 1981: 146–155.

Miller, Seumas and Blackler, John. "Restorative Justice: Retribution Confession and Shame." In H. Strang and J. Braithwaite, (eds.), *Restorative Justice, from Philosophy to Practice.* Hants, England: Dartmouth, 2000.

Miller, Seumas and Blackler, John. *Ethical Issues in Policing.* Aldershot, England: Ashgate, 2005.

Montado, Leo. "Injustice in Harm and Loss." *Social Justice Research* 7 (1994): 5–28,

Montado, Leo and Lerner, Melvin. *Responses to Victimization and Belief in a Just World.* New York: Plenum Press, 1998.

Moore, David. "Shame, Forgiveness and Juvenile Justice." *Criminal Justice Ethics* 12, no. 1, (1993):3–25.

Moore, George E. *Principia Ethica.* Cambridge: Cambridge University Press, 1903.

Morris, Allison. "Critiquing the Critics: A Brief Response to Criticisms of Restorative Justice." *British Journal of Criminology* 42, no. 3 (2002): 596–615.

Morris, Allison and Maxwell, Gabrielle. "Reforming Juvenile Justice: The New Zealand Experiment." *The Prison Journal* 77 (1997): 125–134.

Morris, Herbert. " Guilt and Punishment." *The Personalist* 52 (1971):305–321.

Morris, Herbert, *On Guilt and Innocence.* Berkeley, CA: University of California Press, 1976.

Morris, Martin. "The Paradigm Shift to Communication and the Eclipse of the Object." *South Atlantic Quarterly* 96 (1998): 755–788.

Morris, Norval. "Desert as a Limiting Principle." In A. Von Hirsch and A. Ashworth, (eds.), *Principled Sentencing.* Boston, MA: Northeastern University Press, 1992.

Morris, Norval and Tonry, Michael. *Intermediate Punishments.* New York, NY: Oxford University Press, 1989.

Morris, Ruth. *A Practical Path to Transformative Justice.* Toronto, Ontario, Canada: Rittenhouse Press, 1994.

Murphy, Jeffrey. *Cruel and Unusual Punishments Retribution, Justice and Therapy.* Dordrect, Netherlands: D. Redel, 1985.

Murphy, Jeffrey. "Forgiveness, Mercy, and the Retributive Emotions." *Criminal Justice Ethics* 7 (1988): 3–15

Murphy, Jeffrey. "Two Cheers for Vindictiveness." *Punishment and Society* 2 (2000): 131–143.

Murphy, Jeffrey. "Forgiveness in Counseling: A Philosophical Perspective." In S. Lamb and J. G. Murphy, (eds.), *Before Forgiving: Cautionary Views of Forgiveness in Psychotherapy.* New York, NY: Oxford University Press, 2002: 41–53.

Murphy, Jeffrey and Hampton, Jean. 1988. *Forgiveness and Mercy.* New York, NY: Cambridge University Press, 1988.

Myers, Martha and Hagan, John. "Private and Public: Troubled Prosecutors and the Allocation of Court Resources." *Social Problems* 26 (1979): 439–451.

Nahapiet, Janine. and Ghoshal, Sumantra. "Social Capital, Intellectual Capital, and the Organizational Advantage."*Academy of Management Review* 23 (1998): 242–267.

National Center for Health Statistics. Http://Www.Cdc.Gov/Men/Lcod/04black.Pdf.

Neiburh, Reinhold. "God's Justice and Mercy." In R. M. Brown, (ed.), *The Essential Reinhold Neiburh.* New Haven, CT: Yale University Press, 1986.

Neu, Jerome. "To Understand all is to Forgive all—Or is it?" In S. Lamb and J. G. Murphy, (eds.), *Before Forgiving: Cautionary Views of Forgiveness in Psychotherapy.* New York, NY: Oxford University Press, 2002: 17–40.

Nowak, Martin and Sigmund, Karl. "Tit for Tat in Heterogeneous Populations." *Nature 355* (1992): 250–252.

Nowak, Martin and Sigmund, Karl. "A Strategy of Win-Stay, Lose-Shift That Outperforms Tit-For-Tat in the Prisoner's Dilemma Game." *Nature 364,* (1993): 56–58

Nozick, Robert. *Philosophical Explanations.* Cambridge, MA: Harvard University Press, 1981.

Nugent, William, Williams, Mona and Umbreit, Mark. "Participation in Victim-Offender Mediation and the Prevalence and Severity of Subsequent Delinquent Behavior: A Meta-Analysis." *Utah Law Review* 1 (2003): 137–166

O'Carroll, Patrick and Mercy, James. "Patterns and Recent Trends in Black Homicide." In D. N. Hawkins, (ed.), *Homicide Among Black Americans.* Lanham, MD: University Press of America, 1986.

Office of Juvenile Justice and Delinquency Prevention. *Guide for Implementing the Balanced and Restorative Justice Model.* Washington, D.C.: U.S. Department of Justice, 1998.

Ohbuchi, Kenichi, Agarie, Nariyuki, and Kameda, Masuyo. "Apology as Aggression Control: Its Role in Mediating Appraisal of and Response to Harm." *Journal of Personality and Social Psychology 56* (1989): 219–227.

Ohbuchi, Kenichi and Sato, Kobun. "Children's Reaction to Mitigating Accounts: Apologies, Excuses and Intentionality of Harm." *The Journal of Social Psychology* 134 (1994): 5–17.

Olson, Susan. and Dzur, Albert. "Reconstructing Professional Roles in Restorative Justice Programs." *Utah Law Review* 1 (2003): 57–89.

O'Manique, John. *The Origins of Justice.* Philadelphia: University of Pennsylvania Press, 2003.

Opotow, Susan. "Moral Exclusion and Injustice: An Introduction." *Journal of Social Issues* 1 (1990): 1–20.

Orth, Ulrich. "Does Perpetrator Punishment Satisfy Victim's Feelings of Revenge?" *Aggressive Behavior 30* (2004): 62–70.

Oswald, Margit, Hupfeld, Jorg, Klug, S. and Gabriel, U. "Lay Perspectives on Criminal Deviance, Goals of Punishment and Punitivity." *Social Justice Research* 15 no. 2, (2002): 85–98.

Packer, Herbert. "Two Models of the Criminal Process." *University of Pennsylvania Law Review* 113, no. 1 (1964): 1–68.

Palk, Gerald, Hayes, Hennessy, and Prenzler, Timothy. "Restorative Justice and Community Conferencing: Summary of Findings from a Pilot Study." *Current Issues in Criminal Justice* 10 (1998): 138–155.

Pallone, Nathan and Hennesey, James. "Tinderbox Criminal Violence." In R. Clarke and M. Felson, (ed.), *Routine Activity and Rational Choice.* New Brunswick, NJ: Transactional Publishers, 1993: 127–158.

Pavlich, George. "Deconstructing Restoration: The Promise of Restorative Justice." In E. Weitekamp and H. Kerner, (eds.), *Restorative Justice: Theoretical Foundations*. Portland, OR: Willan, 2002: 90–109.

Pavlich, George. "What Are the Dangers as Well as the Promises of Community Involvement?" In H. Zehr and B. Toews, (eds.), *Critical Issues in Restorative Justice*. Monsey, NY: Criminal Justice Press, 2004: 173–183.

Pepinsky, Hal. *The Geometry of Violence and Democracy.* Bloomington: Indiana University Press, 1991.

Petersilia, Joan. "A Decade of Experimenting with Intermediate Sanctions: What Have We Learned?" *Federal Probation* 62, no. 2 (1999): 3–9.

Petersilia, Joan and Turner, Susan. "Reducing Prison Admissions: The Potential of intermediate Sanctions." *Journal of State Government 62* (1989): 65–69

Petrucci, Carrie. "Apology in the Criminal Justice Setting: Evidence for including Apology as an Additional Component in the Legal System." *Behavioral Sciences and the Law* 20 (2002): 337–362.

Pollard, Charles. "Victims and the Criminal Justice System: A New Vision." *Criminal Law Review* (2000): 5–17.

Porter, Bruce and Dunn, Marvin. *The Miami Riot of 1980: Crossing the Bounds.* Lexington, MA: D.C. Heath, 1984.

Portes, Alejandro. "Social Capital: Its Origins and Applications in Modern Sociology." *Annual Review of Sociology* 24 (1998):1–24.

Poulson, Barton. "A Third Voice: A Review of Empirical Research on the Psychological Outcomes of Restorative Justice." *Utah Law Review* (2003): 167–203.

Prager, Dennis. "The Sin of Forgiveness." *Wall Street Journal*, December 15, 1997.

Pranis, Kay. "Building Community Support for Restorative Justice: Principles and Strategies." In B. Galaway and J. Hudson, (eds.), *Restorative Justice: International Perspectives*. Monsey, NY: Criminal Justice Press, 1996.

Primoratz, Igor. *Justifying Legal Punishment.* London, England: Humanities Press International, 1989.

Proeve, Michael, Smith, David, and Niblo, Diane Mead. "Mitigation Without Definition: Remorse in the Criminal Justice System." *Australian and New Zealand Journal of Criminology* 3 (1999):16–26.

Putnam, Robert. *Making Democracy Work: Civic Traditions in Modern Italy.* Princeton, NJ: Princeton University Press, 1993.

Putnam, Robert. "Tuning in, Tuning Out: The Strange Disappearance of Social Capital in America." *PS: Political Science and Politics* 28, no. 4 (1995): 664–683.

Quinney, Richard. *Class, State, and Crime.* New York: D. McKay Co., 1980.

Rawls, John. *A Theory of Justice.* Oxford, England: Oxford University Press, 1972.

Retzinger, Suzanne, and Scheff, Thomas. "Strategy for Community Conferences: Emotions and Social Bonds." In B. Galaway and J. Hudson, (eds.), *Restorative Justice: International Perspectives.* Monsey, NY: Criminal Justice Press, 1996.

Ridley, Matt. *The Origins of Virtue.* New York: Viking, 1997.

Roberts, Julian and Hough, Mike. *Changing Attitudes to Punishment: Public Opinion, Crime and Justice.* Cullompton, England: Willan, 2002.

Roberts, Julian and Stalans, Loretta. *Public Opinion, Crime and Criminal Justice.* Boulder CO: Westview Press, 1999.

Roberts, Luc and Peters, Tony. "How Restorative Justice Is Able to Transcend the Prison Walls: A Discussion of the 'Restorative Detention' Project." In E. Weitekamp and H.-J. Kerner, (eds.), *Restorative Justice in Context: International Practice and Directions.* Portland, OR: Willan, 2003: 95–122.

Robinson, Paul. "The Virtues of Restorative Processes, the Vices of 'Restorative Justice.'" *Utah Law Review* 2003: 375–388.

Rossi, Peter and Berk, Richard. *Just Punishment: Federal Guidelines and Public Views Compared.* New York: Aldine De Gruyter, 1997.

Sabol, William, and Couture, Heather. *Bureau of Justice Statistics, Prison Inmates at Midyear 2007.* Washington, DC: US Department of Justice, June, 2008.

Sagrestano, Lynda. "The Use of Power and Influence in a Gendered World." *Psychology of Women Quarterly* 16 (1992): 439–447.

Sampson, Robert, Raudenbush, Stephen and Earls, Felton. "Neighborhoods and Violent Crime: A Multilevel Study of Collective Efficacy." *Science,* 277 (1997): 918–924.

Schember, Michael. *The Science of Good and Evil: Why People Cheat, Gossip, Care, Share and Follow the Golden Rule.* New York, NY: Henry Holt, 2004.

Scheff, Thomas. *Emotions, the Social Bond and the Human Reality: Part/Whole Analysis.* New York: Cambridge University Press, 1997.

Scher, Stephen and Darley, John. "How Effective Are the Things People Say to Apologize? Effect of the Realization of the Apology Speech Act." *Journal of Psycholinguistic Research* 26 (1997): 127–140.

Scobie, Enid. and Scobie, Geof. "Damaging Events: The Perceived Need for Forgiveness." *Journal for the Theory of Social Behaviour* 28 (1998): 373–401.

Seligman, Adam. *The Problem of Trust.* Princeton, NJ: Princeton University Press, 1997.

Sessar, Klaus. "Punitive Attitudes of the Public: Myth and Reality." In G. Bazemore and L. Walgrave, (eds.), *Restorative Juvenile Justice: Repairing the Harm of Youth Crime.* Monsey, NY: Criminal Justice Press, 1999.

Sherman, Lawrence, Gottfredson, Denise, Mackenzie, Doris, Eck, John Reuter, Peter and Bushwan, Shawn. *Preventing Crime: What Works What Doesn't, What's Promising: A Report to the United States Congress.* Washington, D.C.: National Institute of Justice, 1997.

Shapland, Joanna. "Victim Assistance and the Criminal Justice System: The Victim's Perspective." In E. Fattah, (ed.). *From Crime Policy to Victim Policy.* London, UK: Macmillan, 1986: 218–233.

Sharpe, Susan. *Restorative Justice: A Vision for Healing and Change.* Edmonton, Alberta : Edmonton Victim Offender Mediation Society, 1998.

Shaw, Clifford and McKay, Henry. *Juvenile Delinquency and Urban Areas.* Chicago, IL: University of Chicago Press, 1942.

Shuman, Daniel and Smith, Alexander. *Justice and the Prosecution of Old Crimes.* Washington, DC: American Psychological Association, 2000.

Silver, Allan. "Friendship and Trust as Moral Ideals: An Historical Approach." *European Journal of Sociology,* 30 (1989):274–297.

Singer, Peter. *The Expanding Circle: Ethics and Sociobiology.* New York, NY: Farrar, Strauss and Giroux, 1981.

Smith, Adam, *The Theory of Moral Sentiments* [1759], Knud Haakonssen, (ed.). Cambridge: Cambridge University Press, 2002.

Solomon, Robert. *A Passion for Justice: Emotions and The Origins of the Social Contract.* Reading, MA: Addison-Wesley, 1990.

Solomon, Robert. *True to Our Feelings: What Our Emotions Are Really Telling Us.* New York, NY: Oxford University Press, 2007.

Spohn, Cassia. "The Sentencing Decisions of Black and White Judges: Expected and Unexpected Similarities." *Law and Society Review* 24 (1990): 1197–1216.

Stossel, Jon. *Myths, Lies and Downright Stupidity.* New York, NY: Hyperion Press, 2006.

Strang, Heather. *Repair or Revenge: Victims and Restorative Justice.* Oxford, England: Clarendon Press, 2002.

Strang, Heather and Braithwaite, John, (eds.). *Restorative Justice, from Philosophy to Practice.* Hants, England: Dartmouth, 2000.

Stubbs, Julie. "Domestic Violence and Women's Safety: Feminist Challenges to Restorative Justice." In H. Strang and J. Braithwaite, (eds.), *Restorative Justice and Family Violence.* Cambridge, England: Cambridge University Press, 2002: 42–61.

Sullivan, Dennis and Tifft, Larry. *Restorative Justice: Healing the Foundations of Our Everyday Lives,* 2nd ed. Monsey, NY: Willow Tree Press, 2005.

Sylvester, Douglas. "Interdisciplinary Perspectives on Restorative Justice: Myth in Restorative Justice History." *Utah Law Review* 1 (2003): 471–522.

Szmania, Susan and Mangis, Daniel. "Finding the Right Time and Place: A Case Study Comparison of the Expression of Offender Remorse in Traditional Justice Restorative Justice Contexts." *Marquette Law Review* 89 (2005): 335–358.

Tavuchis, Nicholas. *Mea Culpa: Sociology of Apology and Reconciliation.* Stanford, CA: Stanford University Press, 1991.

Terez, Tom. "Eager for a Paradigm Shift? Not So Fast." *Workforce* 81 no. 2 (2002): 26–27.

Theibert, Paul. "Manager's Journal: Eschew That Paradigm. Drop the Jargon." *The Wall Street Journal* (August 1, 1994): A14,

Thompson, Randall and Zingiff, Matthew. "Detecting Sentencing Disparity: Some Problems in Evidence." *American Journal of Sociology* 86 (1981): 869–880.

Thorne, Sally, Henderson, Angela, McPherson, Gladys, and Pesut, Barbara. "The Problematic Allure of the Binary in Nursing Theoretical Discourse." *Nursing Philosophy 5* (2005): 208–215.

Thorne, Sally, Reimer, Sheryl and Henderson, Angela. "Ideological Implications of Paradigm Discourse." *Nursing Inquiry 6* (1999):123–131.

Tonry, Michael and Coffee, John C., Jr. "Plea Bargaining and Enforcement of Sentencing Guidelines." In A. Von Hirsch and A. Ashworth, (eds.), *Principled Sentencing*. Boston, MA: Northeastern University Press, 1992.

Tontodonato, Pamela, and Erez, Edna. "Crime, Punishment and Victim Distress." *International Review of Victimology 3* (1994): 33–55.

Trivers, Robert. "The Evolution of Reciprocal Altruism." *Quarterly Review of Biology* 46 (1971): 35–57.

Tunick, Mark. *Punishment: Theory and Practice*. Berkeley: University of California Press, 1992.

Uhlmann, Thomas. "Black Elite Decision Making: The Case of Trial Judges." *American Journal of Political Science* 22 (1978): 884–895.

Umbreit, Marc. "Violent Offenders and their Victims." In M. Wright and B. Galaway, *Mediation and Criminal Justice: Victims, Offenders and Community*. Newbury Park, CA: Sage, 1989.

Umbreit, Marc. "Victim-Offender Mediation with Violent Offenders." In E. Viano, (ed.), *The Victimology Handbook: Research Findings, Treatment and Public Policy*. New York, NY: Garland, 1990.

Umbreit, Marc. "Restorative Justice through Mediation: The Impact of Programs in Four Canadian Provinces." In B. Galaway and J. Hudson , (eds.), *Restorative Justice: International Perspectives*. Monsey, NY: Criminal Justice Press, 1996.

Umbreit, Marc. "Avoiding the Marginalization and 'McDonaldization' of Victim-Offender Mediation: A Case Study in Moving toward the Mainstream." In G. Bazemore and L. Walgrave, (eds.), *Restorative Juvenile Justice: Repairing the Harm of Youth Crime*. Monsey, NY: Criminal Justice Press, 1999: 213–234.

Umbreit, Mark and Armour, Marilyn. "The Paradox of Forgiveness in Restorative Justice." In E. Worthington, Jr., (ed.), *The Handbook of Forgiveness*. New York, NY: Routledge, (2005): 491–502.

Umbreit, Marc and Carey, Mark. "Restorative Justice: Implications for Organizational Change." *Federal Probation* 59 no. 1 (1995): 47–53.

Umbreit, Marc, Coates, Robert and Kalanj, Boris. *Victim Meets Offender: The Impact of Restorative Justice and Mediation*. Monsey, NY: Criminal Justice Press, 1994.

Uslander, Eric. *The Moral Foundations of Trust*. Cambridge, UK: Cambridge University Press, 2002.

Van Dijk, Jan. "Ideological Trends Within the Victims' Movement: An International Perspective." In M. Maguire, and J. Pointing, (eds.), *Victims of Crime: A New Deal?* Milton Keynes, UK: Open University Press, 1988: 115–126.

Van Ness, Daniel. *Crime and its Victims: What We Can Do*. Downer's Grove, IL: Intervarsity Press, 1986.

Van Ness, Daniel. "New Wine and Old Wineskins: Four Challenges of Restorative Justice." *Criminal Law Forum,* 4 no. 2 (1993): 251–276.

Van Ness, Daniel and Strong, Karen *Restoring Justice.* (1st and 3rd editions). Cincinnati, OH: Anderson, 1997, 2006.

Vidmar, Neil. "Retribution and Revenge." In J. Sanders, and V. Hamilton , (eds.), *Handbook of Justice Research in Law* New York: Kluwer, 2000: 31–63.

Vidmar, Neil and Miller, Dale. "Social Psychological Processes Underlying Attitudes toward Legal Punishment." *Law and Society Review* 14 (1980): 401-438.

Von Hirsch, Andrew. *Doing Justice: The Choice of Punishments.* New York, NY: Hill and Wang, 1976.

Von Hirsch, Andrew. *Censure and Sanctions.* Oxford, England: Oxford University Press, 1996.

Von Hirsch, Andrew. "Proportionate Sentencing: A Desert Perspective." In A. Von Hirsch, A. Ashworth and J. Roberts, (eds.), *Principled Sentencing,* 3rd Edition, Oxford, UK: Hart, 2009: 115–125.

Von Hirsch, Andrew, Ashworth, Andrew, and Shearing, Clifford. "Specifying Aims and Limits for Restorative Justice." In A. Von Hirsch, J. Roberts, A. E. Bottoms, K. Roach, and M. Schiff, (eds.), *Restorative Justice and Criminal Justice: Competing or Reconcilable Paradigms?* Oxford, England: Hart, 2003.

Von Hirsch, Andrew, Roberts, Julian, Anthony, Roach, Kent, and Schiff, Mara, (eds.), *Restorative Justice and Criminal Justice: Competing or Reconcilable Paradigms?* Oxford, UK: Hart, 2003.

Wagatsuma, Hiroshi and Rossett, Arthur. "The Implications of Apology: Law and Culture in Japan and the United States." *Law and Society Review* 20 (1986): 461–498.

Wagstaff, Graham. *Making Sense of Justice: On the Psychology of Equity and Desert.* Liverpool, England: Edwin Mellen Press, 1998.

Walgrave, Lode. "Restorative Justice for Juveniles: Just a Technique or a Fully-Fledged Alternative?" *Howard Journal of Criminal Justice* 34 (1995): 228–249.

Walgrave, Lode. "How Pure can a Maximalist Approach to Restorative Justice Remain? Or can a Purist Model of Restorative Justice Become Maximalist?" *Contemporary Justice Review* 3 (2000): 415–432.

Walgrave, Lode. "Has Restorative Justice Appropriately Responded to Retribution Theory and Impulses?" In H. Zehr and B. Toews, (eds.), *Critical Issues in Restorative Justice.* Monsey, NY: Criminal Justice Press, 2004.

Walgrave, Lode and Bazemore, Gordon. "Reflections on the Future of Restorative Justice for Juveniles." In G. Bazemore and M. Schiff, (eds.), *Restorative Community Justice: Repairing Harm and Transforming Communities.* Cincinnati, OH: Anderson, 2002: 359–399.

Walker, Samuel. *A Critical History of Police Reform.* Lexington, MA: Lexington Books, 1977.

Walker, Samuel and Katz, Charles. *The Police in America,* (5th Ed), New York: McGraw-Hill, 2005.

Walker, Samuel, Spohn, Cassia and Delone, Miriam. *The Color of Justice: Race, Ethnicity, and Crime in America.* New York, NY: Wadsworth, 1996.

Walsh, Anthony. "Evolutionary Psychology and the Origins of Justice." *Justice Quarterly* 17, no. 4 (2000): 841–864.

Warr, Mark. "Public Perceptions and Reactions to Crime." In J. Sheley, (ed.), *Criminology: A Contemporary Handbook*. Belmont, CA: Wadsworth, 2000: 13–31.

Wasik, Martin and von Hirsch, Andrew. "Section 29 Revisited: Previous Convictions in Sentencing." *Criminal Law Review* 24 (1994): 409–418.

Weibe, Richard. "The Mental Health Implications of Crime Victims' Rights." In D. Wexler and J. Winick, (eds.) *Developments in Therapeutic Jurisprudence*. Durham, NC: Academic Press, 1996.

Weiner, Bernard, Graham, Sandra, and Reynor Christine. "An Attributional Examination of Retributive and Utilitarian Philosophies of Punishment." *Journal of Justice Research* 10 (1997): 431–452.

Weiseberg, Robert. "Restorative Justice and the Danger of 'Community.'" *Utah Law Review 1* (2003): 343–374.

Weisstub, David. "Victims of Crime in the Criminal Justice System." In E. Fattah, (ed.) *From Crime Policy to Victim Policy: Reorienting the Justice System*. Basingstoke, UK: Macmillan, 1986.

Weitecamp, Elmer. "Can Restitution Serve as a Reasonable Alternative to Imprisonment? An Assessment of the Situation in the USA." In H. Messmer, and H. Otto, (eds.). *Restorative Justice on Trial: Pitfalls and Potentials of Victim-Offender Mediation*. Dordrecht, Netherlands: Kluwer Publishing, 1992.

Weitecamp, Elmer. "The History of Restorative Justice." In G. Bazemore and L. Walgrave, (eds.), *Restorative Juvenile Justice: Repairing the Harm of Youth Crime*. Monsey, NY: Criminal Justice Press, 1999.

Wemmers, Jo-Anne. "Restorative Justice for Victims of Crime: A Victim-oriented Approach to Restorative Justice." *International Review of Victimology* 9 (2002): 43–59.

Wilson, Edward. *Sociobiology: The New Synthesis*. Cambridge, MA: MIT Press, 1975.

Wilson, James and Herrnstein, Richard. *Crime and Human Nature*. New York: Simon and Schuster, 1985.

Wilson, Orlando. *Police Administration*. New York: McGraw Hill, 1950.

Wolgast, Elizabeth. *A Grammar of Justice*. Ithaca, NY: Cornell University Press, 1987.

Woolcock, Michael. "Social Capital and Economic Development: Toward a Theoretical Synthesis and Policy Framework." *Theory and Society,* 27 (1998): 151–208.

Woolcock, Michael. "The Place of Social Capital in Understanding Social and Economic Outcomes." *Canadian Journal of Policy Research 2* (2001):1–27.

Worthington, Everett, Jr., (ed.). *Dimensions of Forgiveness: Psychological Research and theological Perspectives*. Philadelphia, PA: Templeton, 1998.

Wright, Martin. *Justice for Victims and Offenders*. Philadelphia, PA: Open University Press, 1991.

Wright, Martin. "Can Mediation Be An Alternative to Criminal Justice?" In B. Galaway and J. Hudson, (eds.), *Restorative Justice: International Perspectives*. Monsey, NY: Criminal Justice Press, 1996.

Wright, Martin. "The Rights and Needs of Crime Victims in the Criminal Justice Process." In H. Kaptein and M. Malsch, (eds.), *Crime, Victims and Justice: Essays on Principles and Practice*. Aldershot, England: Ashgate, 2004.

Wright, Martin and Galaway, Burt, (eds.) *Mediation and Criminal Justice: Victims Offenders and Community*. Newbury Park, CA: Sage, 1989.

Wu, Jianzhong and Axelrod, Robert. "How to Cope With Noise in the Iterated Prisoner's Dilemma." *Journal of Conflict Resolution* 39 (1995):183–189.

Yancey, Philip. *What's So Amazing About Grace?* Grand Rapids, MI: Bondservant, 1997.

Yates, John. "At Suspect's Church, a Congregation Struggles." *The Wichita Eagle* (February 26, 2005): 1.

Young, Marlene. "A Constitutional Amendment for the Victims of Crime: The Victims' Perspective." *Wayne Law Review* 34 (1987): 51–68.

Zatz, Marjorie. "The Changing Form of Racial/Ethnic Biases in Sentencing." *Journal of Research in Crime and Delinquency* 24 (1987): 69–92.

Zehr, Howard. *Changing Lenses: A New Focus for Crime and Justice*. Scottsdale, PA: Herald Press, 1990.

Zehr, Howard. "Review: The Spiritual Roots of Restorative Justice." *British Journal of Criminology* 43 (1993): 653–654.

Zehr, Howard. "Justice as Restoration, Justice as Respect." *The Justice Professional* 2 (1998): 71–78.

Zehr, Howard. *The Little Book of Restorative Justice*. Intercourse, PA: Good Books, 2002.

Zehr, Howard and Umbreit, Marc. "Victim-Offender Reconciliation: An Incarceration Substitute?" *Federal Probation* 46 (1982): 63–68.

Index

Oswald, Margit, 139 n.101
Otto, Randy, 136 n.21

Packer, Herbert, 90 n.1
Palk, Gerald, 137 n.48
Paradigms, 261-272; Defined, 262-
    263; Dichotomies, formation of,
    263-264; Ideologies and, 264-
    268; Overuse of, 262-265, 269-
    270 n.6; Paradigm shift, 262-263;
    Reform, effect on, 266;
    Rhetorical use of, 263, 268-269;
    Scholarship, effect on, 267-268
Parole. See Probation and Parole, this
    index
Pavlich, George, 220 n.2
Penal abolition, 18
Pepinsky, Hal, 21 n.8
Personal Trust. See Trust, personal,
    this index
Peters, Tony, 272 n.24
Petrucci, Carrie, 135 n.7, n.13; 136
    n.24, n.26; 138 n.90; 313 n.4
Plea bargaining. Purpose of, in
    conventional system, 157-158,
    194-195, 228-229; Restorative
    justice conferencing as alternative
    to, 230-233; Sentence bargaining
    v. charge bargaining, 195-196
Policing. Community support, need
    for, 258; Development of, 284-
    285; Minorities, alienation of,
    284, 325; Restoration of trust
    approach to, 284-288; Restorative
    justice and, 324
Pollard, Charles, 139 n.107
Portes, Alejandro, 220 n.5
Powers, Katharine Ann, case of, 107-
    108
Prager, Dennis, 141 n.168
Prenzler, Timothy, 137 n.48
Prison, expansion of populations, 14,
    246
Prisoners' rights, 14, 181
Private Justice. Disparities resulting
    from, 42; Impartiality, lack of,
    42; Neglect of public interest and,
    42; Problem of, 16-17, 41-45,
    152; Restoration of trust,
    approach to, 191

Probation and parole, 306-308;
    Presentence reports, use of, 307
Proctor, Judith, 139 n.113; 140 n.142
Punishment. Critical nexus,
    component of, 108-109, 118-120;
    Healing, debate on role in, 98-
    103; Public support for, 103-104;
    Reciprocal altruism and, 64, 81-
    84; Reducing reliance on, 189-
    191, 301.302, 319-320;
    Restorative Justice, role in, 103-
    120; Voluntary submission to, 83,
    106-9, 120, 132-133, 146, 189,
    324
Putnam, Robert, 208; 220 n.4, n.6

Quinney, Richard, 55 n.10

Raudenbush, Stephen, 91 n.47; 22
    n.16
Reciprocal Altruism. Benefits of, 70;
    "Cheaters," detection of, 64-70;
    Cultural influences, 74, 88-89;
    Empathy and, 74; Evolution of,
    57-70; Forgiveness and, 70-73;
    Kin altruism distinguished, 60,
    68-69; Origin of justice and, 69-
    70; Pure altruism, distinguished,
    60-62, 80
Reciprocity, 65-86; Golden Rule and,
    84-86; Norms of, 64, 67, 70, 80-
    81, 169, 208-209, 214-215;
    Presumption of, 65-67, 70, 73,
    80-81, 104-105, 118, 120, 215;
    Trust and, 80-90
Rehabilitation. Loss of faith in, 5, 13-
    14; Restoration of trust, condition
    of, 31-32, 51, 146, 162-180, 323
Reintegration. Devising plan for, 154-
    157; Conditions for, 145-146;
    Trust and, 182-184
Reintegrative shaming, 151
Reisig, Michael, 259 n.4
Reschly, Daniel, 271 n.6
Resentment. Disrespect, moral
    response to, 66; Golden Rule.
    relation to, 84-85; Guilt as
    counterpart to, 83; Justice
    response, 63, 64, 203

About the Book

Is there a place for punishment in restorative justice? Can restorative justice be applied to a full range of offenses? Ross London answers both questions with an unequivocal yes.

London proposes that restoration, and especially the restoration of trust, be viewed as the overarching goal of all criminal justice policies and practices. Within that context, he argues that punishment—far from contradicting the goal of restoration—is not only essential for the victim and the community, but also a necessary component for the reintegration of the offender.

Drawing on his experience as a judge, prosecutor, and public defender, London offers a pragmatic vision of restorative justice that integrates its core values with real-world applications for even the most serious violent crimes.

Ross London is professor of criminal justice at Berkeley College.